HISTORY AND RELATED DISCIPLINES
SELECT BIBLIOGRAPHIES
GENERAL EDITOR: R. C. RICHARDSON

UNITED STATES HISTORY

This bibliography provides coverage of the most recent books and articles on the history of the United States. The book reflects the enormous diversity of history research and writing on the United States today.

The bibliography is arranged by seven chronological divisions that cover the sweep of American history, starting with Native Americans before European contact and ending with the era of the Cold War and its aftermath. Each chronological division includes ten topical subdivisions: general histories and anthologies; guides to sources; biography; family and demography; class, gender and society; religion, beliefs, and ideas; work and enterprise; race and identity; space, movement, and place; and the state and the public realm. In this way all current historical approaches and methods are included. This easy access is enhanced by author and subject indexes.

Louise A. Merriam is a librarian in Eau Claire, Wisconsin. James W. Oberly is Professor of History at the University of Wisconsin-Eau Claire.

HISTORY AND RELATED DISCIPLINES
SELECT BIBLIOGRAPHIES
GENERAL EDITOR: R. C. RICHARDSON

Bibliographical guides designed to meet the needs of under-graduates, postgraduates and their teachers in universities and colleges of higher education. All volumes in the series share a number of common characteristics. They are selective, manageable in size, and include those books and articles which are most important and useful. All volumes are edited by practising teachers of the subject and are based on their experience of the needs of students. The arrangement combines chronological with thematic divisions. Many of the items listed receive some descriptive comment.

Already published in the series:

BRITISH ECONOMIC AND SOCIAL HISTORY

THE STUDY OF HISTORY

SOCIETY AND ECONOMY IN
EARLY MODERN EUROPE

BRITISH AND IRISH ARCHAEOLOGY

AFRICA, ASIA AND SOUTH AMERICA
SINCE 1800

WESTERN POLITICAL THOUGHT:
POST-WAR RESEARCH

ANCIENT GREECE AND ROME

EUROPEAN ECONOMIC AND SOCIAL HISTORY

JAPANESE STUDIES

UNITED STATES HISTORY

A BIBLIOGRAPHY OF THE NEW WRITINGS ON AMERICAN HISTORY

COMPILED BY

LOUISE A. MERRIAM
AND JAMES W. OBERLY

MANCHESTER UNIVERSITY PRESS
Manchester and New York

Distributed exclusively in the USA and Canada by St. Martin's Press

Published by
MANCHESTER UNIVERSITY PRESS
Oxford Road, Manchester M13 9NR, UK
and Room 400, 175 Fifth Avenue, New York
NY 100010, USA
Distributed exclusively in the USA and Canada by
St. Martin's Press, Inc., 175 Fifth Avenue, New York
NY 10010, USA

British Library Cataloguing-in-Publication Data
A catalogue record for this book is available from the
British Library

Library of Congress Cataloging-in-Publication Data applied for

ISBN 0 7190 3688 7 *hardback*

Photoset in Linotron Plantin
by Northern Phototypesetting Co. Ltd, Bolton

Printed in Great Britain
by Cromwell Press Ltd, Broughton Gifford

CONTENTS

CONTENTS

vii

CONTENTS

GENERAL EDITOR'S PREFACE

History, to an even greater extent than most other academic disciplines, has developed at a prodigious pace in the twentieth century. Its scope has extended and diversified, its methodologies have been revolutionized, its philosophy has changed, and its relations with other disciplines have been transformed. The number of students and teachers of the subject in the different branches of higher education has vastly increased, and there is an ever-growing army of amateurs, many of them taking adult education courses. Academic and commercial publishers have produced a swelling stream of publications – both specialist and general – to cater for this large and expanding audience. Scholarly journals have proliferated. It is no easy matter even for specialists to keep abreast of the flow of publications in their particular field. For those with more general academic interests the task of finding what has been written on different subject areas can be time-consuming, perplexing, and often frustrating.

It is primarily to meet the needs of undergraduates, postgraduates and their teachers in universities and colleges of higher education, that this series of bibliographies is designed. It will be a no less valuable resource, however, to the reference collection of any public library, school or college.

Though common sense demands that each volume will be structured in the way which is most appropriate for the particular field in question, nonetheless all volumes in the series share a number of important common characteristics. First – quite deliberately – all are *select* bibliographies, manageable in size, and include those books and articles which in the editor's judgement are most important and useful. To attempt an uncritically comprehensive listing would needlessly dictate the inclusion of items which were frankly ephemeral, antiquarian, or discredited and result only in the production of a bulky and unwieldy volume. Like any select bibliography, however, this series will direct the reader where appropriate to other, more specialized and detailed sources of bibliographical information. That would be one of its functions. Second, all the volumes are edited not simply by specialists in the different fields but by practising teachers of the subject, and are based on their experience of the needs of students in higher education. Third, there are common features of arrangement and presentation. All volumes begin with listings of general works of a methodological or historiographical nature, and proceed within broad chronological divisions to arrange their material thematically. Most items will receive some descriptive comment. Each volume, for ease of reference, has an index of authors and editors.

R. C. RICHARDSON

EDITORIAL PREFACE

This bibliography is, quite simply, a selected listing of writings on United States history from the 1980s and early 1990s in English. A few works from the 1970s have crept in because they are the only recent works on a particular subject, or because they are too significant to be left out. These entries – more than 4,000 in all – are arranged in ten chronological categories which are subdivided by subject matter. Each of the categories includes the same subject divisions as the other nine, a feature we hope will encourage the user to compare developments in the same subject area across chronological periods. For example, material on religion in the Civil War period appears under the same headings as books about religion in the late twentieth century. In short, this work is not simply a listing, but an arrangement as well.

The subject categories for each chronological period are, of course, very inclusive. That is why we also provide a subject index which cuts across chronological periods, using more precise terms so that readers can identify resources easily. This benefit is important to this work because we have assumed that it is important to its users: undergraduate history students, graduate students in need of a quick overview of the recent works on a particular subject, librarians and bibliographers looking for the 'best' works in the field, and the general reader. Although it is not designed for subject specialists, there are numerous subject bibliographies on narrow topics listed here.

At least two-thirds of the items listed are books – monographs, bibliographies, atlases, encyclopedias, biographies, and dictionaries. This reflects the nature of historical scholarship: the book is the vehicle that historians use to marshal evidence and present their cases. In contrast to researchers in a field like chemistry, historians use articles in scholarly journals to try out an idea,

report on a small finding, or comment upon someone else's ideas. The full-blown historical argument is generally reserved for a book-length presentation. Consequently, the articles that are listed in this work are mostly review articles (that is, pieces synthesizing a number of books on a particular topic); significant articles that will eventually become part of a large, book-length work; or essays on a topic which, by its nature, does not lend itself to book-length treatment.

Selected from the books and journals are materials on social and political history, using the most broad definitions of these terms. The student will not find much here about art or music history, for example. Literature, except as it affects socio-political developments, is not present, either. Instead, the bibliography focuses on those topics of greatest interest to historians of the United States since 1980: demography, social and class relations, religion and culture, work and enterprise, race and ethnicity, movement and place, and the state and the public realm. These are the areas in which historians have worked most fruitfully in recent years. We leave it to the art, music, and literary historians to compile a similar work for their fields.

These materials were selected for the bibliography according to several criteria. We tried to list all significant books, as determined by our own review and by reviews in major historical journals, and we searched for new syntheses or approaches to standard subjects. No non-English-language works are included here, although there are a number of historians working in the field who produce excellent works in a language other than English. Much of the history of the American South West, for example, has been chronicled and analyzed by scholars writing in Spanish. The diligent student will certainly find works such as these.

Because the bibliography is limited to English-language materials, and because the journal articles listed are from major historical publications, they will be relatively easy to obtain, especially by readers in the English-speaking world. Most journal articles published since 1989 are available through electronic online publishing services. Inter-library loan services have improved to the point where almost anything is available to the student who has the diligence to locate and retrieve the item.

Why, in the age of electronic services such as online catalogs and electronic databases, is there a need for a bibliography such as this? First, unlike computer-based resources, this work pulls together in one place materials not readily available to the beginning or casual searchers of electronic databases. Second, it covers in a handy and useable format – and the book is still the easier format to use for many things – a huge amount of material in a manageable size. Finally, it gives the casual researcher or undergraduate a place to start – in fact, a head start. Searching an electronic database requires that you know some of the search terms in use, but the user of this bibliography needs to know nothing upon starting. We hope that he or she will know much more about developments in the field of United States history when the book goes back on the shelf.

Acknowledgements and dedication

While compiling this work we have accumulated many debts. In particular, we would like to thank Kathy Finder of the University of Wisconsin-Eau Claire for her assistance with software. No book about history is published without the aid of librarians, and this one is no exception. We acknowledge and are grateful for the help given by the staff at McIntyre Library, University of Wisconsin-Eau Claire. We thank the University of Wisconsin-Eau Claire for supporting this project in a concrete way through its research grant program. We are grateful to Deborah Robie for her assistance in proofreading. We appreciate the patience of Roger Richardson, series editor. Finally, we thank our children, Nicholas, William, and Peter for their acceptance of pleasures denied. This book is dedicated to them.

Louise A. Merriam
James W. Oberly

1

GENERALITIES

GUIDES TO SOURCES

General

1.1 **ABC-CLIO**, *America: History and Life*, Santa Barbara, CA, 1964– . Annual index and abstracts to periodical literature, doctoral dissertations, and book reviews for writings about American history, the abstracts are particularly valuable as a shortcut in doing any literature search. Still, this is a clumsy reference source and the online version is notable more for its misses than hits. Much of the database compiled up through the 1980s is available by subject speciality under the names of the ABC-CLIO editors Gail Schlacter and Pamela Byrne.

1.2 **American Historical Association**, *Writings on American History*, irregular series, Washington, DC. A series that dates back to 1903 but with many interruptions. Currently, it is an annual compendium of the book and periodical literature of American history.

1.3 **Beers**, H. P., *Bibliographies in American History. Guide to Material for Research*, New York, 1973.

1.4 **Bell**, Mary McC., **Dwyer**, C., and **Henderson**, W. A., 'Finding manuscript collections. NUCMC, NIDS, and RLIN', *National Genealogical Society Quarterly*, LXXVII, 1989, 208–218.

1.5 **Cassara**, E., *History of the United States of America. A Guide to Information Sources*, Detroit, 1977.

1.6 **Freidel**, F., (ed.), *The Harvard Guide to American History*, Cambridge, MA, 1974. A two-volume set that is a combination of dictionary, encyclopedia, and bibliography, a bit dated now, but still a useful starting place.

1.7 **Goodrum**, C. A., and **Dalrymple**, Helen W., *Guide to the Library of Congress*, Washington, DC, 1988. Periodically updated and quite useful to the researcher before a visit.

1.8 **Hanke**, L., (ed.), *Guide to the Study of United States History outside the U.S., 1945–1980*, White Plains, NY, 1985. Five volume set that mixes a guide to archival sources in collections outside the U.S., along with a bibliography of published writings done by scholars in foreign countries.

1.9 **Howe**, Barbara J., and **Kemp**, E. L., (ed.), *Public History. An Introduction*, Malabar, FL, 1986.

1.10 **Library of Congress**, *National Union Catalog of Manuscript Collections*, Washington, DC, 1959– . The most complete listing of repositories holding manuscript collections, and well indexed by subject, name, and chronology, NUCMC has been superseded by various online indexes, particularly that of RLIN.

1.11 **Library Resources**, Inc., *The Microbook Library of American Civilization*, Chicago, 1972. A 1970s publishing project that placed tens of thousands of documents and primary sources onto ultra-small microfiche, difficult to use but quite a remarkable collection.

1.12 **Prucha**, F. P., *Handbook for Research in American History. A Guide to Bibliographies and Other Reference Works*, Lincoln, NE, 1987. A guide to the use of finding aids.

1.13 **Sharp**, H. S., *Footnotes to American History. A Bibliographic Source Book*, Metuchen, NJ, 1977. Organized by incident, personality, episode, and rumor (e.g., Captain Kidd's treasure), this volume offers a short descriptive entry followed by a list of references.

1.14 **Thelen**, D., 'A round table: Synthesis in American history', *Journal of American History*, LXXIV, 1987, 127–130. Five discussions on history, its synthesis or lack of, and what might or might not be going wrong in history.

1.15 **United States. National Archives and Records**, *Microfilm Resources for Research. A Comprehensive Catalog*, Washington, DC, 1990.

1.16 **United States. National Archives and Records**, *Guide to the National Archives of the United States*, Washington, DC, 1987.

Biography

1.17 **Garraty**, J. A., *New Dictionary of American Biography*, New York, 1992– . A completely new publishing venture that will be the replacement for the Dumas Malone-edited series of early twentieth century volumes.

1.18 **Garraty**, J. A., *Encyclopedia of American Biography*, New York, 1974.

1.19 **Ingham**, J. N., *Biographical Directory of American Business Leaders*, Westport, CT, 1983.

1.20 **Meier**, M. S., *Mexican American Biographies. A Historical Dictionary, 1836–1987*, New York, 1988.

1.21 **Muccigrosso**, R., (ed.), *Research Guide to American Historical Biography*, Washington, DC, 1988.

1.22 **Waserman**, M. J., *Bibliography on Oral History*, New York, 1975.

Demography, family, and health

1.23 **Acock**, A. C., *The Influence of the Family. A Review and Annotated Bibliography of Socialization, Ethnicity, and Delinquency, 1975–1986*, New York, 1986.

1.24 **Beales**, R. W., 'Selected bibliography on children and families in New England', *Dublin Seminar for New England Folklife*, X, 1985, 148–157.

1.25 **Benson-von der Ohe**, Elizabeth, and **Mason**, Valmari M., *An Annotated Bibliography of U. S. Scholarship on the History of the Family*, New York, 1986.

1.26 **Davis**, L. G., *The Black Aged in the United States. An Annotated Bibliography*, Westport, CT, 1980.

1.27 **Davis**, L. G., *The Black Family in the United States. A Selected Bibliography of Annotated Books, Articles, and Dissertations on Black Families in America*, Westport, CT, 1978.

1.28 **DiCanio**, Margaret, *The Encyclopedia of Marriage, Divorce, and the Family*, New York, 1989.

1.29 **Hawes**, J. M., and **Hider**, R. H., (ed.), *American Childhood. A Research Guide and Historical Handbook*, Westport, CT, 1985.

1.30 **Hawes**, J. M., and **Nybakken**, Elizabeth I., (ed.), *American Families. A Research Guide and Historical Handbook*, New York, 1991.

1.31 **McLean**, H. W., and **Fuller**, M. J., 'A conversion guide to using population statistics, 1750–1980', *History Teacher*, XVI, 1983, 519–522.

1.32 **Milden**, J. W., *The Family in Past Time. A Guide to the Literature*, New York, 1977.

1.33 **Momeni**, J. A., *Demography of Racial and Ethnic Minorities in the United States. An Annotated Bibliography with a Review Essay*, Westport, CT, 1984.

1.34 **Myers**, H. F., *Black Child Development in America, 1927–1977. An Annotated Bibliography*, Westport, CT, 1979.

1.35 **Obudo**, R. A., and **Scott**, Jeannine B., *Afro-American Demography and Urban Issues. A Bibliography*, Westport, CT, 1985.

1.36 **Pollock**, Linda, (ed.), *A Lasting Relationship. Parents and Children Over Three Centuries*, Hanover, NH, 1987. Extracts from child-rearing manuals.

1.37 **Sadler**, Judith DeBoard, *Families in Transition. An Annotated Bibliography*, Hamden, CT, 1988.

1.38 **Scott**, D. M., and **Wishy**, B., *America's Families. A Documentary History*, New York, 1982.

1.39 **Wright**, N. E., *Preserving Your American Heritage. A Guide to Family and Local History*, Provo, UT, 1981.

Class, gender, and social relations

1.40 **Bailey**, W. G., *Police Science, 1964–1984. A Selected, Annotated Bibliography*, New York, 1986. A useful bibliography for looking at work on crime and punishment during the period when Americans started becoming more fearful of crime.

1.41 **Bass**, D. C., *Women in American Religious History. An Annotated Bibliography and Guide to Sources*, Boston, 1986.

1.42 **Beach**, M., *A Subject Bibliography of the History of American Higher Education*, Westport, CT, 1984.

1.43 **Booth**, M. W., *American Popular Music. A Reference Guide*, Westport, CT, 1983.

1.44 **Braden**, Donna R., *Leisure and Entertainment in America*, Dearborn, MI, 1988. An encyclopedia of the history of popular sports and amusements.

1.45 **Buhle**, Mari Jo, *Women and the American Left. A Guide to Sources*, Boston, 1983.

1.46 **Chalfant**, H. P., *Sociology of Poverty in the United States. An Annotated Bibliography*, Westport, CT, 1985.

1.47 **Christensen**, T., *Reel Politics. American Political Movies from 'Birth of a Nation' to 'Platoon'*, New York, 1987.

1.48 **Cohen**, H., and **Coffin**, T. P., (ed.), *The Folklore of American Holidays*, Detroit, 1987.

1.49 **Conway**, J. K., *The Female Experience in Eighteenth- and Nineteenth-Century America. A Guide to the History of American Women*, New York, 1982.

1.50 **Cordasco**, F., *Crime in America. Historical Pattern and Contemporary Realities. An Annotated Bibliography*, New York, 1985.

1.51 **Davis**, Gwenn, *Drama by Women to 1900. A Bibliography of American and British Writers*, Toronto, 1992.

1.52 **Diner**, Hasia R., *Women in Urban Society. A Guide to Information Sources*, Detroit, 1979.

1.53 **Drew**, B. A., *Heroines. A Bibliography of Women Series Characters in Mystery, Espionage, Action, Science Fiction, Fantasy, Horror, Western, Romance, and Juvenile Novels*, New York, 1989.

1.54 **Durham**, W. B., *American Theatre Companies, 1749–1887*, New York, 1986. A historical dictionary of all known companies.

1.55 **Durnin**, R. G., *American Education. A Guide to Information Sources*, Detroit, 1982.

1.56 **Fairbanks**, Carol, and **Haakenson**, Bergine, (ed.), *Writings of Farm Women, 1840–1940. An Anthology*, New York, 1990.

1.57 **Fishburn**, K., *Women in Popular Culture. A Reference Guide*, Westport, CT, 1982.

1.58 **Gabaccia**, D. R., *Immigrant Women in the United States. A Selectively Annotated Multidisciplinary Bibliography*, New York, 1989.

1.59 **Goodfriend**, Joyce D., *The Published Diaries and Letters of American Women. An Annotated Bibliography*, Boston, 1987.

1.60 **Hardt**, H., 'The foreign-language press in American press history', *Journal of Communication*, XXXIX, 1989, 114–13.

1.61 **Humphreys**, N. K., *American Women's Magazines. An Annotated Historical Guide*, New York, 1989.

1.62 **Lender**, M. E., *Dictionary of American Temperance Biography. From Temperance Reform to Alcohol Research, the 1600s to the 1980s*, Westport, CT, 1984.

1.63 **Mark**, C., *Sociology of America. A Guide to Information Sources*, Detroit, 1976.

1.64 **McHenry**, R., *Famous American Women. A Biographical Dictionary from Colonial Times to the Present*, New York, 1983.

1.65 **Melvin**, Patricia Mooney, (ed.), *American Community Organizations. A Historical Dictionary*, New York, 1986.

1.66 **Miller**, T., *American Communes, 1860–1960. A Bibliography*, New York, 1990.

1.67 **Nelson**, B. J., *American Women in Politics. A Selected Bibliography and Resource Guide*, New York, 1984.

1.68 **Radelet**, M., and **Vandiver**, Margaret, (ed.), *Capital Punishment in America. An Annotated Bibliography*, New York, 1988.

1.69 **Robinson**, Alice M., (ed.), *Notable Women in the American Theatre. A Biographical Directory*, New York, 1990.

1.70 **Schlacter**, Gail, and **Byrne**, Pamela R., *Crime and Punishment in America. A Historical Bibliography*, Santa Barbara, CA, 1984.

1.71 **Shemanski**, F., *A Guide to Fairs and Festivals in the United States*, Westport, CT, 1984.

1.72 **Shemanski**, F., *Social Reform and Reaction in America. An Annotated Bibliography*, Santa Barbara, CA, 1984.

1.73 **Streib**, V. L., 'Capital punishment

history: moral penance or legal homicide?',
Criminal Justice History, X, 1989, 209–211.
Reviews recent books on the history and
use of capital punishment from an
abolitionist perspective.

1.74 **Sweeney**, P. E., *Biographies of American
Women. An Annotated Bibliography*, Santa
Barbara, CA, 1990.

1.75 **Terris**, V. R., *Women in America. A Guide
to Information Sources*, Detroit, 1980.

1.76 **Tierney**, H., (ed.), *Women's Studies
Encyclopedia*, New York, 1989.

1.77 **Tingley**, D. F., *Social History of the United
States. A Guide to Information Sources*,
Detroit, 1979.

1.78 **Trattner**, W. I., and **Achenbaum**, W. A.,
(ed.), *Social Welfare in America. An
Annotated Bibliography*, Westport, CT,
1983.

1.79 **Wietzman**, D. L., *Underfoot. An Everyday
Guide to the Exploring the American Past*,
New York, 1976.

1.80 **Zophy**, A. H., and **Kavenik**, F. M., (ed.),
Handbook of American Women's History,
New York, 1990.

Religion, beliefs,
ideas, and culture

1.81 **Bowden**, H. W., *Dictionary of American
Religious Biography*, Westport, CT, 1977.

1.82 **Ellis**, J. T., and **Trisco**, R., (ed.), *A Guide
to American Catholic History*, Santa
Barbara, CA, 1982. The second edition of
this work.

1.83 **Gales**, S. H., (ed.), *Encyclopedia of
American Humorists*, New York, 1988.

1.84 **Gohdes**, C. L. F., *Bibliographical Guide to
the Study of the Literature of the U.S.A.*,
Durham, NC, 1984.

1.85 **Hill**, S. S., *Encyclopedia of Religion in the
South*, Macon, GA, 1984.

1.86 **Inge**, M. T., (ed.), *Handbook of American
Popular Culture*, Westport, CT, 1978.

1.87 **Jones**, C. E., *Guide to the Study of the
Pentecostal Movement*, Metuchen, NJ,
1983.

1.88 **Jones**, S. S., *Folklore and Literature in the
United States. An Annotated Bibliography of
Studies of Folklore in American Literature*,
New York, 1984.

1.89 **Landrum**, L. N., *American Popular
Culture. A Guide to Information Sources*,
Detroit, 1982.

1.90 **Levernier**, J. A., and **Wilmes**, D. R.,
(ed.), *American Writers before 1800. A
Biographical and Critical Reference Guide*,
Westport, CT, 1983.

1.91 **Logsdon**, G., (ed.), *'The Whorehouse Bells
were Ringing' and Other Songs Cowboys
Sing*, Urbana, IL, 1989. An annotated
collection of songs by and about cowboys.

1.92 **Melton**, J. G., *Religious Leaders of North
America. A Bibliographical Guide to
Founders and Leaders of Religious Bodies*,
Detroit, 1991.

1.93 **Melton**, J. G., *The Encyclopedia of
American Religions*, Detroit, 1989.

1.94 **Menendez**, A. J., *Religious Conflict in
America. A Bibliography*, New York, 1985.

1.95 **Mitterling**, P. I., *U.S. Cultural History. A
Guide to Information Sources*, Detroit,
1980.

1.96 **Newton**, M., and **Newton**, J. A., (ed.),
*Racial and Religious Violence in America. A
Chronology*, New York, 1991.

1.97 **Sawyer**, K., 'A bibliography of the works
of Jerald C. Brauer', *Church History*, LX,
1991, 263–270. A guide to the writings of
one of the foremost religious historians of
the postwar period.

1.98 **Wallace**, D. D., 'Recent publications on
American religious history: a
bibliographical essay and review',
American Studies International, XIX, 1981,
15–42.

Work and enterprise

1.99 **Davis**, Mary, **Rothstein**, M., and
Stratford, Jean, (ed.), *The History of
California. Agriculture. An Updated
Bibliography*, Davis, CA, 1991.

1.100 **Downard**, W. L., *Dictionary of the History
of the American Brewing and Distilling
Industries*, Westport, CT, 1980.

1.101 **Fink**, G. M., and **Cantor**, M., (ed.),
*Biographical Dictionary of American Labor
Leaders*, Westport, CT, 1984.

1.102 **Gyory**, A., 'Published works of Herbert G.
Gutman: a bibliography', *Labor History*,
XXIX, 1988, 400–405.

1.103 **Hutchinson**, W. K., *American Economic
History. A Guide to Information Sources*,
Detroit, 1980.

1.104 **Levi**, S. C., 'Labor history and Alaska',
Labor History, XXX, 1989, 595–607. A
guide to sources and bibliography.

1.105 **McCusker**, J. J., *How Much Is That In Real Money? A Historical Price Index*, Charlottesville, VA, 1992. A very helpful guide to converting currencies and prices into modern numbers.

1.106 **Neufeld**, M. F., **Leab**, D. J., and **Swanson**, Dorothy, (ed.), *American Working Class History. A Representative Bibliography*, New York, 1983. Representative, that is, of the "New Labor History".

1.107 **Orsagh**, T., *The Economic History of the United States Prior to 1860. An Annotated Bibliography*, Santa Barbara, CA, 1975.

1.108 **Porter**, G., (ed.), *Encyclopedia of American Economic History. Studies of the Principal Movements and Ideas*, New York, 1980.

1.109 **Rasmussen**, W. D., *Agriculture in the United States. A Documentary History*, New York, 1975. A four volume set of primary source documents.

1.110 **Rothenberg**, M., *The History of Science and Technology in the United States. A Critical and Selective Bibliography*, New York, 1982.

1.111 **Schapsmeier**, E. L., *Encyclopedia of American Agricultural History*, Westport, CT, 1975.

1.112 **Thompson**, E. T., *The Plantation. An International Bibliography*, Boston, 1983. Useful for finding comparative literature on the U.S. South and the Caribbean and South America.

Race and ethnic identity

1.113 **Allen**, J. P., and **Turner**, E. J., *We the People. An Atlas of America's Ethnic Diversity*, New York, 1988.

1.114 **Antcil**, P., and **Ramirez**, B., (ed.), *If One Were to Write a History . . . Selected Writings by Robert F. Harney*, Toronto, ONT, 1991. A posthumous festschrift on Harney's lifelong interest, the coming together in North America of the world's different peoples.

1.115 **Bogle**, D., *Blacks in American Films and Television. An Encyclopedia*, New York, 1988.

1.116 **Calloway**, C. G., *Recent Books and Articles on American Indian History*, Chicago, 1985.

1.117 **Center for Afroamericans and African Studies**, *Black Immigration and Ethnicity in the United States. An Annotated Bibliography*, Westport, CT, 1985.

1.118 **Cordasco**, F., *Italian Americans. A Guide mto Information Sources*, Detroit, 1978.

1.119 **Cordasco**, F., *The Immigrant Woman in North America. An Annotated Bibliography of Selected References*, Metuchen, NJ, 1985.

1.120 **Daniel**, W. C., *Black Journals of the United States*, Westport, CT, 1982.

1.121 **Danky**, J. P., (ed.), *Native American Periodicals and Newspapers, 1828–1982. Bibliography, Publishing Record, and Holdings*, Westport, CT, 1984.

1.122 **Davis**, L. G., and **Sims-Wood**, Janet L., *The Ku Klux Klan. A Bibliography*, Westport, CT, 1984.

1.123 **Doezema**, Linda Pegman, *Dutch Americans. A Guide to Information Sources*, Detroit, 1979.

1.124 **Douglas**, W. A., and **Etulain**, R. W., *Basque Americans. A Guide to Information Sources*, Detroit, 1981.

1.125 **Fascial**, J., and **Pinsker**, S., (ed.), *Jewish-American History and Culture. An Encyclopedia*, New York, 1992.

1.126 **Filby**, P. W., and **Meyer**, Mary K., (ed.), *Passenger and Immigration Lists Index. A Guide to Published Arrival Records of About 500,000 Passengers Who Came to the United States and Canada in the Seventeenth, Eighteenth, and Nineteenth Centuries*, Detroit, 1985.

1.127 **Fisher**, W. H., *The Invisible Empire. A Bibliography of the Ku Klux Klan*, Metuchen, NJ, 1980.

1.128 **Gray**, J., *Black Theatre and Performance. A Pan-African Bibliography*, New York, 1990.

1.129 **Green**, Rayna, *Native American Women. A Contextual Bibliography*, Bloomington, IN, 1983.

1.130 **Gurock**, J. S., *American Jewish History. A Bibliographical Guide*, New York, 1983.

1.131 **Hecker**, M., and **Heike**, F., (ed.), *The Greeks in America, 1528–1977. A Chronology and Fact Book*, Dobbs Ferry, NY, 1978.

1.132 **Hill**, E. E., *Guide to Records in the National Archives of the United States Relating to American Indians*, Washington, DC, 1982. The essential guide to the voluminous federal records on the subject, and helpful in indicating the documents available on microfilm.

1.133 **Hughes**, E. C., and **Hughes**, H. M., *Where Peoples Meet. Racial and Ethnic Frontiers*, Westport, CT, 1981.

1.134 **Jenkins**, B., *Black Separatism. A Bibliography*, Westport, CT, 1976. Bibliography of Black Nationalism in the United States.

1.135 **Karklis**, M., *The Latvians in America, 1640–1973. A Chronology and Fact Book*, Dobbs Ferry, NY, 1974.

1.136 **Kim**, H., *The Koreans in America, 1882–1974. A Chronology and Fact Book*, Dobbs Ferry, NY, 1974.

1.137 **Kim**, H., *Dictionary of Asian American History*, New York, 1986.

1.138 **Kim**, H., *Asian American Studies. An Annotated Bibliography and Research Guide*, New York, 1989.

1.139 **Kinloch**, G. C., *Race and Ethnic Relations. An Annotated Bibliography*, New York, 1984.

1.140 **Klein**, B. T., *Reference Encyclopedia of the American Indian*, New York, 1986. The fourth edition.

1.141 **Littlefield**, D. F., *A Biobibliography of Native American Writers, 1772–1924*, Metuchen, NJ, 1985.

1.142 **Masako**, H., *The Japanese in America, 1843–1973. A Chronology and Fact Book*, Dobbs Ferry, NY, 1974.

1.143 **Mehdi**, B. T., *The Arabs in America, 1492–1977. A Chronology and Fact Book*, Dobbs Ferry, NY, 1978.

1.144 **Meier**, M. S., *Bibliography of Mexican American History*, Westport, CT, 1984.

1.145 **Metress**, S. P., *The Irish-American Experience. A Guide to the Literature*, Washington, DC, 1981.

1.146 **Miller**, R. M., and **Smith**, J. D., (ed.), *Dictionary of Afro-American Slavery*, New York, 1988.

1.147 **Miller**, S. M., (ed.), *The Ethnic Press in the United States. A Historical Analysis and Handbook*, Westport, CT, 1987.

1.148 **Newman**, R., *Black Access. A Bibliography of Afro-American Bibliographies*, Westport, CT, 1984.

1.149 **Noonan**, B. C., and **Bowles**, A., (ed.), *Index to Wisconsin Native American Periodicals, 1897–1981*, Westport, CT, 1983.

1.150 **Olson**, J. S., *Slave Life in America. A Historiography and Selected Bibliography*, Lanham, MD, 1983.

1.151 **Peterson**, B. L., *Early Black American Playwrights and Dramatic Writers. A Biographical Directory and Catalog of Plays, Films, and Broadcasting Scripts*, New York, 1990.

1.152 **Rock**, R. O., *The Native American in American Literature. A Selectively Annotated Bibliography*, Westport, CT, 1985.

1.153 **Schlacter**, Gail, and **Byrne**, Pamela R., *The Jewish Experience in America. A Historical Bibliography*, Santa Barbara, CA, 1983.

1.154 **Sims-Wood**, J. L., *The Progress of Afro-American Women. A Selected Bibliography and Resource Guide*, Westport, CT, 1980.

1.155 **Smith**, J. D., *Black Slavery in the Americas. An Interdisciplinary Bibliography, 1865–1980*, Westport, CT, 1982.

1.156 **Sokolyszyn**, A., and **Wertsman**, V., *Ukrainians in Canada and the United States. A Guide to Information Sources*, Detroit, 1981.

1.157 **Southern**, E., *Biographical Dictionary of Afro-American and African Musicians*, Westport, CT, 1982.

1.158 **Stuart**, P., *Nations Within a Nation. Historical Statistics of American Indians*, New York, 1987. A handy one-volume statistical abstract, particularly strong on the twentieth century.

1.159 **Sturtevant**, W. C., (ed.), *Handbook of North American Indians*, Washington, DC, 1978–1990. A fifteen volume set that is encyclopedic in scope, and divided along geographical and topical lines. Relevant volumes for the study of American Indians within the present-day boundaries of the U.S. include Vol. 4 "History of Indian-White Relations"; Vol. 7 "Northwest Coast"; Vol. 8 "California"; Vols. 9 and 10 "Southwest"; Vol. 11 "Great Basin"; and Vol. 15 "Northeast".

1.160 **Suggs**, H. L., (ed.), *The Black Press in the South, 1865–1979*, Westport, CT, 1983.

1.161 **Swierenga**, R. P., (ed.), *The Dutch in America. Immigration, Settlement, and Cultural Change*, New Brunswick, NJ, 1985.

1.162 **Thernstrom**, S., **Orlov**, Ann, and **Handlin**, O., (ed.), *Harvard Encyclopedia of American Ethnic Groups*, Cambridge, MA, 1980. A collection of essays on 106 distinct ethnic groups in American history, along with longer essays on themes of ethnic identity.

1.163 **Tung**, W. L., *The Chinese in America, 1829–1973. A Chronology and Fact Book*, Dobbs Ferry, NY, 1974.

1.164 **Vaughan**, A. T., *Narratives of North American Indian Captivity. A Selective Bibliography*, New York, 1983.

1.165 **Waldman**, C., *Atlas of the North American Indian*, New York, 1985.

1.166 **Waldman**, C., *Encyclopedia of Native American Tribes*, New York, 1988.

1.167 **Werstman**, V., *The Romanian in America and Canada. A Guide to Information Sources*, Detroit, 1980.

1.168 **Wolfson**, Evelyn, *From Abenaki to Zuni. A Dictionary of Native American Tribes*, New York, 1988.

Space, movement, and place

1.169 **Anderson**, J., *The Living History Sourcebook*, Nashville, TN, 1985.

1.170 **Buenker**, J. D., *Urban History. A Guide to Information Sources*, Detroit, 1981.

1.171 **Davis**, R. C., *Encyclopedia of American Forest and Conservation History*, New York, 1983. A two volume set that covers the older literature of timber and logging history, as well as the newer literature on environmental topics.

1.172 **Filby**, P. W., *A Bibliography of American County Histories*, Baltimore, 1985.

1.173 **Grim**, R. E., *Historical Geography of the United States. A Guide to Information Sources*, Detroit, 1982.

1.174 **Hanson**, G. T., and **Moneyhon**, C. H., (ed.), *Historical Atlas of Arkansas*, Norman, OK, 1989.

1.175 **Haskell**, J. D., *Massachusetts. A Bibliography of its History*, Boston, 1976.

1.176 **Hornsby**, A., *Chronology of African-American History. Significant Events and People from 1619 to the Present*, Detroit, 1991.

1.177 **Kaminkow**, M. J., (ed.), *United States Local Histories in the Library of Congress. A Bibliography*, Baltimore, 1975. A four volume set that is an essential starting point for local history.

1.178 **Kyvig**, D. E., *Nearby History. Exploring the Past Around You*, Nashville, TN, 1988.

1.179 **Mechling**, J., *The Pacific Basin. An Annotated Bibliography*, New York, 1985.

1.180 **Parks**, R., (ed.), *Connecticut, A Bibliography of its History*, Hanover, NH, 1986.

1.181 **Peterson**, C. S., *Consolidated Bibliography of County Histories in Fifty States in 1961*, Baltimore, 1973.

1.182 **Roller**, D. C., and **Twyman**, R. W., *The Encyclopedia of Southern History*, Baton Rouge, LA, 1979.

1.183 **Rouse**, J. E., *Urban Housing, Public and Private. A Guide to Information Sources*, Detroit, 1978.

1.184 **Sealock**, R. B., *Bibliography of Place-Name Literature. United States and Canada*, Chicago, 1982.

1.185 **Shearer**, B. F., *States Names, Seals, Flags, and Symbols. A Historical Guide*, New York, 1987.

1.186 **Shumsky**, N. L., and **Crimmins**, T., *Urban America. A Historical Bibliography*, Santa Barbara, CA, 1983. Abstracts of books, articles, and dissertations taken from *America: History and Life*.

1.187 **Socolofsky**, H. E., and **Dean**, V. M., *Kansas History. An Annotated Bibliography*, Westport, CT, 1992. Reviews the secondary literature on the Sunflower State as well as indicating the holdings of the major repositories.

1.188 **Steiner**, M. C., *Region and Regionalism in the United States. A Sourcebook for the Humanities and Social Sciences*, New York, 1988.

1.189 **Stoddard**, E. R., **Nostrand**, R. L., and **West**, J. P., (ed.), *Borderlands Sourcebook. A Guide to the Literature on Northern Mexico and the American Southwest*, Norman, OK, 1983.

1.190 **Wilson**, C. R., and **Ferris**, W., (ed.), *Encyclopedia of Southern Culture*, Chapel Hill, NC, 1989.

1.191 **Yellis**, K., 'Finding the fun in fundamentals: the nearby history series', *Public Historian*, XIII, 1991, 61–69.

The state and the public realm

1.192 **Beaubien**, A. K., *American Politics and Government. Selected Basic Reference Works*, Ann Arbor, MI, 1974.

1.193 **Beede**, B. R., *Intervention and Counterinsurgency. An Annotated Bibliography of the Small Wars of the United States 1898–1984*, New York, 1985.

1.194 **Brune**, L. H., *Chronological History of*

United States Foreign Relations, 1776 to January 20, 1981, New York, 1985. A two volume reference work.

1.195 **Bryson**, T. A., *United States/Middle East Diplomatic Relations, 1784–1978. An Annotated Bibliography*, Metuchen, NJ, 1979.

1.196 **Buenker**, J. D., *Urban History. A Guide to Information Sources*, Detroit, 1981.

1.197 **Buhle**, Mary Jo, **Buhle**, P., and **Georgakas**, D., (ed.), *Encyclopedia of the American Left*, New York, 1990.

1.198 **Burns**, R. D., (ed.), *Guide to American Foreign Relations Since 1700*, Santa Barbara, CA, 1983.

1.199 **Cohen**, N. S., *The American Presidents. An Annotated Bibliography*, Pasadena, CA, 1989.

1.200 **Coletta**, P. E., *A Bibliography of American Naval History*, Annapolis, MD, 1981.

1.201 **Congressional Quarterly**, *American Leaders, 1789–1987. A Biographical Summary*, Washington, DC, 1987.

1.202 **Cook**, B. W., **Chatfield**, C., and **Cooper**, S., (ed.), *The Garland Library of War and Peace. A Collection of 360 Titles Bound in 328 Volumes*, New York, 1971.

1.203 **Davis**, R. C., *Encyclopedia of American Forest and Conservation History*, New York, 1983. A two volume set that covers the older literature of timber and logging history, as well as the newer literature on environmental topics.

1.204 **Filby**, P. W., *A Bibliography of American County Histories*, Baltimore, 1985.

1.205 **Findling**, J. E., *Dictionary of American Diplomatic History*, Westport, CT, 1980.

1.206 **Greene**, J. P., *Encyclopedia of American Political History. Studies of the Principal Movements and Ideas*, New York, 1984. A three volume set.

1.207 **Greenstein**, F. I., *Evolution of the Modern Presidency. A Bibliographical Survey*, Washington, DC, 1977.

1.208 **Grim**, R. E., *Historical Geography of the United States. A Guide to Information Sources*, Detroit, 1982.

1.209 **Higham**, R. D. S., *A Guide to the Sources of the United States Military History*, Hamden, CT, 1975.

1.210 **Hornsby**, A., *Chronology of African-American History. Significant Events and People from 1619 to the Present*, Detroit, 1991.

1.211 **Inter-University Consortium for Political and Social Research**, *Guide to Resources and Services, 1992–93*, Ann Arbor, MI, 1992. Guide to the data archive maintained by ICPSR; most of authors of the "new" history books that employ quantitative methods deposit their computer files with ICPSR, available to be used by other researchers.

1.212 **Jessup**, J. E., and **Coakley**, R. W., (ed.), *A Guide to the Study and Use of Military History*, Washington, DC, 1979.

1.213 **Johnson**, J. W., *Historic U.S. Court Cases, 1690–1990. An Encyclopedia*, New York, 1992.

1.214 **Kadish**, S. H., (ed.), *Encyclopedia of Crime and Justice*, New York, 1983. Four volume reference work that is strongest for the study of modern criminology.

1.215 **Kallenbach**, J. E., *American State Governors, 1776–1976*, Dobbs Ferry, NY, 1979.

1.216 **Kruschke**, E. R., *Encyclopedia of Third Parties in the United States*, Santa Barbara, CA, 1991.

1.217 **Kyvig**, D. E., *Nearby History. Exploring the Past Around You*, Nashville, TN, 1982.

1.218 **Lane**, J. C., *America's Military Past. A Guide to Information Sources*, Detroit, 1980.

1.219 **Levy**, L. W., *Encyclopedia of the American Constitution*, New York, 1986. A four volume set.

1.220 **Lincove**, D. A., *The Anglo-American Relationship. An Annotated Bibliography of Scholarship, 1945–1985*, New York, 1988.

1.221 **Maisel**, L. S., and **Bassett**, C., (ed.), *Political Parties and Elections in the United States. An Encyclopedia*, New York, 1991.

1.222 **McCarrick**, E. M., *U.S. Constitutions. A Guide to Information Sources*, Detroit, 1980.

1.223 **Mechling**, J., *The Pacific Basin. An Annotated Bibliography*, New York, 1985.

1.224 **Miles**, W., *The People's Voice. An Annotated Bibliography of American Presidential Campaign Newspapers, 1828–1984*, New York, 1987.

1.225 **Millett**, S. M., *A Selected Bibliography of American Constitutional History*, Santa Barbara, CA, 1975.

1.226 **Murphy**, T. P., *Urban Politics. A Guide to Information Sources*, Detroit, 1978.

1.227 **Murphy**, T. P., *Urban Politics. A Guide to Information Sources*, Detroit, 1978.

1.228 **Newton**, M., *Terrorism in the United States*

and Europe, 1800–1959. An Annoted
Bibliography, New York, 1988.

1.229 **O'Brien**, S., *American Political Leaders.
From Colonial Times to the Present*, Santa
Barbara, CA, 1991.

1.230 **Okinshevich**, L., *United States History and
Historiography in Postwar Soviet Writing
1945–1970*, Santa Barbara, CA, 1976.

1.231 **Parks**, R., (ed.), *Connecticut, A
Bibliography of its History*, Hanover, NH,
1986.

1.232 **Peterson**, C. S., *Consolidated Bibliography
of County Histories in Fifty States in 1961*,
Baltimore, 1973.

1.233 **Plischke**, E., *U.S. Foreign Relations. A
Guide to Information Sources*, Detroit,
1980.

1.234 **Rockwood**, D. S., *American Third Parties
Since the Civil War. An Annotated
Bibliography*, New York, 1985.

1.235 **Rouse**, J. E., *Urban Housing, Public and
Private. A Guide to Information Sources*,
Detroit, 1978.

1.236 **Sealock**, R. B., *Bibliography of Place-
Name Literature. United States and Canada*,
Chicago, 1982.

1.237 **Shavit**, D., *The United States in Asia. A
Historical Dictionary*, New York, 1990.

1.238 **Shavit**, D., *The United States in the Middle
East. A Historical Dictionary*, New York,
1988.

1.239 **Shearer**, B. F., *States Names, Seals, Flags,
and Symbols. a Historical Guide*, New
York, 1987.

1.240 **Shumsky**, N. L., and **Crimmins**, T.,
Urban America. A Historical Bibliography,
Santa Barbara, CA, 1983. Abstracts of
books, articles, and dissertations taken
from *America: History and Life*.

1.241 **Sobel**, R., (ed.), *Biographical Directory of
the United States Executive Branch,
1774–1977*, Westport, CT, 1977.

1.242 **Socolofsky**, H. E., and **Dean**, V. M.,
Kansas History. An Annotated Bibliography,
Westport, CT, 1992. Reviews the
secondary literature on the Sunflower State
as well as indicating the holdings of the
major repositories.

1.243 **Steiner**, M. C., *Region and Regionalism in
the United States. A Sourcebook for the
Humanities and Social Sciences*, New York,
1988.

1.244 **Stoddard**, E. R., **Nostrand**, R. L., and
West, J. P., (ed.), *Borderlands Sourcebook.
A Guide to the Literature on Northern Mexico
and the American Southwest*, Norman, OK,

1983.

1.245 **Stubbs**, W., *Congressional Committees,
1789–1982. A Checklist*, Westport, CT,
1985.

1.246 **Vexler**, R. I., *The Vice-Presidents and
Cabinet Members. Bibliographies Arranged
Chronologically by Administration*, Dobbs
Ferry, NY, 1975.

1.247 **Wilson**, C. R., and **Ferris**, W., (ed.),
Encyclopedia of Southern Culture, Chapel
Hill, NC, 1989.

1.248 **Wilson**, D. E., *National Planning in the
United States. An Annotated Bibliography*,
Boulder, CO, 1979.

HISTORIOGRAPHY

General

1.249 **Abbot**, A., 'Conceptions of time and
events in social science methods. Causal
and Narrative Approaches', *Historical
Methods*, XXIII, 1990, 140–150. Uses the
analysis of careers and employment to
argue for a general reorientation of how
social science historians should think about
their methods.

1.250 **Achenbaum**, W. A., 'Public history's past,
present, and prospects', *American
Historical Review*, XCII, 1987, 1162–1174.
Reviews recent writings on the practice of
"public" history, or the applied study of
history to solving problems in government
and the private sector.

1.251 **Adams**, W. P., 'American history abroad.
Personal reflections on the conditions of
scholarship in West Germany', *Reviews
in American History*, XIV, 1986,
557–568.

1.252 **Blatti**, Jo, (ed.), *Past Meets Present. Essays
about Historic Interpretation and Public
Audiences*, Washington, DC, 1987.

1.253 **Bogue**, A. G., *Clio and the Bitch Goddess.
Quantification in American Political History*,
Beverly Hills, CA, 1983.

1.254 **Bonazzi**, T., 'American history. The view
from Italy', *Reviews in American History*,
XIV, 1986, 523–541.

1.255 **Bratt**, J. D., 'God, tribe, and nation:
ethno-religious history at middle age. A

review article', *Comparative Studies in Society and History*, XXXIII, 1991, 176–186.

1.256 **Cmiel**, K., 'After objectivity: what comes next in history?', *American Literary History*, II, 1990, 170–181. A review essay about the practice of history in the poststructuralist period.

1.257 **Debouzy**, Marianne, 'American history in France', *Reviews in American History*, XIV, 1986, 542–556. Part of a symposium on American history as seen from abroad, sponsored by the editors of *Reviews in American History*.

1.258 **Fitch**, Nancy, 'Statistical fantasies and historical facts. History in crisis and its methodological implications', *Historical Methods*, XVII, 1984, 239–254. Part of an entire issue of the journal devoted to appraising the state of quantitative history.

1.259 **Fogel**, R. W., and **Elton**, G. R., *Which Road to the Past? Two Views of History*, New Haven, CT, 1983. The two views – quantitative versus narrative – are less like oil and water in this friendly exchange of essays.

1.260 **Foner**, E., *The New American History*, Philadelphia, 1990. A series of pamphlets, sponsored by the American Historical Association, that reviews the findings in various fields of American history.

1.261 **Frisch**, M., 'American history and the structures of collective memory. A modest exercise in empirical iconography', *Journal of American History*, LXXV, 1989, 1130–1155. Reports the results of a questionnaire/survey in his American History classes concerning students' historical knowledge and describes his findings.

1.262 **Frisch**, M., *A Shared Authority. Essays on the Craft and Meaning of Oral and Public History*, Albany, NY, 1990.

1.263 **Guggisberg**, H. R., 'European approaches to American history. The role of religion in American intellectual history as seen from Europe', *Reviews in American History*, XIV, 1986, 569–579. Part of a symposium on the topic of American history as seen from abroad.

1.264 **Hamerow**, T. S., 'The bureaucratization of history', *American Historical Review*, XCIV, 1989, 654–660. An attack on the "new" history as practiced today.

1.265 **Hamerow**, T. S., *Reflections on History and Historians*, Madison, WI, 1987. A critical

look at the historical profession and its recent tendency toward fragmenting into dissonant parts.

1.266 **Haskins**, L., and **Kirk**, J., *Understanding Quantitative History*, Cambridge, MA, 1990.

1.267 **Heale**, M. J., 'American history. The view from Britain', *Reviews in American History*, XIV, 1986, 501–522. One of a set of invited essays by Americanists abroad.

1.268 **Hexter**, J. H., 'Carl Becker, Professor Novick and me, or cheer up, Professor N!', *American Historical Review*, XCVI, 1991, 675–682. Part of an AHR Forum review of Peter Novick's *That Noble Dream*. The Forum also includes the comments of Linda Gordon, D. A. Hollinger, A. Megill, Dorothy Ross, and a response from Novick.

1.269 **Himmelfarb**, Gertrude, 'Some Reflections on the New History', *American Historical Review*, XCIV, 1989, 661–670. A conservative critique of the intellectual and social basis of the writings that make up the "new" history.

1.270 **Hollinger**, D. A., 'The Return of the prodigal. The persistence of historical knowing', *American Historical Review*, XCIV, 1989, 610–621. A critical response to David Harlan's embrace of poststructuralism in an AHR Forum.

1.271 **Jedlicki**, J., 'The image of America in Poland, 1776–1945', *Reviews in American History*, XIV, 1986, 669–688.

1.272 **Kammen**, M. G., (ed.), *The Past Before Us. Contemporary Historical Writing in the United States*, Ithaca, NY, 1980. The official view of the state of the profession at the beginning of the 1980s, as sponsored by the American Historical Association.

1.273 **Kammen**, M. G., *Selvages and Biases. The Fabric of History in American Culture*, Ithaca, NY, 1987.

1.274 **Karamanski**, T. J., (ed.), *Ethics and Public History. An Anthology*, Malabar, FL, 1990.

1.275 **Karsten**, P., and **Modell**, J., (ed.), *Theory, Method, and Practice in Social and Cultural History*, New York, 1992.

1.276 **Kinnell**, Susan K., (ed.), *Historiography. An Annotated Bibliography of Journal Articles, Books, and Dissertations*, Santa Barbara, CA, 1987. A handy summary, taken from the abstracts of ABC-CLIO's *America: History and Life*.

1.277 **Kloppenburg**, J. T., 'Objectivity and historicism. A century of American historical writing', *American Historical Review*, XCVI, 1989, 1011–1030. Reviews Peter Novick's *That Noble Dream* and offers a critique of both the objectivity ideal and the historicist alternative.

1.278 **Kutler**, S. I., and **Katz**, S. N., (ed.), *The Promise of American History*, Baltimore, 1982. A special issue of *Reviews in American History* that carried essays on the new work in most of the new sub-fields; included are review articles on chronological subjects such as Jacksonian America, Reconstruction, and Progressivism, and topical review articles of women's history, social mobility studies, southern history, Native American history, legal history, education history, intellectual history, and diplomatic history.

1.279 **Lears**, T. J. J., 'The concept of cultural hegemony. Problems and possibilities', *American Historical Review*, XC, 1985, 567–593. Considers the burgeoning use of Gramscian analysis and how well the concept fits across different time periods.

1.280 **Leon**, W., and **Rosenzweig**, R., (ed.), *History Museums in the United States. A Critical Assessment*, Urbana, IL, 1989. A dozen essays that survey the state of public history, as practiced in museums.

1.281 **Levine**, L. W., 'The unpredictable past. Reflections on recent American historiography', *American Historical Review*, XCIV, 1989, 671–679. Part of an AHR Forum on the "New History".

1.282 **Mawdsley**, E., *et al.*, (ed.), *History and Computing III. Historians, Computers, and Data. Applications in Research and Teaching*, 1990. A useful how-to guide for the cliometrician.

1.283 **Monkkonen**, E. H., 'The challenge of quantitative history', *Historical Methods*, XVII, 1984, 86–93. Part of a special issue of the journal devoted to taking stock of social science methods in history.

1.284 **Novick**, P., *That Noble Dream. The 'Objectivity Question' and the American Historical Profession*, New York, 1988. A monumental survey that interprets the various schools of American historical writing, and at the same time offers a social history of the profession.

1.285 **Reiff**, Janice L., *Structuring the Past. The Use of Computers in History*, Washington, DC, 1991.

1.286 **Scott**, Joan Wallach, 'History in crisis?

The others' side of the story', *American Historical Review*, XCIV, 1989, 680–692. An attack on the conservative critique of the new history, especially that proposed by Gertrude Himmelfarb.

1.287 **Sternsher**, B., *Consensus, Conflict, and American Historians*, Bloomington, IN, 1975.

1.288 **Thelen**, D., 'Memory and American History', *Journal of American History*, LXXV, 1989, 1117–1129. Describes the role of memory and its uses and shortcomings in history.

1.289 **Thelen**, D., (ed.), 'Toward the internationalization of American history. A round table', *Journal of American History*, LXXIX, 1992, 432–542. A special issue of the *Journal of American History* devoted to the views of Americanists working abroad. Included are short articles by scholars from Germany, the Congo, Quebec, Mexico, France, Algeria, Japan, Great Britain, Russia, Cuba, and Italy.

1.290 **Thomas**, B., *The New Historicism and Other Old-Fashioned Topics*, Princeton, NJ, 1991.

1.291 **Wise**, G., *American Historical Explanations. A Strategy for Grounded Inquiry*, Minneapolis, MN, 1980.

Demography, family, and health

1.292 **Fox**, D. M., 'The new historiography of American medical education', *History of Education Quarterly*, XXVI, 1986, 117–124.

1.293 **Hareven**, Tamara K., 'The history of the family and the complexity of social change', *American Historical Review*, XCVI, 1991, 95–124. Reviews the development of the sub-field of family history and the methodological innovations associated with its practice.

1.294 **Leasure**, J. W., 'United States demographic and family history: a review essay', *Historical Methods*, XVI, 1983, 163–168.

1.295 **Leavitt**, Judith Walzer, 'Medicine in context. A review essay of the history of medicine', *American Historical Review*, XCV, 1990, 1471–1484. Reviews the recent literature and analyzes how the methods and concerns of social history have come to inform the writing of medical history.

1.296 **Marcy**, P. T., 'Factors affecting the fecundity and fertility of historical populations. A review', *Journal of Family History*, VI, 1981, 309–326.

1.297 **O'Connor**, B. C., 'Working-class kinship networks: a marriage of methods', *Journal of Urban History*, X, 1984, 187–194.

1.298 **Smith**, Judith E., 'Family history and feminist history', *Feminist Studies*, XVII, 1991, 349–364.

Class, gender, and social relations

1.299 **DuBois**, Ellen Carol, (ed.), *Feminist Scholarship. Kindling in the Groves of Academe*, Urbana, IL, 1985.

1.300 **Cott**, Nancy F., 'What's in a name? The limits of "social feminism". Or, expanding the vocabulary of women's history', *Journal of American History*, LXXVI, 1989, 809–829. A review of how the term "social feminism" was invented to describe women's reform activities before suffrage, and how that term now limits discourse.

1.301 **Feinberg**, W., 'On a new direction for educational history', *History of Education Quarterly*, XXI, 1981, 223–239.

1.302 **Guttman**, A., 'Who's on first? Or, books on the history of American sports', *Journal of American History*, LXVI, 1979, 348–354. Reviews the first wave of social history books on sports and popular culture.

1.303 **Hoffer**, P. C., 'Counting crime in premodern England and America: a review essay', *Historical Methods*, XIV, 1981, 187–193. Reviews the recent literature on estimating crime from court records in the seventeenth and eighteenth centuries.

1.304 **Howe**, D. W., 'The history of education as cultural history', *History of Education Quarterly*, XXII, 1982, 205–214.

1.305 **LeMahieu**, D. L., 'The history of British and American sport: a review article', *Comparative Studies in Society and History*, XXXII, 1990, 838–844.

1.306 **Lenger**, F., 'Class, culture, and class consciousness in ante-bellum Lynn. A critique of Alan Dawley and Paul Faler', *Social History*, VI, 1981, 317–332.

1.307 **Nugent**, W., *Structures of American Social History*, Bloomington, IN, 1981.

1.308 **Sklar**, Kathryn Kish, 'A call for comparisons', *American Historical Review*, XCV, 1990, 1109–1114. Reviews several articles on women's history that the AHR published and finds that key differences in women's historical experience may be traced to the nature of state power.

1.309 **Sparhawk**, Ruth M., *American Women in Sport, 1887–1987. A 100-year Chronology*, Metuchen, NJ, 1989. Strongest for the postwar period.

1.310 **Tyrrell**, I. R., *The Absent Marx. Class Analysis and Liberal History in Twentieth-Century America*, New York, 1986.

1.311 **Walsh**, Margaret, 'Working women in the United States', *Society for the Study of Labour History Bulletin*, LIV, 1989, 37–53.

1.312 **Zunz**, O., (ed.), *Reliving the Past. The Worlds of Social History*, Chapel Hill, NC, 1985. Includes the practice of North American social history among reviews of the discipline as practiced around the world.

Religion, beliefs, ideas, and culture

1.313 **Bitton**, D., and **Arrington**, L. J., *Mormons and their Historians*, Salt Lake City, UT, 1988.

1.314 **Dolan**, J. P., 'The immigrants and their gods: a new perspective in American religious history', *Church History*, LVII, 1988, 61–72. Suggests that historians of religion look more closely at immigrant beliefs and worship.

1.315 **Harlan**, D., 'Intellectual history and the return of literature', *American Historical Review*, XCIV, 1989, 581–609. Argues that poststructuralism unmasks the illusion of the historian seeking to situate texts in their historical context. Instead, practitioners of intellectual history should cast their work as a dialogue with past thinkers.

1.316 **Hollinger**, D. A., *In the American Province. Studies in the History and Historiography of Ideas*, Bloomington, IN, 1985.

1.317 **Jacoby**, R., 'A new intellectual history?', *American Historical Review*, XCVII, 1992, 405–424. A review of the state of the field.

1.318 **LaCapra**, D., 'Intellectual history and its ways', *American Historical Review*, XCVII, 1992, 425–439.

1.319 **Littman**, R. A., 'The real history of

psychology stands up', *Journal of the History of the Behavioral Sciences*, XXVII, 1991, 204–213.

1.320 **Marty**, M. E., 'Review essay: new visibility for the invisible institution', *Georgia Historical Quarterly*, LXXV, 1991, 385–400. Reviews recent writings on the history of the black church.

1.321 **Merkley**, P., 'Religion and the political prosperity of America. An historian's reflections on recent publications in religious studies', *Canadian Journal of History*, XXVI, 1991, 277–291.

1.322 **Noll**, M. A., 'Evaluating north Atlantic religious history, 1640–1859: a review article', *Comparative Studies in Society and History*, XXXIII, 1991, 415–425. Reviews recent writings on the emergence of an Anglo-American religious persuasion.

1.323 **Parker**, H. M., 'New views of American religion", *Social Science Journal*, LXXXI, 1981, 111–114.

1.324 **Reinitz**, R., *Irony and Consciousness. American Historiography and Reinhold Niebuhr's Vision*, Lewisburg, PA, 1980.

1.325 **Alexander**, T. G., (ed.), '*Great Basin Kingdom' Revisited. Contemporary Perspectives*, Logan, UT, 1991. An historiographical appraisal of Leonard Arrington's 1958 classic.

1.326 **Reising**, R. J., 'Reconstructing Parrington', *American Quarterly*, XLI, 1989, 155–164. A review of the Progressive literary critic/historian and the rise and fall of his views on American culture.

1.327 **Robertson**, R., 'Parsons on the evolutionary significance of American religion', *Sociological Analysis*, XLIII, 1982, 307–325. Reviews the thought of the sociologist Talcott Parsons about the cause and effect relationship of religion in American history.

1.328 **Tucker**, B., 'The new American intellectual history', *Canadian Review of American Studies (Canada)*, XXII, 1991, 91–100. Reviews recent writings in intellectual history and notes the focus on culture as the new subject for the historian of ideas.

1.329 **Wind**, J. P., *Places of Worship. Exploring their History*, Nashville, TN, 1990. A primer about how to do local church history.

Work and enterprise

1.330 **Cutcliffe**, S. H., and **Post**, R. C., (ed.), *In Context. History and the History of Technology. Essays in Honor of Melvin Kranzberg*, Bethlehem, PA, 1989.

1.331 **Helmbold**, Lois Rita, and **Schofield**, Ann, 'Women's labor history, 1790–1945', *Reviews in American History*, XVII, 1989, 1501–1618.

1.332 **Holt**, W., 'The new American labor law history', *Labor History*, XXX, 1989, 275–293.

1.333 **Kealey**, G. S., 'Gutman and Montgomery: politics and direction of U.S. labor and working-class history in the 1980s', *International Labor and Working-Class History*, XXXVII, 1990, 58–68.

1.334 **Norrell**, R. J., 'After thirty years of "new" labour history, there is still no socialism in Reagan country', *Historical Journal*, XXXIII, 1990, 227–238.

1.335 **Staudenmaier**, J. M., 'Comment. Recent trends in the history of technology', *American Historical Review*, XCV, 1990, 715–725. Reviews the recent literature on the history of technology and finds the field split between those with a Whiggish view of progress and those who find all technology reflecting the social relationships of power.

1.336 **Wilentz**, S., and **Stansell**, Christine, 'Gutman's legacy', *Labor History*, XXIX, 1988, 378–390. Reviews the contributions of historian Herbert Gutman to the "new labor history".

Race and ethnic identity

1.337 **Ashworth**, J., 'The relationship between capitalism and humanitarianism', *American Historical Review*, XCII, 1987, 813–828. Comments on Thomas Haskell's 'Capitalism and the origins of the humanitarian sensibility'. Haskell has a rejoinder to Ashworth and David B. Davis immediately following in the same issue of the *AHR*.

1.338 **Chan**, Sucheng, 'In appreciation of Asian American local history', *Amerasia Journal*, XVI, 1990, 247–253. Reviews the recent flowering of writing on Asian-Americans in various locations throughout the American West.

1.339 **Davis**, D. B., 'Reflections on abolitionism and ideological hegemony', *American Historical Review*, XCII, 1987, 797–812. Comments on Thomas Haskell's "Capitalism and the origins of the humanitarian sensibility".

1.340 **Dorries**, R. R., 'German emigration to the United States: a review essay on recent West German publications', *Journal of American Ethnic History*, VI, 1986, 71–83.

1.341 **Dusinberre**, W., 'The aftermath of American slavery', *History*, LXVIII, 1983, 64–79. A review article on the new literature about Reconstruction.

1.342 **Fischer**, D. H., 'Albion and the critics. Further evidence and reflection. "Albion's Seed". Four British folkways in America – A symposium', *William and Mary Quarterly*, XLVIII, 1991, 223–308.

1.343 **Harris**, R. L., Jr., 'The flowering of Afro-American history', *American Historical Review*, XCII, 1987, 1150–1161. Reviews the recent emergence of black history as one of the central themes of the profession, and the contributions of black historians as defining of the field.

1.344 **Haskell**, T. L., 'Capitalism and the origins of the humanitarian sensibility', *American Historical Review*, XC, 1985, 339–361. A two-part article that connects the antislavery appeal with the wider view of a common humanity throughout the world that capitalists experienced via market relations. More of the argument applies to Great Britain, but the American case fits his argument, too.

1.345 **Hine**, Darlene Clark, (ed.), *The State of Afro-American History. Past, Present, and Future*, Baton Rouge, LA, 1986. A collection of papers presented at a 1983 conference that surveyed the scholarship and teaching of black history.

1.346 **Kivisto**, P., and **Blanck**, D., (ed.), *American Immigrants and Their Generations. Studies and Commentaries on the Hansen Thesis after Fifty Years*, Urbana, IL, 1990. Reviews the argument put forward by Marcus Lee Hansen in the late 1930s that immigrants and their descendants altered their ethnic identity according to the number of generations they were removed from Europe.

1.347 **Parish**, P. J., *Slavery. History and Historians*, New York, 1989. Covers the new literature on slavery written in the 1970s and 1980s with an emphasis on the major scholars who transformed the field.

1.348 **Parman**, D. L., and **Price**, Catherine, '"Work in Progress". The emergence of Indian history as a professional field', *Western Historical Quarterly*, XX, 1989, 185–196.

1.349 **Radzilowski**, T. C., 'Old and new wine in new bottles: current books in Polish-American history', *Journal of American Ethnic History*, IX, 1989, 96–107.

1.350 **Sheridan**, T. E., 'Chicano social history', *Journal of the Southwest*, XXXI, 1989, 249–256.

1.351 **Vaughan**, A. T., 'From white man to redskin', *American Historical Review*, LXXXVII, 1982, 917–953.

Space, movement, and place

1.352 **Chavez**, T. E., 'Heartland of the Spanish frontier. A review essay', *New Mexico Historical Review*, LXV, 1990, 357–363.

1.353 **Cronon**, W., 'A place for stories: nature, history, and narrative', *Journal of American History*, LXXVIII, 1992, 1347–1376. Treatment of the history of the American environment through the use of narrative.

1.354 **Cronon**, W., **Miles**, G. and **Gitlin**, J., *Under an Open Sky. Rethinking America's Western Past*, New York, 1992. A collection of essays from practitioners of the "new western history".

1.355 **Dillon**, M. L., *Ulrich Bonnell Phillips. Historian of the Old South*, Baton Rouge, LA, 1985. Part of a continuing reassessment of Phillips, this volume maintains that his work is so flawed by racism that he has little to say to practising historians today.

1.356 **Gillette**, H., and **Miller**, Z. L., (ed.), *American Urbanism. A Historiographical Review*, New York, 1987.

1.357 **Grantham**, D. W., 'Making southern history and culture more accessible: an essay on recent reference works', *Georgia Historical Quarterly*, XXIV, 1990, 433–450.

1.358 **Hall**, K. L., *A Comprehensive Bibliography of American Constitutional and Legal History*, Millwood, NY, 1984.

1.359 **Heard**, J. N., (ed.), *Handbook of the American Frontier. Four Centuries of Indian-White Relationships*, Metuchen, NJ, 1990. A projected five volume series, two of which have appeared through 1994.

1.360 **Luebke**, F. C., *et al.*, (ed.), *Mapping the North American Plains. Essays in the History of Cartography*, Norman, OK, 1987.

1.361 **Malone**, M. P., *Historians and the American West*, Lincoln, NE, 1983. Eighteen essays on what has become the New Western History broadly organized around the theme of the American West as a distinctive region, rather than as a one-time frontier society.

1.362 **Mattson**, V. E., and **Marion**, W. E., (ed.), *Frederick Jackson Turner. A Reference Guide*, Boston, 1985.

1.363 **Nichols**, R. L., (ed.), *American Frontier and Western Issues. A Historiographical Review*, Westport, CT, 1986.

1.364 **Nouailhat**, Y.-H., 'Franco-American relations. French perspectives', *Reviews in American History*, XIV, 1986, 653–668.

1.365 **Ridge**, M., (ed.), *Fredrick Jackson Turner. Wisconsin's Historian of the Frontier*, Madison, WI, 1986.

1.366 **Roper**, J. H., *U. B. Phillips. A Southern Mind*, Macon, GA, 1984. Evaluates the writings of the early twentieth century historian of race and slavery as essentially fixated on white racism and southern themes and less a Progressive historian than other writers have suggested.

1.367 **Runte**, A., 'Public lands and public lives: change and continuity in environmental history', *Public Historian*, XII, 1990, 115–119.

1.368 **Russell**, J. M., 'Regional and national perspectives on American urban history', *Canadian Review of American Studies*, XXI, 1990, 265–274.

1.369 **Russo**, D. J., *Keepers of Our Past. Local Historical Writing in the United States, 1820s–1930s*, Westport, CT, 1988.

1.370 **Schlereth**, T. J., *Cultural History and Material Culture. Everyday Life, Landscapes, Museums*, Ann Arbor, MI, 1990.

1.371 **Shafer**, B. E., (ed.), *The End of Realignment. Interpreting American Electoral Eras*, Madison, WI, 1991.

1.372 **Sherry**, M. S., 'War and weapons: the new cultural history', *Diplomatic History*, XIV, 1990, 433–446.

1.373 **Worster**, D., (ed.), *The Ends of the Earth. Perspectives on Modern Environmental History*, New York, 1988.

The state and the public realm

1.374 **Haines**, G. K., and **Walker**, J. S., (ed.), *American Foreign Relations. A Historiographical Review*, Westport, CT, 1981.

1.375 **Hall**, K. L., *A Comprehensive Bibliography of American Constitutional and Legal History*, Millwood, NY, 1984.

1.376 **Nouailhat**, Y.-H., 'Franco-American relations. French perspectives', *Reviews in American History*, XIV, 1986, 653–668.

1.377 **Shafer**, B. E., (ed.), *The End of Realignment. Interpreting American Electoral Eras*, Madison, WI, 1991.

1.378 **Sherry**, M. S., 'War and weapons: the new cultural history', *Diplomatic History*, XIV, 1990, 433–446.

SURVEYS AND TEXTS

General

1.379 **Handlin**, O., and **Handlin**, Lillian, *Liberty in America. 1600 to the Present*, New York, 1989– . A multi-volume series that places the struggle for liberty at the center of American history.

1.380 **Johnson**, G. R., (ed.), *The Will of the People. The Legacy of George Mason*, Fairfax, VA, 1991. Essays about attempts to implement the popular will from Mason's time to the present.

1.381 **Luedtke**, L. S., *Making America. The Society and Culture of the United States*, Chapel Hill, NC, 1992.

1.382 **Robertson**, J. O., *American Myth, American Reality*, New York, 1980. An extended essay about the national purpose, community, the individual, and the use of power, all as exemplified in some enduring national myths.

1.383 **Smith**, P., *A People's History of the United States*, New York, 1984. An eight volume set that starts American history at the Revolution and continues up to the Second World War. A clear and consistent narrative voice makes this survey distinctive.

1.384 **Stearns**, P. N., *Jealousy. The Evolution of*

an Emotion in American History, New York, 1989.

1.385 **Vance**, W. L., *America's Rome*, New Haven, CT, 1989. A two volume work that examines American views on ancient and Catholic Rome, and how those views have shaped American thought.

1.386 **Walker**, R. H., *Reform in America. The Continuing Frontier*, Lexington, KY, 1985. An attempt to organize the whole of American reform into three categories: the promotion of democracy, the inclusion of the excluded, and the search for utopias.

1.387 **Wilkinson**, R., *The Pursuit of American Character*, New York, 1988.

1.388 **Woodward**, C. V., *The Old World's New World*, New York, 1991.

1.389 **Woodward**, W., 'America as a culture: a fourfold heritage?', *Journal of American Culture*, XI, 1988, 1–32.

1.390 **Zelinsky**, W., *Nation into State. The Shifting Symbolic Foundations of American Nationalism*, Chapel Hill, NC, 1989.

Biography

1.391 **Burton**, D. H., *et al.*, (ed.), *An Anglo-American Plutarch*, Lanham, MD, 1990.

1.392 **Nagel**, P. C., *The Lees of Virginia. Seven Generations of an American Family*, New York, 1990.

1.393 **Rishel**, J. F., *Founding Families of Pittsburgh. The Evolution of a Regional Elite*, Pittsburgh, 1990.

Demography, family, and health

1.394 **Alvarez**, R. R., *Familia, Migration and Adaptation in Baja and Alta California, 1880–1975*, Berkeley, CA, 1987.

1.395 **Anderson**, Margo J., *The American Census. A Social History*, New Haven, CT, 1988. A recounting of the decennial population count that tells the political and bureaucratic history behind each census, along with a discussion of the method used to find and count each American.

1.396 **Bates**, Barbara, *Bargaining for Life. A Social History of Tuberculosis, 1876–1938*, Philadelphia, 1992.

1.397 **Bell**, M., *Major Butler's Legacy. Five Generations of a Slaveholding Family*, Athens, GA, 1987. Follows Pierce Butler from Ireland to the Sea Islands of Georgia in the eighteenth century, and the subsequent four generations of the Butler family up to the twentieth century.

1.398 **Brewer**, Priscilla J., 'The demographic features of the Shaker decline, 1787–1900', *Journal of Interdisciplinary History*, XV, 1984, 31–52.

1.399 **Cable**, Mary, *The Little Darlings. A History of Child Rearing in America*, New York, 1975.

1.400 **Chudacoff**, H. P., *How Old Are You? Age Consciousness in American Culture*, Princeton, NJ, 1989. Surveys the history of thought about age and social categories based upon age.

1.401 **Clement**, Priscilla Ferguson, 'Children and charity: orphanages in New Orleans, 1817–1914', *Louisiana History*, XXVII, 1986, 337–351.

1.402 **Cole**, T. R., *The Journey of Life. A Cultural History of Aging in America*, New York, 1992.

1.403 **Coontz**, Stephanie, *The Social Origins of Private Life. A History of American Families. 1600–1900*, New York, 1988.

1.404 **Degler**, C. N., *At Odds. Women and the Family in America from the Revolution to the Present*, New York, 1980. A survey which finds persistent tension between the aspirations of women and the demands of the family.

1.405 **D'Emilio**, J., and **Freedman**, Estelle B., *Intimate Matters. A History of Sexuality in America*, New York, 1988.

1.406 **Demos**, J. P., *Past, Present and Personal. The Family and the Life Course in American History*, New York, 1986. A set of his collected essays on family history.

1.407 **Duberman**, M. B., **Vicinus**, Martha, and **Chauncey**, G., (ed.), *Hidden from History. Reclaiming the Gay and Lesbian Past*, New York, 1989.

1.408 **Fox**, Vivian C., and **Quitt**, M. H., *Loving, Parenting and Dying. The Family Cycle in England and America, Past and Present*, New York, 1980.

1.409 **Gemery**, H. A., 'European emigration to North America, 1700–1820: numbers and quasi-numbers', *Perspectives in American History*, I, 1984, 283–342.

1.410 **Gevitz**, N., (ed.), *Other Healers. Unorthodox Medicine in America*, Baltimore, 1988. A collection of nine essays on the practice of medicine outside the mainstream, including chiropractic and homeopathy.

1.411 **Gordon**, Linda, *Heroes of Their Own Lives. The Politics and History of Family Violence, Boston, 1880–1960*, New York, 1988.

1.412 **Gordon**, M., (ed.), *The American Family in Social-historical Perspective*, New York, 1983. The third edition.

1.413 **Graff**, H. J., (ed.), *Growing Up in America. Historical Experiences*, Detroit, 1987. A set of essays on the history of childhood and adolescence.

1.414 **Griswold de Castillo**, R., *La Familia. Chicano Families in the Urban Southwest, 1848 to the Present*, Notre Dame, IN, 1985.

1.415 **Haber**, Carole, *Beyond Sixty-Five. The Dilemma of Old Age in America's Past*, New York, 1983.

1.416 **Hareven**, Tamara K., and **Plakans**, A., (ed.), *Family History at the Crossroads. A Journal of Family History Reader*, Princeton, NJ, 1987. Compiled by the editors of the journal to review the state of the field.

1.417 **Harvey**, A. McG., *et al.*, *A Centennial History of Medicine at Johns Hopkins*, Baltimore, 1989. A two volume set that combines text and photographs to explore the history of the great teaching hospital at Baltimore's Johns Hopkins University.

1.418 **Heaton**, T. B., 'Four characteristics of the Mormon family: contemporary research on chastity, conjugality, children, and chauvinism', *Dialogue*, XX, 1987, 101–114.

1.419 **Hunter**, Jean E., and **Mason**, P. T., (ed.), *The American Family. Historical Perspectives*, Pittsburgh, 1991. Thirteen essays that collectively place family history within broader changes in social and economic life.

1.420 **Kett**, J., *Rites of Passage. Adolescence in America, 1790 to the Present*, New York, 1977.

1.421 **Kierner**, Cynthia A., *Traders and Gentlefolk. The Livingstons of New York, 1675–1790*, Ithaca, NY, 1992. Charts the rise and relative decline of the leading merchant-politician family of New York.

1.422 **Klepp**, Susan E., (ed.), 'Demography in early Philadelphia, 1690–1860', *Proceedings of the American Philosophical Society*, CXXXIII, 1989, 85–115. Introductory essay that sets the tone for an entire issue of the journal devoted to the demographic history of the Philadelphia region.

1.423 **Lane**, H., *When the Mind Hears. A History of the Deaf*, New York, 1984. Reviews the controversy between those who insisted on making the deaf understand oral language and those who promoted a separate sign language, with the author carrying the narrative to the present-day struggle of the deaf to gain civil rights.

1.424 **Lasch**, C., *Haven in a Heartless World. The Family Besieged*, New York, 1977.

1.425 **Leavitt**, Judith Walzer, *Brought to Bed. Childbearing in America, 1750–1950*, New York, 1986.

1.426 **Logue**, Barbara J., 'The case for birth control before 1850: Nantucket reexamined', *Journal of Interdisciplinary History*, XV, 1985, 371–391.

1.427 **Long**, Diana Elizabeth, and **Golden**, Janet, (ed.), *The American General Hospital. Communities and Social Contexts*, Ithaca, NY, 1989.

1.428 **Matossian**, Mary Kilbourne, *Poisons of the Past. Molds, Epidemics, and History*, New Haven, CT, 1989. Underscores the importance of regular food poisoning on events in the past, with particular attention paid to explaining mass episodes like religious revivals.

1.429 **Menken**, Jane, **Trussell, J.**, and **Watkins**, Susan, 'The nutrition fertility link: an evaluation of the evidence', *Journal of Interdisciplinary History*, XI, 1981, 425–441.

1.430 **Mintz**, S., and **Kellogg**, Susan, *Domestic Revolutions. A Social History of American Family Life*, New York, 1988. Surveys the change from the colonial patriarchal family to the companionate family of the twentieth century, with attention given to increased pressures on families due to the encroachment of market society.

1.431 **Moch**, Leslie Page, (ed.), *Essays on the Family and Historical Change*, College Station, TX, 1983. A volume of essays on aspects of the family in Europe and North America; notable is an essay on the history of dating among American adolescents.

1.432 **Mount**, F., *The Subversive Family. An Alternative History of Love and Marriage*, New York, 1992.

1.433 **Piven**, Frances Fox, and **Cloward**, R. A., 'Welfare doesn't shore up traditional family roles: a reply to Linda Gordon, "Welfare, and the Family"', *Social Research*, LV, 1988, 631–647.

1.434 **Pleck**, Elizabeth, *Domestic Tyranny. The*

Process of Reform Against Family Violence, New York, 1987.

1.435 **Pollock**, Linda A., *Forgotten Children. Parent-Child Relations from 1500–1900*, New York, 1983.

1.436 **Quale**, Gladys Robina, *A History of Marriage Systems*, New York, 1988. Considers American family history in a wide-ranging cross cultural study.

1.437 **Reid**, R. M., 'Church membership, consanguineous marriage, and migration in a Scotch-Irish frontier population', *Journal of Family History*, XIII, 1988, 397–414.

1.438 **Rosenberg**, C. E., and **Golden**, Janet, (ed.), *Framing Disease. Studies in Cultural History*, New Brunswick, NJ, 1992. Essays that unite cultural history with the history of medicine.

1.439 **Rothman**, Ellen K., *Hands and Hearts. A History of Courtship in America*, New York, 1984.

1.440 **Rotundo**, E. A., 'Body and soul. Changing ideals of American middle class manhood, 1790–1920', *Journal of Social History*, XVI, 1982, 23–38.

1.441 **Savitt**, T. L., and **Young**, J. H., (ed.), *Disease and Distinctiveness in the American South*, Knoxville, TN, 1988. Seven essays by historians on topics ranging from specific diseases like malaria and yellow fever to the use of patent medicines in the South.

1.442 **Schapiro**, M. O., 'Land availability and fertility in the United States, 1760–1870', *Journal of Economic History*, XLII, 1982, 577–600.

1.443 **Seward**, R. R., *The American Family. A Demographic History*, Beverly Hills, CA, 1978.

1.444 **Shammas**, Carole, **Salmon**, Marylynn, and **Dahlin**, M., *Inheritance in America. From Colonial Times to the Present*, New Brunswick, NJ, 1987.

1.445 **Smith**, D. S., 'Child-naming practices, kinship ties, and change in family attitudes in Hingham, Massachusetts, 1641 to 1880', *Journal of Social History*, XIV, 1985, 541–566.

1.446 **Swerdlow**, Amy, *Household and Kin. Families in Flux*, Old Westbury, NY, 1981.

1.447 **Vinovskis**, M. A., 'Family and schooling in colonial and nineteenth-century America', *Journal of Family History*, XII, 1987, 19–37.

1.448 **Walch**, T. J., *Our Family, Our Town. Essays on Family, and Local History Sources in the National Archives*, Washington, DC, 1987.

1.449 **Watkins**, Susan Cott, **Menken**, Jane A., and **Bongaarts**, J., 'Demographic foundations of family change', *American Sociological Review*, LII, 1987, 346–358.

1.450 **Wells**, R. V., *Revolutions in Americans' Lives. A Demographic Perspective on the History of Americans, Their Families, and Their Society*, Westport, CT, 1982. A thorough survey of American population history that also compares the nation's demographic past to that of western Europe.

1.451 **Wells**, R. V., *Uncle Sam's Family. Issues in and Perspectives on American Demographic History*, Albany, NY, 1985.

1.452 **West**, E., and **Petrik**, Paula, (ed.), *Small Worlds. Children and Adolescents in America, 1850–1950*, Lawrence, KS, 1992. A collection of diverse essays about adolescence.

Class, gender, and social relations

1.453 **Alexander**, C. C., *Our Game. An American Baseball History*, New York, 1991.

1.454 **Antler**, Joyce, and **Biklen**, Sari Knopp, (ed.), *Changing Education. Women as Radicals and Conservators*, Albany, NY, 1990. Essays on topics from coeducation at the college level to the training of midwives.

1.455 **Baer**, Judith A., *Women in American Law. The Struggle toward Equality from the New Deal to the Present*, New York, 1991.

1.456 **Baltzell**, E. D., *Puritan Boston and Quaker Philadelphia. Two Protestant Ethics and the Spirit of Class Authority and Leadership*, New York, 1979.

1.457 **Banner**, Lois W., *In Full Flower. Aging Women, Power, and Sexuality. A History*, New York, 1992.

1.458 **Barker-Benfield**, G. J., and **Clinton**, Catherine, (ed.), *Portraits of American Women from Settlement to the Present*, New York, 1991. Twenty-five short biographical sketches of American women, mostly famous ones like Eleanor Roosevelt, but some more obscure like the Cherokee Indian diplomat Nancy Ward.

1.459 **Berkin**, Carol Ruth, and **Norton**, Mary

Beth, *Women of America. A History,* Boston, 1979.

1.460 **Blocker**, J. S., *American Temperance Movements. Cycles of Reform*, Boston, 1989.

1.461 **Bodnar**, J., *Remaking America. Public Memory, Commemoration, and Patriotism in the Twentieth Century*, Princeton, NJ, 1991.

1.462 **Brown**, R. M., *No Duty to Retreat. Violence and Values in American History and Society*, New York, 1991. A survey of the enduring role that personal and organized violence has played in American history and its continuing cultural influence.

1.463 **Bushman**, R. L., *The Refinement of America. People, Houses, Cities*, New York, 1992.

1.464 **Button**, H. W., *History of Education and Culture in America*, Englewood Cliffs, NJ, 1989. Second edition of a survey of the history of schooling.

1.465 **Byrd**, Alicia D., 'Adult educational efforts of the American black church: 1600–1900', *Journal of Religious Thought*, XLIV, 1988, 83–92.

1.466 **Clifford**, Geraldine Joncich, and **Guthrie**, J. W., *Ed. School. A Brief for Professional Education*, Chicago, 1988. Explores the history of teacher training from the nineteenth century normal school through the teacher's college, and on up to today's education schools within the multiversity.

1.467 **Cloud**, Barbara, *The Business of Newspapers on the Western Frontier*, Reno, NV, 1992.

1.468 **Collier**, J. L., *The Rise of Selfishness in America*, New York, 1991.

1.469 **Cowan**, Ruth Schwartz, *More Work for Mother. The Ironies of Household Technology from the Open Hearth to the Microwave*, New York, 1983.

1.470 **Cremin**, L.J., *American Education. The National Experience, 1783–1876*, New York, 1980. The second volume of his trilogy on the history of American education.

1.471 **Cremin**, L. J., *American Education. The Metropolitan Experience, 1876–1980*, New York, 1988. Completes the author's trilogy of the history of American education.

1.472 **Current**, R. N., *Phi Beta Kappa in American Life. The First Two Hundred Years*, New York, 1990. A history of the collegiate honors society from its founding at the College of William and Mary through its spread across higher education.

1.473 **Curry**, R. O., and **Goodheart**, L. B., (ed.), *American Chameleon. Individualism in Trans-National Context*, Kent, OH, 1991.

1.474 **Czitrom**, D. J., *Media and the American Mind. From Morse to McLuhan*, Chapel Hill, NC, 1982.

1.475 **D'Emilio**, J., *Making Trouble. Essays on Gay History, Politics, and the University*, New York, 1992. Essays by the historian in the forefront of writing the history of homosexuality in the U.S.

1.476 **Evans**, Sara M., *Born for Liberty. A History of Women in America*, New York, 1989. The leading survey of women's history published to date.

1.477 **Faderman**, Lillian, *Odd Girls and Twilight Lovers. A History of Lesbian Life in Twentieth Century America*, New York, 1990.

1.478 **Forseth**, R., 'Ambivalent sensibilities: alcohol in history and literature', *American Quarterly*, XLII, 1990, 127–135.

1.479 **Gilfoyle**, T. J., *City of Eros. New York City, Prostitution, and the Commercialization of Sex, 1790–1920*, New York, 1992.

1.480 **Ginsburg**, Faye, and **Tsing**, Anna Lowenhaupt, (ed.), *Uncertain Terms. Negotiating Gender in American Culture*, Boston, 1990.

1.481 **Gordon**, Linda, 'What does welfare regulate? Welfare, and the family', *Social Research*, LV, 1988, 609–630.

1.482 **Groneman**, Carol, and **Norton**, Mary Beth, (ed.), *'To Toil the Livelong Day', America's Women at Work, 1790–1980*, Ithaca, NY, 1987. A collection of sixteen essays on various aspects of women in the workforce.

1.483 **Grover**, Kathryn, (ed.), *Fitness in American Culture. Images of Health, Sport, and the Body, 1830–1940*, Amherst, MA, 1989.

1.484 **Grover**, Kathryn, (ed.), *Hard at Play. Leisure in America, 1840–1940*, Amherst, MA, 1992.

1.485 **Guttman**, A., *A Whole New Ball Game. An Interpretation of American Sports*, Chapel Hill, NC, 1988. Makes use of the Weberian concept of modernization to understand the transformation of sports from playfulness to rational and bureaucratic games.

1.486 **Guttman**, A., *Women's Sports. A History,*

New York, 1991. A thorough survey that includes a section describing the contemporary scene.

1.487 **Heffer**, Jean, and **Rovet**, Jeanine, (ed.), *Why Is There No Socialism in the United States?* Paris, 1988. A collection of essays by political scientists and historians on a perennial puzzler.

1.488 **Hilmes**, Michele, *Hollywood and Broadcasting. From Radio to Cable*, Urbana, IL, 1990.

1.489 **Hindus**, M. S., *Prisons and Plantations. Crime, Justice and Authority in Massachusetts and South Carolina, 1767–1878*, Chapel Hill, NC, 1980.

1.490 **Hoff**, Joan, *Law, Gender, and Injustice. A Legal History of U.S. Women*, New York, 1991.

1.491 **Horowitz**, Helen Lefkowitz, *Campus Life. Undergraduate Cultures from the End of the Eighteenth Century to the Present*, New York, 1987. A review of student life on college campuses that focuses on the social life of students outside their classes and studies.

1.492 **Johnson**, D. R., *Policing the Underworld. The Impact of Crime on the Development of the American Police, 1800–1887*, Philadelphia, 1979.

1.493 **Johnson**, D. R., *American Law Enforcement. A History*, St. Louis, 1984.

1.494 **Johnson**, Loretta T., 'Charivari/shivaree: a European folk ritual on the American plains', *Journal of Interdisciplinary History*, XX, 1990, 371–387.

1.495 **Jones**, Jacqueline, *The Dispossessed. America's Underclasses from the Civil War to the Present*, New York, 1992.

1.496 **Karier**, C. J., *The Individual, Society and Education. A History of American Educational Ideas*, Urbana, IL, 1986.

1.497 **Kennedy**, Susan E., *If All We Did was to Weep at Home. A History of White Working-Class Women in America*, Bloomington, IN, 1979.

1.498 **Kessler-Harris**, Alice, *Out to Work. A History of Wage-Earning Women in the United States*, New York, 1982.

1.499 **Labaree**, D. F., *The Making of an American High School. The Credentials Market and the Central High School of Philadelphia, 1838–1939*, New Haven, CT, 1988.

1.500 **Lundgreen**, P., 'Engineering education in Europe and the U.S.A., 1750–1930: The rise to dominance of school culture and the engineering professions', *Annals of Science* XLVII, 1990, 33–75.

1.501 **McClellan**, B. E., and **Reese**, W. J., (ed.) *The Social History of American Education*, Urbana, IL, 1988.

1.502 **Morn**, F., *The Eye that Never Sleeps. A History of the Pinkerton National Detective Agency*, Bloomington, IN, 1982.

1.503 **Norton**, Mary Beth, 'The evolution of white women's experience in early America', *American Historical Review*, XCIX, 1984, 593–619.

1.504 **Ogden**, Annegret S., *The Great American Housewife. From Helpmate to Wage Earner, 1776–1986*, Westport, CT, 1986.

1.505 **Pessen**, E., *The Log Cabin Myth. The Social Backgrounds of the Presidents*, New Haven, CT, 1984.

1.506 **Popkewitz**, T., (ed.), *The Formation of School Subjects. The Struggle for Creating an American Institution*, Philadelphia, 1987.

1.507 **Radelet**, M. L., 'Executions of whites for crimes against blacks. Exceptions to the rule?', *Sociological Quarterly*, XXX, 1989, 529–544.

1.508 **Richards**, J. H., *Theater Enough. American Culture and the Metaphor of the World State, 1607–1789*, Durham, NC, 1991.

1.509 **Rorabaugh**, W. J., *The Alcoholic Republic. An American Tradition*, New York, 1979.

1.510 **Rosenberg**, Rosalind, *Divided Lives. American Women in the Twentieth Century*, New York, 1992.

1.511 **Rosenzweig**, R., and **Blackmar**, Elizabeth, *The Park and the People. A History of Central Park*, Ithaca, NY, 1992.

1.512 **Rubin**, Joan Shelley, *The Making of Middle-Brow Culture*, Chapel Hill, NC, 1992.

1.513 **Schlissel**, Lillian, **Ruiz**, Vicki L., and **Monk**, Janice, (ed.), *Western Women. Their Land, Their Lives*, Albuquerque, NM, 1988. A collection of essays that is strong on Indian women, Chicanas, and Mormon women.

1.514 **Schwager**, Sally, 'Educating women in America', *Signs*, XII, 1987, 333–372.

1.515 **Seidman**, S., *Romantic Longings. Love in America, 1830–1980*, New York, 1991.

1.516 **Seymour**, H. S., *Baseball. The People's Game*, New York, 1990. Avoids the usual focus on major league baseball in favor of a different look at the game played by people of all walks of life.

1.517 **Sloane**, D. C., *The Last Great Necessity. Cemeteries in American History*, Baltimore,

1991. Traces the movement away from churchyard burial grounds toward pastoral cemeteries that attempted to reflect American ideals.

1.518 **Spring**, J. H., *The American School, 1642–1985. Varieties of Historical Interpretation of the Foundations and Development of American Education*, New York, 1986.

1.519 **Staples**, W. G., *Castles of Our Conscience. Social Control and the American State, 1800–1985*, New Brunswick, NJ, 1990. A survey of the history of prisons and other total institutions.

1.520 **Shore**, E., *et al.*, (ed.), *The German-American Radical Press. The Shaping of a Left Political Culture, 1850–1940*, Urbana, IL, 1992.

1.521 **Stearns**, Carol Z., and **Stearns**, P. N., *Anger. The Struggle for Emotional Control in America's History*, Chicago, 1986.

1.522 **Stearns**, Carol Z., and **Stearns**, P. N., (ed.), *Emotions and Social Change. Toward a New Psychohistory*, New York, 1988.

1.523 **Stearns**, P. N., *Be a Man! Males in Modern Society*, New York, 1979.

1.524 **Swerdlow**, Amy, and **Lessinger**, Hanna, (ed.), *Class, Race, and Sex. The Dynamics of Control*, Boston, 1983.

1.525 **Taylor**, W. R., (ed.), *Inventing Times Square. Commerce and Culture at the Crossroads of the World*, New York, 1991. A collection of essays on the theme of the emergence of a district for popular and dangerous amusements.

1.526 **Tebbel**, J. W., and **Zuckerman**, Mary Ellen, *The Magazine in America, 1741–1990*, New York, 1991.

1.527 **Tyack**, D., **James**, T., and **Benavot**, A., *Law and the Shaping of Public Education, 1785–1954*, Madison, WI, 1987.

1.528 **Van Cleve**, J. V., *A Place of Their Own. Creating the Deaf Community*, Washington, DC, 1989.

1.529 **Walker**, S., *Popular Justice. A History of American Criminal Justice*, New York, 1980.

1.530 **Woloch**, Nancy, *Women and the American Experience*, New York, 1984.

1.531 **Zopf**, P. E., *American Women in Poverty*, New York, 1989.

Religion, beliefs, ideas, and culture

1.532 **Ross-Bryant**, Lynn, 'The land in American religious experience', *Journal of the American Academy of Religion*, LVIII, 1990, 333–356.

1.533 **Albanese**, Catherine L., *Nature Religion in America. From the Algonkian Indians to the New Age*, Chicago, 1990.

1.534 **Ariel**, Y., *On Behalf of Israel. American Fundamentalist Attitudes toward Jews, Judaism, and Zionism, 1865–1945*, Brooklyn, NY, 1991.

1.535 **Baer**, H. A., and **Singer**, M., (ed.), *African-American Religion in the Twentieth Century. Varieties of Protest and Accommodation*, Knoxville, TN, 1992. Collected essays on the transformation of the black church due to social and political factors.

1.536 **Barbour**, H., and **Frost**, J. W., *The Quakers*, Westport, CT, 1988.

1.537 **Barkun**, M., 'The awakening-cycle controversy', *Sociological Analysis*, XLVI, 1985, 425–443.

1.538 **Barth**, G., *Fleeting Moments. Nature and Culture in American History*, New York, 1990. An environmental history of the brief periods in American history when the construct of nature was in balance with human culture.

1.539 **Beckwith**, K., *American Women and Political Participation. The Impacts of Work, Generation, and Feminism*, New York, 1986.

1.540 **Bellah**, R. N., 'Civil religion in America', *Daedalus*, CXVII, 1988, 97–118.

1.541 **Bender**, T., *New York Intellect. A History of Intellectual Life in New York City from 1750 to the Beginnings of our own Time*, New York, 1987.

1.542 **Bennett**, D. H., *The Party of Fear. From Nativist Movements to the New Right in American History*, Chapel Hill, NC, 1988. A linking of nineteenth century anti-immigrant groups to twentieth century anti-communism, resting on the idea that the right wing has always focused its fear on "alien" people or ideas.

1.543 **Bercovitch**, S., *The American Jeremiad*, Madison, WI, 1978. Links the development of American culture to the sermons of decline and doom that characterized the second generation of New England Puritans.

1.544 **Brown**, R. D., *Knowledge Is Power. The Diffusion of Information in Early America, 1700–1865*, New York, 1989.

1.545 **Burnham**, J. C., *Paths into American Culture. Psychology, Medicine, and Morals*, Philadelphia, 1988.

1.546 **Carter**, P. A., *Revolt Against Destiny. An Intellectual History of the United States*, New York, 1989.

1.547 **Chatfield**, C., *The American Peace Movement. Ideals and Activism*, New York, 1992.

1.548 **Crews**, M., *The Church of God. A Social History*, Knoxville, TN, 1990.

1.549 **Davidson**, Cathy N., *Reading in America. Literature and Social History*, Baltimore, 1989. A collection of twelve essays on book publishing and the audience for reading.

1.550 **Davis**, C., *The History of Black Catholics in the United States*, New York, 1990.

1.551 **Dayton**, D. W., and **Johnson**, R. K., (ed.), *The Variety of American Evangelism*, Knoxville, TN, 1991.

1.552 **Dinnerstein**, L., *Uneasy at Home. Antisemitism and the American Jewish Experience*, New York, 1987.

1.553 **Feldman**, E., *Dual Destinies. The Jewish Encounter with Protestant America*, Urbana, IL, 1990. Covers the coexistence of Jews with Protestants from colonial times to the present, with an interesting analysis of how fundamentalists went from anti-Semitism to pro-Zionism in anticipation of the realization of the Book of Revelations.

1.554 **Fox**, R. W., and **Lears**, T. J. J., (ed.), *The Culture of Consumption. Critical Essays in American History, 1880–1980*, New York, 1983.

1.555 **Fox-Genovese**, Elizabeth, 'Two steps forward, one step back. New questions and old models in the religious history of American women', *Journal of the American Academy of Religion*, LIII, 1985, 465–471.

1.556 **Fuller**, R. C., *Alternative Medicine and American Religious Life*, New York, 1989. A work that takes wholistic healing seriously and connects it to the diversity of American religious history.

1.557 **Grenz**, S., 'North American report. Secular saints. Civil religion in America', *Baptist Quarterly*, XXXIII, 1990, 238–243.

1.558 **Hackett**, D. G., *The Rude Hand of Innovation. Religion and Social Order in Albany, New York, 1652–1836*, New York, 1991.

1.559 **Hamm**, T. D., *The Transformation of American Quakerism. Orthodox Friends, 1800–1907*, Bloomington, IN, 1988.

1.560 **Hertzberg**, A., *The Jews in America. Four Centuries of an Uneasy Encounter. A History*, New York, 1989. Stresses that Judaism in America has always had shallow roots, and includes a bleak prediction for the future maintenance of a separate Jewish identity.

1.561 **Holifield**, E. B., 'Religion and order in England and America: a review article', *Comparative Studies in Society and History*, XXV, 1983, 525–534.

1.562 **Karp**, A. J., *Haven and Home. A History of the Jews in America*, New York, 1985.

1.563 **Kauffman**, C. J., (ed.), *Bicentennial History of the Catholic Church in America*, New York, 1989. A six volume set that covers topics such as church organization, the immigrant church, women, and Catholic spirituality.

1.564 **Kuklick**, B., 'The emergence of the humanities', *South Atlantic Quarterly*, XXCIX, 1990, 195–206.

1.565 **Levine**, L. W., 'The folklore of industrial society. Popular culture and its audiences', *American Historical Review*, XCVII, 1992, 1369–1399. A speculative essay about the use of popular culture as a source for historians writing social history.

1.566 **Marty**, M. E., 'Hell disappeared. No one noticed. A civic argument', *Harvard Theological Review*, LXXVIII, 1985, 381–398.

1.567 **Marty**, M. E., *Pilgrims in their Own Land. 500 Years of Religion in America*, Boston, 1984.

1.568 **Mayor**, S. H., 'English nonconformity and the American experience', *Journal of the United Reformed Church Historical Society*, III, 1984, 104–115.

1.569 **Melton**, J. G., 'Spiritualization and reaffirmation. What really happens when prophecy fails', *American Studies*, XXVI, 1985, 17–29.

1.570 **Midgette**, Nancy Smith, *To Foster the Spirit of Professionalism. Southern Scientists and State Academies of Science*, Tuscaloosa, AL, 1991.

1.571 **Moore**, R. L., *Religious Outsiders and the Making of Americans*, New York, 1986. Argues that the effort by schismatic and separate religious groups was central to defining American identity.

1.572 **Noll**, M. A., (ed.), *Religion and American Politics. From the Colonial Period to the*

1980s, New York, 1990.

1.573 **O'Brien**, D., and **Bernadin**, J., 'Public Catholicism', *U.S. Catholic Historian*, VIII, 1989, 89–99. Offers a periodization of American Catholic history and finds that the post-immigrant Church is more of an evangelical ministry.

1.574 **Perry**, L., *Intellectual Life in America. A History*, New York, 1984. A history of ideas as well as a history of the social environment in which ideas take root.

1.575 **Quinby**, L., *Freedom, Foucault, and the Subjects of America*, Boston, 1991.

1.576 **Raboteau**, A. J., 'Down at the cross: Afro-American spirituality', *U.S. Catholic Historian*, VIII, 1989, 33–38.

1.577 **Sachar**, H. M., *A History of the Jews in America*, New York, 1992.

1.578 **Sanders**, R., *Shores of Refuge. A Hundred Years of Jewish Emigration*, New York, 1988.

1.579 **Slotkin**, R., *Gunfighter Nation. The Myth of the Frontier in Twentieth-Century America*, New York, 1992. Continues the author's contribution to American Studies by focusing on violence in films.

1.580 **Tentler**, Leslie Woodcock, *Seasons of Grace. A History of the Catholic Archdiocese of Detroit*, Detroit, 1990. A fine example of the new religious history that blends doctrine, church administration, and the social history of the parishioners.

1.581 **Tentler**, Leslie Woodcock, *The Rites of Assent. Transformations in the Symbolic Construction of America*, New York, 1993.

1.582 **Thorsen**, N. A., 'American religion and the idea of unprecedented violence', *American Studies in Scandinavia*, XVIII, 1986, 53–66.

1.583 **Trachtenberg**, A., *Reading American Photographs. Images as History, Mathew Brady to Walker Evans*, New York, 1989.

1.584 **Vandermeer**, P. R., and **Swierenga**, R. P., (ed.), *Belief and Behavior. Essays in the New Religious History*, New Brunswick, NJ, 1991. A series of essays that blend social science history methods with a respectful approach to the role of faith in history.

1.585 **Veysey**, L., 'Ideological sources of American movements', *Society*, XXV, 1988, 58–61.

1.586 **Wahlman**, Maude S., 'Religious symbols in Afro-American folk art', *New York Folklore*, XII, 1986, 1–24.

1.587 **Wallace**, D. D., 'Sects, cults and mainstream religion: a cultural interpretation of new religious movements in America', *American Studies*, XXVI, 1985, 5–16.

1.588 **Wertheimer**, J., (ed.), *The American Synagogue. A Sanctuary Transformed*, New York, 1988. Looks at the changes in beliefs among American Jews over the past two centuries.

1.589 **Youngs**, J. W. T., *The Congregationalists*, Westport, CT, 1990. A helpful synthesis that traces the denomination from the Puritans up through the twentieth century.

1.590 **Ziff**, L., *Writing in the New Nation. Prose, Print, and Politics in the Early United States*, New Haven, CT, 1991.

Work and enterprise

1.591 **Abramowitz**, M., *Thinking About Growth and Other Essays on Economic Growth and Welfare*, New York, 1989. Collected essays of one of the leaders in the writing of the history of national income accounting.

1.592 **Asher**, R., and **Stephenson**, C., (ed.), *Labor Divided. Race and Ethnicity in United States Labor Struggles, 1835–1960*, Albany, NY, 1990.

1.593 **Baron**, Ava, (ed.), *Work Engendered. Toward a New History of American Labor*, Ithaca, NY, 1991. Essays on work that go beyond simply acknowledging women's work toward an understanding of masculinity and femininity in the workplace.

1.594 **Blackford**, M. G., *A History of Small Business in America*, New York, 1991.

1.595 **Blackford**, M. G., *Portrait Cast in Steel. Buckeye International and Columbus, Ohio, 1881–1980*, Westport, CT, 1982.

1.596 **Blackford**, M. G., and **Kerr**, K. A., *Business Enterprise in American History*, Boston, 1986.

1.597 **Brownlee**, W. E., *Dynamics of Ascent. A History of the American Economy*, Chicago, 1988. The second edition of a helpful survey.

1.598 **Bruchey**, S. W., *The Wealth of the Nation. An Economic History of the United States*, New York, 1988. A short survey by an historian who reads and can translate the language of modern econometricians.

1.599 **Bryant**, K. L., *A History of American Businesses*, Englewood Cliffs, NJ, 1983.

1.600 **Chandler**, A. D., *The Visible Hand. The Managerial Revolution in American*

23

Business, Cambridge, MA, 1977. A history of the rise of the modern corporation and how its internal organization has replaced many market functions.

1.601 **Dethloff**, H. C., *A History of the American Rice Industry*, College Station, TX, 1988.

1.602 **DiBacco**, T. V., *Made in the U. S. A. A History of American Business*, New York, 1987.

1.603 **Dicke**, T. S., *Franchising in America. The Development of a Business Method, 1840–1980*, Chapel Hill, NC, 1992.

1.604 **Doti**, Lynn Pierson, and **Schweikart**, L., *Banking in the American West. From the Gold Rush to Deregulation*, Norman, OK, 1991.

1.605 **Dyson**, L. K., *Farmers Organizations*, Westport, CT, 1986.

1.606 **Engerman**, S. L., and **Gallman**, R. E., (ed.), *Long-Term Factors in American Economic Growth*, Chicago, 1986. Volume 51 in the series "Studies in Income and Wealth", commissioned by the National Bureau of Economic Research. As with volumes 24 and 30, this one represents the summation of the best work in the field by the "new economic historians".

1.607 **Bruchey**, S. W., *Enterprise. The Dynamic Economy of a Free People*, Chicago, 1990.

1.608 **Ficken**, R. E., *The Forested Land. A History of Lumbering in Western Washington*, Cambridge, MA, 1988. From nineteenth century origins around Puget Sound through the maturation of the Washington state economy.

1.609 **Fox-Genovese**, Elizabeth, and **Genovese**, E. D., *Fruits of Merchant Capital. Slavery and Bourgeois Property in the Rise and Expansion of Capitalism*, New York, 1983. A series of essays on the Atlantic world and the role of merchants in the expansion of slavery.

1.610 **Freyer**, T. A., *Regulating Big Business. Antitrust in Great Britain and America, 1880–1990*, New York, 1992.

1.611 **Friedman**, M., and **Schwartz**, Anna Jacobson, *Monetary Trends in the United States and the United Kingdom. Their Relation to Income, Prices and Interest Rates, 1967–1975*, Chicago, 1982. An updating of the two authors' 1963 classic *A Monetary History of the United States*.

1.612 **Frisch**, M., and **Walkowitz**, D. J., *Working-Class America. Essays on Labor, Community and American Society*, Urbana, IL, 1983. A collection of ten essays ranging in topic from labor in the early textile mills through organized labor's contradictory role in World War II.

1.613 **Gardner**, A. D., and **Flores**, Verla R., *Forgotten Frontier. A History of Wyoming Coal Mining*, Boulder, CO, 1989. Reviews the history of deep mining in Wyoming, and the later transitition to surface strip mining and the state's rise to preeminence in the industry.

1.614 **Gelfand**, L. E., and **Neymeyer**, R. J., (ed.), *Agricultural Distress in the Midwest, Past and Present*, Iowa City, IA, 1986. Collects four essays that trace the problem of family farms and market oscillations over the past century.

1.615 **Goldin**, Claudia Dale, and **Rockoff**, H., *Strategic Factors in Nineteenth Century American Economic History. A Volume to Honor Robert W. Fogel*, Chicago, 1992. Essays by the leading economic historians, including an introduction by Stanley Engerman on his two decades of collaboration with Fogel, the 1993 Nobel Prize co-winner in economics.

1.616 **Haber**, S., *The Quest for Authority and Honor in the American Professions, 1750–1900*, Chicago, 1991.

1.617 **Hatch**, N. O., *The Professions in American History*, Notre Dame, IN, 1988. A collection of essays on professions by leading historians in the field.

1.618 **Hidy**, R. W., *et al.*, *The Great Northern Railway. A History*, Boston, 1988. A publishing project first started after World War II, but only recently completed; the railroad's history is charted from its origins in Minnesota through recent mergers.

1.619 **Hughes**, J. R. T., *American Economic History*, Glenview, IL, 1983.

1.620 **Hunter**, L. C., *A History of Industrial Power in the United States, 1780–1930. Volume I, Waterpower in the Century of the Steam Engine*, Charlottesville, VA, 1979. First volume in a series.

1.621 **Hunter**, L. C., *A History of Industrial Power in the United States, 1780–1930. Volume II, Steam Power*, Charlottesville, VA, 1985.

1.622 **Hunter**, L. C., and **Bryant**, L., *A History of Industrial Power in the United States, 1780–1930. Volume III, The Transmission of Power*, Cambridge, MA, 1991. The final volume in Hunter's trilogy covers both the transmission of steam power and electric power.

1.623 **Jacoby**, S. M., (ed.), *Masters to Managers. Historical and Comparative Perspectives on American Employers*, New York, 1991.

1.624 **Kilby**, P. C., *Quantity and Quiddity. Essays in U. S. Economic History*, Middletown, CT, 1987. A festschrift to honor the career of Stanley Lebergott, with essays by some of the most distinguished writers in the field.

1.625 **Kolchin**, P., *Unfree Labor. American Slavery and Russian Serfdom*, Cambridge, MA, 1987. A comparative history of the two types of unfree labor that connects their rise and fall to world capitalism.

1.626 **Lane**, A. T., *Solidarity or Survival? American Labor and European Immigrants, 1830–1924*, Westport, CT, 1987.

1.627 **Lebergott**, S., *The Americans. An Economic Record*, New York, 1984. An economic history survey written by one of the leaders of the "new economic history".

1.628 **Lee**, Susan, and **Passell**, P., *A New Economic View of American History*, New York, 1979. The new economic historians tackle American history from the viewpoint that prices in the market determine behavior and historical outcomes.

1.629 **Licht**, W., *Getting Work. Philadelphia, 1840–1950*, Cambridge, MA, 1992. An in-depth exploration of the functioning of the labor market during the course of industrialization with the finding that informal networks of social relations counted for more than individual achievement.

1.630 **Martin**, A., *Railroads Triumphant. The Growth, Rejection, and Rebirth of a Vital American Force*, New York, 1992.

1.631 **McCraw**, T. K., *The Essential Alfred Chandler. Essays Toward a Historical Theory of Big Business*, Boston, 1988. A festschrift to the dean of modern business historians.

1.632 **North**, D. C., *Institutions, Institutional Change and Economic Performance*, 1990. One of the leading practitioners of the new economic history makes the argument that institutional forces set the parameters for the working of the market; this work helped win the author a share of the 1993 Nobel Prize in economics.

1.633 **O'Malley**, M., *Keeping Watch. A History of American Time*, New York, 1990.

1.634 **Pate**, J'Nell L., *Livestock Legacy. The Fort Worth Stockyards, 1887–1987*, College Station, TX, 1988.

1.635 **Poulson**, B. W., *Economic History of the United States*, New York, 1981.

1.636 **Reverby**, Susan M., *Ordered to Care. The Dilemma of American Nursing, 1850–1945*, New York, 1987.

1.637 **Robertson**, J. O., *American Business*, New York, 1985. A survey of business history that closely examines the conflict between market values and community values.

1.638 **Roediger**, D. R., and **Foner**, P. S., *Our Own Time. A History of American Labor and the Working Day*, Westport, CT, 1989. Places the struggle for the shorter work week and work day at the heart of American labor history.

1.639 **Sexton**, Patricia Cayo, *The War on Labor and the Left. Understanding America's Unique Conservatism*, Boulder, CO, 1991. Argues that the reason for the comparative weakness of the American labor movement was the intense repression from Corporate America.

1.640 **Stapleton**, D. H., *The Transfer of Early Industrial Technologies to America*, Philadelphia, 1987.

1.641 **Steinfeld**, R. J., *The Invention of Free Labor. The Employment Relation in English and American Law and Culture, 1350–1870*, Chapel Hill, NC, 1991.

1.642 **Hughes**, J. T. R., *The Government Habit Redux. Economic Controls from Colonial Times to the Present*, Princeton, NJ, 1991. A survey of the history of government regulation of the market economy. The authors finds that Americans have sought regulation from a misunderstanding and mistrust of the workings of markets.

1.643 **Blackford**, M. E., *The Rise of Modern Business in Great Britain, the United States, and Japan*, Chapel Hill, NC, 1988.

1.644 **Tweedale**, G., *Sheffield Steel and America. A Century of Commercial and Technological Interdependence, 1830–1930*, 1987.

1.645 **Vidich**, A. J., 'The moral, economic, and political status of labor in American society', *Social Research*, XLIX, 1982, 752–790.

1.646 **Weiner**, Lynn V., *From Working Girl to Working Mother. The Female Labor Force in the United States, 1820–1980*, Chapel Hill, NC, 1985. Maintains that nineteenth century attitudes about the place of women in society have hindered the development of social policy to help working women throughout the twentieth century.

1.647 **Whiteside**, J., *Regulating Danger. The Struggle for Mine Safety in the Rocky Mountain Coal Industry*, Lincoln, NE, 1990. Covers a century of conflict between mine owners and miners over the fashioning of work rules that promoted safety rather than maximum production.

1.648 **Wilkins**, Mira, *The History of Foreign Investment in the United States to 1914*, Cambridge, MA, 1989.

Race and ethnic identity

1.649 **Alexander**, Adele Logan, *Ambiguous Lives. Free Women of Color in Rural Georgia, 1789–1879*, Fayetteville, AR, 1991.

1.650 **Aptheker**, H., *Anti-Racism in U.S. History. The First Two Hundred Years*, New York, 1992. The latest work by an author who has been publishing in this subject area for six decades.

1.651 **Archdeacon**, T. J., *Becoming American. An Ethnic History*, New York, 1983.

1.652 **Banton**, M., 'The classification of races in Europe and North America: 1700–1850', *International Social Science Journal (Great Britain)*, XXXIX, 1987, 45–60.

1.653 **Beeth**, H., and **Wintz**, C. D., (ed.), *Black Dixie. Afro-Texan History and Culture in Houston*, College Station, TX, 1992.

1.654 **Berry**, Mary Frances, *Long Memory. The Black Experience in America*, New York, 1982.

1.655 **Boles**, J. B., (ed.), *Masters and Slaves in the House of the Lord. Race and Religion in the American South, 1740–1870*, Lexington, KY, 1988.

1.656 **Bronitsky**, G., 'Indian assimilation in the El Paso area', *New Mexico Historical Review*, LII, 1987, 151–168.

1.657 **Campisi**, J., and **Hauptman**, L. M., *The Oneida Indian Experience. Two Perspectives*, Syracuse, NY, 1988. An unusual set of essays, some written by scholars on the history of the Oneidas from the time of the Iroquois League through subsequent migrations, and the balance written by tribal people today.

1.658 **Cantor**, G., *Historic Landmarks of Black America*, Detroit, 1991.

1.659 **Carlson**, A. W., *The Spanish-American Homeland. Four Centuries in New Mexico' Rio Arriba*, Baltimore, 1990.

1.660 **Cashman**, S. D., *African-Americans and the Quest for Civil Rights, 1900–1990*, New York, 1991.

1.661 **Cassity**, M. J., *Legacy of Fear. American Race Relations to 1900*, Westport, CT, 1985.

1.662 **Clark**, D., 'The Irish in the American economy', *Irish Studies*, IV, 1985, 231–251.

1.663 **Clark**, D., *Erin's Heirs. Irish Bonds of Community*, Lexington, KY, 1991. Looks mainly at Philadelphia and finds a continuing strong Irish identity, many generations after the initial heavy immigration.

1.664 **Davis**, D. B., *Slavery and Human Progress* New York, 1985. Considers some of the paradoxes raised in the author's earlier work, particularly how slavery was often associated with imperial expansion until the nineteenth century when abolition replaced it as the hallmark of human progress.

1.665 **Deloria**, V., *American Indians, American Justice*, Austin, TX, 1983. A survey of U.S. law and Native American rights by one of the foremost writers on the subject

1.666 **Edmunds**, R. D., (ed.), *American Indian Leaders*, Lincoln, NE, 1980. A collection of essays on eighteenth, nineteenth, and twentieth century Native American male leaders and how they conducted intratriba and international relations.

1.667 **Elphick**, R., 'A comparative history of white supremacy', *Journal of Interdisciplinary History*, XIII, 1983, 503–513.

1.668 **Farr**, J. B., *Black Odyssey. The Seafaring Traditions of Afro-Americans*, New York, 1989.

1.669 **Ferguson**, L., *Uncommon Ground. Archaeology and Early African America, 1650–1800*, Washington, DC, 1992.

1.670 **Fields**, Barbara Jeanne, 'Slavery, race an ideology in the United States of America' *New Left Review*, XXXI, 1990, 95–118. leading historian of African-Americans untangles the origins of race-based slaver in North America and finds that the demand for unfree labor preceded a racial caste system.

1.671 **Foner**, P. S., *History of Black Americans*, Westport, CT, 1975–1983. The fruits of a half-century's devotion to the topic.

1.672 **Forbes**, J. D., 'The manipulation of race, caste and identity: classifying Afroamericans, Native Americans, Americans, and Red-Black people', *Journal of Ethnic Studies*, XVII, 1990, 1–5.

1.673 **Fowler**, Loretta, *Shared Symbols, Contested Meanings. Gros Ventre Culture and History, 1778–1984*, Ithaca, NY, 1987. An ethnohistory of the Montana people with an emphasis on the continuity of their lives.

1.674 **Franklin**, J. H., *Race and History. Selected Essays, 1938–1988*, Baton Rouge, LA, 1989. A collection of the life's work of the leading modern historian of the black experience in America, focusing on the writing and telling of history.

1.675 **Fredrickson**, G. M., *White Supremacy. A Comparative Study in American and South African History*, New York, 1981.

1.676 **Fredrickson**, G. M., *The Arrogance of Race. Historical Perspectives on Slavery, Racism, and Social Inequality*, Middletown, CT, 1988. A collection of seventeen essays by one of the leading historians of race relations in the Atlantic world.

1.677 **Frost**, L., *The New Urban Frontier. Urbanisation and City-Building in Australasia and the American West*, Kensington, NSW, 1991. Finds an east-west divide in Australia, much like in the U.S. and Canada, with similar social consequences.

1.678 **Gabbacia**, Donna, *Seeking Common Ground. Multidisciplinary Studies of Immigrant Women in the United States*, Westport, CT, 1992. A set of essays that compares nineteenth and twentieth century immigrant women from the migration process through acculturation.

1.679 **Genovese**, E. D., *From Rebellion to Revolution. Afro-American Slave Revolts in the Making of the Modern World*, Baton Rouge, LA, 1978.

1.680 **Hirsch**, A. R., and **Logsdon**, J., (ed.), *Creole New Orleans. Race and Americanization*, Baton Rouge, LA, 1992.

1.681 **Holloway**, J. E., (ed.), *Africanisms in American Culture*, Bloomington, IN, 1990. A collection of essays that surveys the influence of African culture on American religion and the arts.

1.682 **Hoxie**, F. E., (ed.), *Indians in American History. An Introduction*, Arlington Heights, IL, 1988.

1.683 **Inkori**, J. E., and **Engerman**, S. L., (ed.), *The Atlantic Slave Trade. Effects on Economies, Societies, and Peoples in Africa, the Americas and Europe*, Durham, NC, 1992.

1.684 **Jaynes**, G. D., and **Williams**, R. M., (ed.), *A Common Destiny. Blacks and American Society*, Washington, DC, 1989. A government report on the status of race relations in the U.S. since World War II.

1.685 **Jones**, Jacqueline, *Labor of Love, Labor of Sorrow. Black Women, Work and the Family from Slavery to the Present*, New York, 1985. A broad survey of black women and work which shows how they worked to keep their families and communities whole under the most trying circumstances.

1.686 **Kaplan**, S., and **Austin**, A. D., (ed.), *American Studies in Black and White. Selected Essays, 1949–1989*, Amherst, MA, 1991.

1.687 **Katz**, W. L., *Black Indians. A Hidden Heritage*, New York, 1986. A survey of the extratribal relations between Native Americans and African-Americans from the seventeenth century onward.

1.688A **Kelsey**, H., 'European impact on the California Indians, 1530–1830', *Americas*, XLI, 1985, 494–511.

1.688B **Kenagy**, Suzanne G., 'Stepped cloud and cross: the intersection of Pueblo and European visual symbolic systems', *New Mexico Historical Review*, LXIV, 1989, 325–340.

1.689 **Kestler**, F. R., *The Indian Captivity Narrative. A Woman's View*, New York, 1990.

1.690 **Kroes**, R., and **Neuschafer**, H. O., (ed.), *The Dutch in North-America. Their Immigration and Cultural Continuity*, Amsterdam, 1991.

1.691 **LeMay**, M. C., *From Open Door to Dutch Door. An Analysis of U.S. Immigration Policy since 1820*, New York, 1987.

1.692 **Lewis**, J. R., 'Shamans and prophets: continuities and discontinuities in Native American new religions', *American Indian Quarterly*, XII, 1988, 221–228.

1.693 **Littlefield**, D. F., *Africans and Creeks from the Colonial Period to the Civil War*, Westport, CT, 1979. Considers extratribal relations between the two groups, from marriage and kinship to slaveowning.

1.694 **Luebke**, F. C., *Germans in the New World. Essays in the History of Immigration*, Urbana, IL, 1990.

1.695 **Lurie**, Nancy Oestreich, *Wisconsin Indians*, Madison, WI, 1980. Tells in brief form the history of each of the tribes and bands since Wisconsin became a state in 1848.

1.696 **Machor**, J. L., *Pastoral Cities. Urban Ideals and the Symbolic Landscape of America*, Madison, WI, 1987.

1.697 **Mandle**, J. R., *Not Slave, Not Free. The African American Economic Experience since the Civil War*, Durham, NC, 1992. A continuation of the author's argument for understanding freedom in the South as the "plantation mode of production".

1.698 **Marcus**, J. R., *United States Jewry, 1776–1985*, Detroit, 1989. A monumental four volume survey is planned with the first volume appearing in 1989 and covering the years up to 1840.

1.699 **Marks**, Shula, 'White supremacy', *Comparative Studies in Society and History*, XXIX, 1987, 385–397.

1.700 **Martin**, C., (ed.), *The American Indian and the Problem of History*, New York, 1987.

1.701 **Mathes**, Valerie Sherer, 'Native American women in medicine and the military', *Journal of the West*, XXI, 1982, 41–48.

1.702 **McCool**, D., 'Federal Indian policy and the sacred mountains of the Papago Indians', *Journal of Ethnic Studies*, IX, 1981, 57–69.

1.703 **Merrell**, J. H., *The Indians' New World. Catawbas and their Neighbors from European Contact through the Era of Removal*, Chapel Hill, NC, 1989. Model example of the new ethnohistory that looks at the internal history of an Indian tribe and the changes it faced over time.

1.704 **Miller**, J. R., *Skyscrapers Hide the Heavens. A History of Indian-White Relations in Canada*, Toronto, 1991. Revised edition of a very helpful contrast to the U.S. case.

1.705 **Morgan**, P. D., 'Work and culture: the task system and the world of lowcountry blacks, 1700 to 1880', *William and Mary Quarterly*, XXXIX, 1982, 563–599.

1.706 **Moses**, L. G., and **Wilson**, R., *Indian Lives. Essays on Nineteenth and Twentieth Century Native American Leaders*, Albuquerque, NM, 1985.

1.707 **Nelson**, W. J., 'Racial definition: background for divergence', *Phylon*, XLVII, 1986, 318–326.

1.708 **Noble**, A. G., (ed.), *To Build in a New Land. Ethnic Landscapes in North America*, Baltimore, 1992. Essays on the historical geography of the great wave of immigration and how the immigrants changed the visual basis of the American scene.

1.709 **O'Brien**, D. J., and **Fugita**, S. S., *The Japanese American Experience*, Bloomington IN, 1991. Traces the enduring culture and behavior of Japanese Americans back to mid nineteenth century Japan.

1.710 **O'Connor**, T. H., 'The Irish in New England', *New England Historical and Genealogical Register*, CXXXIX, 1985, 187–195.

1.711 **Oswalt**, W. H., *Bashful No Longer. An Alaskan Eskimo Ethnohistory, 1778–1988*, Norman, OK, 1990.

1.712 **Pacyga**, D. A., *Polish Immigrants and Industrial Chicago Workers on the South Side, 1880–1992*, Columbus, OH, 1991.

1.713 **Palmer**, S., and **Reinhartz**, D., (ed.), *Essays on the History of North American Discovery and Exploration*, College Station TX, 1988. A collection of essays on comparative colonialisms in North America over the past five hundred years.

1.714 **Pencak**, W., **Berrol**, Selma, and **Miller**, R M., (ed.), *Immigration to New York*, Philadelphia, 1991. A collection of conference papers that survey immigrant life in New York with particular attention paid to recent arrivals.

1.715 **Perdue**, Theda, *Slavery and the Evolution of Cherokee Society, 1540–1866*, Knoxville TN, 1979.

1.716 **Perry**, R. J., *Western Apache Heritage. People of the Mountain Corridor*, Austin, TX, 1991.

1.717 **Peterson**, Jacqueline, 'Indians and whites on the Columbia plateau', *Ethnohistory*, XXXV, 1988, 191–196.

1.718 **Phillips**, G. O., 'The Caribbean presence in Maryland, 1634–1984: an overview', *Immigrants and Minorities*, VI, 1987, 277–304.

1.719 **Quarles**, B., *Black Mosaic. Essays in Afro-American History and Historiography*, Amherst, MA, 1988. A collection of essays written between the 1940s and 1980s by one of the leading historians of the African-American experience.

1.720 **Reinhardt**, K. J., 'Critique. Women, religion, and peace in an American Indian ritual', *Explorations in Ethnic Studies*, VII, 1984, 16–38.

1.721 **Reith**, D., 'U.S. Census data. Ethnicity and the American census', *Ethnic Forum*, X, 1990, 98–105.

1.722 **Rice**, C. D., *The Rise and Fall of Black Slavery*, New York, 1988. Second edition of a helpful survey, particularly on the transatlantic nature of nineteenth century abolitionism.

1.723 **Roediger**, D. R., *The Wages of Whiteness. Race and the Making of the American Working Class*, London, 1991.

1.724 **Rountree**, Helen C., *Pocahontas' People. The Powhatan Indians of Virginia Through Four Centuries*, Norman, OK, 1990. Starts with the seventeenth century encounter of the Powhatans with the English and follows them through intermarriage with African slaves and acculturation into the larger Virginia society.

1.725 **Schelbert**, L., 'The historical context of French-Swiss migration to Knoxville, Tennessee', *Swiss American Historical Society Review*, XXVII, 1991, 7–10.

1.726 **Shammas**, Carole, 'Black women's work and the evolution of plantation society in Virginia', *Labor History*, XXVI, 1985, 5–28.

1.727 **Shapiro**, H., *White Violence and Black Response. From Reconstruction to Montgomery*, Amherst, MA, 1988.

1.728 **Shore**, E., *et. al.*, (ed.), *The German-American Radical Press. The Shaping of a Left Political Culture, 1850–1940*, Urbana, IL, 1992.

1.729 **Smith**, Eleanor, 'Black American women and work: a historical review: 1619–1920', *Women's Studies International Forum*, VIII, 1985, 343–349.

1.730 **Smits**, D. D., 'The "squaw drudge". A prime index of savagism', *Ethnohistory*, XXIX, 1982, 281–306.

1.731 **Sollors**, W., *Beyond Ethnicity. Consent and Descent in American Culture*, New York, 1986. A German scholar's look at how Americans have defined themselves and outsiders in the sometimes contradictory notions of lineage and voluntary group membership.

1.732 **Strickland**, R., *The Indians in Oklahoma*, Norman, OK, 1980.

1.733 **Takaki**, R. T., *Iron Cages. Race and Culture in Nineteenth Century America*, New York, 1979.

1.734 **Takaki**, R. T., 'Brains over muscles: the meaning of intelligence and race in American history', *Halcyon*, VI, 1984, 45–54.

1.735 **Thornton**, R., 'Social organization and the demographic survival of the Tolowa',

Ethnohistory, XXXI, 1984, 187–196.

1.736 **Tise**, L. E., *Proslavery. A History of the Defense of Slavery*, Athens, GA, 1987.

1.737 **Vecoli**, R. J., and **Sinke**, Suzanne M., (ed.), *A Century of European Migrations, 1830–1930*, Urbana, IL, 1991.

1.738 **Viola**, H. J., (ed.), *After Columbus. The Smithsonian Chronicle of the North American Indian*, Washington, DC, 1990.

1.739 **Washburn**, W. E., *The Indian in America*, New York, 1975. A handy introduction to the subject from the reliable New American Nation series.

1.740 **Williams**, R. A., *The American Indian in Western Legal Thought. The Discourse of Conquest*, New York, 1990.

1.741 **Williams**, W. L., *The Spirit and the Flesh. Sexual Diversity in American Indian Culture*, Boston, 1986. A review of the different western tribes that practised a form of berdache and how a 'third gender' served many useful social needs.

1.742 **Williams**, W. L., (ed.), *Southeastern Indians Since the Removal Era*, Athens, GA, 1979.

Space, movement, and place

1.743 **Allen**, Barbara, and **Schlereth**, T. J., (ed.), *Sense of Place. American Regional Cultures*, Lexington, KY, 1990. An American Studies approach to persistence among regions within the United States.

1.744 **Bishit**, Catherine W., *et. al.*, *Architects and Builders in North Carolina. A History of the Practice of Building*, Chapel Hill, NC, 1990.

1.745 **Bowman**, S. D., (ed.), *What Made the South Different? Essays and Comments*, Jackson, MS, 1990.

1.746 **Brugger**, R. L., *Maryland. A Middle Temperament*, Baltimore, 1988. A complete history of the state from colonial times to the present.

1.747 **Buisseret**, D., (ed.), *From Sea Charts to Satellite Images. Interpreting North American History Through Maps*, Chicago, 1990. A set of map essays that range from nineteenth century land surveys to computerized geographic information systems displays.

1.748 **Cayton**, A. R. L., and **Onuf**, P. S., *The Midwest and the Nation. Rethinking the History of an American Region*,

Bloomington, IN, 1990. A reformulation of the Turner thesis that argues the American Midwest is distinctive precisely because it was the nineteenth century home of bourgeois values and small business.

1.749 **Chesnutt**, D. R., and **Wilson**, C. N., *The Meaning of South Carolina History. Essays in Honor of George C. Rogers, Jr*, Columbia, SC, 1991.

1.750 **Cobb**, J. C., *The Most Southern Place on Earth. The Mississippi Delta and the Roots of Regional Identity*, New York, 1992.

1.751 **Cunningham**, R., *Apples on the Flood. The Southern Mountain Experience*, Knoxville, TN, 1987. Uses world systems theory to argue that the Appalachian region of the South has always served in a cultural sense as a barrier between the metropolitan core and the wilds within North America.

1.752 **Dudden**, A. P., *The American Pacific. From the Old China Trade to the Present*, New York, 1992.

1.753 **Dunlap**, T. R., *Saving America's Wildlife*, Princeton, NJ, 1988.

1.754 **Earle**, C., *Geographical Inquiry and American Historical Problems*, Stanford, CA, 1992. Collection of essays spanning the range of American history, all with the theme that place matters in the analysis of change over time.

1.755 **Escott**, P. D., and **Crow**, J. J., 'The social order and violent disorder: an analysis of North Carolina in the revolution and the Civil War', *Journal of Southern History*, LII, 1986, 373–402.

1.756 **Foley**, W. E., *The Genesis of Missouri. From Wilderness Outpost to Statehood*, Columbia, MO, 1989.

1.757 **Fraser**, W. J., *Charleston! Charleston! The History of a Southern City*, Columbia, SC, 1989.

1.758 **Gibson**, J. R., *European Settlement and Development in North America. Essays on Geographical Change in Honour and Memory of Andre Hill Clark*, Toronto, 1978. A posthumous festschrift to the Canandian historical geographer. Included are essays on regions within the United States by some of the leading practitioners of historical geography.

1.759 **Glad**, P. W., *The History of Wisconsin. War, a New Era, and Depression, 1914–1940*, Madison, WI, 1990. Part of a six volume series, Glad's contribution gives the war, the 1920s and the Depression equal attention.

1.760 **Hale**, D. K., 'Mineral exploration in the Spanish borderlands, 1513–1846', *Journal of the West*, XX, 1981, 5–20.

1.761 **Hall**, T. D., *Social Change in the Southwest, 1350–1880*, Lawrence, KS, 1989.

1.762 **Hays**, S. P., (ed.), *City at the Point. Essays on the Social History of Pittsburgh*, Pittsburgh, 1989.

1.763 **Hundley**, N., *The Great Thirst. Californians and Water, 1770s-1990s*, Berkeley, CA, 1992.

1.764 **Jordan**, T. G., and **Kaups**, Matti, 'Folk architecture in cultural and ecological context', *Geographical Review*, LXXVII, 1987, 526–575.

1.765 **Kennedy**, L. W., *Planning the City upon a Hill. Boston since 1630*, Amherst, MA, 1992.

1.766 **Knepper**, G. W., *Ohio and its People*, Kent, OH, 1989.

1.767 **Lamar**, H. R., *Texas Crossings. The Lone Star State and the American Far West, 1836–1936*, Austin, TX, 1991.

1.768A **Lamar**, H. R., and **Thompson**, L., (ed.), *The Frontier in History. North America and Southern Africa Compared*, New Haven, CT, 1981.

1.768B **Lawson-Peebles**, R., (ed.), *Views of American Landscapes*, New York, 1989.

1.769 **Lazarus**, E., *Black Hills/White Justice. The Sioux Nation versus the United States, 1775 to the Present*, New York, 1991.

1.770 **Lerda**, V. G., and **Westendorp**, T., (ed.), *The United States South. Regionalism and Identity*, Rome, 1991.

1.771 **Lipsitz**, G., *The Sidewalks of St. Louis. People and Politics in an American City*, Columbia, MO, 1991.

1.772 **Luckingham**, B., *Phoenix. The History of a Southwestern Metropolis*, Tucson, AZ, 1989.

1.773 **MacDonald**, N., *Distant Neighbors. A Comparative History of Seattle and Vancouver*, Lincoln, NE, 1987.

1.774 **Madison**, J. H., *Heartland. Comparative Histories of the Midwestern States*, Bloomington, IN, 1988.

1.775 **Malone**, M., and **Etulain**, R. W., *The American West. A Twentieth Century History*, Lincoln, NE, 1989.

1.776 **Marks**, S. A., *Southern Hunting in Black and White. Nature, History, and Ritual in a Carolina Community*, Princeton, NJ, 1991. An extended essay on the modern masculine culture of hunting, with a historical perspective that shows how killing for food has been transformed into killing for sport.

1.777 **Martin**, C. L., *In the Spirit of the Earth. Rethinking History and Time*, Baltimore, 1992.

1.778 **May**, D. L., *Utah. A People's History*, Salt Lake City, UT, 1987.

1.779 **McWhiney**, G., *Cracker Culture. Celtic Ways in the Old South*, Tuscaloosa, AL, 1988.

1.780 **Mitchell**, R. D., (ed.), *Appalachian Frontiers. Settlement, Society, and Development in the Preindustrial Era*, Lexington, KY, 1991.

1.781 **Mollenkopf**, J. H., (ed.), *Power, Culture, and Place. Essays on New York City*, New York, 1989.

1.782 **Monkkonen**, E. H., *America Becomes Urban. The Development of U.S. Cities and Towns, 1780–1980*, Berkeley, CA, 1988. Standard survey on U.S. urban history that covers political and social history.

1.783 **Monkkonen**, E. H., *Walking to Work. Tramps in America, 1790–1935*, Lincoln, NE, 1984.

1.784 **Moore**, W. B., and **Tripp**, J. F., (ed.), *Looking South. Chapters in the History of an American Region*, New York, 1989.

1.785 **Nelson**, R., *Aesthetic Frontiers. The Machiavellian Tradition and the Southern Imagination*, Jackson, MS, 1990. Uses the concept of republican ideology and civic humanism to understand southern intellectuals in the modern world.

1.786 **Nostrand**, R. L., *The Hispano Homeland*, Norman, OK, 1992. Traces the history of New Mexico from the sixteenth century to the present.

1.787 **O'Brien**, M., *Rethinking the South. Essays in Intellectual History*, Baltimore, 1988. Reviews the thought of leading southern writers from the antebellum period up to the present.

1.788 **Opie**, J., *The Law of the Land. Two Hundred Years of American Farmland Policy*, Lincoln, NE, 1987. Highlights the importance of the rectangular survey in forming the American landscape and how environmental concerns stand in conflict with older notions of dominance over the land.

1.789 **Otto**, J. S., *The Southern Frontiers, 1607–1860. The Agricultural Evolution of the Colonial and Antebellum South*, Westport, CT, 1989. A short survey that blends historical geography with economic history.

1.790 **Pederson**, Jane Marie, *Between Memory and Reality. Family and Community in Rural Wisconsin, 1870–1970*, Madison, WI, 1992.

1.791 **Pyne**, S. J., *Fire in America. A Cultural History of Wildland and Rural Fire*, Princeton, NJ, 1982. An unusual history of the environment that traces the evolution of the human use of fire in North America, and the social struggle over the control of burning.

1.792 **Reid**, R. L., (ed.), *Always a River. The Ohio River and the American Experience*, Bloomington, IN, 1991.

1.793 **Taylor**, W. R., *In Pursuit of Gotham. Culture and Commerce in New York*, New York, 1992. A leading practioner of American Studies turns his attention to the Big Apple and analyzes it as a giant text.

1.794 **Walton**, J., *Western Times and Water Wars. State, Culture, and Rebellion in California*, Berkeley, CA, 1992.

1.795 **West**, J. O., 'Grutas at the crossroads of the Spanish southwest', *Password*, XXXII, 1987, 3–12.

1.796 **White**, R., '*It's Your Misfortune and None of My Own.' A History of the American West*, Norman, OK, 1991. A survey of western U.S. history that, as the title indicates, finds a history of individualism, exploitation, and conflict as continuing themes.

1.797 **Williams**, M., *Americans and their Forests. A Historical Geography*, 1989.

1.798 **Woodward**, C. V., *The Future of the Past*, New York, 1989. A collection of essays by the leading historian of the South mainly written in the 1970s and 1980s.

1.799 **Worster**, D., *Under Western Skies. Nature and History in the American West*, New York, 1992. An environmental history of the West with the emphasis on the importance of land on culture.

1.800 **Wynn**, G., 'Settler societies in geographical focus', *Historical Studies*, XX, 1983, 353–366.

The state and the public realm

1.801 **Arsenault**, R., (ed.), *Crucible of Liberty. 200 Years of the Bill of Rights*, New York, 1991.

1.802 **Beach**, E. L., *The United States Navy. 200 years*, New York, 1986.

1.803 **Becker**, W. H., and **Wells**, S. F., Jr., (ed.), *Economics and World Power. An Assessment of American Diplomacy Since 1789*, New York, 1984. Eight essays that cover the span of American foreign policy and together read as a postrevisionist critique of an economic interpretation of American diplomatic motivation.

1.804 **Blanchard**, Margaret A., *Revolutionary Sparks. Freedom of Expression in Modern America*, New York, 1992. A history of how Americans have made use of their First Amendment rights to free speech in the nineteenth and twentieth centuries.

1.805 **Bodenhammer**, D. J., *Fair Trial. Rights of the Accused in American History*, New York, 1992.

1.806 **Bogue**, A. G., 'Members of the House of Representatives and the processes of modernization, 1789–1960', *Journal of American History*, LXII, 1976, 275–302. Studies the people who served in the House of Representatives and their characteristics.

1.807 **Bothwell**, R., *Canada and the United States. The Politics of Partnership*, New York, 1992.

1.808 **Burns**, J. M., *The American Experiment*, New York, 1989. A three volume political history of the U.S. that stresses the importance of presidential leadership in a pluralist system.

1.809 **Burns**, J. M., and **Burns**, S., *A People's Choice. The Pursuit of Rights in America*, New York, 1991.

1.810 **Bushnell**, Eleanor, *Crimes, Follies, and Misfortunes. The Federal Impeachment Trials*, Urbana, IL, 1992. Covers impeachment actions by the Congress from the 1790s up through the 1980s.

1.811 **Calhoun**, F. S., *The Lawmen. United States Marshals and Their Deputies, 1789–1989*, Washington, DC, 1989.

1.812 **Campbell**, B. A., and **Trilling**, R. J., *Realignment in American Politics. Toward a Theory*, Austin, TX, 1980.

1.813 **Campbell**, Karyln Kohrs, and **Jamieson**, Kathleen Hall, 'Inaugurating the presidency', *Presidential Studies Quarterly*, XV, 1985, 394–411.

1.814 **Cantor**, M., *The Divided Left. American Radicalism, 1900–1975*, New York, 1978.

1.815 **Coffman**, E. M., *The Old Army. A Portrait of the American Army in Peacetime, 1784–1898*, New York, 1986. A descriptive portrait of the officers and enlisted men, as well as their families, that places them in t social context of the nineteenth century.

1.816 **Argersinger**, P. H., *Structure, Process, an Party. Essays in American Political History* New York, 1992.

1.817 **Cohen**, W. I., *East Asian Art and America Culture. A Study in International Relations* New York, 1992.

1.818 **Conant**, M., *The Constitution and the Economy. Objective Theory and Critical Commentary*, Norman, OK, 1991.

1.819 **Cosgrove**, R. A., *Our Lady, the Common Law. An Anglo-American Legal Community, 1870–1930*, New York, 1987.

1.820 **Currie**, D. P., *The Constitution in the Supreme Court. The Second Century, 1888–1986*, Chicago, 1990.

1.821 **Davis**, A. F., (ed.), *For Better or Worse. The American Influence in the World*, Westport, CT, 1981. A collection of essays originally composed for the American Revolution bicentennial (1976) about the extent of American influence overseas from the mundane to the imperial.

1.822 **Davis**, J. W., *The President as Party Leader*, Westport, CT, 1992.

1.823 **DeBenedetti**, C., *The Peace Reform in American History*, Bloomington, IN, 1980

1.824 **DeSario**, J., and **Langton**, S., (ed.), *Citizen Participation in Public Decision Making*, Westport, CT, 1987.

1.825 **Diggins**, J. P., *The Lost Soul of American Politics. Virtue, Self-Interest and the Foundations of Liberalism*, New York, 1984.

1.826 **Dimbleby**, D., and **Reynolds**, D., *An Ocean Apart. The Relationship between Britain and America in the Twentieth Century*, New York, 1988.

1.827 **Dinkin**, R. J., *Campaigning in America. A History of Election Practices*, Westport, CT, 1989. A survey of changes in presidential election campaigns.

1.828 **Dunn**, C. W., 'The theological dimensions of presidential leadership: a classification model', *Presidential Studies Quarterly*, XIV, 1984, 61–72.

1.829 **Ely**, J. W., *The Guardian of Every Other Right. A Constitutional History of Property Rights*, New York, 1992.

1.830 **Finkelman**, P., and **Gottlieb**, S. E., (ed.), *Toward a Usable Past. Liberty Under State Constitutions*, Athens, GA, 1991.

1.831 **Fisher**, R. A., *Tippecanoe and Trinkets Too, The Material Culture of American Presidential Campaigns, 1824–1984*, Urbana, IL, 1988.

1.832 **Graber**, M. A., *Transforming Free Speech. The Ambiguous Legacy of Civil Libertarianism*, Berkeley, CA, 1991.

1.833 **Hagan**, K. J., *This People's Navy. The Making of American Sea Power*, New York, 1991. Surveys the role of the U. S. Navy from the Revolution onward and makes an argument counter to the nineteenth century seapower theorist Dennis Mahan.

1.834 **Hagan**, K. J., and **Roberts**, W. R., (ed.), *Against All Enemies. Interpretations of American Military History from Colonial Times to the Present*, New York, 1986.

1.835 **Hall**, K., *The Magic Mirror. Law in American History*, New York, 1989.

1.836 **Hansen**, J. M., *Gaining Access. Congress and the Farm Lobby, 1919–1981*, Chicago, 1991.

1.837 **Hassler**, W. W., *With Shield and Sword. American Military Affairs, Colonial Times to the Present*, Ames, IA, 1982.

1.838 **Hays**, S. P., *American Political History as Social Analysis*, Knoxville, TN, 1980.

1.839 **Henry**, C. P., *Culture and African American Politics*, Bloomington, IN, 1990. Roots black politics in the culture of the black folk tradition.

1.840 **Higham**, R. D. S., *The United States Army in Peacetime. Essays in Honor the Bicentennial, 1775–1975*, Manhattan, KS, 1975.

1.841 **Horowitz**, M. J., *The Transformation of American Law, 1870–1960. The Crisis of Legal Orthodoxy*, New York, 1992. Continues the author's magisterial survey of the changes in the intellectual shaping of the law.

1.842 **Hovenkamp**, H., *Enterprise and American Law, 1836–1937*, Cambridge, MA, 1991.

1.843 **Howarth**, S., *To Shining Sea. A History of the United States Navy, 1775–1991*, New York, 1991. A brisk narrative that ranges from John Paul Jones to the Cold War.

1.844 **Hoyt**, E. P., *America's Wars and Military Excursions*, New York, 1987.

1.845 **Hunt**, M. H., *Ideology and U. S. Foreign Policy*, New Haven, CT, 1987. Finds that race and the thirst for national greatness have driven American foreign policy for two centuries.

1.846 **Jensen**, Joan M., *Army Surveillance in America, 1775–1980*, New Haven, CT, 1991.

1.847 **Jiang**, A. X., *The United States and China*, Chicago, 1988. A communist history of American foreign policy toward China that carries the story up to the Revolution of 1949.

1.848 **Kammen**, M. G., *A Machine that Would Go of Itself. The Constitution in American Culture*, New York, 1986. A review of the uses to which the Constitution has been put, particularly the periodic anniversary celebrations, including the centennial and sesquicentennial.

1.849 **Karsten**, P., *The Military in America. From the Colonial Era to the Present*, New York, 1980.

1.850 **Kelso**, W. A., *American Democratic Theory, Pluralism and Its Critics*, Westport, CT, 1978.

1.851 **Keve**, P. W., *Prisons and the American Conscience. A History of U.S. Federal Corrections*, Carbondale, IL, 1991.

1.852 **Klaits**, J., and **Haltzel**, M. H., (ed.), *Liberty/Liberté. The American and French Experiences*, Washington, DC, 1991. More reminiscences on both sides of the Atlantic on the occasion of the centennial of the Statue of Liberty.

1.853 **Kleppner**, P., *The Evolution of American Electoral Systems*, Westport, CT, 1981.

1.854 **Kohn**, S. M., *Jailed for Peace. The History of American Draft Law Violators*, Westport, CT, 1986.

1.855 **Kuklick**, B., *The Good Ruler. From Herbert Hoover to Richard Nixon*, New Brunswick, NJ, 1988. Examines the emotional history of the public reaction to presidents as inspiration leaders.

1.856 **Labunski**, R., Libel and the First Amendment. Legal History, *Practice in Print and Broadcasting*, New Brunswick, NJ, 1987.

1.857 **Lasser**, W., *The Limits of Judicial Power. The Supreme Court in American Politics*, Chapel Hill, NC, 1988. Looks at the Court's performance in past judicial crises and finds a basic institutional strength that overcame unpopular decisions.

1.858 **LaFeber**, W., *The American Age. United States Foreign Policy at Home and Abroad Since 1750*, New York, 1988. A survey of American diplomatic history that concentrates on the twentieth century.

1.859 **Lipset**, S. M., *Continental Divide. The Values and Institutions of the United States and Canada*, New York, 1990. An argument for the enduring legacy of the American Revolution in creating two different nations and societies.

1.860 **Love**, R. W., *History of the US Navy,*

1775–1941, Harrisburg, PA, 1992.

1.861 **Lurie**, J., *Arming Military Justice. The Origins of the United States Court of Military Appeals*, Princeton, NJ, 1992.

1.862 **Marsh**, Margaret S., *Anarchist Women, 1870–1920*, Philadelphia, 1981.

1.863 **Millett**, A. R., and **Maslowski**, P., *For the Common Defense. A Military History of the United States of America*, New York, 1984.

1.864 **Moeller**, S. D., *Shooting War. Photography and the American Experience of Combat*, New York, 1989. Covers wartime photography from the Spanish-American War through Vietnam.

1.865 **Palmer**, M. A., *Guardians of the Gulf. A History of America's Expanding Role in the Persian Gulf*, New York, 1992.

1.866 **Parker**, A. C. E., 'Beating the spread. Analyzing American election outcomes', *Journal of American History*, LXVII, 1980, 61–87.

1.867 **Pastor**, R. A., and **Castaneda**, J. G., *Limits to Friendship. The United States and Mexico*, New York, 1988.

1.868 **Randall**, S. J., *Colombia and the United States. Hegemony and Interdependence*, Athens, GA, 1992.

1.869 **Robins**, Natalie, *Alien Ink. The FBI's War on Freedom of Expression*, New York, 1992.

1.870 **Rodgers**, D. T., *Contested Truths. Keywords in American Politics Since Independence*, New York, 1987. Analyzes the use in political discourse of such charged terms as "rights," and "freedom," and finds that control of language has often been the key to power in American history.

1.871 **Rosenberg**, N. L., *Protecting the Best Men. An Interpretive History of the Law of Libel*, Chapel Hill, NC, 1986. Shows how changes in society away from deference led to changes in libel law, and how in recent times, the law has become more contradictory.

1.872 **Ryan**, G. D., and **Nenninger**, T. K., (ed.), *Soldiers and Civilians. The U.S. Army and the American People*, Washington, DC, 1987.

1.873 **Saul**, N. E., *Distant Friends. The United States and Russia, 1763–1867*, Lawrence, KS, 1991. A thorough survey of diplomatic relations between the two nations that finds common ground based on a mutual Anglophobia.

1.874 **Savage**, J. D., *Balanced Budgets and American Politics*, Ithaca, NY, 1988. Shows how concern about federal budget deficits has largely been symbolic and used in the larger discourse within the two-party system.

1.875 **Schaffer**, D., (ed.), *Two Centuries of American Planning*, Baltimore, 1988. A collection of essays that particularly concentrates on the heyday of urban planning, the mid-twentieth century.

1.876 **Schiffrin**, S. H., *The First Amendment, Democracy, and Romance*, Cambridge, MA, 1990.

1.877 **Schlesinger**, A. M., Jr., *The Cycles of American History*, Boston, 1986. Offers a theory, put forward by the author's father, that American politics runs in thirty year cycles of alternating liberal government action and then conservative government quiescence.

1.878 **Sferrazza**, C., *First Ladies. The Saga of the Presidents' Wives and their Power, 1789–1961*, New York, 1990. A two volume work that demonstrates the influence on policy-making of numerous obscure presidential spouses.

1.879 **Silver**, T. B., and **Schramm**, P. W., (ed.), *Natural Right and Political Right. Essays in Honor of Harry V. Jaffa*, Durham, NC, 1984. A festschrift to honor one of the most influential conservative political thinkers of the postwar period.

1.880 **Skocpol**, Theda, *Protecting Soldiers and Mothers. The Political Origins of Social Policy in the United States*, Cambridge, MA, 1992. Explains the lag of the United States in establishing a national retirement pension system to the ongoing system of pensions given to Union Army veterans and widows, and to the system of maternal support that arose in some of the states.

1.881 **Stevens**, E. W., *Literacy, Law, and Social Order*, DeKalb, IL, 1988. Traces the ways in which courts have dealt with illiterate people in civil law, especially voting rights cases.

1.882 **Utley**, R. L., (ed.), *The Promise of American Politics. Principles and Practice after Two Hundred Years*, Lanham, MD, 1989. A collection of essays by public intellectuals as part of a series known as the Tocqueville Forum.

1.883 **White**, G. E., *Tort Law in America. An Intellectual History*, New York, 1980.

1.884 **Wiecek**, W. M., *Liberty Under Law. The Supreme Court in American Life*, Baltimore, 1988.

1.885 **Williams**, T. H., *The History of American Wars from 1745 to 1918*, New York, 1981.

2

NORTH AMERICAN HISTORY
AND THE
EUROPEAN ENCOUNTER

GENERAL

2.1   **Axtell**, J., *Beyond 1492. Encounters in Colonial North America*, New York, 1992. A set of essays by one of the leading ethnohistorians about the interpretation of the 500th anniversary of what has become known as the Columbian Encounter.

2.2   **Beechert**, E. D., *Honolulu. Crossroads of the Pacific*, Columbia, SC, 1991.

2.3   **Brennan**, L. A., *Artifacts of North America*, Harrisburg, PA, 1975.

2.4   **Gorenstein**, Shirley, (ed.), *North America*, New York, 1975. Part of St. Martin's Press "Series in Prehistory".

2.5   **Kellar**, J. H., *An Introduction to the Prehistory of Indiana*, Indianapolis, IN, 1983.

2.6   **Kopper**, P., *The Smithsonian Book of North American Indians. Before the Coming of the Europeans*, Washington, DC, 1986.

2.7   **Kraft**, H. C., *The Lenape. Archaeology, History, and Ethnography*, Newark, NJ, 1986. A review of the history of the Lenape people who inhabited what is now New Jersey, and how they were scattered after European contact to the far reaches of North America.

2.8   **Plog**, F., *The Study of Prehistoric Change*, New York, 1974.

2.9   **Quimby**, I. M. G., *Material Culture and the Study of American Life*, New York, 1977. Proceedings of a Winterthur Museum conference on Southwest Indian antiquities.

2.10 **Quinn**, D. B., *North America from Earliest Discovery to First Settlements. The Norse Voyages to 1612*, New York, 1977.

2.11 **Riley**, C. L., and **Hedrick**, B. C., *Across the Chicimec Sea. Papers in Honor of J. Charles Kelley*, Carbondale, IL, 1978. A festschrift with essays on the Native Americans of the Southwest before European contact.

2.12 **Rogers**, J. D., *Objects of Change. The Archaeology and History of Arikara Contact with Europeans*, Washington, DC, 1990.

2.13 **Sale**, K., *The Conquest of Paradise. Christopher Columbus and the Columbian Legacy*, New York, 1990. A brief account of Columbus's first voyage, combined with a highly critical interpretation of the motives that impelled European expansion in the fifteenth century and the kind of American society the invaders soon destroyed.

2.14 **Snow**, D. R., *The Archaeology of North America*, New York, 1976.

2.15 **Stannard**, D. E., *American Holocaust. Columbus and the Conquest of the New World*, New York, 1992. A highly critical treatment of the European discovery and its consequences.

2.16 **Tooker**, Elisabeth, (ed.), *The Development of Political Organization in Native North America*, Philadelphia, PA, 1983.

2.17 **Tyler**, S. L., *Two Worlds. The Indian Encounter with the European, 1492–1509*, Salt Lake City, UT, 1988. An early contribution to the Columbian quincentenary.

2.18 **Viola**, H. J., and **Margolis**, Carolyn, (ed.), *Seeds of Change. A Quincentennial Commemoration*, Washington, DC, 1991.

An anthology of essays covering the Columbian Encounter, including perspectives on the Native Americans, Europeans, and Africans at the end of the fifteenth century.

2.19 **Walthall**, J. A., *Prehistoric Indians of the Southeast. Archaeology of Alabama and the Middle South*, University, AL, 1980.

GUIDE TO SOURCES

Atlases and dictionaries

2.20 **Jelks**, E. B., and **Jelks**, Juliet C., (ed.), *Historical Dictionary of North American Archaeology*, New York, 1988.
2.21 **Prucha**, F. P., *Atlas of American Indian Affairs*, Lincoln, NE, 1990. Helpful for pre-contact times, but stronger for the eighteenth and nineteenth centuries.
2.22 **Tanner**, Helen Hornbeck, *Atlas of Great Lakes Indian History*, Norman, OK, 1987. Carefully drawn maps accompanied by splendid narrative and bibliography, strongest for the eighteenth and early nineteenth centuries, but helpful for pre-contact times.

Bibliographies

2.23 **Blaine**, Martha Royce, *The Pawnees. A Critical Bibliography*, Bloomington, IN, 1980. One in a series of more than two dozen bibliographies of tribal people produced by the Newberry Library's Center for the History of the American Indian.
2.24 **Cashman**, M., *Bibliography of American Ethnology*, Rye, NY, 1976.
2.25 **Dobyns**, H. F., *Native American Historical Demography. A Critical Bibliography*, Bloomington, IN, 1976.
2.26 **Dobyns**, H. F., *Indians of the Southeast. A Critical Bibliography*, Bloomington, IN, 1980.
2.27 **Edmunds**, R. D., (ed.), *Kinsmen Through Time. An Annotated Bibliography of Potawatomi History*, Metuchen, NJ, 1987.

2.28 **Fogelson**, R. D., *The Cherokees. A Critical Bibliography*, Bloomington, IN, 1978.
2.29 **Green**, M. D., *The Creeks. A Critical Bibliography*, Bloomington, IN, 1979.
2.30 **Grumet**, R. S., *Native Americans of the Northwest Coast. A Critical Bibliography*, Bloomington, IN, 1979.
2.31 **Haas**, Marilyn L., *Indians of North America. Methods and Sources for Library Research*, Hamden, CT, 1983.
2.32 **Heizer**, R. F., *The Indians of California. A Critical Bibliography*, Bloomington, IN, 1976.
2.33 **Hoebel**, E. A. *The Plains Indians. A Critical Bibliography*, Bloomington, IN, 1977.
2.34 **Hoover**, H. T., *The Sioux. A Critical Bibliography*, Bloomington, IN, 1979.
2.35 **Hoxie**, F. E., and **Markowitz**, H., *Native Americans, an Annotated Bibliography*, Pasadena, CA, 1991.
2.36 **Iverson**, P., *The Navajos. A Critical Bibliography*, Bloomington, IN, 1976.
2.37 **Kersey**, H. A., *The Seminole and Miccosukee Tribes. A Critical Bibliography*, Bloomington, IN, 1987.
2.38 **Kidwell**, Clara Sue, *The Choctaws. A Critical Bibliography*, Bloomington, IN, 1980.
2.39 **Martin**, M. Marlene, and **O'Leary**, T. J., *Ethnographic Bibliography of North America*, New Haven, CT, 1990.
2.40 **Melody**, M. E., *The Apaches. A Critical Bibliography*, Bloomington, IN, 1977.
2.41 **Porter**, F. W., *Indians in Maryland and Delaware. A Critical Bibliography*, Bloomington, IN, 1979.
2.42 **Powell**, P. J., *The Cheyennes, Maheoo's People. A Critical Bibliography*, Bloomington, IN, 1980.
2.43 **Salisbury**, N., *The Indians of New England. A Critical Bibliography*, Bloomington, IN, 1982.
2.44 **Schuster**, Helen H., *The Yakimas. A Critical Bibliography*, Bloomington, IN, 1982.
2.45 **Stewart**, O. C., *Indians of the Great Basin. A Critical Bibliography*, Bloomington, IN, 1982.
2.46 **Tanner**, Helen Hornbeck, *The Ojibways. A Critical Bibliography*, Bloomington, IN, 1976.
2.47 **Thornton**, R., *The Urbanization of American Indians. A Critical Bibliography*, Bloomington, IN, 1982.
2.48 **Tooker**, Elisabeth, *The Indians of the*

Northeast. A Critical Bibliography, Bloomington, IN, 1978.

Historiography

2.49 **Calloway**, C. G., (ed.), *New Directions in American Indian History*, Norman, OK, 1988.

2.50 **Hirschfelder**, Arlene B., **Byler**, Mary Gloyne, and **Dorris**, M. A., *Guide to Research on North American Indians*, Chicago, 1983.

2.51 **Swagerty**, W. R., (ed.), *Scholars and the Indian Experience. Critical Reviews of Recent Writing in the Social Sciences*, Bloomington, IN, 1984.

2.52 **Thornton**, R., and **Grasmick**, Mary K., *Bibliography of Social Science Research and Writings on American Indians*, Minneapolis, MN, 1979.

2.53 **White**, R., 'New world populations and postcontact epidemics', *Ethnohistory*, XXXVII, 1989, 66–70. Reviews the recent literature on the quantitative dimensions of the Native American population loss.

DEMOGRAPHY, FAMILY, AND HEALTH

2.54 **Becker**, M. J., 'Lenape population at the time of European contact. Estimating native numbers in the lower Delaware Valley', *Transactions of the American Philosophical Society*, CXXXIII, 1989, 112–122.

2.55 **Chisholm**, J. S., *Navajo Infancy. An Ethnological Study of Child Development*, Hawthorne, NY, 1983.

2.56 **Crosby**, A. W., *The Columbian Exchange. Biological and Cultural Consequences of 1492*, Westport, CT, 1973.

2.57 **Denevan**, W. M., *The Native Population of the Americas in 1492*, Madison, WI, 1992.

2.58 **Dobyns**, H. F., *Their Number Become Thinned. Native American Population Dynamics in Eastern North America*, Knoxville, TN, 1983. Extrapolates a figure of eighteen million native people in the present-day lower forty-eight states, based

on carrying capacity of various village sites; definitely the upper bound of estimates of pre-contact population estimates.

2.59 **Grumet**, R. S., 'A new ethnohistorical model for North American Indian demography', *North American Archaeologist*, XI, 1990, 29–41.

2.60 **Haegert**, Dorothy, *Children of the First People*, Vancouver, 1989.

2.61 **Hann**, J. H., 'Demographic patterns and changes in mid-seventeenth century Timucua and Apalachee', *Florida Historical Quarterly*, LXIV, 1986, 371–392.

2.62 **Kay**, Jeanne. 'The fur trade and Native American population growth', *Ethnohistory*, XXXI, 1984, 265–287. Disputes any connection between population loss and the depletion of fur-bearing animals.

2.63 **Kennedy**, Brenda, *Marriage Patterns in Archaic Population*, Ottawa, 1981.

2.64 **Larsen**, C. S., (ed.), *Native American demography in the Spanish Borderlands*, New York, 1991.

2.65 **Moore**, J. H., and **Campbell**, G. R., 'An ethnohistorical perspective on Cheyenne demography', *Journal of Family History*, IV, 1989, 17–42.

2.66 **Nelson**, Kjerstie, *Marriage and Divorce Practices in Native California*, Berkeley, CA, 1975.

2.67 **Palkovich**, Ann M., 'Historic population of the eastern pueblos: 1540–1910', *Journal of Anthropological Research*, XLI, 1985, 401–426.

2.68 **Ramenofsky**, Ann F., *Vectors of Death. The Archaeology of European Contact*, Albuquerque, NM, 1987.

2.69 **Reidhead**, V. A., *A Linear Programming Model of Prehistoric Subsistence Optimization. A Southeastern Indiana Example*, Indianapolis, IN, 1981.

2.70 **Snow**, D. R., and **Starna**, W. A., 'Sixteenth-century depopulation: a view from the Mohawk Valley', *American Anthropologist*, XCI, 1989, 142–149.

2.71 **Thornton**, R., *American Indian Holocaust and Survival. A Population History Since 1492*, Norman, OK, 1987. The most thorough demographic survey on the question of Native American population, both before European contact and since.

2.72 **Thornton**, R., *The Cherokees. A Population History*, Lincoln, NE, 1990. A demographic survey of the southeastern tribe that follows the people through nineteenth century removal to Oklahoma and twentieth century migration to California.

2.73 **Witherspoon**, G., *Navajo Kinship and Marriage*, Chicago, 1975.

SOCIAL HISTORY

Gender relations

2.74 **Gridley**, Marion Eleanor, *American Indian Women*, New York, 1974.
2.75 **Niethammer**, Carolyn J., *Daughters of the Earth. The Lives and Legends of American Indian Women*, New York, 1977.
2.76 **Norbeck**, E., and **Farrer**, Claire R., (ed.), *Forms of Play of Native North Americans*, St. Paul, MN, 1979.
2.77 **Oxendine**, J. B., *American Indian Sports Heritage*, Champaign, IL, 1988.

RELIGION, BELIEFS, IDEAS AND CULTURE

2.78 **Bierhorst**, J., *The Mythology of North America*, New York, 1985.
2.79 **Collins**, J. J., *Native American Religions. A Geographical Survey*, Lewiston, NY, 1991.
2.80 **Erdoes**, R., and **Ortiz**, A., (ed.), *American Indian Myths and Legends*, New York, 1984.
2.81 **Feest**, C. F., *Native Arts of North America*, New York, 1980.
2.82 **Fenton**, W. N., *The False Faces of the Iroquois*, Norman, OK, 1987. An investigation into the secret religious meaning of the masks worn by some of the Iroquois tribes.
2.83 **Finn**, Rosemary R., 'The belief system of the Powhatan Indians', *Archeological Society of Virginia Quarterly Bulletin*, XLII, 1987, 150–158.
2.84 **Furst**, P., and **Furst**, Jill Leslie, *North American Indian Art*, New York, 1982.

2.85 **Hausman**, G., *Turtle Island Alphabet. A Lexicon of Native American Symbols and Culture*, New York, 1992.
2.86 **Highwater**, J., *Ritual of the Wind. North American Indian Ceremonies*, New York, 1984.
2.87 **Hultkrantz**, A., *Belief and Worship in Native North America*, Syracuse, NY, 1981.
2.88 **Jacka**, J. D., *Beyond Tradition. Contemporary Indian Art and its Evolution*, Flagstaff, AZ, 1988.
2.89 **Merkur**, D., *Becoming Half Hidden. Shamanism and Initiation Among the Inuit*, Stockholm, 1985.
2.90 **Morton**, E. D., *To Touch the Wind. An Introduction to Native American Philosophy and Beliefs*, Dubuque, IA, 1988.
2.91 **Powers**, W. K., *Oglala Religion*, Lincoln, NE, 1977.
2.92 **Schaafsma**, Polly, *Indian Rock Art of the Southwest*, Albuquerque, NM, 1979.
2.93 **Wade**, E. L., (ed.), *The Arts of the North American Indian. Native Traditions in Evolution*, New York, 1986.
2.94 **Williamson**, R. A., *Living the Sky. The Cosmos of the American Indian*, Boston, 1984.
2.95 **Williamson**, R. A., and **Farrer**, Claire R., *Earth and Sky Visions of the Cosmos in Native American Folklore*, Albuquerque, NM, 1992.

WORK AND ENTERPRISE

2.96 **Ebeling**, W., *Handbook of Indian Foods and Fibers of Arid America*, Berkeley, CA, 1986. In addition to food, this extensive volume covers textile manufacturing.
2.97 **Ford**, R. I., (ed.), *Prehistoric Food Production in North America*, Ann Arbor, MI, 1985.
2.98 **Frison**, G. C., *The Casper Site. A Hell Gap Bison Kill on the High Plains*, New York, 1974.
2.99 **Kindscher**, Kelly, *Edible Wild Plants of the Prairie. An Ethnobotanical Guide*, Lawrence, KS, 1987.
2.100 **Kipp**, H. W., *Indians in Agriculture. An*

Historical Sketch, Washington, DC, 1988.

2.101 **Larsen**, L. H., *Aboriginal Subsistence Technology on the Southeastern Coastal Plain During the Late Prehistoric Period*, Gainesville, FL, 1980.

2.102 **Moerman**, D. E., *Medicinal Plants of Native America*, Ann Arbor, MI, 1986.

2.103 **Munson**, P. J., *Experiments and Observations on Aboriginal Wild Plant Food Utilization in Eastern North America*, Indianapolis, IN, 1984.

2.104 **Nabhan**, G. P., *Enduring Seeds. Native American Agriculture and Wild Plant Conservation*, San Francisco, 1989.

2.105 **Neusius**, Sarah W., (ed.), *Foraging, Collecting and Harvesting. Archaic Period Subsistence and Settlement in the Eastern Woodlands*, Carbondale, IL, 1986.

2.106 **Seeman**, M. F., *The Hopewell Interaction Sphere. The Evidence for Interregional Trade and Structural Complexity*, Indianapolis, IN, 1979.

2.107 **Vennum**, T., *Wild Rice and the Ojibway People*, St. Paul, MN, 1988. A study in ethnobotany that considers the value of wild rice in the diet and culture of the Ojibway (Chippewa) people of the Lake Superior region.

2.108 **Winterhalder**, B., and **Smith**, E. A., (ed.), *Hunter-gatherer Foraging Strategies. Ethnographic and Archeological Analyses*, Chicago, 1981.

RACE AND ETHNIC IDENTITY

2.109 **Baugh**, T. G., 'Culture history and protohistoric societies in the southern plains', *Plains Anthropologist*, 1986, XXXI, 167–187.

2.110 **Clifton**, J. A., *Being and Becoming Indian. Biographical Studies of North American Frontiers*, Chicago, 1989.

2.111 **Greenberg**, A. M., and **Morrison**, J., 'Group identities in the boreal forest: the origin of the Northern Ojibwa', *Ethnohistory*, XXIX, 1982, 75–102.

2.112 **Russell**, H. S., *Indian New England Before the Mayflower*, Hanover, NH, 1980.

SPACE, MOVEMENT, AND PLACE

2.113 **Brose**, D. S., and **Greber**, Naomi, (ed.), *Hopewell Archaeology. The Chillicothe Conference*, Kent, OH, 1979.

2.114 **Cordell**, Linda S., *Prehistory of the Southwest*, Orlando, FL, 1984.

2.115 **Danziger**, E. J., *The Chippewas of Lake Superior*, Norman, OK, 1978.

2.116 **Ferguson**, W. M., *Anasazi Ruins of the Southwest in Color*, Albuquerque, NM, 1987.

2.117 **Hann**, J. H., *Apalachee. The Land Between the Rivers*, Gainesville, FL, 1988. An ethnohistory of the people who lived in what now is northern Florida, and how they were ultimately destroyed at the end of the seventeenth century.

2.118 **Hill**, Beth, and **Hill**, R., *Indian Petroglyphs of the Pacific Northwest*, Seattle, 1975.

2.119 **Johnson**, E., *The Prehistoric Peoples of Minnesota*, St. Paul, MN, 1978. Surveys existing knowledge about the Paleo-Indian, Eastern Archaic, Woodland and Mississippian cultures.

2.120 **Martin**, P. S., *The Archaeology of Arizona. A Study of the Southwest Region*, Garden City, NY, 1973.

2.121 **Mason**, R. J., *Great Lakes Archaeology*, New York, 1981.

2.122 **Morse**, D. F., *Archaeology of the Central Mississippi Valley*, New York, 1983.

2.123 **Niemczycki**, Mary Ann Palmer, 'The Genesee connection. The origins of Iroquois culture in West-Central New York', *North American Archaeologist*, VII, 1986, 15–44.

2.124 **Prufer**, O. H., and **McKenzie**, D. H., *Studies in Ohio Archaeology*, Kent, OH, 1975.

2.125 **Ritzenthaler**, R. E., *Prehistoric Indians of Wisconsin*, Milwaukee, 1985. Third edition of a still useful booklet, written by a veteran anthropologist.

2.126 **Roper**, Donna C., *Archaeological Survey and Settlement Pattern Models in Central Illinois*, Kent, OH, 1979. Looks at land use patterns in the Sangamon Valley of present-day Illinois.

2.127 **Sando**, J. S., *Pueblo Nations. Eight Centuries of Pueblo Indian History*, Santa Fe, NM, 1992. Revised edition of the 1976 volume with new material on recent developments in the Southwest.

2.128 **Snow**, D., *The Iroquois*, New York, 1992. Considers the formation of the Iroquois League in pre-contact times and continues their history up to the eighteenth century.

2.129 **Stewart**, Hilary, *Indian Artifacts of the Northwest Coast*, Seattle, 1975.

2.130 **Stuart**, D. E., *Prehistoric New Mexico. Background for Survey*, Albuquerque, NM, 1984.

2.131 **Weisman**, B. R., *Like Beads on a String. A Culture History of the Seminole Indians in Northern Peninsular Florida*, Tuscaloosa, AL, 1989.

2.132 **Wright**, G. A., *People of the High Country. Jackson Hole Before the Settlers*, New York, 1984.

3

CONQUEST AND RESETTLEMENT:
EUROPEANS, AFRICANS, AND
NATIVE AMERICANS, 1600–1760

GENERAL HISTORIES
AND ANTHOLOGIES

3.1 **Agnew**, J.-C., *Worlds Apart. The Market and the Theater in Anglo-American Thought*, New York, 1986.

3.2 **Bailyn**, B., and **Morgan**, P. D., *Strangers Within the Realm. Cultural Margins of the First British Empire*, Chapel Hill, NC, 1991. A set of essays on the relations between the imperial center and its periphery, from Ireland and Scotland to Native Americans and the slave colonies of the West Indies.

3.3 **Cornell**, S., 'Land, labour and group formation: Blacks and Indians in the United States', *Ethnic and Racial Studies*, XIII, 1990, 368–388.

3.4 **Craven**, W., *Colonial American Portraiture. The Economic, Religious, Social, Cultural, Philosophical, Scientific, and Aesthetic Foundations*, New York, 1986.

3.5 **Daniels**, B. C., *The Fragmentation of New England. Comparative Perspectives on Economic, Political, and Social Divisions in the Eighteenth Century*, New York, 1988.

3.6 **Davis**, R. B., *Intellectual Life in the Colonial South, 1585–1763*, Knoxville, TN, 1978.

3.7 **Fischer**, D. H., *Albion's Seed. Four British Folkways in America*, New York, 1989. Argues that the culture of East Anglia, the South of England, the North Midlands and the Scottish Borderlands respectively shaped the distinctive folkways of New England, Virginia, Pennsylvania and Appalachia.

3.8 **Greenblatt**, S., *Marvelous Possessions. The Wonder of the New World*, Chicago, 1991.

3.9 **Greene**, J. P., *Pursuits of Happiness. The Social Development of Early Modern British Colonies and the Formation of American Culture*, Chapel Hill, NC, 1988. Surveys the social history of the British North American and Caribbean colonies and finds that the Chesapeake region was closest in standing to that of Great Britain.

3.10 **Greene**, J. P., *Imperatives, Behaviors, and Identities. Essays in Early American Cultural History*, Charlottesville, VA, 1992.

3.11 **Greene**, J. P., and **Pole**, J. R., *Colonial British America. Essays in the New History of the Early Modern Era*, Baltimore, MD, 1984. A collection of essays organized around social science themes, reflecting the influence of the Annales school on the study of American colonial history.

3.12 **Hall**, D. D., **Murrin**, J. M., and **Tate**, T. W., *Saints and Revolutions. Essays on Early American History*, New York, 1984.

3.13 **Hawke**, D. F., *Everyday Life in Early America*, New York, 1988.

3.14 **Henretta**, J. A., **Kammen**, M., and **Katz**, S., (ed.), *The Transformation of Early American History. Society, Authority, and Ideology*, New York, 1991. A festschrift to honor Bernard Bailyn, with essays by some of the leading historians of colonial America.

3.15 **Meinig**, D. W., *The Shaping of America. A Geographical Perspective on 500 Years of History, Atlantic America, 1492–1800*, New Haven, CT, 1986. The Atlantic world and the North American continent as seen with some strikingly original maps by a historical geographer.

3.16 **Middleton**, R., *Colonial America. A History, 1607–1760*, 1992. A survey of the era that emphasizes the differences among the colonies and the unity of the period as something other than a prelude to the Revolution.

3.17 **Olson**, Alison Gilbert, *Making the Empire Work. London and American Interest Groups, 1690–1790*, Cambridge, MA, 1992. Considers how family and trade relationships helped influence the making of imperial policy in Great Britain.

3.18 **Salisbury**, N., *Manitou and Providence. Indians, Europeans, and the Making of New England, 1500–1643*, New York, 1982.

3.19 **Selesky**, H. E., *War and Society in Colonial Connecticut*, New Haven, CT, 1990.

3.20 **Tate**, T. W., and **Ammerman**, D. L., (ed.), *The Chesapeake in the Seventeenth Century. Essays on Anglo-American Society and Politics*, Chapel Hill, NC, 1979. An influential volume of essays that features new work on the demographic and geographic history of the Maryland and Virginia settlements around Chesapeake Bay.

3.21 **Thomas**, D. H., *Archaeological and Historical Perspectives on the Spanish Borderlands West*, Washington, DC, 1989.

3.22 **Todorov**, T., *The Conquest of America. The Question of the Other*, New York, 1984. A reexamination of the Spanish chronicles of exploration.

3.23 **Trigger**, B. G., *Natives and Newcomers. Canada's 'Heroic Age' Reconsidered*, Kingston, ONT, 1985. Particular focus on the Iroquois wars.

Diary of Elizabeth Drinker, Boston, 1991. A three volume set of the daily writing of a Philadelphia Quaker woman that spans the second half of the eighteenth century.

3.26 **Dunn**, R. S., and **Dunn**, Mary Maples, (ed.), *The Papers of William Penn*, Philadelphia, 1975. Five volumes have appeared in the series through 1987.

3.27 **Jennings**, F. J., (ed.), *The History and Culture of Iroquois Diplomacy. An Interdisciplinary Guide to the Treaties of the Six Nations and their League*, Syracuse, NY, 1985.

3.28 **Klepp**, Susan E., and **Smith**, B. G., (ed.), *The Unfortunate. The Voyage and Adventures of William Moraley, an Indentured Servant*, University Park, PA, 1992. Account of an eighteenth century Englishman who sold himself into indentured servitude and unsuccessfully sought his fortune in Philadelphia.

3.29 **LaFantasie**, G. W., (ed.), *The Correspondence of Roger Williams*, Hanover, NH, 1988. A two volume set of Williams' letters, many never before published.

3.30 **Lockridge**, K. A., *The Diary, and Life, of William Byrd II of Virginia, 1674–1744*, Chapel Hill, NC, 1987.

3.31 **Namias**, June, *A Narrative of the Life of Mrs. Mary Jemison*, Norman, OK, 1992. Captivity account of a woman who was captured by the Senecas as a child and chose to live with them the rest of her life.

3.32 **Peyser**, J. L., (ed.), *Letters from New France. The Upper Country, 1686–1783*, Urbana, IL, 1992. A collection of letters, mainly from the St. Joseph settlement in present-day Michigan, that sheds light on the dealings between the French and Indians.

3.33 **Russo**, Jean E., 'The constables' lists: An invaluable resource', *Maryland Historical Magazine*, LXXXV, 1990, 164–170.

GUIDES TO SOURCES

Primary sources

3.24 **Barbour**, P. L., *The Complete Works of Captain John Smith, 1580–1631*, Chapel Hill, NC, 1986. A three volume set of the writings of the leader of the Jamestown colony.

3.25 **Crane**, Elaine Forman, *et al.*, (ed.), *The*

Bibliographies and dictionaries

3.34 **Borne**, Pamela R., and **Kinnell**, Susan K., (ed.), *Pioneers and Explorers In North America. Summaries of Biographical Articles in History Journals*, Santa Barbara, CA, 1988. Taken from the abstracts of *America, History and Life*, there are similar volumes from the same editors for business and industry, the arts, politics, and religion.

3.35 **Lydon**, J. G., *Struggle for Power. A Bibliography of the French and Indian War*, New York, 1986.

3.36 **O'Donnell**, J. H., *Southeastern Frontiers. Europeans, Africans, and American Indians, 1513–1840. A Critical Bibliography*, Bloomington, IN, 1982. Another of the Newberry Library's series of bibliographies of tribal people.

3.37 **Ronda**, J. P., and **Axtell**, J. L., *Indian Missions. A Critical Bibliography*, Bloomington, IN, 1978. Another of the Newberry Library's series of bibliographies on the aspects of American Indian history.

Historiography

3.38 **Axtell**, J., 'Colonial America without the Indians. Counterfactual reflections', *Journal of American History*, LXXIII, 1987, 891–996.

3.39 **Harlan**, D., 'A people blinded from birth. American history according to Sacvan Bercovitch', *Journal of American History*, LXXVIII, 1991, 949–971. A review of the influence on Puritan studies of Bercovitch's *The American Jeremiad*: see also the immediate rejoinder by Bercovitch on pp. 972–987 of the same issue of the *JAH*.

3.40 **Merwick**, Donna, ' "Being There". Some theoretical aspects of writing history at a distance', *Reviews in American History*, XIV, 1986, 487–500. An essay about how the Australian scholar uses cultural anthropology to understand colonial America.

3.41 **Poyo**, G. E., and **Hinojosa**, G. M., 'Spanish Texas and Borderlands historiography in transition. Implications for United States history', *Journal of American History*, LXXV, 1988, 393–416. A plea for more and better research into the role and importance of Spain's experience in North American and U.S. History.

3.42 **Roberts**, G. B., 'New sources for seventeenth-century New England and the pioneer population of 1750 to 1850. A review essay', *New England Historical and Genealogical Register*, CXXXV, 1981, 57–68.

3.43 **Walsh**, Lorena S., 'The historian as census taker: individual reconstitution and the reconstruction of censuses for a colonial Chesapeake county', *William and Mary Quarterly*, XXXVIII, 1981, 242–260.

3.44 **Yentsch**, Anne, 'Minimum vessel lists as evidence of change in folk and courtly traditions of food use', *Historical Archaeology*, XXIV, 1990, 24–53. A blend of archaeological analysis of pottery fragments in seventeenth century Maryland with evidence from probate records to chart social change.

BIOGRAPHY

3.45 **Flexner**, J. T., *Lord of the Mohawks. A Biography of Sir William Johnson*, Boston, 1979. A revised edition of the 1959 biography.

3.46 **Gragg**, L., *A Quest for Security. The Life of Samuel Parris, 1653–1720*, Westport, CT, 1990. A biography of the minister who led and supported the witchcraft trials in Salem.

3.47 **Hall**, M. G., *The Last American Puritan. The Life of Increase Mather, 1639–1723*, Middletown, CT, 1988. Treats Mather's life and thought amid the problem of the second generation of New England Puritans, from the half-way covenant through the Salem witch trials and the decline of Puritan orthodoxy.

3.48 **Johnson**, R. R., *John Nelson, Merchant Adventurer. A Life Between Empires*, New York, 1991. A biography of a trader active in the late seventeenth century, and who dealt on the margins between the French, Indians, and English.

3.49 **Kershaw**, G. E., *James Bowdoin II. Patriot and Man of the Enlightenment*, Lanham, MD, 1991.

3.50 **LeMay**, J. A. L., *The American Dream of Captain John Smith*, Charlottesville, VA, 1991.

3.51 **McCully**, B. T., 'Governor Francis Nicholson, patron par excellence of religion and learning in colonial America', *William and Mary Quarterly*, XXXIX, 1982, 319–333.

3.52 **Morgan**, E. S., 'The world of William Penn', *Proceedings of the American Philosophical Society*, CXXVII, 1983, 291–315.

3.53 **Potts**, L. W., *Arthur Lee. A Virtuous Revolutionary*, Baton Rouge, LA, 1981.

3.54 **Price**, J. M., *Perry of London. A Family on the Seaborne Frontier, 1615–1753*, Cambridge, MA, 1992. A collective biography of the family members in a tobacco trading firm that linked the Chesapeake to the metropolis.

3.55 **Quitt**, M. H., 'The English cleric and the Virginia adventurer: the Washingtons, father and son', *Virginia Magazine of History and Biography*, XCVII, 1989, 163–184.

3.56 **Silverman**, K., *The Life and Times of Cotton Mather*, New York, 1984. A sympathetic biography of Mather that places him in a larger Atlantic world context as the first American-born writer who contributed to English ideas.

3.57 **Simmonds**, M., *The Last Conquistador. Juan de Onate and the Settling of the Far Southwest*, Norman, OK, 1991. A life of the governor of New Mexico at the beginning of the seventeenth century.

3.58 **Spalding**, P., and **Jackson**, H. H., (ed.), *Oglethorpe in Perspective. Georgia's Founder after Two Hundred Years*, Tuscaloosa, AL, 1989.

DEMOGRAPHY, FAMILY, AND HEALTH

3.59 **Altman**, Ida, and **Horn**, J., (ed.), 'To Make America'. *European Emigration in the Early Modern Period*, Berkeley, CA, 1991.

3.60 **Anderson**, T. L., 'From the parts to the whole: modeling Chesapeake population. Methodological problems in determining population growth in the 17th century Chesapeake colonies', *Explorations in Economic History*, XVII, 1981, 399–414.

3.61 **Anderson**, Virginia DeJohn, 'Migrants and motives: Religion and the settlement of New England', *New England Quarterly*, LVIII, 1985, 339–383.

3.62 **Archer**, R., 'New England mosaic: A demographic analysis for the seventeenth century', *William and Mary Quarterly*, XLVII, 1990, 477–502. Makes use of printed family geneaologies to analyze the demographic history of the first generation of New England towns.

3.63 **Byers**, E., 'Fertility transition in a New England commercial center: Nantucket Massachusetts, 1680–1840', *Journal of Interdisciplinary History*, XIII, 1982, 17–40.

3.64 **Calvert**, Karin, 'Children in American family portraiture, 1670 to 1810', *William and Mary Quarterly*, XXXIX, 1982, 87–113. Charts the changes in how adults viewed children by an analysis of portraits.

3.65 **Coclanis**, P. A., 'Death in early Charleston: an estimate of the crude death rate for the white population of Charleston, 1722–1732', *South Carolina Historical Magazine*, LXXXV, 1984, 280–291.

3.66 **Greven**, P. J., *Spare the Child. The Religious Roots of Punishment and the Psychological Impact of Physical Abuse*, New York, 1991.

3.67 **Greven**, P. J., *The Protestant Temperament. Patterns of Child-Rearing, Religious Experience, and the Self in Early America*, New York, 1977.

3.68 **Henderson**, R. C., 'Demographic patterns and family structure in eighteenth-century Lancaster County, Pennsylvania', *Pennsylvania Magazine of History and Biography*, CXIV, 1990, 349–383.

3.69 **Jimenez**, Mary Ann, *Changing Faces of Madness. Early American Attitudes and Treatment of the Insane*, Hanover, NH, 1987.

3.70 **Jordan**, W. D., and **Skemp**, Sheila L. (ed.), *Race and Family in the Colonial South. Essays*, Jackson, MS, 1987.

3.71 **Levy**, B., *Quakers and the American Family. British Settlement in the Delaware Valley*, New York, 1988. Places British Quaker migrants at the center of the transformation of the family from patriarchal form to child-centered domesticity.

3.72 **Menard**, R. R., 'Population, economy, and society in seventeenth-century Maryland', *Maryland Historical Magazine*, LXXIX, 1984, 71–92.

3.73 **Moran**, G. F., and **Vinovskis**, M. A., 'The Puritan family and religion: a critical reappraisal', *William and Mary Quarterly*, XXIX, 1982, 29–63.

3.74 **Narrett**, D. E., *Inheritance and Family Life in Colonial New York City*, Ithaca, NY, 1992. Traces the changes in estate law from the Dutch regime up to the Revolution and links those changes to family history.

3.75 **Numbers**, R. L., (ed.), *Medicine in the New World. New Spain, New France, and New England*, Knoxville, TN, 1987.

3.76 **Reff**, D. T., *Disease, Depopulation, and Culture Change in Northwestern New Spain, 1518–1764*, Salt Lake City, UT, 1991.

3.77 **Rink**, O. A., 'The people of New Netherland: notes on non-English immigration to New York in the seventeenth century', *New York History*, CXII, 1981, 5–42.

3.78 **Schweitzer**, Mary M., *Custom and Contract. Household, Government and the Economy in Colonial Pennsylvania*, New York, 1987. Finds the origins of the productive market economy of Chester County, Pennsylvania in its households, and shows how the household was the basic unit of production, investment, and trade.

3.79 **Smith**, D. B., *Inside the Great House. Planter Family Life in Eighteenth-Century Chesapeake Society*, Ithaca, NY, 1980.

3.80 **Smith**, D. S., ' "All in Some Degree Related to Each Other". A demographic and comparative resolution of the anomaly of New England kinship', *American Historical Review*, XCIV, 1989, 44–79. Links the weakening bonds of kinship relations in New England to the region's subsequent emergence as the American "Lancashire", "Prussia", and "Athens" all rolled into one.

3.81 **Tebbenhoff**, E., 'Tacit rules and hidden structures. Naming practices and godparentage in Schenectady, New York, 1680–1800', *Journal of Social History*, XIV, 1985, 567–585.

3.82 **Thistlewaite**, F., *Dorset Pilgrims. The Story of West Country Pilgrims Who Went to New England in the 17th Century*, 1989. Analyzes the passage from England of migrants who settled and made the town of Windsor, Connecticut.

3.83 **Wall**, Helena M., *Fierce Communion. Family and Community in Early America*, Cambridge, MA, 1990.

3.84 **Weissbach**, L. S., 'The townes of Massachusetts. A pilot study in geneaology and family history', *Essex Institute Historical Collections*, CXVIII, 1982, 200–220.

SOCIAL RELATIONS

Class and community

3.85 **Allen**, D. G., *In English Ways. The Movement of Societies and the Transferral of English Local Law and Custom to the Massachusetts Bay in the Seventeenth Century*, Chapel Hill, NC, 1981. Traces the founders of five Massachusetts towns back to England and finds that the differences among New England settlements mirrored differences also found between English regions.

3.86 **Crane**, Elaine Forman, *A Dependent People. Newport, Rhode Island in the Revolutionary Era*, New York, 1985. Analyzes the prosperity of prewar Newport and finds that its basis in the rum trade was shattered by imperial regulations in the 1760s, and that the port town never regained its colonial prominence.

3.87 **Goodfriend**, Joyce D., *Before the Melting Pot. Society and Culture in Colonial New York City, 1664–1730*, Princeton, 1992.

3.88 **Heyrman**, Christine Leigh, *Commerce and Culture. The Maritime Communities of Colonial Massachusetts, 1690–1750*, New York, 1984.

3.89 **Innes**, S., *Labor in a New Land. Economy and Society in Seventeenth Century Springfield*, Princeton, 1983. Shows the extent to which the Pynchon family dominated the early town of Springfield, Massachusetts and how different the settlement was from other Puritan towns.

3.90 **King**, Julia A., 'A comparative midden analysis of a household and inn in St. Mary's City Maryland', *Historical Archaeology*, XXII, 1988, 17–39.

3.91 **Klingelhofer**, E., 'Aspects of early Afro-American material culture: artifacts from the slave quarters in Garrison Plantation, Maryland', *Historical Archaeology*, XXI, 1987, 112–119.

3.92 **Konig**, D. T., *Law and Society in Puritan Massachusetts. Essex County, 1629–1692*, Chapel Hill, NC, 1979.

3.93 **Main**, Gloria, *Tobacco Colony. Life in Early Maryland, 1650–1719*, Princeton, 1982. A detailed look at the social structure and daily life of the servants and planters of Maryland through the study of more than 3,000 probate inventories.

3.94 **Main**, J. T., *Society and Economy in*

Colonial Connecticut, Princeton, 1985. Examines wealthholding and property distribution in the colony through an examination of probate records and finds a high level of prosperity and well-being for a majority of the population.

3.95 **Nellis**, E. G., 'The working poor of pre-revolutionary Boston', *Historical Journal of Massachusetts*, XVII, 1989, 137–159.

3.96 **Perry**, J. R., *The Formation of a Society on Virginia's Eastern Shore, 1615–1655*, Chapel Hill, NC, 1990. Finds the origins of a stable society of landowners early on in the history of Virginia, based on land and kinship with the church playing a reduced role.

3.97 **Purvis**, T., 'Economic diversification and labour utilization among the rural elite of the British mid-atlantic colonies. A case study from the Delaware valley', *Social History*, XIVV, 1986, 57–71.

3.98 **Roeber**, A. G., *Faithful Magistrates and Republican Lawyers. Creators of Virginia's Legal Culture, 1680–1810*, Chapel Hill, NC, 1981.

3.99 **Rutman**, D. B., and **Rutman**, Anita H., *A Place in Time. Middlesex County, Virginia, 1650–1750*, New York, 1984. A community of the South that parallels the New England town studies done in the 1970s; the Rutmans trace the emergence of a society of planters, yeomen, and slaves in the Tidewater region.

3.100 **Waterhouse**, R., 'The development of elite culture in the colonial American south: a study of Charles Town, 1670–1770', *Australian Journal of Politics and History*, XXVIII, 1982, 391–404.

3.101 **Wolf**, E., *The Book Culture of a Colonial American City. Philadelphia Books, Bookmen, and Booksellers*, New York, 1988. Reconstructs the tastes of the reading public from records of private libraries and booksellers.

Gender relations

3.102 **Breitwieser**, M. R., *American Puritanism and the Defense of Mourning. Grief and Ethnology in Mary White Rowlandson's Captivity Narrative*, Madison, WI, 1990. A literary analysis of the famous account of a Puritan minister's wife, held hostage in King Philip's War.

3.103 **Gutierrez**, R. A., *When Jesus Came, the Corn Mothers Went Away. Marriage, Sexuality, and Power in New Mexico, 1500–1846*, Stanford, CA, 1991.

3.104 **Koehler**, L., *A Search for Power. The 'Weaker Sex' in Seventeenth-Century New England*, Urbana, IL, 1980.

3.105 **Thompson**, R., *Sex in Middlesex. Popular Mores in a Massachusetts County, 1649–1699*, Amherst, MA, 1986. A look at the history of Puritan sex with an emphasis on the deviant and criminal, as reflected in court records.

3.106 **Thompson**, R., 'Attitudes towards homosexuality in the seventeenth century New England colonies', *Journal of American Studies*, XXIII, 1989, 27–40.

3.107 **Ulrich**, Laure Thatcher, *Good Wives. Image and Reality in the Lives of Women in Northern New England, 1650–1750*, New York, 1982. Analyzes the types of lives that Puritan women led and matches them to biblical characters as a way of understanding the social world of early New England.

Education

3.108 **Chase**, T., 'Harvard student disorders in 1770', *New England Quarterly*, LXI, 1988, 25–54.

3.109 **Fletcher**, Charlotte, 'An endowed King William's school plans to become a college', *Maryland Historical Magazine*, LXXX, 1985, 157–166.

3.110 **Herbst**, J., *From Crisis to Crisis. American College Government, 1636–1819*, Cambridge, MA, 1982.

3.111 **Simpson**, A., 'Robert Carter's schooldays', *Virginia Magazine of History and Biography*, XCIV, 1986, 161–188.

3.112 **Szasz**, Margaret, *Indian Education in the American Colonies, 1607–1783*, Albuquerque, NM, 1988.

3.113 **Wright**, B., ' "For the children of the infidels"? American Indian education in the colonial colleges', *American Indian Culture and Research Journal*, XII, 1988, 1–14.

Crime and punishment

3.114 **Bragdon**, Kathleen Joan, 'Crime and punishment among the Indians of Massachusetts, 1675–1750', *Ethnohistory*,

XXVIII, 1981, 23–32.

3.115 **Cahn**, M. D., 'Punishment, discretion, and the codification of prescribed penalties in colonial Massachusetts', *American Journal of Legal History*, XXXIII, 1989, 107–136.

3.116 **Cohen**, D. A., 'A fellowship of thieves: property criminals in eighteenth-century Massachusetts', *Journal of Social History*, XXII, 1988, 65–92.

3.117 **Flaherty**, D. H., 'Crime and social control in provincial Massachusetts', *Historical Journal*, XXIV, 1981, 339–360.

3.118 **Gaskins**, R., 'Changes in the criminal law in eighteenth-century Connecticut', *American Journal of Legal History*, XXV, 1981, 309–342.

3.119 **Gildrie**, R. P., 'Taverns and popular culture in Essex County, Massachusetts, 1678–1686', *Essex Institute Historical Collections*, CXXIV, 1988, 158–185.

3.120 **Greenberg**, D., 'Crime, law enforcement, and social control in colonial America', *American Journal of Legal History*, XXVI, 1982, 293–325.

3.121 **Hirsch**, A. J., *The Rise of the Penitentiary. Prisons and Punishment in Early America*, New Haven, CT, 1992. Traces the origins of the penitentiary back to early modern England.

3.122 **Hull**, N. E. H., *Female Felons. Women and Serious Crime in Colonial Massachusetts*, Urbana, IL, 1987.

3.123 **Konig**, D. T., ' "Dae's laws" and the non-common law origins of criminal justice in Virginia', *American Journal of Legal History*, XXVI, 1982, 354–375.

3.124 **Morgan**, K., 'Convict runaways in Maryland, 1745–1775', *Journal of American Studies*, XXIII, 1989, 253–268.

3.125 **Preyer**, Kathryn, 'Penal measures in the American colonies: an overview', *American Journal of Legal History*, XXVI, 1982, 326–353.

3.126 **Spindel**, Donna J., *Crime and Society in North Carolina, 1663–1776*, Baton Rouge, LA, 1989. A descriptive analysis of court records that places violent crime in its historical context.

3.127 **Williams**, D. E., 'Rogues, rascals and scoundrels: the underworld literature of early America', *American Studies*, XXIV, 1983, 5–19.

3.128 **Williams**, D. E., ' "Behold a tragic scene strangely changed into a theater of mercy". The structure and significance of criminal

conversion narratives in early New England', *American Quarterly*, XXXVIII, 1986, 827–847.

3.129 **Wood**, Betty, ' "Until he shall be dead, dead, dead". The judicial treatment of slaves in eighteenth-century Georgia', *Georgia Historical Quarterly*, LXXI, 1987, 377–398.

RELIGION, BELIEFS, IDEAS, AND CULTURE

3.130 **Anesko**, M., 'So discreet a zeal: slavery and the Anglican church in Virginia 1680–1730', *Virginia Magazine of History and Biography*, XCIII, 1985, 247–278.

3.131 **Balmer**, R., *A Perfect Babel of Confusion. Dutch Religion and English Culture in the Middle Colonies*, New York, 1989. Examines how the English superimposed the Church of England on Dutch Reformed settlers and the varied reaction of the Dutch in New York City and the Hudson Valley.

3.132 **Bolton**, S. C., *Southern Anglicanism. The Church of England in Colonial South Carolina*, Westport, CT, 1982.

3.133 **Bonomi**, Patricia, *Under the Cope of Heaven. Religion, Society, and Politics in Colonial America*, New York, 1986.

3.134 **Bonomi**, Patricia, and **Eisenstadt**, P. R., 'Church adherence in the eighteenth-century British American colonies', *William and Mary Quarterly*, XXXIX, 1982, 245–286.

3.135 **Brauer**, J. C., 'Regionalism and religion in America', *Church History*, LIV, 1985, 366–378.

3.136 **Burkhart**, Louise M., *The Slippery Earth. Nahua-Christian Moral Dialogue in Sixteenth Century Mexico*, Tucson, AZ, 1989. Analyzes how Catholic dogma was translated into the native language Nahua and how inexact the fit was between Christianity and native cosmology.

3.137 **Commager**, H. S., *The Empire of Reason. How Europe Imagined and America Realized the Enlightenment*, Garden City, NY, 1977.

3.138 **Gain**, Alison M., 'Quaker revivals as an

organizing process in Nantucket, Massachusetts, 1698–1708', *Quaker History*, LXXIX, 1990, 57–76.

3.139 **Holifield**, E. B., *Era of Persuasion. American Thought and Culture, 1521–1680*, Boston, 1989.

3.140 **Hopple**, L. C., 'Germanic European origins and geographical history of the southeastern Pennsylvania Schwenkfelders', *Pennsylvania Folklife*, XXXII, 1982, 72–95.

3.141 **Nord**, D. P., 'Teleology and news: the religious roots of American journalism', *Journal of American History*, LXXVII, 1990, 9–38.

3.142 **Pahl**, J., *Paradox Lost. Free Will and Political Liberty in American Culture, 1637–1760*, Baltimore, 1992. Traces the Protestant debates over determinism into the political realm of the eighteenth century.

3.143 **Pestana**, Carla Gardina, *Quakers and Baptists in Colonial Massachusetts*, New York, 1991.

3.144 **Sandos**, J. A., 'Junipero Serra's canonization and the historical record', *American Historical Review*, XCIII, 1988, 1253–1269. Reviews the role that historians play as experts in Roman Catholic canonization proceedings, and in the case of Serra and his actions in California, notes the protest of Native American groups at the prospect of his sainthood.

3.145 **Sawyer**, J. K., 'Benefit of clergy in Maryland and Virginia', *American Journal of Legal History*, XXXIV, 1990, 49–68.

3.146 **Warner**, M., *The Letters of the Republic. Publication and the Public Sphere in Eighteenth Century America*, Cambridge, MA, 1990. Connects the emergence of printing and publishing in the colonies to the development and dissemination of republican ideas.

Puritanism

3.147 **Anderson**, Virginia DeJohn, 'Religion, the common thread', *New England Quarterly*, LIX, 1986, 418–424. A dissenting comment on David G. Allen's article in the same issue. Anderson argues that the Puritan migration made little economic sense for the migrants.

3.148 **Bozeman**, T. D., *To Live Ancient Lives. The Primitivist Dimension in Puritanism*, Chapel Hill, NC, 1988. A work with insights on nearly every aspect of the Puritan theological outlook, especially on the millennialist strain of thought in the founders of the Massachusetts Bay colony, and on the jeremiad of their children.

3.149 **Breen**, T. H., *Puritans and Adventurers. Change and Persistence in Early America*, New York, 1980. A comparative look at the separate development of New England and Virginia that traces their divergence from the origins of each region and colonial purpose.

3.150 **Brumm**, Ursula, ' "What went you out into the wilderness to see?" Nonconformity and the wilderness in Cotton Mather's *Magnalia Christi Americana*', *Prospects*, VI, 1981, 1–15.

3.151 **Canup**, J., *Out of the Wilderness. The Emergence of an American Identity in Colonial New England*, Middletown, CT, 1990.

3.152 **Cohen**, C. L., *God's Caress. The Psychology of Puritan Religious Experience*, New York, 1986. Concentrates on the Puritans' views on sin and salvation.

3.153 **Delbanco**, A., *The Puritan Ordeal*, Cambridge, MA, 1989.

3.154 **Fiering**, N., *Moral Philosophy at Seventeenth-Century Harvard. A Discipline in Transition*, Chapel Hill, NC, 1981.

3.155 **Foster**, S., *The Long Argument. English Puritanism and the Shaping of New England Culture, 1570–1700*, Chapel Hill, NC, 1991.

3.156 **Gaustad**, E. S., *Liberty of Conscience. Roger Williams in America*, Grand Rapids, MI, 1991. Analyzes Williams' religious thought in its seventeenth century context and also explains why he has become so celebrated in the twentieth century as a relevant figure.

3.157 **Gura**, P. F., *A Glimpse of Sion's Glory. Puritan Radicalism in New England, 1620–1650*, Middletown, CT, 1984. An examination of dissenting strains of New England Puritans.

3.158 **Hall**, D. D., *Worlds of Wonder, Days of Judgement. Popular Religious Belief in Early New England*, New York, 1989. A cultural history of the blending of Puritan beliefs with earlier pre-Reformation religious sensibilities, as worked out between the Congregational ministry and laity.

3.159 **Holstun**, J., *A Rational Millenium. Puritan Utopias of Seventeenth-Century England and America*, New York, 1987.

3.160 **Hughes**, R. T., *Illusions of Innocence. Protestant Primitivism in America, 1630–1875*, Chicago, 1988.

3.161 **Levin**, D., 'Giants in the earth: science and the occult in Cotton Mather's letters to the Royal Society', *William and Mary Quarterly*, XLV, 1988, 751–770.

3.162 **Pettit**, N., 'Prelude to mission: Brainerd's expulsion from Yale', *New England Quarterly*, LIX, 1986, 28–50. Analyzes Jonathan Edwards' writings on David Brainerd and the Arminian controversy at Yale.

3.163 **Solberg**, W. U., 'Science and religion in early America: Cotton Mather's Christian Philosopher', *Church History*, LVI, 1987, 73–92.

3.164 **Stout**, H. S., *The New England Soul. Preaching and Religious Culture in Colonial New England*, New York, 1986.

3.165 **Toulouse**, Teresa, *The Art of Prophesying. New England Sermons and the Shaping of Belief*, Athens, GA, 1987.

3.166 **Turner**, E., 'Earwitnesses to resonance in space: an interpretation of Puritan psalmody in early eighteenth-century New England', *American Studies*, XXV, 1984, 25–47.

3.167 **Watson**, Patricia A., *The Angelical Conjunction. The Preacher-Physicians of Colonial New England*, Knoxville, TN, 1991.

3.168 **Winship**, M. P., 'Encountering Providence in the seventeenth century: the experiences of a yeoman and a minister', *Essex Institute Historical Collections*, CXXVI, 1990, 27–36.

3.169 **Zakai**, A., *Exile and Kingdom. History and Apocalypse in the Puritan Migration to America*, New York, 1992.

The Great Awakening

3.170 **Butler**, J., *Awash in a Sea of Faith. Christianizing the American People*, Cambridge, MA, 1990. Finds the concept of the Great Awakening something of an artificial construct.

3.171 **Crawford**, M. J., *Seasons of Grace. Colonial New England's Revival Tradition in its British Context*, New York, 1991. Outlines the connections between Jonathan Edwards, George Whitefield, and John Wesley.

3.172 **Fraser**, J. W., 'The great awakening and new patterns of Presbyterian theological education', *Journal of Presbyterian History*, LX, 1982, 189–208.

3.173 **Guelzo**, A. C., *Edwards on the Hill. A Century of American Theological Debate*, Middletown, CT, 1989. Analyzes the arguments of Jonathan Edwards' *Freedom of the Will* and the subsequent debate of the "New Theology".

3.174 **Hatch**, N. O., and **Stout**, H. S., (ed.), *Jonathan Edwards and the American Experience*, New York, 1988. A collection of essays that appraises the state of scholarship on Edwards in history, theology, and philosophy.

3.175 **Hoopes**, J., 'Jonathan Edwards' religious psychology', *Journal of American History*, LXIX, 1983, 849–865.

3.176 **Jenson**, R. W., *America's Theologian. A Recommendation of Jonathan Edwards*, New York, 1988. Finds Edwards to be a religious thinker with much to say to readers today, as well as a leading exponent of the Great Awakening.

3.177 **Lacey**, Barbara E., 'The world of Hannah Heaton: the autobiography of an eighteenth-century farm woman', *William and Mary Quarterly*, XLV, 1988, 280–304.

3.178 **Lambert**, F., ' "Pedlar in Divinity". George Whitefield and the Great Awakening, 1737–1745', *Journal of American History*, LXXVII, 1990, 812–837. Emphasizes Whitefield's organizational skills as a religious entrepreneur as a key explanation for his popular reception.

3.179 **Lee**, S. H., *The Philosophical Theology of Jonathan Edwards*, Princeton, NJ, 1988.

3.180 **Porterfield**, Amanda, 'The mother in eighteenth-century American conception of man and God', *Journal of Psychohistory*, XV, 1987, 189–206.

3.181 **Schmidt**, L. E., *Holy Fairs. Scottish Communions and American Revivals in the Early Modern Period*, Princeton, NJ, 1989.

3.182 **Tracy**, Patricia J., *Jonathan Edwards, Pastor. Religion and Society in Eighteenth-Century Northampton*, New York, 1979. A biography of Edwards that places him in the social and economic history of the Connecticut Valley, and connects the Great Awakening in Northampton to increased materialism and the pressures of the encroaching market.

3.183 **Weber**, D., 'The figure of Jonathan Edwards', *American Quarterly*, XXXV, 1983, 556–564.

Witchcraft

3.184 **Boyer**, P., and **Nissenbaum**, S., *Salem Possessed. The Social Origins of Witchcraft*, Cambridge, MA, 1974.

3.185 **Demos**, J. P., *Entertaining Satan. Witchcraft and the Culture of Early New England*, New York, 1982.

3.186 **Gildrie**, R. P., 'Visions of evil. Popular culture, Puritanism and the Massachusetts witchcraft crisis of 1692', *Journal of American Culture*, VIII, 1985, 17–34.

3.187 **Gragg**, L., *The Salem Witch Crisis*, Westport, CT, 1992.

3.188 **Knight**, Janice, 'Learning the language of God: Jonathan Edwards and the typology of nature', *William and Mary Quarterly*, XLVIII, 1991, 531–551.

WORK AND ENTERPRISE

3.190 **Carr**, Lois Green, **Menard**, R. R., and **Walsh**, L. S., *Robert Cole's World. Agriculture and Society in Early Maryland*, Chapel Hill, NC, 1991. A micro-level study of one yeoman farm in the seventeenth century Tidewater region, and the people who worked it.

3.191 **Cohen**, D. S., *The Dutch-American Farm*, New York, 1992.

3.192 **Horn**, J. P., ' "The bare necessities": standards of living in England and the Chesapeake, 1650–1700', *Historical Archaeology*, XXII, 1988, 74–91.

3.193 **Innes**, S., (ed.), *Work and Labor in Early America*, Chapel Hill, NC, 1988.

3.194 **Mancall**, P. C., *Valley of Opportunity. Economic Culture along the Upper Susquehanna, 1700–1800*, Ithaca, NY, 1991. Recounts the coming of the market economy to rural New York, with careful attention paid to environmental transformations and to Indian-White

relations.

3.195 **McCusker**, J. J., and **Menard**, R. R., *The Economy of British America, 1607–1789*, Chapel Hill, NC, 1985. An extended review of economic history literature; the authors hold that the domestic and international linkages created by the export of agricultural staples were the decisive factors leading to colonial growth and development.

3.196 **Perkins**, E. J., *The Economy of Colonial America*, New York, 1980. A useful survey of colonial economic history.

3.197 **Price**, J. M., *Capital and Credit in British Overseas Trade. The View from the Chesapeake, 1700–1776*, Cambridge, MA, 1980. A study of the sources of credit for the colonial tobacco trade, finding that a host of middlemen, particularly warehouse operators in British port towns, played critical roles in financing transatlantic commerce.

3.198 **Rediker**, M., ' "Good hands, stout hearts, and fast feet". The history and culture of working people in early America', *Labour*, X, 1982, 123–144.

3.199 **Remer**, Rosalind, 'Old lights and new money: a note on religion, economics, and the social order in 1740 Boston', *William and Mary Quarterly*, XLVII, 1990, 566–573.

3.200 **Sacks**, D. H., *The Widening Gate. Bristol and the Atlantic Economy, 1450–1700*, Berkeley, CA, 1991.

3.201 **Shammas**, Carole, *The Pre-Industrial Consumer in England and America*, New York, 1990.

3.202 **Truxes**, T. M., *Irish-American Trade, 1660–1783*, New York, 1988.

3.203 **Usner**, D. H., *Indians, Settlers, and Slaves in a Frontier Exchange Economy. The Lower Mississippi Valley before 1783*, Chapel Hill, NC, 1992.

3.204 **Vickers**, D., 'Nantucket whalemen in the deep-sea fishery. The changing anatomy of an early American labor force', *Journal of American History*, LXXII, 1985, 277–296.

Slavery, unfree labor, and the plantation system

3.205 **Breen**, T. H., and **Innes**, S., '*Myne Owne Ground*', *Race and Freedom on Virginia's Eastern Shore, 1640–1676*, New York, 1980.

3.206 **Carr**, Lois Green, and **Menard**, R. R., 'Land, labor, and economies of scale in early Maryland. Some limits to growth in the Chesapeake system of husbandry', *Journal of Economic History*, XLIX, 1989, 407–418.

3.207 **Clemens**, P. G. E., *The Atlantic Economy and Colonial Maryland's Eastern Shore. From Tobacco to Grain*, Ithaca, NY, 1980.

3.208 **Coughtry**, J., *The Notorious Triangle. Rhode Island and the African Slave Trade, 1700–1807*, Philadelphia, 1981.

3.209 **Ekrich**, A. R., *Bound for America. The Transportation of British Convicts to the Colonies, 1718–1775*, 1987. Traces the fortunes of the 50,000 convicts from England and Ireland who were reprieved from the gallows and sentenced to indentured servitude in the English North American colonies.

3.210 **Galenson**, D., *White Servitude in Colonial America*, New York, 1981. The most complete account of indentured servitude in the colonies, based on quantitative analysis of samples of indenture contracts from seventeenth century Bristol and eighteenth century London.

3.211 **Galenson**, D., *Traders, Planters, and Slaves. Market Behavior in Early English America*, New York, 1986. A comparative history of plantation and slave-based agriculture in the West Indies and mainland colonies, written from the perspective of the "new economic history".

3.212 **Kellow**, Margaret, 'Indentured servants in eighteenth-century Maryland', *Social History*, XVII, 1984, 229–255.

3.213 **Kim**, S. B., *Landlord and Tenant in Colonial New York. Manorial Society, 1664–1775*, Chapel Hill, NC, 1978.

3.214 **Kulikoff**, A., *Tobacco and Slaves. The Development of Southern Cultures in the Chesapeake, 1680–1800*, Chapel Hill, NC, 1986. A social and demographic history of the tobacco regime that flourished in the Tidewater region.

3.215 **Rawley**, J. A., *The Transatlantic Slave Trade. A History*, New York, 1981.

3.216 **Solow**, Barbara L., (ed.), *Slavery and the Rise of the Atlantic System*, New York, 1991. Essays on the economic history of the slave trade.

3.217 **Walsh**, Lorena, 'Plantation Management in the Chesapeake, 1620–1820', *Journal of Economic History*, XLIX, 1989, 393–406.

3.218 **Van der Zee**, J., *Bound Over. Indentured Servitude and American Conscience*, New York, 1985.

RACE AND ETHNIC IDENTITY

African-Americans

3.219 **Chase**, Jeanne, 'The 1741 conspiracy to burn New York: black plot or black magic?', *Social Science Information*, XXII, 1983, 969–981.

3.220 **Cody**, Cheryl Ann, 'There was no "Absalom" on the Ball plantations. Slave-naming practices in the South Carolina low country, 1720–1865', *American Historical Review*, XCII, 1987, 563–596. Traces a sample of more than two thousand slaves and their names; an initial pattern of maintaining African names slowly gave way to a naming pattern that by the Civil War was more patriarchal, biblical, and similar to white patterns.

3.221 **Davidson**, T. E., 'Free blacks in old Somerset county, 1745–1755', *Maryland Historical Magazine*, LXXX, 1985, 151–156.

3.222 **Davis**, T. J., *A Rumor of Revolt. The "Great Negro Plot" in Colonial New York*, New York, 1985. A comprehensive history of the suppression of a supposed slave revolt with white accessories, this volume argues for the reality of the plot without justifying the savage official repression that followed it.

3.223 **Glasrud**, B. A., and **Smith**, A. M., (ed.), *Race Relations in British North America, 1607–1783*, Chicago, 1982.

3.224 **Hall**, Gwendolyn Midlo, *Africans in Colonial Louisiana. The Development of Afro-Creole Culture in the Eighteenth Century*, Baton Rouge, LA, 1992.

3.225 **Hall**, R. L., 'Slave resistance in Baltimore city and county, 1747–1790', *Maryland Historical Magazine*, LXXXIV, 1989, 305–318.

3.226 **Johnson**, J., 'New Orleans's Congo Square: an urban setting for early Afro-American culture formation', *Louisiana History*, XXXII, 1991, 117–157.

3.227 **Kay**, M. L. M., and **Cary**, Lorin Lee, ' "They are indeed the constant plague of their tyrants": slave defence of a moral economy in colonial North Carolina, 1748–1772', *Slavery and Abolition*, VI, 1985, 37–56.

3.228 **Morgan**, P. D., 'Black life in eighteenth-century Charleston', *Perspectives in American History*, I, 1984, 187–232.

3.229 **Piersen**, W. D., *Black Yankees. The Development of an Afro-American Sub-Culture in Eighteenth-Century New England*, Amherst, MA, 1988. Looks at the rapid acculturation of African slaves into New England society and how a distinctive brand of backwater Afro-American culture emerged.

3.230 **Sobel**, M., *The World They Made Together. Black and White Values in Eighteenth Century Virginia*, Princeton, NJ, 1987. An unusual interpretation of colonial race relations that stresses how much the Africans and English had in common, and how they collaborated to form a genuinely integrated premodern culture.

3.231 **Thornton**, J., *Africa and Africans in the Making of the Atlantic World, 1400–1680*, New York, 1992. Survey of the influence of Africa on the Americas.

3.232 **Wax**, D. D., ' "The great risque we run": the aftermath of slave rebellion at Stono, South Carolina, 1739–1745', *Journal of Negro History*, LXVII, 1982, 136–147.

Native Americans

3.233 **Aquila**, R., *The Iroquois Restoration. Iroquois Diplomacy on the Colonial Frontier, 1701–1754*, Detroit, 1983.

3.234 **Axtell**, J., *The European and the Indian. Essays in the Ethnohistory of Colonial North America*, New York, 1981.

3.235 **Axtell**, J., *The Invasion Within. The Contest of Cultures in Colonial North America*, New York, 1985. A series of essays that contrasts the relative success of French religious overtures to the American Indians with the British, and also considers the response of natives to outsiders.

3.236 **Axtell**, J., *After Columbus. Essays in the Ethnohistory of Colonial North America*, New York, 1988. A collection of the essays by the leading historian of the encounter between Europeans and American Indians.

3.237 **Bowden**, H. W., *American Indian and Christian Missions. Studies in Cultural Conflict*, Chicago, 1981.

3.238 **Bradley**, J. W., *Evolution of the Onondaga Iroquois. Accommodating Change, 1500–1655*, Syracuse, NY, 1987.

3.239 **Brandon**, W., *New Worlds for Old. Reports from the New World and their Effect on the Development of Social Thought in Europe, 1500–1800*, Athens, OH, 1986. Emphasizes the importance on European thought of the stark differences between the conquerors and the Native Americans, and as well, how the distinctive American environment permanently altered the European settlers.

3.240 **Calloway**, C. G., *The Western Abenkais of Vermont, 1600–1800. War, Migration, and the Survival of an Indian People*, Norman, OK, 1990. The ethnohistory of the Algonkian-speaking tribe, and something of its travails in the Iroquois wars, as well as its subsequent struggle to maintain a tribal identity.

3.241 **Cave**, A. E., 'Canaanites in a promised land. The American Indian and the providential theory of empire', *American Indian Quarterly*, XII, 1988, 277–297.

3.242 **Ceci**, Lynn, 'Squanto and the pilgrims', *Society*, XXVII, 1990, 40–44. Looks at the initial contact at Plymouth and highlights pre-1620 contacts in the region between Europeans and Native Americans.

3.243 **Devens**, Carol, *Countering Colonization. Native American Women and Great Lakes Missions, 1630–1900*, Berkeley, CA, 1992.

3.244 **Ferling**, J. E., *A Wilderness of Miseries. War and Warriors in Early America*, Westport, CT, 1980. Surveys the colonial wars between the English settlers and the Native Americans.

3.245 **Forbes**, J. D., *Black Africans and Native Americans. Color, Race, and Caste in the Evolution of Red-Black Peoples*, New York, 1988.

3.246 **Galloway**, Patricia, 'Choctaw factionalism and civil war, 1746–1750', *Journal of Mississippi History*, XLIV, 1982, 289–327.

3.247 **Hauptmann**, L. M., and **Wherry**, J. D., (ed.), *The Pequots in Southern New England. The Fall and Rise of an American Indian Nation*, Norman, OK, 1990. Covers the seventeenth century demise of the tribe after their encounter with the Puritans, but also their persistence in Connecticut and recent cultural and economic revival.

3.248 **Heard**, J. N., *White into Red. A Study of the*

Assimilation of White Persons Captured by Indians, Metuchen, NJ, 1973.

3.249 **Jennings**, F., *The Ambiguous Iroquois Empire. The Covenant Chain Confederation of Indian Tribes with English Colonies from its Beginnings to the Lancaster Treaty of 1774*, New York, 1984.

3.250 **Jennings**, F., *Empire of Fortune. Crowns, Colonies, and Tribes in the Seven Years War in America*, New York, 1988. Continues the argument started in his *Ambiguous Iroquois Empire* that the Iroquois alliance with the British was fundamental to military success against France in the Pennsylvania theater during the Seven Years War.

3.251 **John**, Elizabeth Ann Harper, *Storms Brewed in Other Men's Worlds. The Confrontation of Indians, Spanish, and French in the Southwest, 1540–1795*, College Station, TX, 1975.

3.252 **Jones**, Dorothy V., *License for Empire. Colonialism by Treaty in Early America*, Chicago, 1982.

3.253 **Kupperman**, Karen Ordahl, *Settling with the Indians. The Meeting of English and Indian Cultures in America, 1580–1640*, Totowa, NJ, 1980.

3.254 **McConnell**, M. N., *A Country Between. The Upper Ohio Valley and its Peoples, 1724–1774*, Lincoln, NE, 1992.

3.255 **Miller**, C. L., and **Hammel**, G. R., 'A new perspective on Indian-white contact. Cultural symbols and colonial trade', *Journal of American History*, LXXIII, 1986, 311–328. Addresses Native American motivation in regard to the trinkets and baubles that they traded for and their role in Indian-white relations.

3.256 **Peacock**, J., 'Principles and effects of Puritan appropriation of Indian land and labor', *Ethnohistory*, XXXI, 1984, 39–44.

3.257 **Richter**, D. K., *The Ordeal of the Longhouse. The Peoples of the Iroquois League in the Era of European Colonization*, Chapel Hill, NC, 1992.

3.258 **Rountree**, Helen C., *The Powhatan Indians of Virginia. Their Traditional Culture*, Norman, OK, 1989. An ethnohistory of the Native Americans who met the Jamestown settlement, and what their world looked like in the early seventeenth century.

3.259 **Schlesier**, K. H., 'Rethinking the midewiwin and the plains ceremonial called the sun dance', *Plains Anthropologist*, XXXV, 1990, 1–27.

3.260 **Sheehan**, B. W., *Savagism and Civility. Indians and Englishmen in Colonial Virginia*, New York, 1980.

3.261 **Simmonds**, W. S., 'Cultural bias in the New England Puritans' perception of Indians', *William and Mary Quarterly*, XXXVIII, 1981, 56–72.

3.262 **Trigger**, B. G., 'Early native North American responses to European contact. Romantic versus rationalistic interpretations', *Journal of American History*, LXXVII, 1991, 1195–1215. Looks at how the Native Americans reacted to the arrival of the Europeans.

3.263 **White**, R., *The Middle Ground. Indians, Empires, and Republics in the Great Lakes Region, 1650–1815*, New York, 1991. A study of the region the French called the 'pays d'haut' and how a new hybrid culture emerged out of the disparate peoples, Indian and European.

3.264 **Wood**, P. H., (ed.), *Powhatan's Mantle. Indians in the Colonial Southeast*, Lincoln, NE, 1989. A set of essays on the initial contact between the Virginia natives and the English who settled in the seventeenth century.

European-Americans

3.265 **Butler**, J., *The Huguenots in America. A Refugee People in New World Society*, Cambridge, MA, 1983.

3.266 **Cohen**, D. S., 'How Dutch were the Dutch of New Netherland?', *New York History*, LXII, 1981, 43–60.

3.267 **Cressy**, D., *Coming Over. Migration and Communication between England and New England in the Seventeenth Century*, New York, 1987. Firmly situates the New England migrants in their English context for almost a century after their departure, tracing the transatlantic connection through ideas, money, and family.

3.268 **Merwick**, Donna, *Possessing Albany, 1630–1720. The Dutch and the English Experiences*, 1990. Uses semiotic theory to understand the differences between the social construction of Dutch Fort Orange and English Albany, with the key difference being the Dutch "navigated" the land, and the English "occupied" the soil.

3.269 **Roeber**, A.G., 'In German ways? Problems and potentials of eighteenth-century German social and emigration history', *William and Mary Quarterly*, XLIV, 1987, 750–774.

3.270 **Tully**, A. W., 'Ethnicity, religion and politics in early Pennsylvania', *Pennsylvania Magazine of History and Biography*, CVII, 1983, 491–536.

3.271 **Weber**, D. J., *The Spanish Frontier in North America*, New Haven, CT, 1992. A sweeping survey of the Spanish regime from the sixteenth century through Mexican independence.

3.272 **Wockek**, Marianne, 'The flow and the composition of German immigration to Philadelphia, 1727–1775', *Pennsylvania Magazine of History and Biography*, CV, 1981, 249–278.

SPACE, MOVEMENT, AND PLACE

3.273 **Brandon**, W., *Quivira. Europeans in the Region of the Santa Fe Trail, 1540–1820*, Athens, OH, 1990.

3.274 **Carr**, Lois Green, **Morgan**, P. D., and **Russo**, Jean B., (ed.), *Colonial Chesapeake Society*, Chapel Hill, NC, 1988.

3.275 **Dunn**, R. S., 'William Penn and the selling of Pennsylvania, 1681–1685', *Proceedings of the American Philosophical Society*, CXXVII, 1983, 322–329.

3.276 **Gough**, R. J., 'The myth of the "Middle Colonies". An analysis of regionalization in early America', *Pennsylvania Magazine of History and Biography*, CVIII, 1983, 394–419. Argues that the so-called middle colonies of New York, New Jersey, Pennsylvania, and Delaware actually constituted two separate regions, one centered around New York City and the other around Philadelphia.

3.277 **Hoffman**, P. E., *A New Andalucia and a Way to the Orient. The American Southeast During the Sixteenth Century*, Baton Rouge, LA, 1990. Treats the history of Spanish colonization of the present-day states of South Carolina, Georgia, and Florida from two perspectives: the search for an American colony with a climate and geography similar to the Spanish province

of Andalusia, and the search for a more direct water route to the Pacific.

3.278 **Jordan**, T. G., and **Kaups**, M., *The American Backwoods Frontier. An Ethnic and Ecological Interpretation*, Baltimore, 1989. Argues that an overlooked immigrant group – the Finns – were the first in the seventeenth century to settle th' region away from the Atlantic coast and that their experience in clearing forests wa' the model for subsequent migrants.

3.279 **Quinn**, D. B., *Set Fair for Roanoke. Voyages and Colonies, 1584–1606*, Chapel Hill, NC, 1985. A history of the Lost Colony of Roanoke.

3.280 **Thompson**, R., 'State of the art: early modern migration', *Journal of American Studies*, XXV, 1991, 59–69.

3.281 **Walsh**, Lorena S., 'Staying put or getting out. Findings for Charles County, Maryland, 1650–1720', *William and Mary Quarterly*, XLIV, 1987, 89–103.

Colonial towns

3.282 **Baker**, Nancy T., 'Annapolis, Maryland, 1695–1730', *Maryland Historical Magazine*, XXCI, 1986, 191–209.

3.283 **Cruz**, G. R., *Let There Be Towns. Spanish Municipal Origins in the American Southwest, 1610–1810*, College Station, TX, 1988.

3.284 **Martin**, J., *Profits in the Wilderness. Entrepreneurship and the Founding of New England Towns in the Seventeenth Century*, Chapel Hill, NC, 1991.

3.285 **Wolf**, Stephanie Grauman, *Urban Village Population, Community, and Family Structure in Germantown, Pennsylvania, 1683–1800*, Princeton, NJ, 1976.

The colonial landscape

3.286 **Cronon**, W., *Changes in the Land. Indians Colonists, and the Ecology of New England* New York, 1983. A work that looks at the contrasting attitudes to the land as shown by Native Americans and English settlers

3.287 **Merchant**, Carolyn, *Ecological Revolutions. Nature, Gender, and Science i' New England*, Chapel Hill, NC, 1989.

3.288 **Silver**, T., *A New Face on the Countryside Indians, Colonists, and Slaves in South Atlantic Forests, 1500–1800*, New York,

1990. An environmental perspective on the clash of cultures in the colonial South.

3.289 **Stilgoe**, J. R., *Common Landscape of America, 1580 to 1845*, New Haven, CT, 1982. A description of how European settlement and enterprise reshaped the rural landscape.

THE STATE AND THE PUBLIC REALM

Government and politics

3.290 **Billings**, W. M., *Virginia's Viceroy. Their Majesties' Governor General. Francis Howard, Baron Howard of Effingham*, Fairfax, VA, 1991. An account of the governorship of Effingham who ruled the Virginia Colony during the Glorious Revolution.

3.291 **Bushman**, R. L., *King and People in Provincial Massachusetts*, Chapel Hill, NC, 1992. Divides the Bay Colony into two groups, one dependent on royal authority and a much larger one that associated itself with the independent people.

3.292 **Cook**, E. M., *The Fathers of the Towns. Leadership and Community Structure in Eighteenth-Century New England*, Baltimore, 1976.

3.293 **Jordan**, D. W., *Foundations of Representative Government in Maryland, 1632–1715*, New York, 1987.

3.294 **Mann**, B. H., *Neighbors and Strangers. Law and Community in Early Connecticut*, Chapel Hill, NC, 1987. Looks at lawsuits and the resort to legal methods to resolve disputes as a gauge for the change from Puritan community to Yankee individualism.

3.295 **Morgan**, E. S., *Inventing the People. The Rise of Popular Sovereignty in England and America*, New York, 1988. A set of essays that covers a wide range of topics in Anglo-American political history, from the opposition to the divine right of kings through the folkways of local elections.

3.296 **Nobles**, G. H., *Divisions throughout the Whole. Politics and Society in Hampshire County, Massachusetts, 1740–1760*, New York, 1983.

3.297 **Pencak**, W., and **Wright**, C. E., (ed.), *Authority and Resistance in Early New York*, New York, 1988. Nine essays on law and society in colonial New York.

3.298 **Ritchie**, R. C., *Captain Kidd and the War against Pirates*, Cambridge, MA, 1986. Connects the English pirate William Kidd to New York politics and the crushing of Leisler's Rebellion, and shows how rivalries within the British Empire led to a crackdown on piracy and Kidd's eventual capture and execution.

3.299 **Shields**, D. S., *Oracles of Empire. Poetry, Politics, and Commerce in British America, 1690–1750*, Chicago, 1990. An unusual work that examines the colonial poetry and belles lettres as a source for understanding the British empire.

3.300 **Sosin**, J. M., *English America and the Restoration Monarchy of Charles II. Transatlantic Politics, Commerce, and Kinship*, Lincoln, NE, 1980.

3.301 **Webb**, S. S., *The Governors-General. The English Army and the Definition of the Empire, 1569–1681*, Chapel Hill, NC, 1979.

3.302 **Webb**, S. S., *1676. The End of American Independence*, New York, 1984. Argues that the twin blows of Bacon's Rebellion and King Philip's War led imperial authorities to assume a much greater control over the affairs of the colonies.

Warfare

3.303 **Ahearn**, Marie L., *The Rhetoric of War. Training Day, the Militia, and the Military Sermon*, Westport, CT, 1989. Connects religious history, based on sermons, to the military history of local forces in New England.

3.304 **Anderson**, F., *A People's Army. Massachusetts Soldiers and Society in the Seven Years' War*, Chapel Hill, NC, 1984. Analyzes the men who served in the last colonial war against France and their relations with regular British troops and how that common service had lasting consequences after the war.

3.305 **Ferling**, J. E., 'Soldiers for Virginia: who served in the French and Indian war?', *Virginia Magazine of History and Biography*, XCIV, 1986, 317–328.

3.306 **Harding**, R. H., 'The growth of Anglo-

American alienation: the case of the American regiment, 1740–42', *Journal of Imperial and Commonwealth History*, XVII, 1989, 161–184.

3.307 **Leach**, D. E., *Roots of Conflict. British Armed Forces and Colonial Americans, 1677–1763*, Chapel Hill, NC, 1986.

3.308 **Malone**, P. M., *The Skulking Way of War. Technology and Tactics among the New England Indians*, Lanham, MD, 1991.

3.309 **Puglisi**, M. J., *Puritans Besieged. The Legacies of King Philip's War in Massachusetts Bay Colony*, Lanham, MD, 1991.

3.310 **Shomette**, D. G., and **Haslach**, R. D., *Raid on America. The Dutch Naval Campaign of 1672–1674*, Columbia, SC, 1988.

3.311 **Steele**, I. K., *Betrayals. Fort William Henry and the 'Massacre'*, New York, 1990.

3.312 **Swanson**, C. E., *Predators and Prizes. American Privateering and Imperial Warfare, 1739–1748*, Columbia, SC, 1991.

3.313 **Titus**, J., *The Old Dominion at War. Society, Politics, and Warfare in Late Colonial Virginia*, Columbia, SC, 1991. A history of how the Virginia squirearchy fought the French and Indian War, and how social factors were always at the forefront of thinking during the war.

4

THE MAKING OF
THE UNITED STATES,
1760–1790

GENERAL

4.1 **Bailyn**, B., *Faces of Revolution. Personalities and Themes in the Struggle for American Independence*, New York, 1990.

4.2 **Brown**, R. M., and **Fehrenbacher**, D. E., (ed.), *Tradition, Conflict, and Modernization. Perspective on the American Revolution*, New York, 1977.

4.3 **Countryman**, E., *The American Revolution*, New York, 1985. A survey of the conflict that stresses the crisis in society and how Whig and republican ideas solved the split between notions of community and individualism.

4.4 **Davis**, D. B., *Revolutions. Reflections on American Equality and Foreign Liberations*, Cambridge, MA, 1990. A series of lectures by one of the leading historians of slavery and freedom on major themes of the Age of Revolution.

4.5 **Egnal**, M., *A Mighty Empire. The Origins of the American Revolution*, Ithaca, NY, 1988. An interpretation of the Revolution as an internal struggle among the urban elite, separated into two grand factions over political economy.

4.6 **Ferguson**, E. J., *The American Revolution. A General History, 1763–1790*, Homewood, IL, 1979.

4.7 **Gilje**, P., and **Pencak**, W., (ed.), *New York in the Age of Constitution*, Cranbury, NJ, 1992.

4.8 **Hibbert**, C., *Redcoats and Rebels. The American Revolution through British Eyes*, New York, 1990.

4.9 **Hoffman**, R., and **Albert**, P. J., (ed.), *Arms and Independence. The Military Character of the American Revolution*, Charlottesville, VA., 1984. A set of papers presented at the Capitol Historical Society on the New Military History of the Revolution.

4.10 **Kammen**, M. G., *A Season of Youth. The American Revolution and the Historical Imagination*, New York, 1978.

4.11 **Leckie**, R., *George Washington's War. The Saga of the American Revolution*, New York, 1992.

4.12 **Martin**, J. K., *In the Course of Human Events. An Interpretive Exploration of the American Revolution*, Arlington Heights, IL, 1979.

4.13 **Martin**, J. K., *A Respectable Army. The Military Origins of the Republic, 1763–1789*, Arlington Heights, IL, 1982.

4.14 **Middlekauf**, R., *The Glorious Cause. The American Revolution, 1763–1789*, New York, 1981. Particularly strong on the military campaigns of the war.

4.15 **Morris**, R. B., *The Forging of the Union, 1781–1789*, New York, 1987. Part of the reinvigorated *New American Nation* set of surveys.

4.16 **Olson**, L. C., *Emblems of American Community in the Revolutionary Era. A Study in Rhetorical Iconology*, Washington, DC, 1991. A study of visual images that served to further the Revolutionary cause.

4.17 **Shalhope**, R. E., *The Roots of Democracy. American Thought and Culture, 1760–1800*, Boston, 1990.

4.18 **Tuchman**, Barbara W., *The First Salute,*

New York, 1988. The celebrated historian's final book.

4.19 **Weber**, D., *Rhetoric and History in Revolutionary New England*, New York, 1988.

4.20 **Wills**, G., *Cincinnatus. George Washington and the Enlightenment*, Garden City, NY, 1984. Shows Washington to have been acutely aware of classical parallels and that he tempered his actions to fit the eighteenth century distrust of power and ambition.

GUIDES TO SOURCES

Primary sources

4.21 **Abbott**, W. W., (ed.), *The Papers of George Washington*, Charlottesville, VA, 1983– . Ongoing series of nine volumes that covers Washington's life up until the outbreak of the Revolution.

4.22 **Bickford**, Charlene B., and **Veit**, Helen E., (ed.), *Documentary History of the First Federal Congress, 1789–1791*, Baltimore, 1986.

4.23 **Butler**, J. P., (ed.), *The Papers of the Continental Congress, 1774–1789*, Washington, DC, 1978. A five volume set.

4.24 **Carter**, E., II, (ed.), *The Papers of Benjamin Henry LaTrobe*, Baltimore, 1984. This series comes in several parts with correspondence and sketchbooks of the Maryland engineer.

4.25 **Chesnutt**, D. R., *et al.*, (ed.), *Papers of Henry Laurens*, Columbia, SC, 1985.

4.26 **Cohen**, L. H., *The Revolution Histories. Contemporary Narratives of the American Revolution*, Ithaca, NY, 1980.

4.27 **Ferguson**, E. J., (ed.), *The Papers of Robert Morris*, Pittsburgh, PA, 1973– . A seven volume set of the papers of the leading financier of the Revolutionary War era.

4.28 **Jones**, Alice Hanson, (ed.), *American Colonial Wealth. Documents and Methods*, New York, 1978. A three volume set of typescripts of probate inventories from the colonies in the year 1774, these records form the basis for the editor's subsequent book *Wealth of a Nation to Be*.

4.29 **Kaminski**, J. P., and **Saladino**, G. J., *Documentary History of the Ratification of The Constitution*, Madison, WI, 1981.

4.30 **Koenig**, W. J., *European Manuscript Sources of the American Revolution*, 1974.

4.31 **Mooney**, J. E., *Loyalist Imprints Printed America, 1774–1785*, Worcester, MA, 1974.

4.32 **Oberg**, Barbara B., *et al.*, (ed.), *The Papers of Benjamin Franklin*, New Haven, CT, 1959. More than two dozen volumes have appeared to date, taking Franklin's life into the Revolutionary War.

4.33 **Prince**, E., *et al.*, (ed.), *The Papers of William Livingston*, New Brunswick, NJ 1979– . Five volumes have appeared in this collection of the papers of the governor of New Jersey.

4.34 **Showman**, R. K., (ed.), *The Papers of Nathaniel Greene*, Chapel Hill, NC, 1976–1991. A four volume set that concentrates on Greene's correspondence as commander of the southern armies during the Revolutionary War.

4.35 **Stagg**, J. A., (ed.), *The Papers of James Madison*, Charlottesville, VA, 1984– . Seventeen volumes have appeared through 1991 tracing Madison's correspondence up through the year 1801.

4.36 **Syrett**, H., (ed.), *The Papers of Alexander Hamilton*, New York, 1961– . More than two dozen volumes have appeared in this series.

4.37 **United States Superintendent of Documents**, *American Revolution*, Washington, DC, 1991.

4.38 **Wehmann**, H. W., *A Guide to Pre-Federal Records in the National Archives*, Washington, DC, 1989.

Atlases, bibliographies, and encyclopedias

4.39 **Adams**, T. R., *The American Controversy. A Bibliographical Study of the British Pamphlets About the American Disputes*, Providence, RI, 1980.

4.40 **Blanco**, R. L., *The War of the American Revolution. A Selected Annotated Bibliography of Published Sources*, New York, 1984.

4.41 **Cappon**, L. J., (ed.), *Atlas of Early American History. The Revolutionary Era, 1760–1790*, Princeton, NJ, 1976.

4.42 **Capps**, Marie T., and **Stroup**, T. G., *U.S.*

Military Academy Library Map Collection. The Period of the American Revolution, 1753–1800, West Point, NY, 1971.

4.43 **Faragher**, J. M., *The Encyclopedia of Colonial and Revolutionary America*, New York, 1990. Strongest on biographical entries, but helpful on topical entries, too.

4.44 **Gephart**, R. M., *Revolutionary America, 1763–1789. A Bibliography*, Washington, DC, 1983. A two volume work.

4.45 **Greene**, J. P., and **Pole**, J. R., (ed.), *The Blackwell Encyclopedia of the American Revolution*, Cambridge, MA, 1991. A thorough reference work that covers by topic the elements of the Revolutionary Era, written by the leading scholars in the field; an extra strength is its attention to British politics in the eighteenth century.

4.46 **Nebenzahl**, K., *A Bibliography of Printed Battle Plans of the American Revolution, 1775–1795*, Chicago, 1975.

4.47 **Ontiveros**, Suzanne Robitaille, (ed.), *The Dynamic Constitution. A Historical Bibliography*, Santa Barbara, CA, 1986.

4.48 **Smith**, M. J., *Navies in the American Revolution. A Bibliography*, Metuchen, NJ, 1973.

4.49 **Symonds**, C. L., *A Battlefield Atlas of the American Revolution*, Annapolis, MD, 1986.

4.50 **Wheeler**, R. R., *The Writing and Ratification of the U.S. Constitution. A Bibliography*, Washington, DC, 1986.

4.51 **York**, G., *The American Revolution, 1763–1783. Selected Reference Works*, Ann Arbor, MI, 1976.

4.52 **Zink**, S. D., 'Location and analysis of the historical publications produced by agencies of the United States government during the era of the American Revolution Bicentennial, 1974–1976', *Publishing History*, XXVII, 1990, 77–100.

Historiography

4.53 **Bonwick**, C., 'The American Revolution as a social movement revisited', *Journal of American Studies*, XX, 1986, 355–373.

4.54 **Clark**, J., 'The American Revolution. A war of religion?', *History Today*, XXXIX, 1989, 10–16.

4.55 **Cunliffe**, M., *In Search of America. Transatlantic Essays, 1951–1990*, New York, 1991. A collection of writings by one of the leading English scholars of American history.

4.56 **Drozdowski**, M. M., **Krzyzanowski**, L., and **Kapolka**, G. T., 'George Washington in Polish historiography and historical periodicals', *Polish Review*, XXXIV, 1989, 127–172.

4.57 **Fogleman**, A., 'The people of early America. Two studies by Bernard Bailyn. A review article', *Comparative Studies in Society and History*, XXII, 1989, 605–614.

4.58 **Gordon**, C., 'Crafting a usable past. Consensus, ideology, and historians of the American Revolution', *William and Mary Quarterly*, XXXXVI, 1989, 671–695.

4.59 **Greene**, J. P., 'The American Revolution and modern revolutions', *Amerikastudien/ American Studies*, XXXIII, 1988, 241–249.

4.60 **Higginbotham**, D., and **Adelman**, J. R., 'Armies in the age of the American Revolution. Some comparative dimensions', *Consortium on Revolutionary Europe 1750–1850*, XVIII, 1988, 496–506.

4.61 **Huffstetler**, J. W., 'Henry Lee and Banastre Tarleton. How historians use their memoirs', *Southern Historian*, VI, 1985, 12–19.

4.62 **Kerber**, Linda K., *et al.*, 'Four conversations on future directions in Revolutionary War historiography', *Storia Nordamericana*, II, 1985, 105–119.

4.63 **Lopez**, Claude-Anne, 'Benjamin Franklin and William Dodd. A new look at an old cause celebre', *Proceedings of the American Philosophical Society*, CXXIX, 1988, 260–267.

4.64 **McDermott**, G. R., 'Civil religion in the American Revolutionary period. An historiographic analysis', *Christian Scholar's Review*, XVIII, 1989, 346–362.

4.65 **Wellenreuther**, H., 'Labor in the era of the American Revolution. A discussion of recent concepts and theories', *Labor History*, XXII, 1981, 573–600.

4.66 **Wellenreuther**, H., *et al.*, 'Rejoinder, labor in the era of the American Revolution. An exchange', *Labor History*, XXIV, 1983, 440–454.

BIOGRAPHY

4.67 **Alden**, J. R., *George Washington. A Biography*, Baton Rouge, LA, 1984. A judicious appraisal of Washington's personality, ambition, and talents.

4.68 **Ayer**, A. J., *Thomas Paine*, New York, 1988.

4.69 **Bennett**, C. E., *A Quest for Glory. Major General Robert Howe and the American Revolution*, Chapel Hill, NC, 1991.

4.70 **Faragaher**, J. M., *Daniel Boone. The Life and Legend of an American Pioneer*, New York, 1992.

4.71 **Ferling**, J. E., *John Adams. A Life*, Knoxville, TN, 1992.

4.72 **Ferling**, J. E., *The First of Men. A Life of George Washington*, Knoxville, TN, 1988. A full-length biography that stresses the balance in his life between ambition and self-control.

4.73 **Flexner**, J. T., *The Young Hamilton. A Biography*, Boston, 1978.

4.74 **Flower**, M. E., *John Dickinson, Conservative Revolutionary*, Charlottesville, VA, 1983.

4.75 **Gerlach**, D. R., *Proud Patriot. Philip Schuyler and the War of Independence, 1775–1783*, Syracuse, NY, 1987.

4.76 **Hargrove**, R. J., *General John Burgoyne*, Newark, DE, 1983.

4.77 **Kelsay**, Isabel Thompson, *Joseph Brant, 1743–1807. Man of Two Worlds*, Syracuse, NY, 1984.

4.78 **Kimball**, Marie G., *Jefferson, the Road to Glory, 1743 to 1776*, Westport, CT, 1977.

4.79 **Longmore**, P. K., *The Invention of George Washington*, Berkeley, CA, 1988. A biography that seeks to determine where the contemporary image of Washington left off from the real man, and finds that the subject himself was a consummate actor, continually playing a changing role in public life.

4.80 **MacDougall**, W. L., *American Revolutionary. A Biography of General Alexander McDougall*, Westport, CT, 1977.

4.81 **Malone**, D., *Thomas Jefferson as Political Leader*, Westport, CT, 1975.

4.82 **McCants**, D. A., *Patrick Henry, the Orator*, Westport, CT, 1990.

4.83 **Nelson**, P. D., *Anthony Wayne, Soldier of the Early Republic*, Bloomington, IN, 1985.

4.84 **Rakove**, J. N., *James Madison and the Creation of the American Republic*, Glenview, IL, 1990.

4.85 **Randall**, W. S., *Benedict Arnold. Patriot and Traitor*, New York, 1990.

4.86 **Rea**, R. R., *Major Robert Farmar of Mobile*, Tuscaloosa, AL, 1990.

4.87 **Shaffer**, A. H., *To Be an American. David Ramsay and the Making of the American Consciousness*, Columbia, SC, 1991.

4.88 **Skemp**, Sheila L., *William Franklin. Son of a Patriot, Servant of a King*, New York, 1990.

4.89 **Tagg**, J., *Benjamin Franklin Bache and the Philadelphia 'Aurora'*, Philadelphia, 1991. A biography of Franklin's grandson that places him in the context of the Age of Reason.

4.90 **Thomas**, L. D., *Rise to be a People. A Biography of Paul Cuffee*, Urbana, IL, 1986. A biography of the New England-born black abolitionist who sought to repatriate freed people to Sierra Leone; the author terms this the first instance of "pan-Africanism".

4.91 **Wright**, E., 'The political education of James Madison', *History Today*, XXXI, 1981, 17–23.

DEMOGRAPHY, FAMILY, AND HEALTH

4.92 **Bailyn**, B., *The Peopling of British America. An Introduction*, New York, 1986. A companion volume to *Voyagers to the West* that emphasizes the historical geography of the place of origin of the British immigrants.

4.93 **Bailyn**, B., *Voyagers to the West. A Passage in the Peopling of America on the Eve of the Revolution*, New York, 1986. A quantitative study of British immigrants based on the official Emigration Register with an analysis of the fate of the newcomers in America.

4.94 **Ditz**, Toby L., *Property and Kinship. Inheritance in Early Connecticut, 1750–1820*, Princeton, NJ, 1986.

4.95 **Fliegelman**, J., *Prodigals and Pilgrims. The American Revolution Against Patriarchal

Authority, 1750–1800, New York, 1982. Examines eighteenth century literature to trace the changes in family structure and attitudes.

4.96 **Grubb**, F., 'British immigration to Philadelphia. The reconstruction of ship passenger lists from May 1772 to October 1773', *Pennsylvania History*, LV, 1988, 118–141.

4.97 **Klepp**, Susan E., 'The demographic characteristics of Philadelphia, 1788–1801. Zachariah Poulson's bills of mortality', *Pennsylvania History*, LIII, 1986, 201–221.

4.98 **McDonald**, F., and **McDonald**, Ellen Shapiro, (ed.), 'The population of the United States, 1790, a symposium', *William and Mary Quarterly*, XLIV, 1984, 85–135.

4.99 **Zuckerman**, M., ' "Penmanship exercises for saucy sons." Some thoughts on the colonial Southern family', *South Carolina Historical Magazine*, LXXXIV, 1983, 152–166. A study of the school notebooks produced by planters' sons that suggests that obedience to patriarchy was not considered a virtue, at least not until after adolescence.

SOCIAL RELATIONS

Class and community

4.100 **Beeman**, R. R., *The Evolution of the Southern Backcountry. A Case Study of Lunenburg County, Virginia, 1746–1832*, Philadelphia, 1984. A look at a Southside Virginia county that did not evolve into a stratified Tidewater society and one in which white males enjoyed a rough egalitarianism.

4.101 **Breen**, T. H., *Tobacco Culture. The Mentality of the Great Tidewater Planters on the Eve of Revolution*, Princeton, NJ, 1985. Links the crisis in the tobacco business of the 1760s and 1770s to the planters' fear of dependence and ultimately to their choice to join the rebellion against royal authority.

4.102 **Cray**, R. E., *Paupers and Poor Relief in New York City and its Rural Environs, 1700–1830*, Philadelphia, 1988. A quantitative analysis of the creation of the

almshouse as the principal method of poor relief in New York.

4.103 **Klein**, H. S., and **Willis**, E. P., 'The distribution of wealth in late eighteenth-century New York City', *Social History*, XVIII, 1985, 259–283.

4.104 **Klein**, Rachel N., *Unification of a Slave State. The Rise of the Planter Class in the South Carolina Backcountry, 1760–1808*, Chapel Hill, NC, 1990.

4.105 **Pencak**, W., 'In search of the American character. French travellers in eighteenth century Pennsylvania', *Pennsylvania History*, LV, 1985, 2–55.

4.106 **Smith**, B. G., 'Inequality in late colonial Philadelphia. A note on its nature and growth', *William and Mary Quarterly*, XLII, 1984, 629–645.

Gender relations

4.107 **Bloch**, Ruth H., 'The gendered meanings of virtue in revolutionary America', *Signs*, XIII, 1987, 37–58.

4.108 **Bodle**, W., 'Jane Bartram's application. Her struggle for survival, stability, and self-determination in revolutionary Pennsylvania', *Pennsylvania Magazine of History and Biography*, CXV, 1991, 185–220.

4.109 **Boyle**, Susan, 'Did she generally decide? Women in Ste. Genevieve, 1750–1805', *William and Mary Quarterly*, XLIV, 1987, 775–789.

4.110 **Buel**, Joy Day, and **Buel**, R., *The Way of Duty. A Woman and Her Family in Revolutionary America*, New York, 1984. Links the individual story of Mary Fish with the sweep of the Revolution.

4.111 **Erkkila**, Betsy, 'The Federal mother. Whitman as revolutionary son', *Prospects*, X, 1985, 423–441.

4.112 **Gundersen**, Joan R., 'Independence, citizenship, and the American Revolution', *Signs*, XIII, 1987, 59–77.

4.113 **Hoffman**, R., and **Albert**, P. J., (ed.), *Women in the Age of the American Revolution*, Charlottesville, VA, 1989.

4.114 **Kerber**, Linda K., *Women of the Republic. Intellect and Ideology in Revolutionary America*, Chapel Hill, NC, 1980.

4.115 **Kerber**, Linda K., ' "I have done much to carrey on the warr". Women and the shaping of republican ideology after the American Revolution', *Journal of Women's*

History, I, 1990, 231–243.

4.116 **Lane**, L. M., and **Lane**, Judith J., 'The Columbian patriot. Mercy Otis Warren and the Constitution', *Women and Politics*, X, 1990, 17–32.

4.117A **Norton**, Mary Beth, *Liberty's Daughters. The Revolutionary Experience of American Women*, Boston, 1980.

4.117B **Samuelson**, Nancy B., 'Revolutionary war women and the second oldest profession', *Minerva. Quarterly Report on Women and the Military*, VII, 1989, 16–25.

Education

4.118 **Louis**, E. D., 'William Shippen's unsuccessful attempt to establish the first school for physick in the American colonies in 1762', *Journal of the History of Medicine and Allied Sciences*, XLIV, 1989, 218–239.

4.119 **Miller**, E. F., 'On the American founders' defense of liberal education in a republic', *Review of Politics*, XLVI, 1984, 65–90.

Crime and punishment

4.120 **Cromwell**, P. F., 'Quaker reforms in American criminal justice. The penitentiary and beyond', *Criminal Justice History*, X, 1989, 77–94.

4.121 **Dumm**, T. L., *Democracy and Punishment. Disciplinary Origins of the United States*, Madison, WI, 1987. Connects the emergence of democracy in the late eighteenth and early nineteeth centuries to the simultaneous construction of the penitentiary and asylum.

4.122 **Kealey**, Linda, 'Patterns of punishment. Massachusetts in the eighteenth century', *American Journal of Legal History*, XXX, 1986, 163–186.

4.123 **Palmer**, R., and **Presser**, S. B., 'The federal common law of crime', *Law and History Review*, IV, 1986, 267–323.

4.124 **Preyer**, Kathryn, 'Crime, the criminal law and reform in post-revolutionary Virginia', *Law and History Review*, I, 1983, 53–85.

4.125 **Rowe**, G. S., 'Women's crime and criminal administration in Pennsylvania, 1763–1790', *Pennsylvania Magazine of History and Biography*, CIX, 1985, 335–368.

RELIGION, BELIEFS, IDEAS, AND CULTURE

4.126 **Bergman**, M., 'Destiny, virtue, and piety. Variations on a Thanksgiving theme', *Fides et Historia*, XXI, 1989, 18–37.

4.127 **Bloch**, Ruth, *Visionary Republic. Millennial Themes in American Thought, 1756–1800*, New York, 1985.

4.128 **Frost**, J. W., *A Perfect Freedom. Religious Liberty in Pennsylvania*, New York, 1990.

4.129 **Garrett**, G. C., *Spirit Possession and Popular Religion. From the Camisards to the Shakers*, Baltimore, 1987.

4.130 **Gura**, P. F., 'The role of the "black regiment". Religion and the American Revolution', *New England Quarterly*, LXI, 1988, 439–454.

4.131 **Kessel**, Elizabeth A., ' "A mighty fortress is our God". German religous and educational organizations on the Maryland frontier, 1734–1800', *Maryland Historical Magazine*, LXXVII, 1982, 370–387.

4.132 **Kloos**, J., ' "Feast of reason/flow of soul". Benjamin Rush's public piety', *American Presbyterians*, LXIX, 1991, 49–58.

4.133 **Mason**, K., 'Localism, evangelicalism, and loyalism. The sources of discontent in the revolutionary Chesapeake', *Journal of Southern History*, LVI, 1990, 23–54.

4.134 **Peterson**, M. D., and **Vaughan**, R., (ed.), *The Virginia Statute for Religious Freedom. Its Evolution and Consequences in American History*, New York, 1988. A collection of essays on the history of disestablishment in the eighteenth century.

4.135 **Richey**, R. E., *Early American Methodism*, Bloomington, IN, 1991.

4.136 **Soderlund**, Jean R., *Quakers and Slavery. A Divided Spirit*, Princeton, NJ, 1985.

4.137 **Stark**, R., and **Finke**, R., 'American religion in 1776. A statistical portrait', *Sociological Analysis*, XLIX, 1988, 39–51.

4.138 **Terrar**, T., 'Episcopal-Roman Catholic ecumenism and church democracy during North America's revolutionary era. The life and times of liberation theologian Charles H. Wharton', *Anglican and Episcopal History*, LVI, 1987, 163–192.

4.139 **Thorp**, D. B., *The Moravian Community in Colonial North Carolina. Pluralism on the Southern Frontier*, Knoxville, TN, 1989. A study of the Wachovia settlement in the mid-eighteenth century and how the Moravians established generally tolerant relations with their English neighbors in North Carolina.

4.140 **Valeri**, M., 'The new divinity and the American Revolution', *William and Mary Quarterly*, XLVI, 1989, 741–769.

4.141 **Vincent**, B., 'Masons as builders of the republic. The role of freemasonry in the American Revolution', *European Contributions to American Studies*, XIV, 1988, 132–150.

Republicanism

4.142 **Banner**, J. M., 'France and the origins of American political culture', *Virginia Quarterly Review*, LXIV, 1988, 651–670.

4.143 **Brooke**, J. L., *The Heart of the Commonwealth. Society and Political Culture in Worcester County, Massachusetts, 1713–1861*, New York, 1989.

4.144 **Bullock**, S., 'The revolutionary transformation of American Freemasonry, 1752–1792', *William and Mary Quarterly*, XLVII, 1990, 347–369.

4.145 **Fruchtman**, J. F., 'Nature and revolution in Paine's "Common Sense" ', *History of Political Thought*, X, 1989, 421–438.

4.146 **Greenbaum**, F., 'Empire and autonomy. The American and Netherlandish revolutions', *International Social Science Review*, LXIV, 1989, 9–19.

4.147 **Henretta**, J. A., 'Society and republicanism. America in 1787', *This Constitution*, XV, 1987, 20–26.

4.148 **Higonnet**, P., *Sister Republics. The Origins of French and American Republicanism*, Cambridge, MA, 1988.

4.149 **Kloppenberg**, J. T., 'The virtues of liberalism. Christianity, republicanism, and ethics in early American political discourse', *Journal of American History*, LXXIV, 1987, 9–33. Attempts to map out a "rediscovery of the virtues of liberalism".

4.150 **Kramnick**, I., *Republicanism and Bourgeois Radicalism. Political Ideology in Late Eighteenth Century England and America*, Ithaca, NY, 1990. Describes the Anglo-American world in the Age of Revolution as a place where the liberalism of the emerging middle coexisted in a type of pluralism with Christian doctrines and the older republican tradition.

4.151 **Lause**, M. A., 'The "unwashed infidelity". Thomas Paine and early New York City labor history', *Labor History*,

XXVII, 1986, 385–409.

4.152 **Pangle**, T. L., *The Spirit of Modern Republicanism. The Moral Vision of the American Founders and the Philosophy of Locke*, Chicago, 1988.

4.153 **Rahe**, P. A., *Republics Ancient and Modern. Classical Republicanism and the American Revolution*, Chapel Hill, NC, 1992.

4.154 **Sheldon**, G. W., *The Political Philosophy of Thomas Jefferson*, Baltimore, 1991.

4.155 **Sinopoli**, R., *The Foundations of American Citizenship. Liberalism, the Constitution, and Civic Virtue*, New York, 1992.

4.156 **Smith**, J. A., *Franklin and Bache. Envisioning the Enlightened Republic*, New York, 1990. Treats the relationship between Franklin and his grandson, B. F. Bache, particularly the way in which Bache carried on his grandfather's traditions as a journalist and political critic.

4.157 **Voss**, F., 'Honoring a scorned hero. America's monument to Thomas Paine', *New York History*, LXVIII, 1987, 132–150.

4.158 **Webking**, R. H., *The American Revolution and the Politics of Liberty*, Baton Rouge, LA, 1988.

4.159 **White**, M. G., *The Philosophy of the American Revolution*, New York, 1978.

Aftermath of the Great Awakening

4.160 **Andrews**, S., 'Classicism and the American Revolution', *History Today*, XXXVII, 1987, 37–42.

4.161 **Handlin**, O., and **Handlin**, Lilian, 'Who read John Locke? Words and acts in the American Revolution', *American Scholar*, LVIII, 1989, 545–556.

4.162 **Jaffee**, D., 'The village enlightenment in New England, 1760–1820', *William and Mary Quarterly*, XLVII, 1990, 327–346.

4.163 **Lovejoy**, D. S., *Religious Enthusiasm in the New World. Heresy to Revolution*, Cambridge, MA, 1985. Spans the colonial period and is strongest on the Great Awakening.

4.164 **Post**, D. M., 'Jeffersonian revisions of Locke. Education, property-rights, and liberty', *Journal of the History of Ideas*, XLVII, 1986, 147–159.

4.165 **Sher**, R. B., and **Smitten**, J. R., (ed.), *Scotland and America in the Age of the*

Enlightenment, Princeton, NJ, 1990.

4.166 **Spurlin**, P. M., *The French Enlightenment in America. Essays on the Times of the Founding Fathers*, Athens, GA, 1984.

4.167 **Starkey**, A., 'War and culture, a case study. The enlightenment and the conduct of the British army in America, 1755–1781', *War and Society*, VIII, 1990, 1–28.

4.168 **Sweretz**, S. M., *The Unvarnished Doctrine. Locke, Liberalism, and the American Revolution*, Durham, NC, 1990.

4.169 **Vetterli**, R., and **Bryner**, G., *In Search of the Republic. Public Virtue and the Roots of American Government*, Totowa, NJ, 1987.

WORK AND ENTERPRISE

4.170 **Carrington**, S. H. H., 'The American Revolution and the British West Indies' economy', *Journal of Interdisciplinary History*, XVII, 1987, 823–850.

4.171 **Clark**, C., 'Economics and culture. Opening up the rural history of the early American northeast', *American Quarterly*, XLIII, 1991, 279–301. A review essay of the recent literature on capitalism in the countryside in the colonial period; much of the social history looks at the 'mentalité' of the market and of non-market economic relations.

4.172 **Doerflinger**, T. M., *A Vigorous Spirit of Enterprise. Merchants and Economic Development in Revolutionary Philadelphia*, Chapel Hill, NC, 1986. Places risk-taking merchants at the center of colonial economic growth.

4.173 **Grubb**, F., 'Immigrant servant labor. Their occupational and geographic distribution in the late eighteenth-century mid-Atlantic economy', *Social Science History*, IX, 1985, 249–276.

4.174 **Grubb**, F., 'The incidence of servitude in trans-Atlantic migration, 1771–1804', *Explorations in Economic History*, XXII, 1985, 316–339.

4.175 **Jones**, Alice Hanson, *Wealth of a Nation to Be. The American Colonies on the Eve of the Revolution*, New York, 1980.

4.176 **Linebaugh**, P., and **Rediker**, M., 'The

many-headed hydra. Sailors, slaves, and the Atlantic working class in the eighteenth century', *Journal of Historical Sociology*, III, 1990, 225–252.

4.177 **Liss**, Peggy K., *Atlantic Empires. The Network of Trade and Revolution, 1713–1826*, Baltimore, 1983.

4.178 **Littlefield**, D. R., 'Eighteenth-century plans to clear the Potomac river. Technology, expertise, and labor in a developing nation', *Virginia Magazine of History and Biography*, XCIII, 1985, 291–322.

4.179 **Morgan**, K., 'The organization of the convict trade to Maryland. Stevenson, Randolph, and Cheston, 1768–1775', *William and Mary Quarterly*, XLII, 1985, 201–227.

4.180 **Morgan**, K., 'Shipping patterns and the Atlantic trade of Bristol, 1749–1770', *William and Mary Quarterly*, XLVI, 1989, 506–538.

4.181 **Rediker**, M., *Between the Devil and the Deep Blue Sea. Merchant Seamen, Pirates, and the Anglo-American Maritime World, 1700–1750*, New York, 1987.

4.182 **Salinger**, Sharon V., *"To Serve Well and Faithfully". Labor and Indentured Servants in Pennsylvania, 1682–1800*, New York, 1987. Examines the rise of indentured servitude in Penn's colony from a rural institution to one that characterized subservient labor in Philadelphia, and ultimately the decline of servitude and move to free labor after the Revolution.

4.183 **Smith**, B. G., *The "Lower Sort". Philadelphia's Laboring People, 1750–1800*, Ithaca, NY, 1990. A study of the plebeian population of Philadelphia in the Revolutionary era as the city grew from a small port into a large city.

4.184 **York**, N. L., *Mechanical Metamorphosis. Technological Change in Revolutionary America*, Westport, CT, 1985.

RACE AND ETHNIC IDENTITY

African-Americans

4.185 **Levesque**, G. A., and **Baumgarten**, Nikola A., ' "A monstrous inconsistency". Slavery, ideology and politics in the age of the American Revolution', *Contributions in Black Studies*, VIII, 1986–87, 20–34.

4.186 **Nash**, G. B., *Race and Revolution*, Madison, WI, 1990.

4.187 **Nash**, G. B., and **Soderlund**, Jean R., *Freedom by Degrees. Emancipation in Pennsylvania and Its Aftermath*, New York, 1991.

4.188 **Nicholls**, M. L., 'Passing through this troublesome world. Free blacks in the early southside', *Virginia Magazine of History and Biography*, XCII, 1984, 50–70.

4.189 **White**, S., *Somewhat More Independent. The End of Slavery in New York City, 1770–1810*, Athens, GA, 1991.

Native Americans

4.190 **Cashin**, E. J., *Lachlan McGillivray, Indian Trader. The Shaping of the Southern Colonial Frontier*, Athens, GA, 1992.

4.191 **Dowd**, G. E., *A Spirited Resistance. The North American Indian Struggle for Unity, 1745–1815*, Baltimore, 1992. Examines the period as one in which political movements to oppose the expansion of European settlement overlapped religious and cultural revitalization movements.

4.192 **Holmes**, J. D. L., 'Benjamin Hawkins and United States attempts to teach farming to the southeastern Indians', *Agricultural History*, LX, 1986, 216–232.

4.193 **Kirkby**, Dianne, 'Colonial policy and native depopulation in California and New South Wales, 1770–1840', *Ethnohistory*, XXXI, 1984, 1–16.

4.194 **Olmstead**, E. P., *Blackcoats among the Delaware. David Zeisberger on the Ohio Frontier*, Kent, OH, 1991. A study of Moravian missionaries to the Delaware Indians and in particular one missionary's struggle to protect the tribe from white pressures.

4.195 **Shipek**, Florence E., 'A native American adaptation to drought. The Kumeyyay as seen in the San Diego Mission records, 1770–1798', *Ethnohistory*, XXVIII, 1981, 295–312.

SPACE, MOVEMENT, AND PLACE

4.196 **Bowling**, K. R., *The Creation of Washington, D.C. The Idea and Location of the American Capital*, Fairfax, VA, 1991.

4.197 **Brasseaux**, C. A., *The Founding of New Acadia. The Beginnings of Acadian Life in Louisiana, 1765–1803*, Baton Rouge, LA, 1987.

4.198 **Eckert**, A. W., *Gateway to Empire. A Narrative*, Boston, 1983. An account of the Indian-white conflict in the Old Northwest.

4.199 **Griffin**, Patricia, *Mullet on the Beach. The Minorcans of Florida, 1768–1788*, Jacksonville, FL, 1991. A history of the colony around New Smyrna, Florida, and the Mediterranean islanders who settled it and persisted in Florida into the twentieth century.

4.200 **Liljegren**, E. R., 'Zalmon Coley. The second Anglo-American in Santa Fe', *New Mexico Historical Review*, LXII, 1987, 263–286.

4.201 **Muller**, H. N., ' "The nursery of hardy soldiers". A review essay on migration from Vermont', *Vermont History*, LII, 1984, 180–189.

4.202 **Purvis**, T. L., 'The national origins of New Yorkers in 1790', *New York History*, LXVII, 1986, 132–153.

4.203 **Wood**, J. S., 'Elaboration of a settlement system. The New England village in the federal period', *Journal of Historical Geography*, X, 1984, 331–356.

THE STATE AND THE PUBLIC REALM

The coming of the Revolution

4.204 **Becker**, R. A., *Revolution, Reform, and the Politics of American Taxation, 1763–1783*, Baton Rouge, LA, 1980.

4.205 **Bradley**, J. E., *Popular Politics and the American Revolution in England. Petitions, The Crown, and Public Opinion*, Macon, GA, 1986.

4.206 **Bullion**, J. L., *A Great and Necessary Measure. George Grenville and the Genesis of the Stamp Act, 1763–1765*, Columbia, MO, 1982.

4.207 **Calhoon**, R. M., *The Loyalist Perception and Other Essays*, Columbia, SC, 1989. Examines the thought of leading Tories and the complex set of reasons why some people chose Loyalism.

4.208 **Clayton**, T. R., 'Sophistry, security, and socio-political structures in the American revolution. Or why Jamaica did not rebel', *Historical Journal*, XXIX, 1986, 319–394.

4.209 **Conser**, W. H., et al., (ed.), *Resistance, Politics, and the American Struggle for Independence, 1765–1775*, Boulder, CO, 1986. Examines the colonial opposition to imperial policies as a form of non-violence with lessons for the modern world.

4.210 **Countryman**, E., *A People in Revolution. The American Revolution and Political Society in New York, 1760–1790*, Baltimore, 1981.

4.211 **Davis**, D. B., 'American equality and foreign revolutions', *Journal of American History*, LXXVI, 1989, 729–752.

4.212 **Gilje**, P., *The Road to Mobocracy. Popular Disorder in New York City, 1763–1834*, Chapel Hill, NC, 1987. Traces the role of the crowd in New York's history from the Revolution through the racial and religious riots of the 1830s.

4.213 **Ireland**, O. S., 'The crux of politics, religion and party in Pennsylvania, 1778–1789', *William and Mary Quarterly*, XLII, 1985, 453–475.

4.214 **Klein**, M. M., 'Corruption in colonial America', *South Atlantic Quarterly*, LXXVIII, 1981, 57–72.

4.215 **Lerner**, R., *The Thinking Revolutionary. Principle and Practice in the New Republic*, Ithaca, NY, 1987. A work that uses the political philosophy of Leo Strauss to examine the leading American revolutionaries as men who articulated timeless thoughts and moved to translate those thoughts into action.

4.216 **Maier**, P., *The Old Revolutionaries. Political Lives in the Age of Samuel Adams*, New York, 1980.

4.217 **Marston**, Jerrilyn Greene, *King and Congress. The Transfer of Political Legitimacy, 1774–1776*, Princeton, NJ, 1987. Argues that the second Continental Congress acted most effectively as an executive agency rather than simply an intercolonial legislature, and that in the revolutionary crisis of 1774–76 it acquired a legitimacy previously reserved for royal authority.

4.218 **Nash**, G. B., *The Urban Crucible. Social Change, Political Consciousness and the Origins of the American Revolution*, Cambridge, MA, 1979.

4.219 **Padover**, S. K., *The World of the Founding Fathers*, South Brunswick, NJ, 1977.

4.220 **Rakove**, J. N., *The Beginnings of National Politics*, New York, 1979.

4.221 **Ranlet**, P., *The New York Loyalists*, Knoxville, TN, 1986.

4.222 **Reid**, J. P., *In Defiance of the Law. The Standing-Army Controversy, the Two Constitutions, and the Coming of the American Revolution*, Chapel Hill, NC, 1981.

4.223 **Reid**, J. P., *Constitutional History of the American Revolution. The Authority to Legislate*, Madison, WI, 1991.

4.224 **Rowe**, G. S., and **Knott**, A. W., 'The Longchamps affair (1784–86), the law of nations, and the shaping of early American foreign policy', *Diplomatic History*, X, 1986, 199–220.

4.225 **Shaw**, P., *American Patriots and the Rituals of Revolution*, Cambridge, MA, 1981. An anthropological look at the crowd's behavior in revolutionary crises, mainly in Massachusetts, with the hypothesis that a general anxiety and an adolescent revolt against parental authority best explain the American Revolution.

4.226 **Shy**, J. W., *The American Revolution*, Northbrook, IL, 1973.

4.227 **Steffen**, G., *The Mechanics of Baltimore. Workers and Politics in the Age of Revolution, 1763–1812*, Urbana, IL, 1984. Traces the emergence of a distinct community of artisans who became the shock troops of the revolutionary movement, and after the war, devotees of republicanism.

4.228 **Thomas**, P. D. G., 'George III and the American Revolution', *History*, LXXX, 1985, 16–31.

4.229 **Thomas**, P. D. G., *The Townshend Duties Crisis. The Second Phase of the American Revolution, 1767–1773*, New York, 1987. A study of the Grafton ministry in Great Britain and how it sought but failed to use the Townshend Duties to reach a permanent political settlement over the taxation issue with the colonies.

4.230 **Tucker**, R. W., and **Hendrickson**, D., *The Fall of the First British Empire. Origins of the War of American Independence*, Baltimore, 1982.

4.231 **Tyler**, J. W., *Smugglers and Patriots. Boston Merchants and the Advent of the American Revolution*, Boston, 1986.

4.232 **Yazawa**, M., *From Colonies to Commonwealth. Familial Ideology and the Beginnings of the American Republic*, Baltimore, 1985.

Independence

4.233 **Dinkin**, R. J., *Voting in Revolutionary America. A Study of Elections in the Original Thirteen States, 1776–1789*, Westport, CT, 1982.

4.234 **Flaumenhaft**, H., *The Effective Republic. Administration and Constitution in the Thought of Alexander Hamilton*, Durham, NC, 1992.

4.235 **Greene**, J. P., 'From the perspective of law. Context and legitimacy in the origins of the American Revolution', *South Atlantic Quarterly*, LXXXV, 1986, 56–77.

4.236 **Henderson**, H. J., 'Taxation and political culture. Massachusetts and Virginia, 1760–1800', *William and Mary Quarterly*, XLVII, 1990, 90–114.

4.237 **Hoffer**, P., and **Hull**, N. E. H., *Impeachment in America, 1635–1805*, New Haven, CT, 1984. Traces the origins of the constitutional provision for impeachment of officers, and finds a surge in use of the method by the new states.

4.238 **Hoffert**, R. W., *A Politics of Tensions. The Articles of Confederation and American Political Ideas*, Niwot, CO, 1992.

4.239 **Johnson**, R. R., ' "Parliamentary egotisms".

The clash of legislatures in the making of the American Revolution', *Journal of American History*, LXXIV, 1987, 338–362.

4.240 **Lutz**, D., *The Origins of American Constitutionalism*, Baton Rouge, LA, 1988. Places the 1787 federal constitution in the context of earlier state constitution-making and finds an essential continuity of ideas.

4.241 **Morris**, R. B., 'The Great Peace of 1783', *Massachusetts Historical Society Proceedings*, XCV, 1983, 29–51.

4.242 **O'Callaghan**, J. A., 'The western lands, 1776–84. Catalyst for nationhood', *Journal of Forest History*, XXXI, 1987, 133–138.

4.243 **Ousterhout**, Anne M., *A State Divided. Opposition in Pennsylvania to the American Revolution*, Westport, CT, 1987.

4.244 **Potter**, Janice, *The Liberty We Seek. Loyalist Ideology in Colonial New York and Massachusetts*, Cambridge, MA, 1983.

4.245 **Reid**, J. P., *Constitutional History of the American Revolution. The Authority to Tax*, Madison, WI, 1987. The second volume of a trilogy that seeks to place the American Revolution in the context of English constitution law. The Revolution, the author insists, had everything to do with the dispute over Parliament's power to tax the colonies.

4.246 **Sainsbury**, J., *Disaffected Patriots. London Supporters of Revolutionary America, 1769–1782*, Kingston, ONT, 1987.

4.247 **Thomas**, P. D. G., *Tea Party to Independence. The Third Phase of the American Revolution, 1773–1776*, New York, 1991. Completes the author's trilogy on the coming of the Revolution.

4.248 **Toohey**, R. E., *Liberty and Empire. British Radical Solutions to the American Problem, 1774–1776*, Lexington, KY, 1978.

4.249 **Wood**, G. S., *The Radicalism of the American Revolution*, New York, 1992.

4.250 **Yarbrough**, Jean, 'Race and the moral foundation of the American republic. Another look at the Declaration, and the Notes on Virginia', *Journal of Politics*, LIII, 1991, 90–105.

4.251 **York**, N. L., 'Our first "good" war. Selective memory, special pleading, and the war of American independence', *Peace and Change*, XV, 1990, 371–390.

Warfare

4.252 **Albertson**, Karla Klein, 'The Society of

the Cincinnati', *Early American Life*, XX, 1989, 32–36.

4.253 **Born**, J. D., 'Sailing on the dead sea. American privateersmen in Old Mill Prison during the revolution', *Psychohistory Review*, XIV, 1985, 23–33.

4.254 **Carp**, E. W., *To Starve the Army at Pleasure. Continental Army Administration and American Political Culture, 1775–1783*, Chapel Hill, NC, 1984. Examines the tension between the revolutionaries' fear of centralized power and their need for authority to maintain an armed rebellion; the tension was resolved most effectively by the supply officers within the army itself.

4.255 **Clary**, D. A., and **Whitehorne**, J. W. A., *The Inspectors General of the United States Army, 1777–1903*, Washington, DC, 1987. Gives particular attention to Baron Von Steuben's role in establishing the office that reported to Congress about army actions and spending.

4.256 **Conway**, S., 'To subdue America. British army officers and the conduct of the revolutionary war', *William and Mary Quarterly*, XLIII, 1986, 381–407.

4.257 **Conway**, S., ' "The great mischief complain'd of". Reflections on the misconduct of British soldiers in the revolutionary war', *William and Mary Quarterly*, XLVII, 1990, 370–390.

4.258 **Dull**, J. R., 'Was the Continental Navy a mistake?', *American Neptune*, XLIV, 1984, 167–170.

4.259 **Dull**, J. R., *A Diplomatic History of the American Revolution*, New Haven, CT, 1985. A survey of the continental and North American diplomacy that led to the 1783 Peace of Paris.

4.260 **Dull**, J. R., 'Mahan, sea power, and the war for American independence', *International History Review*, X, 1988, 59–67.

4.261 **Frey**, Sylvia R., *The British Soldier in America. A Social History of Military Life in the Revolutionary Period*, Austin, TX, 1981.

4.262 **Haefele**, W. R., 'General George Washington. Espionage chief', *American History Illustrated*, XXIV, 1989, 22–27.

4.263 **Higginbotham**, D., *War and Society in Revolutionary America. The Wider Dimensions of the Conflict*, Columbia, SC, 1988.

4.264 **Hutson**, J. H., *John Adams and the Diplomacy of the American Revolution*, Lexington, KY, 1980.

4.265 **Huston**, J. A., *Logistics of Liberty. American Services of Supply in the Revolutionary War*, Newark, DE, 1991. A volume on the Revolutionary War by the foremost historian of wartime logistics.

4.266 **Kaplan**, R., 'The hidden war. British intelligence operations during the American Revolution', *William and Mary Quarterly*, XLVII, 1990, 115–138.

4.267 **Knight**, Betsy, 'Prisoner exchange and parole in the American Revolution', *William and Mary Quarterly*, XLVIII, 1991, 201–222.

4.268 **Moore**, C., *The Loyalists. Revolution, Exile, Settlement*, Toronto, ONT, 1984.

4.269 **Nelson**, P. D., 'British conduct of the American revolutionary war. A review of interpretations', *Journal of American History*, LXV, 1978, 623–653. Takes the stand that Britain lost the war, not that America won it, and analyzes why.

4.270 **Rosswurm**, S., *Arms, Country, and Class. The Philadelphia Militia and the 'Lower Sort' during the American Revolution*, New Brunswick, NJ, 1987. Examines how the laboring poor of Philadelphia achieved political consciousness and political power when organized as the city's militia.

4.271 **Schaffel**, K., 'The American Board of War, 1776–1781', *Military Affairs*, L, 1986, 185–189.

4.272 **Tracy**, N., *Navies, Deterrence, and American Independence. Britain and Seapower in the 1760s and 1770s*, Vancouver, BC, 1988.

4.273 **Wood**, W. J., *Battles of the Revolutionary War, 1775–1781*, Chapel Hill, NC, 1990.

(a) NEW ENGLAND PHASE, 1775–1776

4.274 **Burrows**, E. G., ' "Notes on settling America". Albert Gallatin, New England and the American Revolution', *New England Quarterly*, LVIII, 1985, 442–453.

4.275 **Emery**, Deborah Day, 'The monarch of Hampshire. Israel Williams', *Historical Journal of Massachusetts*, XVII, 1989, 119–136.

4.276 **Hankins**, Jean F., 'A different kind of loyalist. The Sandemanians of New England during the revolutionary war', *New England Quarterly*, LX, 1987, 223–249.

4.277 **Villers**, D. H., 'The search for the Connecticut loyalist in the American Revolution. An historiographical survey', *Connecticut History*, II, 1985, 60–76.

(b) MID-ATLANTIC PHASE, 1776–1778

4.278 **Allen**, S. L., 'Choosing sides. A quantitative study of the personality determinants of loyalist and revolutionary political affiliations in New York', *Journal of American History*, LXV, 1978, 344–66.
4.279 **Calderhead**, W. L., 'Thomas Carney. Unsung soldier of the American Revolution', *Maryland Historical Magazine*, LXXXIV, 1989, 319–326.
4.280 **Countryman**, E., 'The uses of capital in revolutionary America. The case of the New York loyalist merchants', *William and Mary Quarterly*, XLIX, 1992, 3–28.
4.281 **Kashatus**, W., 'A Quaker testimony to the American Revolution', *Pennsylvania Heritage*, XVI, 1990, 18–23.
4.282 **Kierner**, Cynthia A., 'Landlord and tenant in revolutionary New York. The case of Livingston Manor', *New York History*, LXX, 1989, 135–152.
4.283 **Koenigsberger**, H. G., 'Composite states, representative institutions and the American Revolution', *Historical Research*, LXII, 1989, 135–153.
4.284 **Mintz**, M. M., *The Generals of Saratoga. John Burgoyne and Horatio Gates*, New Haven, CT, 1990.
4.285 **Pancake**, J. S., *1777. The Year of the Hangman*, University, AL, 1977.
4.286 **Speidel**, Judithe D., 'The artistic spy. A note on the talents of Major Andre', *New York History*, LVIII, 1987, 394–406.
4.287 **Stevens**, P. L., ' "To keep the indians of the Wabache in his majesty's interest". The Indian diplomacy of Edward Abbott, British lieutenant governor of Vincennes, 1776–1778', *Indiana Magazine of History*, LXXXIII, 1987, 141–172.
4.288 **Tiedemann**, J. S., 'Patriots by default. Queens County, New York, and the British army, 1776–1783', *William and Mary Quarterly*, XLIII, 1986, 35–63.
4.289 **Tiedemann**, J. S., 'A revolution foiled. Queens County, New York, 1775–1776', *Journal of American History*, LXXV, 1988, 417–444.
4.290 **Ward**, H. M., *Major General Adam Stephen and the Cause of American Liberty*, Charlottesville, VA, 1989. A military biography of the Scottish immigrant who made good in Virginia and thrived in the Continental Army until disgraced in the 1777 campaign.
4.291 **Wright**, E., 'A patriot for whom? Benedict Arnold and the loyalists', *History Today*, XXXVI, 1986, 29–35.

(c) SOUTHERN PHASE, 1779–1781

4.292 **Cashin**, E. J., *The King's Ranger. Thomas Brown and the American Revolution on the Southern Frontier*, Athens, GA, 1989. A biography of the foremost Tory irregular in Georgia and how he made a wartime alliance between loyalists and the Creeks and Cherokees.
4.293 **Clodfelter**, M. A., 'Between virtue and necessity. Nathanael Greene and the conduct of civil-military relations in the South, 1780–1782', *Military Affairs*, LII, 1988, 169–175.
4.294 **Ferling**, J. E., (ed.), *The World Turned Upside Down. The American Victory in the War of Independence*, New York, 1988.
4.295 **Frey**, Sylvia R., *Water from the Rock. Black Resistance in a Revolutionary Age*, Princeton, NJ, 1991. Looks at blacks who joined the Loyalist side in the Revolution as a way of striking at slavery, and how the polarized relations between rebellious colonists and imperial authorities actually worked to strengthen slavery.
4.296 **Hoffman**, R., **Tate**, T. W., and **Albert**, P. J., (ed.), *An Uncivil War. The Southern Backcountry During the American Revolution*, Charlottesville, VA, 1985.
4.297 **Kennett**, L. B., *The French Forces in America, 1780–1783*, Westport, CT, 1977.
4.298 **Lennon**, D. R., ' "The graveyard of American commanders". The Continental Army's southern department, 1776–1778', *North Carolina Historical Review*, LXVII, 1990, 133–158.
4.299 **Lumpkin**, H., *From Savannah to Yorktown. The American Revolution in the South*, Columbia, SC, 1981.
4.300 **Massey**, G. DeV., 'The British expedition to Wilmington, January–November, 1781', *North Carolina Historical Review*, LVI, 1989, 387–411.
4.301 **Olwell**, R. A., ' "Domestick enemies". Slavery and political independence in South Carolina, May 1775–March 1776',

Journal of Southern History, LV, 1989, 21–48.

4.302 **Posey**, J. T., ' "The turbulent spirit". A Virginia battalion in the southern campaign of 1782', *Virginia Cavalcade*, XL, 1990, 4–13.

4.303 **Royster**, E., *Light-Horse Harry Lee and the Legacy of the American Revolution*, New York, 1981.

4.304 **Selby**, J. E., *The Revolution in Virginia*, Williamsburg, VA, 1988. Covers the political history of the conflict, as well as some of the military history.

4.305 **Troxler**, Carole Watterson, 'Refuge, resistance, and reward. The southern loyalists' claim on east Florida', *Journal of Southern History*, LV, 1989, 563–596.

4.306 **Zuckerman**, M., 'Thermidor in America. The aftermath of independence in the South', *Prospects*, VIII, 1983, 349–368.

The Constitution and its interpretation

4.307 **Ackerman**, B., *We the People. Foundations*, Cambridge, MA, 1991. First of a three volume constitutional history of the United States, this volume focuses on the 1780s as a time when popular demands forced a radical break with the past.

4.308 **Anastaplo**, G., *The Constitution of 1787. A Commentary*, Baltimore, 1989.

4.309 **Ball**, T., and **Pocock**, J. G. A., (ed.), *Conceptual Change and the Constitution*, Lawrence, KS, 1988. Nine essays about the connections between the political discourse of eighteenth century Americans and the federal constitution of 1787.

4.310 **Barlow**, J. J., **Levy**, L. W., and **Masugi**, K., (ed.), *The American Founding. Essays on the Formation of the Constitution*, New York, 1988.

4.311 **Beeman**, R., **Botein**, S., and **Carter**, E., (ed.), *Beyond Confederation. Origins of the Constitution and American National Identity*, Chapel Hill, NC, 1987.

4.312 **Belz**, H., **Hoffman**, R., and **Albert**, P. J., *To Form a More Perfect Union. The Critical Ideas of the Constitution*, Charlottesville, VA, 1992.

4.313 **Borden**, M., *Jews, Turks, and Infidels*, Chapel Hill, NC, 1984. Looks at the constitutional protections and limitations of non-Christians in America.

4.314 **Cohler**, Anne M., *Montesquieu's Comparative Politics and the Spirit of American Constitutionalism*, Lawrence, KS, 1988. Compares the spirit of the laws with the Constitution and finds a great debt of the framers to Montesquieu.

4.315 **Cronin**, T. E., (ed.), *Inventing the American Presidency*, Lawrence, KS, 1989. An anthology on the debates at the Constitutional Convention about Article II and the role of the Executive.

4.316 **Curry**, T. J., *The First Freedoms. Church and State in America to the Passage of the First Amendment*, New York, 1986.

4.317 **Ely**, J. H., *Democracy and Distrust. A Theory of Judicial Review*, Cambridge, MA, 1980.

4.318 **Foley**, M., *Laws, Men and Machines. Modern American Government and the Appeal of Newtonian Mechanics*, 1990. Links constitutional thought to rational scientific thought at the end of the eighteenth century.

4.319 **Gillespie**, M. A., and **Lienesch**, M., (ed.), *Ratifying the Constitution*, Lawrence, KS, 1989. A state-by-state account of the ratification process.

4.320 **Grinde**, D. A., and **Johansen**, B. E., *Exemplar of Liberty. Native America and the Evolution of Democracy*, Los Angeles, 1991. Argues that much of the federal constitution was lifted outright from the Iroquois Confederacy.

4.321 **Halbrook**, S., *That Every Man Be Armed. The Evolution of a Constitutional Right*, Albuquerque, NM, 1985. A passionate defense of the view that the Second Amendment envisioned individual citizens with arms coming together in defense, rather than a collective right to bear arms only within a militia.

4.322 **Kammen**, M., *Sovereignty and Liberty. Constitutional Discourse in American Culture*, Madison, WI, 1988.

4.323 **Kohn**, R. H., (ed.), *The United States Military Under the Constitution of the United States, 1789–1989*, New York, 1991. Collected essays that evaluate civilian control of military power, and how that control has been affected by constitutional provisions.

4.324 **Levinson**, S., *Constitutional Faith*, Princeton, NJ, 1988. Traces the evolution of the Constitution as a document revered by Americans who may nonetheless disagree with much of its contents.

4.325 **Levy**, L. W., *The Establishment Clause*.

Religion and the First Amendment, New York, 1986.

4.326 **Levy**, L. W., *Original Intent and the Framers' Constitution*, New York, 1988. An argument against modern claims that the Supreme Court can decide constitutional law by divining the "original intent" of the document's framers; instead, the author advocates a doctrine of support for an ever broader expansion of rights and liberties.

4.327 **Levy**, L. W., *Constitutional Opinions. Aspects of the Bill of Rights*, New York, 1985. A collection of essays on the history behind judicial interpretations of the Bill of Rights.

4.328 **Levy**, L. W., *Emergence of a Free Press*, New York, 1985. A reworking of an earlier volume by the leading constitutional historian of the First Amendment.

4.329 **Matson**, Cathy D., and **Onuf**, P. S., *A Union of Interests. Political and Economic Thought in Revolutionary America*, Lawrence, KS, 1990. Argues that the 1780s presented a true crisis to the Revolutionary generation which could only be solved by a stronger federal union.

4.330 **McDonald**, F., and **McDonald**, Ellen, *Requiem. Variations on Eighteenth Century Themes*, Lawrence, KS, 1988. Places the 1787 federal constitution within the context of eighteenth century liberal ideology.

4.331 **McWilliams**, W., and **Gibbons**, M. T., (ed.), *The Federalists, the Antifederalists, and the American Political Tradition*, New York, 1992.

4.332 **Millican**, E., *One United People. The Federalist Papers and the National Idea*, Lexington, KY, 1990.

4.333 **Nedelsky**, Jennifer, *Private Property and the Limits of American Constitutionalism. The Madisonian Framework and its Legacy*, Chicago, 1990. Locates Madison's concern for controlling factions in a republic within his fear that a majority of the population would seek to infringe on private property rights; constitutionalism thus became a very real limit on democracy.

4.334 **Onuf**, P. S., *Statehood and Union. A History of the Northwest Ordinance*, Bloomington, IN, 1987. A volume written for the bicentennial of the most successful and enduring accomplishment of the Confederation Congress.

4.335 **Pacheco**, Josephine F., (ed.), *Antifederalism. The Legacy of George Mason*, Fairfax, VA, 1992.

4.336 **Sandoz**, E., *A Government of Laws. Political Theory, Religion, and the American Founding*, Baton Rouge, LA, 1990. An intellectual history of the Constitution's authors that stresses their religious inheritance as much as their Lockean values.

4.337 **Rakove**, J. N., *Interpreting the Constitution. The Debate over Original Intent*, Boston, 1990.

4.338 **Simmons**, R., (ed.), *The United States Constitution. The First 200 Years*, 1989. An anthology of writings from a University of Birmingham conference that treats both the history of the Constitution and its current status.

4.339 **Smith**, J. A., *Printers and Press Freedom. The Ideology of Early American Journalism*, New York, 1988. Considers the state of the press by the late eighteenth century to have been quite, and thus the First Amendment guarantee simply ratified the status quo.

4.340 **Snowiss**, Sylvia, *Judicial Review and the Law of the Constitution*, New Haven, CT, 1990. Examines John Marshall's role in making the federal judiciary the main interpreter of the meaning of the Constitution.

4.341 **Sosin**, J. M., *The Aristocracy of the Long Robe. The Origins of Judicial Review in the United States*, Westport, CT, 1989.

4.342 **White**, M., *Philosophy, The Federalist, and the Constitution*, New York, 1987. Grounds the arguments of Publius, in the Federalist Papers, in the philosophy of Locke and Hume.

4.343 **Wills**, G., *Explaining America. The Federalist*, Garden City, NY, 1981. Continues his *Inventing America* in linking the political thought of Madison and the other constitutional convention delegates to the Scottish Enlightenment.

5

THE NEW NATION,
1790–1848

GENERAL HISTORIES
AND ANTHOLOGIES

5.1 **Jehlen**, Myra, *American Incarnation. The Individual, the Nation, and the Continent*, Cambridge, MA, 1986. Links the ideas about individualism in the early republic to territorial expansion.

5.2 **Larkin**, J., *The Reshaping of Everyday Life, 1790–1840*, New York, 1988. A portrait of the changes in many aspects of American life wrought by the market revolution of the early nineteenth century.

5.3 **Saum**, L. O., *The Popular Mood of Pre-Civil War America*, Westport, CT, 1980.

5.4 **Wiebe**, R., *The Opening of American Society from the Adoption of the Constitution to the Eve of Disunion*, New York, 1984. An interpretive synthesis about the effects of nationalism, democracy, and capitalism on the American people.

GUIDES TO SOURCES

Primary sources

5.5 **Bartlett**, Elizabeth Ann, (ed.), *Sara Grimke. Letters on the Equality of the Sexes and Other Essays*, New Haven, CT, 1988. A collection of Grimke's unpublished letters that highlights her attempt to find a biblical grounding for gender equality.

5.6 **Blassingame**, J. W., (ed.), *The Frederick Douglass Papers*, New Haven, CT, 1979– . Five volumes in this series have appeared taking Douglass's life up through 1880.

5.7 **Blewett**, Mary H., (ed.), *We Will Rise in Our Might. Workingwomen's Voices from Nineteenth-Century New England*, Ithaca, NY, 1991.

5.8 **Boyd**, J. P., (ed.), *The Papers of Thomas Jefferson*, Princeton, NJ, 1950– . Twenty-five volumes have appeared through 1992 in the longest-running documentary editing project.

5.9 **Brady**, Patricia, (ed.), *George Washington's Beautiful Nelly. The Letters of Eleanor Parke Custis Lewis to Elizabeth Bordley Gibson, 1794–1851*, Columbia, SC, 1991.

5.10 **Chance**, J. E., (ed.), *The Mexican War Journal of Captain Franklin Smith*, Jackson, MS, 1991. An officer in the First Mississippi Volunteers, Smith had much to say about the war and also about the Mexican society he encountered.

5.11 **Crawford**, M. J., and **Kane**, J. D. H., *The Naval War of 1812. A Documentary History*, Washington, DC, 1985.

5.12 **Cullen**, C. T., (ed.), *The Papers of John Marshall*, Chapel Hill, NC, 1974– .

5.13 **DenBoer**, G., (ed.), *Documentary History of the First Federal Elections, 1788–1790*, Madison, WI, 1984.

5.14 **Ferrell**, R. H., (ed.), *Monterrey Is Ours. The Mexican War Letters of Lieutenant Dana, 1845–1847*, Lexington, KY, 1990.

5.15 **Foner**, P. S., (ed.), *The Democratic-

Republican Societies, 1790–1800. A Documentary Sourcebook of Constitutions, Declarations, Addresses, Resolutions, and Toasts, Westport, CT, 1976.

5.16 **Hopkins**, J. F., (ed.), *The Papers of Henry Clay*, Lexington, KY, 1959–1990. Ten volumes in this series that concludes with the final volume covering Clay's 1844 bid for the White House and his actions in the Compromise of 1850.

5.17 **Hutchinson**, W. T., (ed.), *The Papers of James Madison*, Chicago, 1962– . A lengthy series subdivided into Madison's writings outside of government, and his papers as Secretary of State under Jefferson, and then as President.

5.18 **King**, A. J., (ed.), *The Papers of Daniel Webster. Legal Papers*, Hanover, NH, 1989– .

5.19 **Lint**, G. L., (ed.), *The Papers of John Adams*, Cambridge, MA, 1977– .

5.20 **McLaughlin**, J., (ed.), *To His Excellency Thomas Jefferson. Letters to a President*, New York, 1991.

5.21 **McLean**, M. D., (ed.), *Papers Concerning Robertson's Colony in Texas*, Arlington, TX, 1974– . Volumes on the Tennessee settlers who moved to Mexico in the 1820s and were instrumental in the Texas uprising against Mexican authority that led to an independent Texas.

5.22 **Meriwether**, R. L., (ed.), *The Papers of John C. Calhoun*, Columbia, SC, 1959.

5.23 **Middleton**, S., (ed.), *The Black Laws in the Old Northwest. A Documentary History*, Westport, CT, 1992. A collection of statutes and other official papers dealing with free blacks in the states carved out of the post-1785 Northwest Territory.

5.24 **Miller**, Lilian B., (ed.), *The Selected Papers of Charles Wilson Peale and His Family*, New Haven, CT, 1980.

5.25 **Moulton**, G. E., (ed.), *The Papers of Chief John Ross*, Norman, OK, 1985. A two volume set of the papers of the principal chief of the Cherokees before, during, and after the tumultuous removal from the Southeast to present-day Oklahoma.

5.26 **Moulton**, G. E., (ed.), *Journals of the Lewis and Clark Expedition*, Lincoln, NE, 1983–1991. A seven volume set that includes an atlas to accompany the journal notations for the three-year expedition.

5.27 **O'Connell**, B., (ed.), *On Our Own Ground. The Complete Writings of William Apess, A Pequot*, Amherst, MA, 1992.

5.28 **Owsley**, Harriet Chappell, (ed.), *The Papers of Andrew Jackson*, Knoxville, TN, 1980– .

5.29 **Reingold**, N., (ed.), *The Papers of Joseph Henry*, Washington, DC, 1972–1992. A six volume set of the papers of the noted physicist.

5.30 **Ulrich**, Laurel Thatcher, (ed.), *A Midwife's Tale. The Life of Martha Ballard, Based on Her Diary, 1785–1812*, New York, 1990.

5.31 **Weaver**, H. W., (ed.), *Correspondence of James K. Polk*, Nashville, TN, 1969– .

5.32 **West**, Lucy Fisher, (ed.), *The Papers of Martin Van Buren. Guide and Index to General Correspondence and Miscellaneous Documents*, Alexandria, VA, 1989.

5.33 **Wiltse**, C. M., (ed.), *The Papers of Daniel Webster*, Hanover, NH, 1974–1989. A fourteen volume set that includes his speeches, correspondence, and papers from his legal career.

Bibliographies

5.34 **Fredriksen**, F. C., (ed.), *Free Trade and Sailors' Rights. A Bibliography of the War of 1812*, Westport, CT, 1985.

5.35 **Shuffleton**, F., (ed.), *Thomas Jefferson. A Comprehensive Annotated Bibliography of Writings About Him, 1826–1980*, New York, 1983.

5.36 **Smith**, D. L., (ed.), *The War of 1812. An Annotated Bibiliography*, New York, 1985.

5.37 **Tutorow**, N. E., (ed.), *The Mexican-American War. An Annotated Bibliography*, Westport, CT, 1981.

Historiography

5.38 **Cave**, A. A., *Jacksonian Democracy and the Historians*, Westport, CT, 1980.

5.39 **Formisano**, R. P., 'Toward a reorientation of Jacksonian politics: a review of the literature, 1959–1975', *Journal of American History* 1976, LXIII, 42–65. As the title states, "a review of the literature" on the "Age of Jackson".

5.40 **Jentz**, J. B., 'Industrialization and class formation in antebellum America: a review of recent case studies', *Amerikastudien/American Studies*, XXX, 1985, 303–325.

5.41 **Lofaro**, M. A., and **Cummings**, J. (ed.),

Crockett at Two Hundred. New Perspectives on the Man and the Myth, Knoxville, TN, 1989. A collection of essays on the meaning of Davy Crockett for American culture, with more attention paid to the myth than to the facts of his life.

5.42 **Rodgers**, D. T., 'Republicanism: the career of a concept', *Journal of American History*, LXXIX, 1992, 11–38.

5.43 **Rugeley**, T., 'Savage and statesman. Changing historical interpretations of Tecumseh', *Indiana Magazine of History*, LXXXV, 1989, 289–311.

BIOGRAPHY

5.44 **Abzug**, R. H., *Passionate Liberator. Theodore Dwight Weld and the Dilemma of Reform*, New York, 1980. A full-length biography of the life of the abolitionist reformer that finds his conversion experience in the 1820s led him to challenge much of his family upbringing and attempt to bring reform to numerous areas of American life.

5.45 **Andrew**, J. A., III, *From Revivals to Removals. Jeremiah Evarts, the Cherokee Nation, and the Search for the Soul of America*, Athens, GA, 1992. Biography of the Congregational minister who led the popular opposition to Indian Removal.

5.46 **Arrington**, L. J., *Brigham Young. American Moses*, New York, 1985. Explores the personality and talents of the Mormon leader who took many of the faithful to found the settlement in present-day Utah.

5.47 **Bauer**, K. J., *Zachary Taylor. Soldier, Planter, Statesman of the Old Southwest*, Baton Rouge, LA, 1985. A biography of Old Rough and Ready that details the emergence of Taylor's American nationalism through his many years of Army service.

5.48 **Baxter**, M. G., *One and Inseparable. Daniel Webster and the Union*, Cambridge, MA, 1984. An account of Webster's public life that focuses on his political and legal exploits.

5.49 **Bergeron**, P. H., *The Presidency of James K. Polk*, Lawrence, KS, 1987. This exploration of Polk's presidency depicts Polk as moderate in his expansionist goals, but unable to control the complicated demands of sectional party politics.

5.50 **Bremer**, R. G., *Indian Agent and Wilderness Scholar. The Life of Henry Rowe Schoolcraft*, Mount Pleasant, MI, 1987. A biography of the U.S. representative to the Lake Superior region tribes, as well as their ethnographer.

5.51 **Brown**, C. M., *Benjamin Silliman. A Life in the Young Republic*, Princeton, NJ, 1989. A biography of Yale University's first chemistry professor and founder of its medical school; the author locates Silliman in Federalist Connecticut but shows how he exploited his opportunities in Jeffersonian America.

5.52 **Chavez**, T. E., *Manuel Alvarez, 1794–1856. A Southwestern Biography*, Niwot, CO, 1990. A biography of the U. S. representative in Santa Fe before the Mexican War and an important figure in the subsequent military conquest.

5.53 **Clifford**, Deborah Pickman, *Crusader for Freedom. A Life of Lydia Maria Child*, Boston, 1992.

5.54 **Cunningham**, N., *In Pursuit of Reason. The Life of Thomas Jefferson*, Baton Rouge, LA, 1987. A one-volume biography by a leading Jefferson scholar that emphasizes Jefferson's contribution to republican thought.

5.55 **Eckhardt**, Celia Morris, *Fanny Wright. Rebel in America*, Cambridge, MA, 1984. Traces Wright's life and career from a feminist viewpoint, and considers how and why Wright became so isolated in the 1830s and 1840s.

5.56 **Farrell**, J. M., 'John Adams's autobiography: the ciceronian paradigm and the quest for fame', *New England Quarterly*, LXII, 1989, 505–528.

5.57 **Godbold**, E. S., and **Russell**, Mattie U., *Confederate Colonel and Cherokee Chief. The Life of William Holland Thomas*, Knoxville, TN, 1990. A biography of the adopted Cherokee Thomas that places his life against the dramatic backdrop of Indian Removal and the fight to remain in North Carolina.

5.58 **Horsman**, R., *Josiah Nott of Mobile. Southerner, Physician, and Racial Theorist*, Baton Rouge, LA, 1987. A biography of the influential Alabamian who wrote on topics ranging from the causes of yellow fever to human intelligence.

5.59 **Jeffrey**, Julie Roy, *Converting the West. A Biography of Narcissa Whitman*, Norman, OK, 1991. A biography of the nineteenth century missionary who was caught in a cultural conflict between race and gender roles in frontier Oregon.

5.60 **Marks**, Paula Mitchell, *Turn Your Eyes toward Texas. Pioneers Sam and Mary Maverick*, College Station, TX, 1989. A biography of the South Carolinian who relocated to Texas just before the Texas Revolution, and of his wife who together established one of the leading families of San Antonio.

5.61 **Mathews**, Jean V., *Rufus Choate. The Law and Civic Virtue*, Philadelphia, 1980.

5.62 **McCoy**, D., *The Last of the Fathers. James Madison and the Republican Legacy*, New York, 1989. Portrays Madison as a conservative unionist and the last of the Revolutionary generation who lived an active political life for a half century after he helped write the Constitution.

5.63 **McLaughlin**, J., *Jefferson and Monticello. The Biography of a Builder*, New York, 1988.

5.64 **Newmyer**, R. K., *Supreme Court Justice Joseph Story. Statesman of the Old Republic*, Chapel Hill, NC, 1985. A biography that places the New England jurist at the center of the capitalist transformation of the law.

5.65 **Niven**, J., *Martin Van Buren. The Romantic Age of American Politics*, New York, 1983. A thorough life of Van Buren and the political party milieu he helped to build.

5.66 **Niven**, J., *John C. Calhoun and the Price of Union. A Biography*, Baton Rouge, LA, 1988. Part of LSU Press's Southern Biography series, this book finds Calhoun consistent in his politics as defender of southern interests.

5.67 **Remini**, R. V., *Henry Clay. Statesman for the Union*, New York, 1991.

5.68 **Remini**, R. V., *Andrew Jackson and the Course of American Empire, 1767–1821*, New York, 1977. Volume one of a magisterial biography of Jackson that emphasizes his exploits in the War of 1812 and in opening up the South to white settlement.

5.69 **Remini**, R. V., *Andrew Jackson and the Course of American Freedom, 1822–1832*, New York, 1981. A republican interpretation of Jackson's political career, including his first two tries for the White House, that stresses Jackson's belief that the nation had strayed too far from the Revolutionary Era truths.

5.70 **Remini**, R. V., *Andrew Jackson and the Course of American Democracy, 1833–1845*, New York, 1984. The third volume of the biography stresses the lasting ways in which Andrew Jackson and his Democratic Party changed the American political culture from one of elite factionalism to a mass-based party system.

5.71 **Richards**, L. L., *The Life and Times of Congressman John Quincy Adams*, New York, 1986. A biography that focuses on Adams' career in the House of Representatives as the leader of the emerging antislavery group of northerners.

5.72 **Rollins**, R. M., *The Long Journey of Noah Webster*, Philadelphia, 1980.

5.73 **Smith**, E. B., *Francis Preston Blair*, New York, 1980.

5.74 **Stewart**, J. B., *Wendell Phillips. Liberty's Hero*, Baton Rouge, LA, 1986. A biography of the abolitionist leader that places him within the tradition of classical republicanism.

5.75 **Tomes**, Nancy, *A Generous Confidence. Thomas Story Kirkbride and the Art of Asylum-Keeping, 1840–1883*, New York, 1984. A biography of the superintendent of the Pennsylvania Hospital for the Insane for four decades and the influence he wielded in mental health treatment.

5.76 **Vipperman**, C. J., *William Lowndes and the Transition of Southern Politics, 1782–1822*, Chapel Hill, NC, 1989.

DEMOGRAPHY, FAMILY, AND HEALTH

5.77 **Cassedy**, J. H., *Medicine and American Growth, 1800–1860*, Madison, WI, 1986. An inquiry into the habit of statistic-collecting by nineteenth century American physicians and what their data can tell us about the medical and demographic history of the country.

5.78 **Censer**, Jane Turner, *North Carolina Planters and Their Children, 1800–1860*,

Baton Rouge, LA, 1984. Analyzes large slaveholders in 1830 in terms of marriage and childrearing, and finds a modern family type emerged to replace the patriarchy of earlier times.

5.79 **Dwyer**, Ellen, *Homes for the Mad. Life inside Two Nineteenth-Century Asylums*, New Brunswick, NJ, 1987. Analyzes the medical and pyschological regimen in two New York asylums and finds that the routine of the workhouse quickly overshadowed that of the physician.

5.80 **Fox-Genovese**, Elizabeth, *Within the Plantation Household. Black and White Women of the Old South*, Chapel Hill, NC, 1988. Argues that the Old South can best be understood as grand patriarchy as much as a time and region of class or racial hegemony; the great family headed by the male planter worked to limit the lives of women of both colors but produced little in the way of opposition by women.

5.81 **Herman**, B. L., 'Delaware's orphans court valuations and the reconstitution of historic landscapes, 1785–1830', *Dublin Seminar for New England Folklife*, XII, 1987, 121–139.

5.82 **Hoffert**, S. D., *Private Matters. American Attitudes toward Childbearing and Infant Nurture in the Urban North, 1800–1860*, Urbana, IL, 1989.

5.83 **Jackson**, R. H., 'Gentile recruitment and population movements in the San Francisco Bay area missions', *Journal of California and Great Basin Anthropology*, VI, 1984, 225–229.

5.84 **Johnson**, P. E., 'The modernization of Mayo Greenleaf patch: land, family, and marginality in New England, 1766–1818', *New England Quarterly*, LV, 1982, 488–516.

5.85 **Lewis**, Jan, *The Pursuit of Happiness. Family and Values in Jefferson's Virginia*, New York, 1983. Analyzes the letters and diaries of Virginia planters to find that evangelical religion and a relatively declining economy drove them to create a tightly bound emotion-laden family.

5.86 **Linden-Ward**, Blanche, *Silent City on a Hill. Landscapes of Memory and Boston's Mount Auburn Cemetery*, Columbus, OH, 1989.

5.87 **Malone**, Ann Patton, *Sweet Chariot. Slave Family and Household Structure in Nineteenth-Century Louisiana*, Chapel Hill, NC, 1992. A detailed look at three

plantation communities that links the history of the black family to changes in the slave economy and society.

5.88 **McMillen**, Sally G., *Motherhood in the Old South. Pregnancy, Childbirth, and Infant Rearing*, Baton Rouge, LA, 1990.

5.89 **Murphy**, L. R., *Enter the Physician. The Transformation of Domestic Medicine, 1760–1860*, Tuscaloosa, AL, 1991. Based on a reading of advice books that show the slow emergence of a physician-dominated medicine with a subsidiary role for patient self-help.

5.90 **Nissenbaum**, S., *Sex, Diet, and Debility in Jacksonian America. Sylvester Graham and Health Reform*, Westport, CT, 1980.

5.91 **Numbers**, R. L., and **Savitt**, T. L. (ed.), *Science and Medicine in the Old South*, Baton Rouge, LA, 1989.

5.92 **Reinier**, Jacqueline S., 'Rearing the republican child: attitudes and practices in post-revolutionary Philadelphia', *William and Mary Quarterly*, XXXIX, 1982, 150–163.

5.93 **Ryan**, Mary P., *Cradle of the Middle Class. The Family in Oneida County, New York, 1790–1865*, New York, 1981.

5.94 **Spurlock**, J. C., *Free Love. Marriage and Middle-Class Radicalism in America, 1825–1860*, New York, 1988.

SOCIAL RELATIONS

Class and community

5.95 **Blackmar**, Elizabeth, *Manhattan for Rent, 1785–1850*, Ithaca, NY, 1989. Examines the emergence of a real estate market in New York City and how it became an arena of social conflict.

5.96 **Burton**, O. V., *In My Father's House are Many Mansions. Family and Community in Edgefield, South Carolina*, Chapel Hill, NC, 1985.

5.97 **Cecil-Fronsman**, B., *Common Whites. Class and Culture in Antebellum North Carolina*, Lexington, KY, 1992. Finds the non-slaveholding whites constituted a separate class from planters but never organized an effective opposition.

5.98 **Gerber**, D. A., *The Making of an American Pluralism. Buffalo, New York, 1825–1860*, Urbana, IL, 1989. An analysis of the overlapping identities of class, religion, ethnicity, and group, and how political parties in the mid-nineteenth century worked to bring different groups together.

5.99 **Gough**, R. J., 'Officering the American Army, 1798', *William and Mary Quarterly*, XLIII, 1986, 460–471.

5.100 **Hahn**, S., and **Prude**, J., *The Countryside in the Age of Capitalist Transformation. Essays in the Social History of Rural America*, Chapel Hill, NC, 1985. A set of essays that apply many of the approaches of E. P. Thompson to the study of class relations in rural America.

5.101 **Hebert**, Catherine, 'Demise of the American dream: the French experience of American life in the age of the French Revolution', *Social History*, XXIII, 1990, 219–248.

5.102 **Johns**, Elizabeth, *American Genre Painting. The Politics of Everyday Life*, New Haven, CT, 1991. Links the social history of the antebellum years with the types of canvasses painted.

5.103 **Kulikoff**, A., *The Agrarian Origins of American Capitalism*, Charlottesville, VA, 1992. A set of essays on the struggle over rights and customs in the countryside and how market forces overcame tradition.

5.104 **Mandler**, P., (ed.), *The Uses of Charity. The Poor on Relief in the Nineteenth Century Metropolis*, Philadelphia, 1990. A collection of essays about public policy toward the poor in Europe and the U.S.

5.105 **Pease**, W. H., and **Pease**, Jane H., *The Web of Progress. Private Values and Public Styles in Boston and Charleston, 1828–1843*, New York, 1985. Contrasts the individualism of Boston with the communitarianism of antebellum Charleston.

5.106 **Story**, R., *The Forging of an Aristocracy. Harvard & the Boston Upper Class, 1800–1870*, Middletown, CT, 1980.

Gender relations

5.107 **Banta**, Martha, *Imaging American Women. Idea and Ideals in Cultural History*, New York, 1987.

5.108 **Chambers-Schiller**, Lee Virginia, *Liberty, a Better Husband. Single Women in America. The Generations of 1780–1840*, New Haven, CT, 1984. Argues that a sample of one hundred never-married women made a self-conscious choice to stay single so that they could pursue other interests.

5.109 **Conrad**, Susan Avery Phinney, *Perish the Thought. Intellectual Women in Romantic America, 1830–1860*, New York, 1976.

5.110 **Grimshaw**, Patricia, *Paths of Duty. American Missionary Women in Nineteenth Century Hawaii*, Honolulu, 1989.

5.111 **Jensen**, Joan M., 'Not only ours but others: The Quaker teaching daughters of the Mid-Atlantic, 1790–1850', *History of Education Quarterly*, XXIV, 1984, 3–19.

5.112 **Kasson**, J. F., *Rudeness and Civility. Manners in Nineteenth Century America*, New York, 1990. Studies nineteenth century etiquette books and finds an increase in prescriptive advice and, by implication, an improvement in actual behavior.

5.113 **Kasson**, Joy S., *Marble Queens and Captives. Women in Nineteenth Century American Sculpture*, New Haven, CT, 1990.

5.114 **Kornfeld**, Eve, 'Women in post-revolutionary American culture: Susanna Haswell Rowson's American career, 1792–1824', *Journal of American Culture*, VI, 1983, 56–62.

5.115 **Leach**, W., *True Love and Perfect Union. The Feminist Reform of Sex and Society*, New York, 1980. An intellectual history of nineteenth century feminism that ties the leaders of the movement to other reform movements of the era.

5.116 **Leverenz**, D., *Manhood and the American Renaissance*, Ithaca, NY, 1989. Reinterprets leading literary figures, especially Melville and Hawthorne, as part of a struggle for the definition of masculinity.

5.117 **McLaurin**, M. A., *Celia. A Slave*, Athens, GA, 1991. Uses a Missouri court case where a slave was tried and hanged for murdering her owner; the facts of the case bring out the sexual exploitation of slave women by their masters.

5.118 **Nagel**, P. C., *The Adams Women. Abigail and Louisa Adams, Their Sisters and Daughters*, New York, 1987.

5.119 **Pease**, Jane H., and **Pease**, W. H., *Ladies, Women and Wenches. Choice and Constraint in Antebellum Charleston & Boston*, Chapel Hill, NC, 1990.

5.120 **Premo**, Terri L., *Winter Friends. Women*

Growing Old in the New Republic,
1785–1835, Urbana, IL, 1990.

5.121 **Stansell**, Christine, *City of Women. Sex*
and Class in New York, 1789–1860, New
York, 1986.

5.122 **Zwiep**, Mary, *Pilgrim Path. The First*
Company of Women Missionaries to Hawaii,
Madison, WI, 1991.

Education

5.123 **Carter**, B. K., and **Kobylka**, J. F., 'The IC
Community: education, leadership, and
participation in James Madison's
thought', *Review of Politics,* LII, 1990,
32–63.

5.124 **Cohen**, Patricia Cline, *A Calculating*
People. The Spread of Numeracy in Early
America, Chicago, 1982. Links the spread
of widespread popular facility with
numbers and counting to the politics of
what was counted.

5.125 **Dolan**, J. P., 'Catholic education in the
early republic', *History of Education*
Quarterly, XXI, 1981, 205–211.

5.126 **Gilmore**, W. J., *Reading Becomes a*
Necessity of Life. Material Culture and
Cultural Life in Rural New England,
1780–1835, Knoxville, TN, 1989. Traces
the impact of commercial capitalism on
southern Vermont and finds that it
depended upon a system of mass literacy
and mass communications.

5.127 **Herbst**, J., 'American higher education in
the age of the college', *History of*
Universities, VII, 1988, 37–59.

5.128 **Kornfeld**, Eve, ' "Republican machines"
or pestalozzian bildung? Two visions of
moral education in the early republic',
Canadian Review of American Studies, XX,
1989, 157–172.

5.129 **Lieberman**, C., 'The constitutional and
political bases of federal aid to higher
education, 1787–1862', *International Social*
Science Review, LXIII, 1988, 3–13.

5.130 **Peeler**, D. P., 'Thomas Jefferson's nursery
of republican patriots: the University of
Virginia', *Journal of Church and State,*
XXVIII, 1986, 79–93.

5.131 **Simpson**, D., *The Politics of American*
English, 1776–1850, New York, 1986.
Uses the Gramscian notion of hegemony to
explain the emergence of a distinctly
bourgeois American language in the early
republic.

5.132 **Tyack**, D., and **Hansot**, Elisabeth,
Learning Together. A History of Coeducation
in American Schools, New Haven, CT,
1990. Examines the paradox of nineteenth
century coeducation in the public schools
at the same time that much of the rest of
society was becoming gender-segregated;
the cost-effectiveness of coeducation was
one of its principal strengths.

Recreation, entertainment, and sport

5.133 **Click**, Patricia C., *The Spirit of the Times.*
Amusements in Nineteenth Century
Baltimore, Norfolk, and Richmond,
Charlottesville, VA, 1989.

5.134 **Crouthamel**, J. L., *Bennett's* New York
Herald *and the Rise of the Popular Press,*
Syracuse, NY, 1989. A history of the
leading Democratic paper of New York
City and its influence on politics and
journalism history.

5.135 **Kirsch**, G. B., *The Creation of American*
Team Sports. Baseball and Cricket,
1838–1872, Urbana, IL, 1989.

5.136 **McKinsey**, Elizabeth R., *Niagara Falls.*
Icon of the American Sublime, New York,
1985. A review of how writers and artists
viewed Niagara Falls.

5.137 **Mulvey**, C., *Transatlantic Manners. Social*
Patterns in Nineteenth-Century Anglo-
American Travel Literature, New York,
1990.

5.138 **Stefanelli**, Maria Anita, 'Anglo-American
interaction: writings of the new nation and
their reception in British periodicals',
Revue Francaise d'Etudes Americaines, XII,
1987, 363–375.

Crime and punishment

5.139 **Carrico**, R. L., 'Spanish crime and
punishment. The Native American
experience in colonial San Diego,
1769–1830', *Western Legal History,* III,
1990, 21–33.

5.140 **Chapin**, B., 'Felony law reform in the early
republic', *Pennsylvania Magazine of*
History and Biography, CXIII, 1989,
163–183.

5.141 **Masur**, L., *Rites of Execution. Capital*
Punishment and the Transformation of

American Culture, 1776–1865, New York, 1989. Traces the changing attitudes toward capital punishment, especially the movement away from public executions.

RELIGION, BELIEFS, IDEAS, AND CULTURE

5.143 **Bercovitch**, S., 'Representing revolution. The example of Hester Prynne', *European Contributions to American Studies*, XIV, 1988, 29–51.

5.144 **Ferguson**, R. A., *Law and Letters in American Culture*, Cambridge, MA, 1984. Examines the writings of lawyers as a form of literature in the early republic.

5.145 **Goodman**, R. B., *American Philosophy and the Romantic Tradition*, New York, 1991.

5.146 **Kupke**, R. J., (ed.), *American Catholic Preaching and Piety in the Time of John Carroll*, Lanham, MD, 1991.

5.147 **Lawson-Peebles**, R., *Landscape and Written Expression in Revolutionary America. The World Turned Upside Down*, New York, 1988. Analyzes the writings and art of leading Americans to show that they retained a European perspective on the landscape of the New World, even after formal political independence.

The Second Great Awakening

5.148 **Barkun**, M., *Crucible of the Millennium. The Burned-Over District of New York in the 1840s*, Syracuse, NY, 1986. An analysis of the region in New York State that produced so many social reform movements in the Second Great Awakening.

5.149 **Bilhartz**, T. D., *Urban Religion and the Second Great Awakening. Church and Society in Early National Baltimore*, Rutherford, NY, 1986.

5.150 **Conkin**, P. K., *Cane Ridge. America's Pentecost*, Madison, WI, 1990. An anatomy of a nineteenth century revival that is traced back to its Scots Presbyterian roots.

5.151 **Cray**, R. E., 'Memorialization and enshrinement. George Whitefield and popular religious culture, 1770–1850', *Journal of the Early Republic*, X, 1990, 339–361.

5.152 **Davis**, H., *Joshua Leavitt. Evangelical Abolitionist*, Baton Rouge, LA, 1990. Places the New Yorker and his abolitionism of the 1830s within the context of evangelism and an otherwise socially conservative outlook.

5.153 **Fraser**, J. W., *Pedagogue for God's Kingdom. Lyman Beecher and the Second Great Awakening*, Lanham, MD, 1985.

5.154 **Hardman**, K. J., *Charles Grandison Finney, 1792–1875. Revivalist and Reformer*, Syracuse, NY, 1987. Ties Finney's life to the theological and intellectual history of the Second Great Awakening that Finney led.

5.155 **Hatch**, N. O., *The Democratization of American Christianity*, New Haven, CT, 1989. A new view of the Second Great Awakening that argues the popularization of religion preceded other changes in society and politics.

5.156 **Howard**, V. B., *Conscience and Slavery. The Evangelistic Calvinist Domestic Missions, 1837–1861*, Kent, OH, 1990. Focuses on the missionary work of the Congregationalists and Presbyterians against slavery, and maintains that the moral impulse to antislavery was the key to the origins of the Civil War.

5.157 **Johnson**, C. D., *Islands of Holiness. Rural Religion in Upstate New York, 1790–1860*, Ithaca, NY, 1990. A quantitative analysis of the various denominations of Cortland County, New York and how the Second Great Awakening transformed worship and religion.

5.158 **Johnson**, P. E., *A Shopkeeper's Millennium. Society and Revivals in Rochester, New York, 1815–1837*, New York, 1978.

5.159 **Loveland**, Anne C., *Southern Evangelicals and the Social Order, 1800–1860*, Baton Rouge, LA, 1980. Distinguishes southern clergy in the Second Great Awakening from their northern counterparts by the strict concentration of southerners on the immediate task of saving souls and a related unwillingness to engage in reform movements.

5.160 **Roth**, R. A., *The Democratic Dilemma. Religion, Reform, and the Social Order in the Connecticut River Valley of Vermont, 1791–1850*, New York, 1987. Examines how the stress of commercial growth and population change was salved to some extent by the revivals of the Second Great Awakening.

5.161 **Stein**, S. J., *The Shaker Experience in America. A History of the United Society of Believers*, New Haven, CT, 1992. An account of American adherents of the Shakers with a treatment of their subsequent decline.

5.162 **Wyatt-Brown**, B., *Yankee Saints and Southern Sinners*, Baton Rouge, LA, 1985. A collection of essays on both abolitionists and proslavery advocates.

The culture of reform

5.163 **Boylan**, Anne M., *Sunday School. The Formation of an American Institution, 1790–1880*, New Haven, CT, 1988.

5.164 **Brumberg**, Joan Jacobs, *Mission for Life. The Story of the Family of Adoniram Judson, the Dramatic Events of the First American Foreign Mission, and the Course of Evangelical Religion in the Nineteenth Century*, New York, 1980. Studies two generations of the Judson family of domestic and overseas missionaries, and concentrates on the role of the three wives of Adoniram Judson in breaking down notions of separate spheres for men and women.

5.165 **Cayleff**, Susan E., *Wash and Be Healed. The Water-Cure Movement and Women's Health*, Philadelphia, 1987.

5.166 **Cayton**, Mary Kupiec, *Emerson's Emergence. Self and Society in the Transformation of New England, 1800–1845*, Chapel Hill, NC, 1989. Locates Emerson's change in thought from communitarianism to individualism in the changes taking place in Massachusetts Unitarianism, and shows that these changes were linked to larger changes in the social order.

5.167 **Dannenbaum**, J., *Drink and Disorder. Temperance Reform in Cincinnati from the Washingtonian Revival to the WCTU*, Urbana, IL, 1984. An exploration of working-class temperance.

5.168 **Donegan**, Jane B., *'Hydropathic Highway to Health'. Women and Water Cure in Antebellum America*, New York, 1986.

5.169 **Foster**, L., *Women, Family, and Utopia. Communal Experiments of the Shakers, the Oneida Community, and the Mormons*, Syracuse, NY, 1991.

5.170 **Goodman**, P., *Towards a Christian Republic. Antimasonry and the Great Transition in New England, 1826–1836*, New York, 1988. An explanation of the politics and culture of anti-masonry that emphasizes the ways in which the capitalist transformation of urban and rural New England unsettled many people and set them looking for conspiracies that would make sense of their changed world.

5.171 **Gougeon**, L., *Virtue's Hero. Emerson, Antislavery, and Reform*, Athens, GA, 1990.

5.172 **Guarneri**, C. J., *The Utopian Alternative. Fourierism in Nineteenth Century America*, Ithaca, NY, 1991. A sympathetic account of how American reformers used Charles Fourier's ideas to build communities that were self-consciously critical of the emerging American free labor ideology of the 1840s.

5.173 **Hampel**, R. L., *Temperance and Prohibition in Massachusetts, 1813–1852*, Ann Arbor, MI, 1982. Examines the ways that prohibitionists tried to influence others to follow their example and explores how the movement expanded as a result of a growth in evangelical religion.

5.174 **Kolmerten**, Carol A., *Women in Utopia. The Ideology of Gender in the American Owenite Communities*, Bloomington, IN, 1990.

5.175 **Miller**, C. A., *Jefferson and Nature. An Interpretation*, Baltimore, 1988. An intellectual history of the influences of Locke and Bacon on Jefferson's thought.

5.176 **Tyrrell**, I., *Sobering Up. From Temperance to Prohibtion in Antebellum America, 1800–1860*, Westport, CT, 1979. Traces the temperance movement to evangelicals in the 1820s who sought uplift more than social control, and then continues the story of how working-class people embraced temperance in the 1840s, and the movement for state-based prohibition in the 1850s.

5.177 **Walters**, R. E., *American Reformers, 1815–1860*, New York, 1978.

5.178 **Wright**, C. E., (ed.), *American Unitarianism, 1805–1865*, Boston, 1989. A collection of essays that employs social history methods to understand liberal religion.

5.179 **Wright**, C. E., *The Transformation of*

Charity in Postrevolutionary New England, Boston, 1992.

5.180 **Ziegler**, V. H., *The Advocates of Peace in Antebellum America*, Bloomington, IN, 1992.

Republicanism and liberalism

5.181 **Appleby**, Joyce, *Capitalism and a New Social Order. The Republican Vision of the 1790s*, New York, 1984. .

5.182 **Boesche**, R., *The Strange Liberalism of Alexis de Tocqueville*, Ithaca, NY, 1987.

5.183 **Cayton**, A. R. L., *The Frontier Republic. Ideology and Politics in the Ohio Country, 1780–1825*, Kent, OH, 1986. A political history of the early settlements in Ohio with an emphasis on the continuing tension between republicanism and liberalism in a mobile society.

5.184 **Kloppenberg**, J. T., 'The virtues of liberalism: Christianity, republicanism, and ethics in early American political discourse', *Journal of American History*, LXXIV, 1987, 9–33.

5.185 **Lamberti**, J.-C., *Tocqueville and the Two Democracies*, Cambridge, MA, 1989.

5.186 **Lienesch**, M., *New Order of the Ages. Time, the Constitution, and the Making of Modern American Political Thought*, Princeton, NJ, 1988. A work that argues for a continuation of a mix of liberal and classical republican ideas that extended not just into the nineteenth century but up to the present.

5.187 **Nelson**, J. R., *Liberty and Property. Political Economy and Policymaking in the New Nation, 1789–1812*, Baltimore, 1987.

5.188 **Wilson**, D. A., *Paine and Cobbett. The Transatlantic Connection*, Kingston, ONT, 1988.

The Mormons

5.189 **Allen**, J. B., *Trials of a Discipleship. The Story of William Clayton, a Mormon*, Urbana, IL, 1987. Traces Clayton's life in the nineteenth century from Lancashire to Utah, and how he led a Mormon life with four wives and thirty-three children.

5.190 **Barlow**, P. L., *Mormons and the Bible. The Place of the Latter-Day Saints in American Religion*, New York, 1991.

5.191 **Beecher**, Maureen Ursenbach, and **Anderson**, Lavina Fielding, (ed.), *Sisters in Spirit. Mormon Women in Historical and Cultural Perspective*, Urbana, IL, 1987.

5.192 **Bennett**, R. E., *Mormons at the Missouri, 1846–1852. 'And Should We Die'*, Norman, OK, 1987.

5.193 **Bringhurst**, N. G., *Brigham Young and the Expanding American Frontier*, Boston, 1986.

5.194 **Bushman**, R. L., *Joseph Smith and the Beginnings of Mormonism*, Urbana, IL, 1984. A biography of the prophet of the Latter Day Saints, written from the Mormon perspective by a Church member and distinguished social historian.

5.195 **Firmage**, E. B., and **Mangrum**, R. C., *Zion in the Courts. A Legal History of the Church of Jesus Christ of Latter-Day Saints, 1830–1900*, Urbana, IL, 1988. Especially strong in its analysis of the Mormons' residence at Nauvoo, Illinois and their problems with the courts.

5.196 **Hansen**, K. J., *Mormonism and the American Experience*, Chicago, 1981.

5.197 **Hardy**, B. C., *Solemn Covenant. The Mormon Polygamous Passage*, Urbana, IL, 1992.

5.198 **Hill**, M. S., *Quest for Refuge. The Mormon Flight from American Pluralism*, Salt Lake City, UT, 1989. Looks at Mormon history up through the Nauvoo settlement in the mid-1840s and finds a persistent theme within Mormonism of hostility to outsiders, which in turn was more than reciprocated by non-Mormons.

5.199 **LeSueuer**, S. C., *The 1838 Mormon War in Missouri*, Columbia, MO, 1987.

5.200 **Moorman**, D. R., *Camp Floyd and the Mormons. The Utah War*, Salt Lake City, UT, 1992.

5.201 **Shipps**, Jan, *Mormonism. The Story of a New Religious Tradition*, Urbana, IL, 1985. Analyzes the founding and propagation of the Latter Day Saints as a separate religion comparable to the ancient Hebrews and Christians.

5.202 **Van Noord**, R., *King of Beaver Island. The Life and Assassination of James Jesse Strang*, Urbana, IL, 1988. A biography of one of Joseph Smith's Mormon followers who established a rival church to the Utah branch in Michigan, and was ultimately killed by his own followers.

5.203 **Winn**, K. H., *Exiles in a Land of Liberty. Mormons in America, 1830–1846*, Chapel Hill, NC, 1989.

Proslavery v. antislavery

5.204 **Fladeland**, Betty, *Abolitionists and Working-Class Problems in the Age of Industrialization*, Baton Rouge, LA, 1984. Considers the tensions in Anglo-American abolitionism between devotion to anti-slavery and capitalism.

5.205 **Genovese**, E. D., *The Slaveholders' Dilemma. Freedom and Progress in Southern Conservative Thought, 1820–1860*, Columbia, SC, 1992.

5.206 **Gerteis**, L. S., *Morality and Utility in American Antislavery Reform*, Chapel Hill, NC, 1987. Links the emergence of a reforming abolitionist movement in the 1830s to new doctrines in political economy and argues that the two came together in an intellectual and political sense before the Civil War, and that this ideological underpinning helps explain why many northerners abandoned the freedmen after the war.

5.207 **Greenberg**, K. S., *Masters and Statesmen. The Political Culture of American Slavery*, Baltimore, 1985. Connects the dialectics of master-slave relations with the republican legacy of a fear of tyranny and power in explaining the peculiar politics of the Old South.

5.208 **Horsman**, R., *Race and Manifest Destiny. The Origins of American Racial Anglo-Saxonism*, Cambridge, MA, 1981.

5.209 **Oakes**, J., *The Ruling Race. A History of American Slaveholders*, New York, 1982.

5.210 **Oakes**, J., *Slavery and Freedom. An Interpretation of the Old South*, New York, 1990. Finds southern slave society to be a hybrid between liberal capitalism and pre-bourgeois paternalism, in contrast to Eugene Genovese.

5.211 **Perry**, L., and **Fellman**, M., (ed.), *Antislavery Reconsidered. New Perspectives on the Abolitionists*, Baton Rouge, LA, 1979.

5.212 **Saxton**, A., *The Rise and Fall of the White Republic. Class, Politics and Mass Culture in Nineteenth Century America*, New York, 1990. Plays off ideas of racial solidarity among whites and their simultaneous commitment to democracy and capitalism.

5.213 **Stowe**, S. M., *Intimacy and Power in the Old South. Ritual in the Lives of the Planters*, Baltimore, 1987. A careful examination of the inner meaning of the correspondence generated by slaveholders through an examination of how men and women encountered honor, coming of age and courtship and marriage.

5.214 **Tushnet**, M., *The American Law of Slavery, 1810–1860. Considerations of Humanity and Interest*, Princeton, NJ, 1981.

5.215 **Walther**, E. H., *The Fire-Eaters*, Baton Rouge, LA, 1992.

5.216 **Wyatt-Brown**, B., *Southern Honor. Ethics and Behavior in the Old South*, New York, 1982. An investigation of the psychology of the master class.

5.217 **Wyatt-Brown**, B., 'God and honor in the Old South', *Southern Review*, XXV, 1989 283–296.

WORK AND ENTERPRISE

5.219 **Clark**, C., *The Roots of Rural Capitalism. Western Massachusetts, 1780–1860*, Ithaca NY, 1990. Uses the Connecticut Valley as test case to examine the spread of market relations, wage labor, interest-bearing credit, and other forms of modern capitalism in rural areas.

5.220 **Conkin**, P. K., *Prophets of Prosperity. America's First Political Economists*, Bloomington, IN, 1980.

5.221 **Gawalt**, G. W., *The Promise of Power. The Emergence of the Legal Profession in Massachusetts, 1760–1840*, Westport, CT, 1979.

5.222 **Gibson**, J. R., *Otter Skins, Boston Ships, and China Goods. The Maritime Fur Trade of the Northwest Coast, 1785–1841*, Seattle WA, 1992.

5.223 **Glickstein**, J. A., *Concepts of Free Labor in Antebellum America*, New Haven, CT, 1991.

5.224 **Hardeman**, N. P., *Shucks, Shocks, and Hominy Blocks. Corn as a Way of Life in Pioneer America*, Baton Rouge, LA, 1981.

5.225 **Jensen**, Joan M., 'Butter making and economic development in mid-Atlantic America from 1750 to 1850', *Signs*, XIII, 1988, 813–829.

5.226 **LaCroix**, S. J., and **Roumasset**, J., 'An economic theory of political change in premissionary Hawaii', *Explorations in Economic History*, XXI, 1984, 151–168.

5.227 **Langum**, D. J., *Law and Community on the Mexican California Frontier. Anglo-American Expatriates and the Clash of Legal Traditions, 1821–1846*, Norman, OK, 1987.

5.228 **Lindstrom**, Diane, *Economic Development in the Philadelphia Region, 1810–1850*, New York, 1978. Shows how the development of a system of transport improvements led to a surge in local trade between Philadelphia and its back country.

5.229 **McCoy**, D., *The Elusive Republic. Political Economy in Jeffersonian America*, Chapel Hill, NC, 1980.

5.230 **Moore**, J. H., *The Emergence of the Cotton Kingdom in the Old Southwest. Mississippi, 1770–1860*, Baton Rouge, LA, 1988.

5.231 **Sellers**, C., *The Market Revolution. Jacksonian America, 1815–1846*, New York, 1991. An interpretation that stresses the revolutionary aspects of the spread of market relations to many areas of American life.

5.232 **Shaw**, R. E., *Canals for A Nation. The Canal Era in the United States, 1790–1860*, Lexington, KY, 1990. A survey of the state level enterprises that were critical in the Transportation Revolution.

5.233 **Soltow**, L., *Distribution of Wealth and Income in the United States in 1798*, Pittsburgh, 1989. Uses special tax records from the year 1798 to prepare wealth and income estimates; the author maintains that the wealth distribution in the early republic was highly uneven and little different than that at the time of the Civil War.

5.234 **Werner**, W., and **Smith**, S. T., *Wall Street*, New York, 1991. A history of the formation of the early capital market for securities.

The American Industrial Revolution

5.235 **Clark**, Jennifer, 'The American image of technology from the Revolution to 1840', *American Quarterly*, XXXIX, 1987, 431–449.

5.236 **Cochran**, T. C., *Frontiers of Change. Early Industrialization in America*, New York, 1981.

5.237 **Dalzell**, R. F., *Enterprising Elite. The Boston Associates and the World They Made*, Cambridge, MA, 1987. Combines business history of the origins of the mechanized

textile industry with the social history of the formation of a distinct upper class within a democracy.

5.238 **Dawley**, A., *Class and Community. The Industrial Revolution in Lynn*, Cambridge, MA, 1976. An account of the transformation of shoemaking from handicraft to factory enterprise.

5.239 **Hawke**, D. F., *Nuts and Bolts of the Past. A History of American Technology, 1776–1860*, New York, 1988.

5.240 **Hindle**, B., *Engines of Change. The American Industrial Revolution, 1790–1860*, Washington, DC, 1986.

5.241 **Hoke**, D. R., *Ingenious Yankees. The Rise of the American System of Manufactures in the Private Sector*, New York, 1990.

5.242 **Mohanty**, Gail Fowler, 'Experimentation in textile technology, 1788–1790, and its impact on handloom weaving and weavers in Rhode Island', *Technology and Culture*, XXIX, 1988, 1–31.

5.243 **Scranton**, P., *Proprietary Capitalism. The Textile Manufacture at Philadelphia, 1800–1885*, New York, 1984. Examines how the small textile firms of the Philadelphia region came to specialize in particular domestic markets and flourish in the face of competition from their larger New England rivals.

5.244 **Steinberg**, T., *Nature Incorporated. Industrialization and the Waters of New England*, New York, 1991. An environmental history of the river systems that provided power to the new textile manufacturing establishments.

5.245 **Tucker**, Barbara M., *Samuel Slater and the Origins of the American Textile Industry, 1790–1860*, Ithaca, NY, 1984. An examination of how Slater devised factory production in textiles around New England values, including a deference to patriarchal control of families.

5.246 **Zonderman**, D. A., *Aspirations and Anxieties. New England Workers and the Mechanized Factory System, 1815–1850*, New York, 1992.

The new working class

5.247 **Boydston**, Jeanne, *Home and Work. Housework, Wages, and the Ideology of Labor in the Early Republic*, New York, 1990. Attempts to trace the ideological change in women's status as laborers from productive partner to domestic dependent, and then estimates the actual impact of women's labor on the newly emerging market economy.

5.248 **Brody**, D., 'Time and work during early American industrialism', *Labor History*, XXX, 1989.

5.249 **Cohen**, I., 'Workers' control in the cotton industry: A comparative study of British and American mule spinning', *Labor History*, XXVI, 1985, 53–85.

5.250 **Dublin**, T., *Women at Work. The Transformation of Work and Community in Lowell, Massachusetts, 1826–1860*, New York, 1979.

5.251 **Jones**, D. P., *The Economic and Social Transformation of Rural Rhode Island, 1780–1850*, Boston, 1992. Traces the coming of market relations to the back country of Rhode Island and the subsequent changes in society and religion.

5.252 **Laurie**, B., *Working People of Philadelphia, 1800–1850*. Philadelphia, 1980.

5.253 **Levine**, B., *The Spirit of 1848. German Immigrants, Labor Conflict, and the Coming of the Civil War*, Urbana, IL, 1992.

5.254 **Murphy**, Teresa Anne, *Ten Hours' Labor. Religion, Reform, and Gender in Early New England*, Ithaca, NY, 1992.

5.255 **Prude**, J., *The Coming of Industrial Order. Town and Factory Life in Rural Massachusetts, 1810–1860*, New York, 1983. A study of the textile industry that appeared in Worcester County, especially the mills established by Samuel Slater that sought to merge enterprise with patriarchal family attitudes.

5.256 **Rorabaugh**, W. J., *The Craft Apprentice. From Franklin to the Machine Age in America*, New York, 1986. Connects republican ideology to the downfall of the master–apprentice system and also to the degradation of skills brought on by mechanization.

5.257 **Schlereth**, T. J. 'The New York artisan in the early republic. A portrait from graphic evidence', *Material Culture*, XXI, 1989, 1–31.

5.258 **Tomlins**, C. L., *Law, Labor, and Ideology in the Early American Republic*, New York, 1993.

5.259 **Wilentz**, S., *Chants Democratic. New York City and the Rise of the American Working Class, 1788–1850*, New York, 1984. Examines the origins of a New York City working class out of the diverse trades and small manufactories.

RACE AND ETHNIC IDENTITY

African-Americans

5.260 **Abrams**, R. D., *Singing the Master. The Emergence of African-American Culture in the Plantation South*, New York, 1992.

5.261 **Aptheker**, H., *Abolitionism. A Revolutionary Movement*, Boston, 1989. An account by a practioner of six decades of historical writing about the revolutionary class and race ideas of the abolitionists.

5.262 **Bolster**, W. J., ' "To Feel like a Man." Black seamen in the Northern states, 1800–1860', *Journal of American History*, LXXVI, 1990, 1173–1199. An investigation of the world of black merchant marinemen; finds that a greater degree of tolerance and freedom was available to free black men at sea than on land.

5.263 **Cornelius**, Janet Duitsman, *'When I Can Read My Title Clear'. Literacy, Slavery, and Religion in the Antebellum South*, Columbia, SC, 1991. Shows that the Old South had a substantial number of literate slaves, and that the Protestant imperative of worshippers reading the Bible often overrode concerns about security for masters.

5.264 **Creel**, Margaret Washington, *'A Peculiar People'. Slave Religion and Community-Culture Among the Gullahs*, New York, 1988. Considers the extent to which an African-shaped Christianity emerged among the Low Country slaves, and how they used it as a form of resistance to slavery.

5.265 **Dillon**, M. L., *Slavery Attacked. Southern Slaves and their Allies, 1619–1865*, Baton Rouge, LA, 1990. Chronicles the opponents of slavery, white and black, with a focus on nineteenth century abolitionists.

5.266 **Hurt**, R. D., *Agriculture and Slavery in Missouri's Little Dixie*, Columbia, MO, 1992.

5.267 **Johnson**, M. P., 'Runaway slaves and the slave communities in South Carolina, 1799 to 1830', *William and Mary Quarterly*, XXXVIII, 1981, 418–441.

5.268 **Jones**, N. T., *Born a Child of Freedom, Yet a Slave. Mechanisms of Control and Strategies of Resistance in Antebellum South Carolina*, Hanover, NH, 1990. Denies the effectiveness of planter control or planter hegemony on the plantation, instead finding that slavery was a constant struggle between master and slave.

5.269 **Mills**, G. B., 'Miscegenation and the free Negro in antebellum "anglo" Alabama. A reexamination of southern race relations', *Journal of American History*, LXVIII, 1981, 16–34.

5.270 **Schwartz**, P., *Twice Condemned. Slaves and the Criminal Laws of Virginia, 1705–1865*, Baton Rouge, LA, 1988. A study of over 4,000 trial cases involving Virginia slaves that finds the slave code was ameliorated in line with other reforms of the criminal law.

5.271 **Slaughter**, T. P., *Bloody Dawn. The Christiana Riot and Racial Violence in the Antebellum North*, New York, 1991. An account of the federal investigation of the aftermath to an armed resistance to the return of runaway slaves from Maryland hiding out in Christiana, Pennsylvania.

5.272 **Stuckey**, S., *Slave Culture. Nationalist Theory and the Foundations of Black America*, New York, 1987.

5.273 **Winch**, Julie, *Philadelphia's Black Elite. Activism, Accommodation, and the Struggle for Autonomy, 1787–1848*, Philadelphia, 1988.

5.274 **Wyatt-Brown**, B., 'The mask of obedience. Male slave psychology in the old South', *American Historical Review*, XCIII, 1988, 1228–1252. An application of psychological models to the analysis of slave personality that updates the older Elkins thesis about a "Sambo" type personality.

Native Americans

5.275 **Calloway**, C. G., *Crown and Calumet. British-Indian Relations, 1783–1815*, Norman, OK, 1987. Useful for studying the continuing commercial and political relations between the British and tribes formally within U.S. boundaries.

5.276 **Edmunds**, R. D., *The Shawnee Prophet*, Lincoln, NE, 1983.

5.277 **Griffith**, B. W., *McIntosh and Weatherford. Creek Indian Leadership*, Tuscaloosa, AL, 1988. A dual biography that contrasts the approaches to tribalism and intercultural identity shown by two rival Creek leaders before, during, and after the War of 1812.

5.278 **Herring**, J. B., *Kenekuk, the Kickapoo Prophet*, Lawrence, KS, 1988.

5.279 **Joslyn Art Museum**, *Karl Bodmer's America*, Lincoln, NE, 1984. A collection of the artists' sketches and watercolors of the northern Great Plains tribes early in the nineteenth century.

5.280 **Littlefield**, D. F., *Africans and Seminoles. From Removal to Emancipation*, Westport, CT, 1977.

5.281 **Martin**, J. W., *Sacred Revolt. The Muskogee's Struggle for a New World*, Boston, 1991.

5.282 **McLoughlin**, W. G., *Cherokees and Missionaries, 1789–1839*, New Haven, CT, 1984. An account of the reciprocal relations between Protestant missionaries in the Southeast and the Cherokees in the midst of a Cherokee cultural renascence.

5.283 **McLoughlin**, W. G., *Cherokee Renascence in the New Republic*, Princeton, NJ, 1987. Recounts the revitalization movement among the southern Cherokees, in areas such as politics, religion, and the economy; the book also deals with the changes in white racial attitudes that led to the Jacksonian removal policy of the 1830s.

5.284 **Milloy**, J. S., *The Plains Cree. Trade, Diplomacy and War, 1790 to 1870*, Winnipeg, MAN, 1988.

5.285 **Moore**, J. H., 'The developmental cycle of Cheyenne polygyny', *American Indian Quarterly*, XV, 1991, 311–328.

5.286 **Peterson**, Jacqueline, and **Brown**, Jennifer S. H., (ed.), *The New Peoples. Being and Becoming Metis in North America*, Lincoln, NE, 1985. A collection of articles mainly about the French-Indian people in Canada, but includes an essay by Peterson about the origins of the metis community around Lake Michigan.

5.287 **Wozniak**, J. S., *Contact, Negotiation and Conflict. An Ethnohistory of the Eastern Dakota, 1819–1839*, Washington, DC, 1978.

5.288 **Wright**, J. L., *Creeks and Seminoles. Destruction and Regeneration of the Muscogulge People*, Lincoln, NE, 1986.

Untangles the diverse ethnic origins of the Muscogulge people of the Southeast by making clear that only the Europeans saw them as a monolithic nation; the author reinterprets the so-called "Creek War" of 1813 in similar ethnic terms.

(a) INDIAN REMOVAL

5.289 **Agnew**, B., *Fort Gibson. Terminal on the Trail of Tears*, Norman, OK, 1980.

5.290 **Dippie**, B. W., *Catlin and his Contemporaries. The Politics of Patronage*, Lincoln, NE, 1990.

5.291 **Finger**, J. R., *The Eastern Band of Cherokees, 1819–1900*, Knoxville, TN, 1984. A history of the Cherokees who stayed behind after the Removal of the 1830s, and the culture they maintained in the Appalachian Mountains.

5.292 **Green**, M. D., *The Politics of Indian Removal. Creek Government and Society in Crisis*, Lincoln, NE, 1982.

5.293 **Maddox**, Lucy, *Removals. Nineteenth Century American Literature and the Politics of Indian Affairs*, New York, 1991.

5.294 **Perdue**, Theda, (ed.), *Nations Remembered. An Oral History of the Five Civilized Tribes, 1865–1907*, Westport, CT, 1980. A small sampler of the interviews done with Indian people in the 1930s as part of the oral history done by the Works Progress Administration.

5.295 **Prucha**, F. P., *The Great Father. The United States Government and the American Indians*, Lincoln, NE, 1984. Magisterial two volume set that is strongest for its coverage of the Removal Era.

5.296 **Satz**, R. N., *Chippewa Treaty Rights. The Reserved Rights of Wisconsin's Chippewa Indians in Historical Perspective*, Madison, WI, 1991.

5.297 **Satz**, R. N., 'The Cherokee Trail of Tears. A sesquicentennial perspective', *Georgia Historical Quarterly*, LXXIII, 1989, 431–466. Part of an entire issue of the journal devoted to an appraisal of the removal of the Cherokees from Georgia in the late 1830s.

5.298 **Viola**, H. J., *Diplomats in Buckskins. A History of Indian Delegations in Washington City*, Washington, DC, 1981. Covers the negotiations and rituals of treaty-making between unequal partners.

5.299 **Wilkins**, T., *Cherokee Tragedy. The Ridge Family and the Decimation of a People.*

Norman, OK, 1986. The story of Cherokee Removal and its effects on John Ridge's family.

5.300 **Young**, Mary, 'Racism in red and black. Indians and other free people of color in Georgia law, politics, and removal policy', *Georgia Historical Quarterly*, LXXIII, 1989, 492–518.

European-Americans

5.301 **Din**, G. C., *The Canary Islanders of Louisiana*, Baton Rouge, LA, 1988. Traces the history of the Hispanic people who came to Louisiana late in the eighteenth century and how they persisted as a distinct community until the twentieth.

5.302 **Grabbe**, H.-J., 'European immigration to the United States in the early national period, 1783–1820', *Proceedings of the American Philosophical Society*, CXXXII, 1989, 190–214.

5.303 **McCaffrey**, L. J., *Textures of Irish America*, Syracuse, NY, 1992.

5.304 **Sarna**, J. D., *Jacksonian Jew. The Two Worlds of Mordecai Noah*, New York, 1981.

SPACE, MOVEMENT, AND PLACE

Explorers and mappers

5.305 **Lavender**, D., *The Way to the Western Sea. Lewis and Clark Across the Continent*, New York, 1988. A useful survey of the expedition.

5.306 **Lavender**, D., *Colorado River Country*, New York, 1982. A history of the explorers of the Colorado.

5.307 **Nichols**, R. L., and **Halley**, P. L., *Stephen Long and American Frontier Exploration*, Newark, DE, 1980.

5.308 **Ronda**, J. P., (ed.), *Lewis and Clark Among the Indians*, Lincoln, NE, 1984.

5.309 **Ronda**, J. P., *Astoria and Empire*, Lincoln, NE, 1990.

5.310 **Savage**, H., *Discovering America, 1700–1875*, New York, 1979. A history of the explorers and their descriptions of the American environment.

The farmer's frontier

5.311 **Cashin**, Joan E., *A Family Venture. Men and Women on the Southern Frontier*, New York, 1991.

5.312 **Clark**, T. D., and **Guice**, J. W., *Frontiers in Conflict. The Old Southwest, 1795–1830*, Albuquerque, NM, 1989. The frontier in question was that of the region that became the Cotton South, and the conflict was between Spain, Great Britain, France, the United States, and the Native Americans for control of the region.

5.313 **Faragher**, J. M., *Sugar Creek. Life on the Illinois Prairie*, New Haven, CT, 1986.

5.314 **Garrison**, J. R., *Landscape and Material Life in Franklin County, Massachusetts, 1770–1860*, Knoxville, TN, 1991.

5.315 **Oberly**, J. W., 'Westward who? Estimates of native white interstate migration after the War of 1812', *Journal of Economic History*, XLVI, 1986, 431–440.

5.316 **Rohrbough**, M. J., *The Trans-Appalachian Frontier. People, Societies, and Institutions, 1775–1850*, New York, 1978.

5.317 **Southerland**, H. deL., and **Brown**, J. E., *The Federal Road through Georgia, the Creek Nation, and Alabama, 1806–1836*, Tuscaloosa, AL, 1989.

5.318 **Taylor**, A., *Liberty Men and Great Proprietors. The Revolutionary Settlement on the Maine Frontier, 1760–1820*, Chapel Hill, NC, 1990. Describes the conflict between large landowners and poor settlers over political, geographical, and religious control in Maine.

5.319 **Waldrep**, C., 'Immigration and opportunity along the Cumberland River in Western Kentucky', *Register of the Kentucky Historical Society*, LXXX, 1982, 392–407.

5.320 **Wyckoff**, W., *The Developer's Frontier. The Making of the Western New York Landscape*, New Haven, CT, 1988. A history of the land speculation by the Holland Land Company and how the geographical pattern of land alienation influenced future generations.

Urban America

5.321 **Adler**, J. S., *Yankee Merchants and the Making of the Urban West. The Rise and Fall of Antebellum St. Louis*, New York, 1991.

5.322 **Daniels**, B. C., 'Opportunity and urbanism: population growth in New England's secondary cities, 1790–1860', *Canadian Review of American Studies*, XXII, 1991, 173–193.

5.323 **Goodstein**, Anita Shafer, *Nashville, 1780–1860. From Frontier to City*, Gainesville, FL, 1989. Explains how Nashville emerged as a mid-South entrepot and center of Whig Party strength.

5.324 **Hamer**, D., *New Towns in the New World. Images and Perceptions of the Nineteenth-Century Urban Frontier*, New York, 1990.

5.325 **Hartog**, H., *Public Property and Private Power. The Corporation of the City of New York in American Law, 1730–1870*, Chapel Hill, NC, 1983.

5.326 **Kennedy**, R. G., *Orders from France. The Americans and the French in a Revolutionary World, 1780–1820*, New York, 1989. An architectural history of how France influenced American design.

5.327 **Mahoney**, T. R., *River Towns in the Great West. The Structure of Provincial Urbanization in the American Midwest, 1820–1870*, New York, 1990. Argues for a regional identity of the American Midwest, based at first on the commercial connections of the Mississippi River system, and later on the railroads.

5.328 **Nash**, G. B., *Forging Freedom. The Formation of Philadelphia's Black Community, 1720–1840*, Cambridge, MA, 1988.

5.329 **Pencak**, W., and **Wright**, C. E. (ed.), *New York and the Rise of American Capitalism. Economic Development and the Social and Political History of an American State, 1780–1870*, New York, 1989. A collection of essays that focuses more on the political and social history of the city with its economic and demographic growth as a background.

5.330 **Seelye**, J., *Beautiful Machine. Rivers and the Republican Plan, 1755–1825*, New York, 1991.

5.331 **Sharpless**, J. B., *City Growth in the United States, England, and Wales, 1820–1861*, New York, 1976.

5.332 **Stott**, R. B., *Workers in the Metropolis. Class, Ethnicity, and Youth in Antebellum New York City*, Ithaca, NY, 1990. Traces the emergence of a distinctive working-class culture that was exclusive in almost every sense, and was formed largely outside the workplace.

5.333 **Thornton**, Tamara Plakins, *Cultivating Gentlemen. The Meaning of Country Life Among the Boston Elite, 1785–1860*, New Haven, CT, 1989. Analyzes the cultural shifts in taste from productive agriculture to the cultivation of flowers and plants as decorative items by Boston's wealthy.

5.334 **Vitz**, R. C., *The Queen and the Arts. Cultural Life in Nineteenth-Century Cincinnati*, Kent, OH, 1989.

5.335 **Weiss**, Ellen, *City in the Woods. The Life and Design of an American Camp Meeting on Martha's Vineyard*, New York, 1987. An architectural history of the Methodist tent city and its culture in the 1830s.

THE STATE AND THE PUBLIC REALM

The party system

5.336 **Anbinder**, T., *Nativism and Slavery. The Northern Know Nothings and the Politics of the 1850s*, New York, 1992.

5.337 **Ashworth**, J., *'Agrarians' and 'Aristocrats'. Party Ideology in the United States, 1837–1846*, 1983. An ideological interpretation of the two-party system of Democrats and Whigs that focuses on the extreme element in each party, as defined by the fiercest attacks of the opposition.

5.338 **Baker**, Jean H., *Affairs of Party. The Political Culture of Northern Democrats in the Mid-Nineteenth Century*, Ithaca, NY, 1983.

5.339 **Banning**, L., (ed.), *After the Constitution. Party Conflict in the New Republic*, Belmont, CA, 1989.

5.340 **Brown**, T., *Politics and Statesmanship. Essays on the American Whig Party*, New York, 1985. Locates the changes in the opposition to Jacksonian Democrats in a renewal of republican ideas from the Revolutionary generation.

5.341 **Cain**, L. P., 'Carving the Northwest Territory into states', *Research in Economic History*, VI, 1991, 153–168.

5.342 **Clinton**, R. L., *Marbury v. Madison and Judicial Review*, Lawrence, KS, 1989.

5.343 **Cole**, D. B., *Martin Van Buren and the American Political System*, Princeton, NJ 1984. Places Van Buren at the center of th emergence of a mass-based party politics

5.344 **Ellis**, R. E., *The Union at Risk. Jacksonia Democracy, States' Rights and the Nullification Crisis*, New York, 1987.

5.345 **Ellis**, R. E., and **Wildavsky**, A., ' "Greatness" revisited: evaluating the performance of early American president in terms of cultural dilemmas', *Presidenti Studies Quarterly*, XXI, 1991, 15–34.

5.346 **Feller**, D., *The Public Lands in Jacksonia Politics*, Madison, WI, 1984. Tells the story of the importance of public land policy in the making of congressional political parties in the 1820s and 1830s.

5.347 **Finkelman**, P., *An Imperfect Union. Slavery, Federalism, and Comity*, Chapel Hill, NC, 1981.

5.348 **Formisano**, R. P., *The Transformation of Political Culture. Massachusetts Parties, 1790s-1840s*, New York, 1983.

5.349 **Freehling**, W. W., *The Road to Disunion Secessionists at Bay, 1776–1854*, New York 1990. The first of two projected volumes, this book analyzes antebellum politics in the Old South and finds a core group of lo country South Carolinians and Tidewate Virginians who turned almost every national issue into a defense of slavery.

5.350 **Gunn**, L. R., *The Decline of Authority. Public Economic Policy and Political Development in New York, 1800–1860*, Ithaca, NY, 1988.

5.351 **Hall**, K. L., *The Politics of Justice. Lowe Federal Judicial Selection and the Second Party System, 1829–61*, Lincoln, NE, 1980.

5.352 **Heale**, M. J., *The Presidential Quest. Candidates and Images in American Political Culture, 1787–1852*, 1982. A detailed study of the changes in campaig styles of men seeking the presidency, particularly with the arrival of Andrew Jackson and a merging of the republican tradition of shunning a campaign and the new democratic one of mobilizing public opinion behind a candidate and hi party.

5.353 **Henderson**, D. F., *Congress, Courts, and Criminals. The Development of Federal Criminal Law, 1801–1829*, Westport, CT 1985.

5.354 **Hoadley**, J. F., *Origins of American Political Parties, 1789–1803*, Lexington, KY, 1986.

5.355 **Hoffer**, P. C., *The Law's Conscience.*

Equitable Constitutionalism in America,
Chapel Hill, NC, 1990. Connects the
evolution of the American judiciary to
changes in the understanding of the law of
equity, and finds support for modern
judicial activism in Jefferson's writings on
equity law.

5.356 **Jeffrey**, T. E., *State Parties and National
Politics. North Carolina, 1815–1861,*
Athens, GA, 1989.

5.357 **Kielbowicz**, R. B., *News in the Mail. The
Press, Post Office, and Public Information,
1700–1860s,* Westport, CT, 1989.

5.358 **Knupfer**, P. B., *The Union As It Is.
Constitutional Unionism and Sectional
Compromise, 1787–1861,* Chapel Hill, NC,
1991.

5.359 **Kohl**, L. F., *The Politics of Individualism.
Parties and the American Character in the
Jacksonian Era,* New York, 1989. Finds
that how people responded to the new
market society of the nineteenth century
determined their political preferences, too.

5.360 **Maizlish**, S. E., *The Triumph of
Sectionalism. The Transformation of Ohio
Politics, 1844–1856,* Kent, OH, 1983.
Argues against an ethnocultural
interpretation of Ohio politics, and instead
contends that the slavery issue ended the
Second Party system thanks to the
leadership of politicians like Salmon P.
Chase.

5.361 **Orth**, J. V., *The Judicial Power of the
United States. The Eleventh Amendment in
American History,* New York, 1987.
Analyzes the role of states in federal law in
the 1790s and traces the subsequent history
of state immunity under the Eleventh
Amendment.

5.362 **Perkins**, E. J., 'Lost opportunities for
compromise in the bank war. A
reassessment of Jackson's veto message',
Business History Review, LXI, 1987,
531–550.

5.363 **Peterson**, Norma Lois, *The Presidencies of
William Henry Harrison and John Tyler,*
Lawrence, KS, 1989. Another in the
University Press of Kansas series on the
American presidency, Peterson sticks
mainly to recounting the Tyler
Administration's executive policies.

5.364 **Rash**, Nancy, *The Painting and Politics of
George Caleb Bingham,* New Haven, CT,
1991. An explication of Bingham's art,
particularly his series on Missouri's
flatboatmen and rivermen, set against the

Whig Party politics of the painter.

5.365 **Resch**, J. P., 'Politics and public culture:
The revolutionary war pension act of
1818', *Journal of the Early Republic,* VIII,
1988, 139–158.

5.366 **Rutland**, R. A., *The Presidency of James
Madison,* Lawrence, KS, 1990. Part of the
publisher's American Presidents series,
this volume is generally sympathetic to
Madison's leadership and conduct of the
War of 1812.

5.367 **Silbey**, J. H., *The Partisan Imperative. The
Dynamics of American Politics Before the
Civil War,* New York, 1985. Essays by a
historian who has long called attention to
the strength of political parties in
Jacksonian America.

5.368 **Siry**, S. E., *De Witt Clinton and the
American Political Economy. Sectionalism,
Politics, and Republican Ideology,
1787–1828,* New York, 1990.

5.369 **Slaughter**, T. P., *The Whiskey Rebellion.
Frontier Epilogue to the American
Revolution,* New York, 1986.

5.370 **Stinchcombe**, W. C., *The XYZ Affair,*
Westport, CT, 1980. Unravels the
complexities of the political and diplomatic
scandal that was backdrop to the 1798
Quasi-War with France.

5.371 **Tachau**, Mary K. Bonsteel, *Federal Courts
in the Early Republic. Kentucky,
1789–1816,* Princeton, NJ, 1978.

5.372 **Watson**, H. L., *Liberty and Power. The
Politics of Jacksonian America,* New York,
1990. Traces the impact of commercial
capitalism or the "market revolution" on
the American political system, and finds
that older republican notions still
dominated the dialogue between
Democrats and Whigs.

5.373 **White**, G. E., *The Oliver Wendell Holmes
Devise History of the Supreme Court of the
United States,* New York, 1988. Volumes
III and IV of the official history that cover
the later years of the Marshall Court and
extend legal history to matters of American
culture.

5.374 **Wilson**, M. L., *The Presidency of Martin
Van Buren,* Lawrence, KS, 1984. Part of
the University Press of Kansas's
presidential history series, Wilson
concentrates on Van Buren's banking
policy and his subsequent defeat in his
1840 reelection bid.

5.375 **Winkle**, K. J., *The Politics of Community.
Migration and Politics in Antebellum Ohio,*

New York, 1988. Emphasizes the importance of political parties in shaping allegiances at a time when massive internal migration would otherwise have made politics and elections chaotic.

5.376 **Zagarri**, Rosemarie, *The Politics of Size. Representation in the United States, 1776–1850*, Ithaca, NY, 1987.

Warfare

5.377 **Barr**, A., *Texans in Revolt. The Battle for San Antonio, 1835*, Austin, TX, 1990.

5.378 **Berton**, P., *Flames Across the Border. The Canadian-American Tragedy, 1813–1814*, Boston, 1981.

5.379 **Chance**, J. E., *Jefferson Davis's Mexican War Regiment*, Jackson, MS, 1991.

5.380 **Clary**, D. A., *Fortress America. The Corps of Engineers, Hampton Roads, and United States Coastal Defense*, Charlottesville, VA, 1990.

5.381 **Crackel**, T. J., *Mr. Jefferson's Army. Political and Social Reform of the Military Establishment, 1801–1809*, New York, 1987. Argues that Jefferson's administration did not so much try to dismantle the army as make it more republican through defining new missions for the military such as engineering and scientific explorations.

5.382 **Cress**, L. D., *Citizens in Arms. The Army and the Militia in American Society to the War of 1812*, Chapel Hill, NC, 1982.

5.383 **del Castillo**, R. G., *The Treaty of Guadalupe Hidalgo. A Legacy of Conflict*, Norman, OK, 1990.

5.384 **Egan**, C. L., *Neither War Nor Peace. Franco-American Relations, 1803–1812*, Baton Rouge, LA, 1983.

5.385 **Eisenhower**, J. S. D., *So Far From God. The U. S. War with Mexico*, New York, 1989.

5.386 **Hatzenbuehler**, R. L., *Congress Declares War. Rhetoric, Leadership, and Partisanship in the Early Republic*, Kent, OH, 1983.

5.387 **Hickey**, D. J., *The War of 1812. A Forgotten Conflict*, Urbana, IL, 1989. The newest synthesis of writing on the war, including a treatment of the military, naval, and especially domestic political history of the war years.

5.388 **Hietala**, T. R., *Manifest Design. Anxious Aggrandizement in Late Jacksonian America*, Ithaca, NY, 1985. Shows how a combination of racism and anglophobia worked to create an ideology that underlay American expansion.

5.389 **Johannsen**, R. W., *To the Halls of Montezuma. The Mexican War in the American Imagination*, New York, 1985. A cultural history of the home front as well as the Army during the Mexican War.

5.390 **Johnson**, J. J., *A Hemisphere Apart. The Foundations of United States Policy toward Latin America*, Baltimore, 1990.

5.391 **Kaplan**, L. S., *Entangling Alliances with None. American Foreign Policy in the Age of Jefferson*, Kent, OH, 1987.

5.392 **Lack**, P. D., *The Texas Revolutionary Experience. A Political and Social History, 1835–1836*, College Station, TX, 1992.

5.393 **Lander**, E. M., *Reluctant Imperialists. Calhoun, the South Carolinians, and the Mexican War*, Baton Rouge, LA, 1980.

5.394 **Long**, D. F., *Gold Braid and Foreign Relations. Diplomatic Activities of U.S. Naval Officers, 1798–1883*, Annapolis, MD, 1988.

5.395 **Oberly**, J. W., *Sixty Million Acres. American Veterans and the Public Lands before the Civil War*, Kent, OH, 1990. A study of the veterans of the War of 1812 and the politics and economics of the pensions that they received in land.

5.396 **Owsley**, F. L., Jr., *Struggle for the Gulf Borderlands. The Creek War and the Battle of New Orleans, 1812–1815*, Gainesville, FL, 1981.

5.397 **Pacquette**, R. L., *Sugar is Made with Blood. The Conspiracy of La Escalera and the Conflict between Empires over Slavery in Cuba*, Middletown, CT, 1988.

5.398 **Palmer**, M. A., *Stoddert's War. Naval Operations during the Quasi-War with France, 1798–1801*, Columbia, SC, 1987.

5.399 **Stagg**, J. C. A., *Mr. Madison's War. Politics, Diplomacy, and Warfare in the Early American Republic, 1783–1830*, Princeton, NJ, 1983.

5.400 **Stevens**, K. R., *Border Diplomacy. The Caroline and McLeod Affairs in Anglo-American-Canadian Relations, 1837–1842*, Tuscaloosa, AL, 1989.

5.401 **Sugden**, J., *Tecumseh's Last Stand*, Norman, OK, 1985. A military history of the 1813 Battle of Thames where the Shawnee leader was killed and his forces defeated.

5.402 **Tucker**, R. W., and **Hendrickson**, D. C. *Empire of Liberty. The Statecraft of Thom*

Jefferson, New York, 1990.

5.403 **Tutorow**, N. E., *Texas Annexation and the Mexican War. A Political Study of the Old Northwest*, Palo Alto, CA, 1978.

5.404 **Watts**, S., *The Republic Reborn. War and the Making of Liberal America, 1790–1820*, Baltimore, 1987.

5.405 **Weeks**, W. E., *John Quincy Adams and American Global Empire*, Lexington, KY, 1992.

5.406 **Welsh**, W. J., and **Skaggs**, D. C., (ed.), *War on the Great Lakes. Essays Commemorating the 175th Anniversary of the Battle of Lake Erie*, Kent, OH, 1991.

5.407 **Whipple**, A. B. C., *To The Shores of Tripoli. The Birth of the U. S. Navy and Marines*, New York, 1991.

6

THE CRISIS OF
THE UNION
AND AFTER, 1848–1898

GENERAL

6.1 **Baum**, D., *The Civil War Party System. The Case of Massachusetts, 1848–1876*, Chapel Hill, NC, 1984. A quantitative study of electoral results that finds statewide realignments before the tumultuous 1850s and again at the end of Reconstruction.

6.2 **Foner**, E., *Slavery, the Civil War, and Reconstruction*, Washington, DC, 1990.

6.3 **Kousser**, J. M., and **McPherson**, J. M., *Region, Race, and Reconstruction. Essays in Honor of C. Vann Woodward*, New York, 1982. A collection of pieces by the students of the foremost American historian of the South and the American Dilemma.

6.4 **McPherson**, J. M., *Battle Cry of Freedom. The Civil War Era*, New York, 1988. A survey that updates the author's *Ordeal by Fire* by an integration of the recent work on slavery and freedom before and during the war.

6.5 **Ransom**, R. L., *Conflict and Compromise. The Political Economy of Slavery, Emancipation, and the American Civil War*, New York, 1989. A handy one volume survey that covers the slavery extension dispute, the war, and the emergence of sharecroppping after the war.

6.6 **Rose**, Anne C., *Victorian America and the Civil War*, New York, 1992.

6.7 **Schlereth**, T. J., *Victorian America. Transformations in Everyday Life, 1876–1915*, New York, 1991.

6.8 **Simpson**, L. P., *Mind and the American

Civil War. A Meditation on Lost Causes*, Baton Rouge, LA, 1989. The published lectures given by the author in the Walter Lynwood Fleming series at Louisiana State University, the essays consider the destructive effects of the Civil War on southern nationalism and what the author calls New England nationalism.

6.9 **Sutherland**, D. E., *The Expansion of Everyday Life, 1860–1876*, New York, 1989. Part of Harper and Row's series on Everyday Life in America.

6.10 **Utley**, R. M., *Billy the Kid. A Short and Violent Life*, Lincoln, NE, 1989. A look more at how Billy the Kid has been treated in literature than at the facts of his life.

GUIDES TO SOURCES

Primary sources

6.11 **Adams**, Virginia Matzke, (ed.), *On the Altar of Freedom. A Black Soldier's Civil War Letters from the Front*, Amherst, MA, 1991. Letters from a corporal in the famou Fifty-Fourth Massachusetts regiment tha comprised one of the first all-black units.

6.12 **Arkush**, R. D., and **Lee**, L. O., (ed.), *Land Without Ghosts. Chinese Impressions America from the Mid-Nineteenth Century t the Present*, Berkeley, CA, 1989.

6.13 **Barnett**, Susanne Wilson, and **Fairbank**, J. K., (ed.), *Christianity in China. Early Protestant Missionary Writings*, Cambridge, MA, 1985.

6.14 **Beers**, H. P., *Guide to the Archives of the Government of the Confederate States of America*, Washington, DC, 1986.

6.15 **Bergeron**, P., *et al.*, (ed.), *The Papers of Andrew Johnson*, Knoxville, TN, 1967– .

6.16 **Beveridge**, C. E., *et al.*, (ed.), *The Papers of Frederick Law Olmsted*, Baltimore, 1979– . This series alternately concentrates on Olmsted's career in landscape design and his anti-slavery activities.

6.17 **Bleser**, Carol, (ed.), *Secret and Sacred. The Diaries of James Henry Hammond, a Southern Slaveholder*, New York, 1988. A single diary of the South Carolinian that covers the years of his public life, 1841–1862.

6.18 **Blight**, D. W., (ed.), *When This Cruel War is Over. The Civil War Letters of Charles Harvey Brewster*, Amherst, MA, 1992. A junior officer's letters about life and combat in the Army of the Potomac.

6.19 **Crawford**, M., (ed.), *William Howard Russell's Civil War. Private Diary and Letters, 1861–1862*, Athens, GA, 1992. Impressions of the American Civil War by the military correspondent of the London Times.

6.20 **Crist**, Lynda Lasswell, *et al.*, (ed.), *The Papers of Jefferson Davis*, Baton Rouge, LA, 1971– .

6.21 **Drago**, E. L., (ed.), *Broke by the War. Letters of a Slave Trader*, Columbia, SC, 1991. A series of letters that reveal the business side of slave-trading in the Old South just before the Civil War.

6.22 **Ellsworth**, Maria S., (ed.), *Mormon Odyssey. The Story of Ida Hunt Udall, Plural Wife*, Urbana, IL, 1992. A collection of letters and documents that examine the life of a woman who at a young age became the number two wife of a leading Mormon.

6.23 **Harris**, Trudier, (ed.), *Selected Works of Ida B. Wells-Barnett*, New York, 1991. A new edition of Wells-Barnett's work that includes the extraordinary reporting of southern lynching that Wells-Barnett wrote as a young Memphis editor.

6.24 **Hay**, Melba Porter, *et al.*, (ed.), *The Papers of Henry Clay*, Lexington, KY, 1955–1992. Eleven volume set of the papers of the "Great Pacificator".

6.25 **Johnson**, M. P., and **Roark**, J. L., (ed.), *No Chariot Let Down. Charleston's Free People of Color on the Eve of the Civil War*, Chapel Hill, NC, 1984. Papers of the Ellison family.

6.26 **Kamphoefner**, W. D., *et al.*, (ed.), *News from the Land of Freedom. German Immigrants Write Home*, Ithaca, NY, 1991.

6.27 **Kaufman**, S. B., (ed.), *The Samuel Gompers Papers*, Urbana, IL, 1986– .

6.28 **Laas**, Virginia Jean, (ed.), *Wartime Washington. The Civil War Letters of Elizabeth Blair Lee*, Urbana, IL, 1991. More than three hundred letters that give the viewpoint of a woman who by birth and marriage was related to many in the Union and Confederate high commands.

6.29 **Lasser**, Carol, and **Merrill**, Marlene Deahl, (ed.), *Friends and Sisters. Letters between Lucy Stone and Antoinette Brown Blackwell, 1846–1893*, Urbana, IL, 1987. A collection that traces the lives of the two women who attended college together and then married a pair of brothers, and how their personal lives intersected with the politics of suffrage.

6.30 **Madsen**, B. D., *Exploring the Great Salt Lake. The Stansbury Expedition of 1849–50*, Salt Lake City, UT, 1989. Includes all the journals and notebooks of an army surveying party, including their accounts of meeting the Mormon settlers.

6.31 **Maintain**, K. W., *Guide to Federal Archives Relating to the Civil War*, Washington, DC, 1986.

6.32 **Maoris**, R. M., *The Children of Pride*, New Haven, CT, 1983. The second, expanded edition of a remarkable set of letters that show the downfall of the planter class during the war and into Reconstruction.

6.33 **Moynihan**, Ruth B., **Armitage**, Susan, and **Dichamp**, Christiane Fischer, (ed.), *So Much to Be Done. Women Settlers on the Mining and Ranching Frontier*, Lincoln, NE, 1990. A collection of letters and diary extracts that show the range of women's experiences in the nineteenth century West.

6.34 **Overfield**, L. J., *The Little Big Horn, 1876*, Lincoln, NE, 1990. A set of documents concerning the defeat of Custer's command.

6.35 **Palmer**, Beverly Wilson, (ed.), *The Selected Letters of Charles Sumner*, Boston, 1990. A two volume set that features the most interesting of Sumner's correspondence, along with complete annotations, culled from the massive microfilm collection of his papers.

6.36 **Perdue**, Theda, (ed.), *Nations Remembered. An Oral History of the Five Civilized Tribes, 1865–1907*, Westport, CT, 1980. A small sampler of the interviews done with Indian people in the 1930s as part of the oral history done by the Works Progress Administration.

6.37 **Rawick**, G., *The American Slave*, Westport, CT, 1972. A nineteen volume set of interviews with ex-slaves, taken in the 1930s by the Works Progress Administration.

6.38 **Reilly**, W. E., *Sarah Jane Foster, Teacher of the Freedmen. A Diary and Letters*, Charlottesville, VA, 1990. A diary of a Maine woman who taught freed blacks in West Virginia and South Carolina as part of a Baptist mission.

6.39 **Rischin**, M., (ed.), *Grandma Never Lived in America. The New Journalism of Abraham Cahan*, Bloomington, IN, 1985. A collection of the writings of the editor of the Jewish Daily Forward.

6.40 **Rosenblatt**, E., and **Rosenblatt**, Ruth, *Hard Marching Every Day. The Civil War Letters of Private Wilbur Fisk, 1861–1865*, Lawrence, KS, 1992. Account of a New England private that gives a first-hand view of life on the front line.

6.41 **Simon**, J. Y., (ed.), *The Papers of Ulysses S. Grant*, Carbondale, IL, 1967– .

6.42 **Skinner**, J. L., *The Autobiography of Henry Merrell. Industrial Missionary to the South*, Athens, GA, 1991. A Yankee textile promoter who moved South, married a southerner, and wound up in the Confederate Army.

6.43 **Steinbach**, R. H., *A Long March. The Lives of Frank and Alice Baldwin*, Austin, TX, 1989. Unusual combination of diaries, journals, and letters that serve as a collected autobiography of a marriage between an Army officer in the Civil War, and later on the Great Plains, and his spouse.

6.44 **Woodward**, C. V., (ed.), *Mary Chesnut's Civil War*, New Haven, CT, 1981. Contains the edited text of the diary along with a wise introduction by Woodward.

Bibliographies and dictionaries

6.45 **Gale**, R. L., *The Gay Nineties in America. A Cultural Dictionary of the 1890s*, Westport, CT, 1992. Entries include note persons and events.

6.46 **Menendez**, A. J., *Civil War Novels. An Annotated Bibliography*, New York, 1986.

6.47 **Wakelyn**, J. L., *Biographical Dictionary the Confederacy*, Westport, CT, 1977.

6.48 **Murdock**, E. C., *The Civil War in the North. A Selective Annotated Bibliography* New York, 1987. Over five thousand entries on all aspects of the war.

6.49 **Osterreich**, S. A., *The American Indian Ghost Dance, 1870–1890. An Annotated Bibliography*, New York, 1991.

6.50 **Scharnhorst**, G., *Charlotte Perkins Gilman. A Bibliography*, Metuchen, NJ, 1985. A listing of the writings by and about the noted feminist and economist.

6.51 **Smith**, D. L., *The American and Canadia West. A Bibliography*, Santa Barbara, CA 1979.

6.52 **Smith**, M. J., *American Civil War Navies A Bibliography*, Metuchen, NJ, 1973.

6.53 **Warner**, E. J., and **Yearns**, W. B., *Biographical Register of the Confederate Congress*, Baton Rouge, LA, 1975.

Historiography

6.54 **Anderson**, E., and **Moss**, A. A., (ed.), *Th Facts of Reconstruction. Essays in Honor o John Hope Franklin*, Baton Rouge, LA, 1991. Nine essays on Reconstruction written mainly by former students of Franklin.

6.55 **Bodnar**, J., 'Symbols and servants. Immigrant America and the limits of public history', *Journal of American History*, 1986, 137–151. Discusses the symbolism behind the Statue of Liberty.

6.56 **Boritt**, G. S., (ed.), *The Historian's Lincoln* Urbana, IL, 1988. A collection of essays, first presented at a Gettysburg College symposium, that features the work of leading Lincoln biographers.

6.57 **Current**, R. N., *Arguing with Historians. Essays on the Historical and the Unhistorica* Middletown, CT, 1987.

6.58 **Dinges**, B. J., 'New directions in frontier military history: a review essay', *New Mexico Historical Review*, LXVI, 1991, 103–116.

6.59 **Fehrenbacher**, D. S., *Lincoln in Text and Context. Collected Essays*, Stanford, CA, 1987. A set of essays by one of the leading historians of the Civil War era that concentrates for the most part on how historians and popular writers have treated Lincoln.

6.60 **Johannsen**, R. W., *Lincoln, the South, and Slavery. The Political Dimension*, Baton Rouge, LA, 1991. Reflections by the premier scholar of Stephen Douglas on his Illinois rival.

6.61 **Limerick**, Patricia Nelson and **Milner**, C. A., (ed.), *Trails. Toward a New Western History*, Lawrence, KS, 1991.

6.62 **Rabinowitz**, H. N., 'More than the Woodward thesis: assessing "The Strange Career of Jim Crow" ', *Journal of American History*, LXXV, 1988, 842–856. Discussion of the impact and importance of *The Strange Career of Jim Crow* by C. Vann Woodward.

6.63 **Singal**, D. J., 'Ulrich B. Phillips: the old South as the new', *Journal of American History*, LXIII, 1977, 871–891. Analyzes Ulrich Phillips and puts his writings into a new forward looking light.

6.64 **Woodward**, C. V., ' "Strange Career" critics: long may they persevere', *Journal of American History*, LXXV, 1988, 857–868. Woodward responds to his critics with a little self criticism and a discussion on his book and the scholarship it has produced.

BIOGRAPHY

6.65 **Akin**, E. N., and **Flagler**, *Rockefeller Partner and Florida Baron*, Kent, OH, 1988. A business biography of Henry Flagler, and how late in life he switched from the oil business to the real estate business in developing the South Atlantic coast of Florida.

6.66 **Allmendinger**, D. F., *Ruffin. Family and Reform in the Old South*, New York, 1990. A biography of Edmund Ruffin, the Virginia agricultural reformer and leader of the secession cause in 1861.

6.67 **Baker**, Jean H., *Mary Todd Lincoln. A Biography*, New York, 1987. A sympathetic biography of Mrs. Lincoln that places her in the context of her Kentucky upbringing as well as within the new scholarship on nineteenth century women.

6.68 **Baker**, P. R., *Stanny. The Gilded Life of Stanford White*, New York, 1989. A biography of the leading architect of the American Renaissance at the end of the nineteenth century that places his professional achievements and personal life within the context of the city's changes.

6.69 **Ballard**, M. B., *Pemberton. A Biography*, Jackson, MS, 1991. A biography of the Confederate commander who surrendered the garrison at Vicksburg, Pennsylvania-born John C. Pemberton.

6.70 **Blue**, F. J., *Salmon P. Chase. A Life in Politics*, Kent, OH, 1987. Detailing the career of Chase from his start in Ohio anti-slavery circles to his position in Lincoln's cabinet, Blue asserts that despite his personal ambitions for the presidency, Chase's first goal was the overthrow of what he called the Slave Power.

6.71 **Bordin**, Ruth, *Frances Willard. A Biography*, Chapel Hill, NC, 1986. A biography of the leader of the Women's Christian Temperance Union that locates its subject in the nineteenth century women's movement.

6.72 **Braden**, W. W., *Abraham Lincoln. Public Speaker*, Baton Rouge, LA, 1988. A summary of observers' and listeners' accounts of Lincoln as a stump speaker.

6.73 **Burnside**, W. H., *The Honorable Powell Clayton*, Conway, AR, 1991. Biography of the leading Republican in Reconstruction Arkansas.

6.74 **Calhoun**, C. W., *Gilded Age Cato. The Life of Walter Q. Gresham*, Lexington, KY, 1988. Biography of the diplomat who played a central role in the bringing of Hawaii under American control.

6.75 **Carlson**, P. H., '*Pecos Bill*'. *A Military Biography of William R. Shafter*, College Station, TX, 1989. Covers the life of the colorful soldier in the Plains Wars and on through the Spanish-American War.

6.76 **Coryell**, Janet, *Neither Heroine Nor Fool. Anna Ella Carroll of Maryland*, Kent, OH, 1990.

6.77 **Davis**, W. C., *Jefferson Davis. The Man and His Hour*, New York, 1991. A full biography that gives ample coverage to the Confederate president while in Richmond, as well as his career before secession.

6.78 **Debo**, Angie, *Geronimo. The Man, His Time, His Place*, Norman, OK, 1976. A biography of the Apache leader, written by one of the leading twentieth century historians of Native Americans.

6.79 **d'Entremont**, J., *Southern Emancipator. Moncure Conway, the American Years, 1832–1865*, New York, 1987. A biography that explores how the son of a Virginia slaveholder came to reject the Old South and embrace abolitionism and Unitarianism.

6.80 **Eckert**, R. L., *John Brown Gordon. Soldier, Southerner, American*, Baton Rouge, LA, 1989. A biography of the Georgian that gives equal attention to his leadership in the Army of Northern Virginia and to his postwar resistance to Reconstruction.

6.81 **Faust**, Drew Gilpin, *James Harvey Hammond. A Program for Mastery of the Old South*, Baton Rouge, LA, 1982. A biography of the South Carolina fire-eater.

6.82 **Forgie**, G. B., *Patricide in the House Divided. A Psychological Interpretation of Lincoln and his Age*, New York, 1979.

6.83 **Franklin**, J. H., *George Washington Williams. A Biography*, Chicago, 1985. A biography of the first great black historian of the nineteenth century that also places Williams in the context of northern black society.

6.84 **Fry**, J. A., *John Tyler Morgan and the Search for Southern Autonomy*, Knoxville, TN, 1992. Biography of the Alabama senator who became a leading champion of American imperialism in the 1880s.

6.85 **Gara**, L., *The Presidency of Franklin Pierce*, Lawrence, KS, 1991. A political biography that does little to rescue the reputation of the hapless Pierce.

6.86 **Geer**, Emily Apt, *First Lady. The Life of Lucy Webb Hayes*, Kent, OH, 1984. Biography of the wife of Rutherford B. Hayes.

6.87 **Harlan**, L. D., *Booker T. Washington. The Making of a Black Leader, 1856–1901*, New York, 1972.

6.88 **Hermann**, Janet Sharp, *Joseph E. Davis. Pioneer Patriarch*, Jackson, MS, 1990. A biography of the slaveowner and proprietor of the Davis Bend Plantation, famous for its experiments in slave autonomy, but nonetheless destroyed in the Civil War.

6.89 **Herr**, Pamela, *Jessie Benton Fremont.*

American Woman of the 19th Century, New York, 1987. A biography of the daughter of one famous politician, and wife of another, links Fremont's life to the wider themes of women's history.

6.90 **Ilisevich**, R. D., *Galusha A. Grow. The People's Candidate*, Pittsburgh, 1988. A biography of the free-soiler who helped pass the Homestead Act in 1862.

6.91 **Jordan**, D. M., *Winfield Scott Hancock. A Soldier's Life*, Bloomington, IN, 1988. A biography of one of the leading corps commanders in the Union's Army of the Potomac, and after the war, an unsuccessful seeker of the presidency.

6.92 **Kalfus**, M., *Frederick Law Olmsted. The Passion of a Public Artist*, New York, 1990. A biography that finds the lasting influence of a difficult childhood on Olmsted's design work.

6.93 **Kasper**, Shirl, *Annie Oakley*, Norman, OK, 1992. A biography of the Wild West Show gunslinger.

6.94 **Lane**, Ann J., *To Herland and Beyond. The Life and Work of Charlotte Perkins Gilman*, New York, 1990.

6.95 **Launius**, R. D., *Joseph Smith III, Pragmatic Prophet*, Urbana, IL, 1988.

6.96 **Leiren**, T. I., *Marcus Thrane. A Norwegian Radical in America*, Northfield, MN, 1987. A biography of the Norwegian labor leader who spent the last half of his life in the U.S., but maintained ties to the Norwegian Left.

6.97 **Martin**, W. E., Jr., *The Mind of Frederick Douglass*, Chapel Hill, NC, 1984.

6.98 **Marvel**, W., *Burnside*, Chapel Hill, NC, 1991. A biography of the failed Army of the Potomac commander that finds Burnside less to blame for his errors than poor staff work.

6.99 **Mathes**, Valerie Sherer, *Helen Hunt Jackson and Her Indian Reform Legacy*, Austin, TX, 1990. A biography of the woman author of the 1881 book *A Century of Dishonor*; the author argues that Jackson differed from other "friends" of the Indians by opposing forced acculturation and assimilation for the California tribes.

6.100 **Mathew**, W. M., *Edmund Ruffin and the Crisis of Slavery in the Old South. The Failure of Agricultural Reform*, Athens, GA, 1988.

6.101 **May**, R. E., *John A. Quitman. Old South Crusader*, Baton Rouge, LA, 1985. A biography of one of Mississippi's leading secessionists.

6.102 **McFeely**, W. S., *Frederick Douglass*, New York, 1991. A biography that covers the subject's life from slavery to freedom, and on to Douglass's long career as an orator and writer on the problem of race in American life.

6.103 **McFeely**, W. S., *Grant. A Biography*, New York, 1981. A full-length biography of the Union Army's commander that stresses the great disjuncture between the failures in his early life and his dramatic wartime accomplishment and subsequent political career.

6.104 **Minus**, P. M., *Walter Rauschenbusch. American Reformer*, New York, 1988.

6.105 **Moses**, L. G., *The Indian Man. A Biography of James Mooney*, Urbana, IL, 1984. The life of the leading ethnologist for the Smithsonian Institution and an account of his researches into American Indian life.

6.106 **Moses**, W. J., *Alexander Crummell. A Study of Civilization and Discontent*, New York, 1989. Life and thought of the black abolitionist and philosopher.

6.107 **Muhlenfeld**, Elisabeth, *Mary Boykin Chesnut. A Biography*, Baton Rouge, LA, 1981. Biography of the most famous southern wartime diarist, and her social status as wife of a leading South Carolina planter and politician.

6.108 **Neely**, M. E., and **McMurty**, R. G., *The Insanity File. The Case of Mary Todd Lincoln*, Carbondale, IL, 1986. Reviews the question of Mrs. Lincoln's sanity that arose after a family rupture with her only surviving son, Robert Todd Lincoln, and finds that she received a fair hearing when she was deemed insane.

6.109 **Orr**, O. H., *Saving American Birds. T. Gilbert Pearson and the Founding of the Audubon Movement*, Gainesville, FL, 1992.

6.110 **Parrish**, T. M., *Richard Taylor. Soldier Prince of Dixie*, Chapel Hill, NC, 1992. Biography of President Zachary Taylor's son and how his antipathy toward the Republicans overcame his unionism and led him into a career as a general in the Confederate army.

6.111 **Phillips**, C., *Damned Yankee. The Life of General Nathaniel Lyon*, Columbia, MO, 1990. Biography of the Union general in the Missouri theater who secured the state in the early fighting of 1861.

6.112 **Porter**, J. C., *Paper Medicine Man. John Gregory Bourke and his American West*, Norman, OK, 1986.

6.113 **Pryor**, Elizabeth Brown, *Clara Barton. Professional Angel*, Philadelphia, 1987. A full biography of the life and work of the prominent Civil War nurse and founder of the American Red Cross.

6.114 **Reid**, R. F., *Edward Everett. Unionist Orator*, Westport, CT, 1990. Biography of the man most noted for giving the two hour address at the dedication of the Gettysburg cemetery, and noteworthy for the new attention paid by communications scholars to rhetoric in the past.

6.115 **Rolle**, A., *John Charles Fremont. Character as Destiny*, Norman, OK, 1991. A biography that attempts to explain Fremont's many failings in life on account of his inner character.

6.116 **Samuels**, E., *Henry Adams*, Cambridge, MA, 1989. A condensed version of the author's three volume biography of Adams that emphasizes his public roles as reformer and historian.

6.117 **Schott**, T. E., *Alexander H. Stephens of Georgia. A Biography*, Baton Rouge, LA, 1988. Biography of the Georgia Whig who became Vice President of the Confederacy and remained a largely unreconstructed rebel after the war.

6.118 **Schutz**, W. J., and **Trenerry**, W. N., *Abandoned by Lincoln. A Military Biography of General John Pope*, Urbana, IL, 1990. Account of the Union general who made a reputation for himself in the West, and then was completely overwhelmed by Lee in Virginia, and forgotten thereafter.

6.119 **Sears**, S. W., *George B. McClellan. The Young Napoleon*, New York, 1988.

6.120 **Sicherman**, Barbara, *Alice Hamilton. A Life in Letters*, Cambridge, MA, 1984. A biography of the woman scientist who also worked at Chicago's Hull House.

6.121 **Simpson**, B. D., *Let Us Have Peace. Ulysses S. Grant and the Politics of War and Reconstruction, 1861–1868*, Chapel Hill, NC, 1991.

6.122 **Simpson**, C. M., *A Good Southerner. The Life of Henry A. Wise of Virginia*, Chapel Hill, NC, 1985. Treats the long political and military career of Wise from Jacksonian politics to the Confederate Army.

6.123 **Smith**, E. B., *The Presidencies of Zachary Taylor & Millard Fillmore*, Lawrence, KS, 1988.

6.124 **Thomas**, E. M., *Bold Dragoon. The Life of J. E. B. Stuart*, New York, 1986.

6.125 **Tomin**, B., and **Burgoa**, C., *Susan B. Anthony*, Santa Rosa, CA, 1983.

6.126 **Trautmann**, T. R., *Lewis Henry Morgan and the Invention of Kinship*, Berkeley, CA, 1989. Life of the pioneering ethnologist.

6.127 **Trefousse**, H. L., *Andrew Johnson. A Biography*, New York, 1989. Finds Johnson's chief fault as President was to squander the opportunity in the summer of 1865 to impose a firm Reconstruction policy.

6.128 **Trowbridge**, Carol, *Andrew Taylor Still, 1828–1917*, Kirksville, MO, 1991. A biography of a leader of the movement to promote osteopathic healing in the U.S.

6.129 **Trulock**, Alice Rains, *In the Hands of Providence. Joshua L. Chamberlain and the American Civil War*, Chapel Hill, NC, 1992. A biography of the Bowdoin College professor turned regimental commander who won a Congressional medal of honor at Gettysburg.

6.130 **Turner**, F., *Rediscovering America. John Muir in His Time and Ours*, New York, 1985. A lyrical biography about the naturalist and the origins of the environmental movement.

6.131 **Twombly**, R., *Louis Sullivan. His Life and Work*, New York, 1986. A biography of the architect that finds his repressed homosexuality expressed in some of his designs.

6.132 **Utley**, R. M., *Cavalier in Buckskin. George Armstrong Custer and the Western Military Frontier*, Norman, OK, 1988. The most distinguished historian of the frontier army's view of the enigmatic Custer.

6.133 **Waggenspack**, Beth M., *The Search for Self-Sovereignty. The Oratory of Elizabeth Cady Stanton*, Westport, CT, 1989.

6.134 **Wills**, B. S., *A Battle from the Start. The Life of Nathan Bedford Forrest*, New York, 1992. A biography of the Confederate cavalryman that confronts his mixed reputation for both gallantry and criminality.

6.135 **Winks**, R. W., *Frederick Billings. A Life*, New York, 1991. A biography of the nineteenth century lawyer and naturalist who was instrumental in establishing Yosemite National Park.

6.136 **Yates**, W. R., *Joseph Wharton. Quaker Industrial Pioneer*, Bethlehem, PA, 1987. A biography of the industrialist associated with Bethlehem Steel, and later the benefactor of the nation's first business school at the University of Pennsylvania.

DEMOGRAPHY, FAMILY, AND HEALTH

6.137 **Bean**, L. L., **Mineau**, Geraldine P., and **Anderton**, D. L., *Fertility Change on the American Frontier. Adaptation and Innovation*, Berkeley, CA, 1990. Analyzes 185,000 Mormon families in Utah and the West in the nineteenth century and places their demographic history into the larger historiography of the transition from high to low fertility.

6.138 **Bleser**, Carol, (ed.), *In Joy and In Sorrow. Women, Family, and Marriage in the Victorian South, 1830–1900*, New York, 1991. A set of essays on the southern family, white and black, and the changing mix of race and gender before and after the Civil War.

6.139 **Dowling**, H. F., *City Hospitals. The Undercare of the Underprivileged*, Cambridge, MA, 1982.

6.140 **Drachman**, Virginia G., *Hospital With a Heart. Women Doctors and the Paradox of Separatism at the New England Hospital, 1862–1969*, Ithaca, NY, 1984. The story of a hospital for women, staffed by women, focuses mainly on the nineteenth century origins but tells the story of the hospital's closing in 1969.

6.141 **Duffy**, J., *The Sanitarians. A History of American Public Health*, Urbana, IL, 1990. A survey of public health in the United States. Duffy contrasts the American experience with that of Europe and suggests that in the U.S., traditions of libertarianism delayed the development of state and national public health establishments.

6.142 **Fellman**, Anita Clair, and **Fellman**, M., *Making Sense of Self. Medical Advice Literature in Late Nineteenth Century America*, Philadelphia, 1981.

6.143 **Fraser**, W. L., **Saunders**, R. F., and **Wakelyn**, J. L., *The Web of Southern Social Relations. Women, Family, and Education*, Athens, GA, 1985.

6.144 **Fye**, W. B., *The Development of American Physiology. Scientific Medicine in the Nineteenth Century*, Baltimore, 1987. A history of the American Physiological Society and how its founders helped place scientific medicine within an academic setting.

6.145 **Galishoff**, S., *Newark. The Nation's Unhealthiest City, 1832–1895*, New Brunswick, NJ, 1988. Covers the origins of public health in New Jersey's largest city. Public and private leaders disdained health measures throughout most of the nineteenth century until finally in 1895 the Board of Health took positive action to curb epidemics.

6.146 **Ginzburg**, Lori D., *Women and the Work of Benevolence. Morality, Politics, and Class in the 19th Century United States*, New Haven, CT, 1990. Finds an ongoing tension before and after the Civil War between gender solidarity among women and class solidarity of men and women, with the latter coming to dominate most domestic reform by the close of the century.

6.147 **Griswold del Castillo**, R., ' "Only for my family . . ." Historical dimensions of chicano family solidarity-the case of San Antonio in 1860', *Aztlan*, XVI, 1985, 145–176.

6.148 **Griswold del Castillo**, R., *Family and Divorce in California, 1850–1890. Victorian Illusions and Everyday Realities*, Albany, NY, 1982.

6.149 **Grossberg**, M., *Governing the Hearth. Law and the Family in Nineteenth Century America*, Chapel Hill, NC, 1985. Considers the laws in the various states on the subjects of marriage and parent-child relations, tying changes to class and gender.

6.150 **Haller**, J. S., *American Medicine in Transition, 1840–1910*, Urbana, IL, 1981.

6.151 **Hareven**, Tamara K., *Transitions. The Family and the Life Course in Historical Perspective*, New York, 1978. A set of essays that first made use of the analytical technique of life course analysis, using Essex County, Massachusetts as the object of study.

6.152 **Hareven**, Tamara K., and **Vinovskis**, M. A., (ed.), *Family and Population in Nineteenth Century America*, Princeton, NJ, 1978.

6.153 **Holloran**, P. C., *Boston's Wayward Children. Social Services for Homeless Children, 1830–1930*, Rutherford, NJ, 1989.

6.154 **Holt**, Marilyn Irvin, *The Orphan Trains. Placing Out in America*, Lincoln, NE, 1992. Treats the story of the 200,000 New York orphans who were transported to the West for ostensibly benevolent purposes, but who, in many cases, wound up as forced laborers.

6.155 **Kleinberg**, S. J., *The Shadow of the Mills. Working Class Families in Pittsburgh, 1870–1907*, Pittsburgh, 1989.

6.156 **Leavitt**, Judith Walzer, *The Healthiest City. Milwaukee and the Politics of Health Reform*, Princeton, NJ, 1982.

6.157 **Lystra**, Karen, *Searching the Heart. Women, Men, and Romantic Love in Nineteenth Century America*, New York, 1989. Rejects the notion that nineteenth century Americans were prudish, finding instead that diaries and letters were filled with expressions of sexual love. The author also rejects the notion that "separate spheres" characterized nineteenth century gender relations.

6.158 **Manfra**, Jo Ann, and **Dykstra**, R. R., 'Serial marriage and the origins of the black stepfamily. The Rowanty evidence', *Journal of American History*, LXXII, 1985, 18–44.

6.159 **May**, Elaine Tyler, *Great Expectation. Marriage and Divorce in Post-Victorian America*, Chicago, 1980.

6.160 **McDannell**, Colleen, *The Christian Home in Victorian America, 1840–1900*, Bloomington, IN, 1986.

6.161 **Meckel**, R. A., *Save the Babies. American Public Health Reform and the Prevention of Infant Mortality, 1850–1929*, Baltimore, 1990.

6.162 **Mineau**, Geraldine P., **Bean**, L. L., and **Anderson**, D. L., 'Description and evaluation of linkage of the 1880 census to family genealogies: implications for Utah fertility research', *Historical Methods*, XXII, 1989, 144–157.

6.163 **Mintz**, S., *A Prison of Expectations. The Family in Victorian Culture*, New York, 1983. Compares the English and American middle-class family.

6.164 **Mohr**, J. C., *Abortion in America. The Origins and Evolution of National Policy, 1800–1900*, New York, 1978.

6.165 **Pernick**, M. S., *A Calculus of Suffering. Pain, Professionalism and Anesthesia in Nineteenth-Century America*, New York, 1985. Examines the ideology among practitioners and critics of the use of anesthesia and surgery in medical treatment.

6.166 **Preston**, S. H., and **Haines**, M. R., *Fatal Years. Child Mortality in Late Nineteenth Century America*, Princeton, NJ, 1991. Makes use of census data to make estimates about infant and child mortality linked to socioeconomic variables such as race and occupation.

6.167 **Reagan**, Leslie J., ' "About to meet her maker". Women, doctors, dying declarations, and the state's investigation of abortion, Chicago, 1867–1940', *Journal of American History*, LXXVII, 1991, 1240–1264. Analyzes criminal prosecutions of midwives in Chicago, particularly how judicial power as well as the medical establishment coerced dying women to identify the midwives.

6.168 **Rosenberg**, C. E., *The Care of Strangers. The Rise of America's Hospital System*, New York, 1987. A synthesis of the history of the nineteenth century hospital that shows how the institution changed from one that received charity cases to one that emphasized teaching and the surgical care of the public at large.

6.169 **Rosner**, D., *A Once Charitable Enterprise. Hospitals and Health Care in Brooklyn and New York, 1885–1915*, New York, 1982. An account of the factors inside and outside medicine that shaped hospitals and public health.

6.170 **Stern**, M. J., *Society and Family Strategy. Erie County, New York, 1850–1920*, Albany, NY, 1987.

6.171 **Strozier**, C. B., *Lincoln's Quest for Union. Public and Private Meanings*, Urbana, IL, 1987. Connects Lincoln's social thought with his family arrangements, particularly his marriage to Mary Todd Lincoln.

6.172 **Verbrugge**, Martha H., *Able-Bodied Womanhood. Personal Health and Social Change in Nineteenth Century Boston*, New York, 1988. Ties the emergence of women's voluntary institutions to efforts on the part of middle-class women to seek personal health and well-being.

6.173 **Vogel**, M. J., *The Invention of the Modern Hospital. Boston, 1870–1930*, Chicago, 1980.

6.174 **Waller**, Altina L., *Feud. Hatfields, McCoys, and Social Changes in Appalachia, 1860–1900*, Chapel Hill, NC, 1988.

6.175 **West**, E., *Growing Up with the Country.*

Childhood on the Far Western Frontier, Albuquerque, NM, 1989.

6.176 **Williams**, Marilyn Thornton, *Washing 'The Great Unwashed'. Public Baths in Urban America, 1840–1920*, Columbus, OH, 1991. Treats the public bath movement as part of the larger public health initiative, set within an urban political milieu beset by conflicts of class and ethnicity.

SOCIAL RELATIONS

Class and community

6.177 **Bailey**, F. A., *Class and Tennessee's Confederate Generation*, Chapel Hill, NC, 1987. An analysis of a questionnaire developed in the 1920s by the Tennessee Department of Archives and History. Athough the intent of the Tennessee survey was that of an apology for the culture of the Old South, Bailey's examination of the questionnaires concludes that the Old South was not a seamless democracy, but rather a culture of class extremes.

6.178 **Bernstein**, I., *The New York City Draft Riots. Their Significance for American Society and Politics in the Age of the Civil War*, New York, 1990. A social history of the wartime draft riot that places the upheaval in the context of class, ethnicity, and local politics.

6.179 **Buhle**, Mari Jo, *Women and American Socialism, 1870–1920*, Urbana, IL, 1981.

6.180 **Clawson**, Mary Ann, *Constructing Brotherhood. Class, Gender, and Fraternalism*, Princeton, NJ, 1989.

6.181 **Coughlin**, M. E., **Hamilton**, C. H., and **Sullivan**, M. A., (ed.), *Benjamin R. Tucker and the Champions of Liberty. A Centenary Anthology*, St. Paul, MN, 1987. Celebrates the writings of Tucker and other anarchists.

6.182 **Doyle**, D. H., *The Social Order of a Frontier Community. Jacksonville, Illinois, 1825–1870*, Urbana, IL, 1978.

6.183 **Einhorn**, Robin L., *Property Rules. Political Economy in Chicago, 1833–1872*, Chicago, 1991.

6.184 **Fogelson**, R. M., *America's Armories. Architecture, Society, and Public Order*, Cambridge, MA, 1989.

6.185 **Griffen**, C., and **Griffen**, Sally, *Natives and Newcomers. The Ordering of Opportunity in Mid-Nineteenth Century Poughkeepsie*, Cambridge, MA, 1978.

6.186 **Hahn**, S., 'Class and state in postemancipation societies. Southern planters in comparative perspective', *American Historical Review*, XCV, 1990, 75–98. Compares the loss of national power by southern planters after their defeat with the ability of rural elites in Germany and Brazil to forge new alliances.

6.187 **Halttunen**, Karen, *Confidence Men and Painted Women. A Study of Middle-Class Culture in America, 1830–1870*, New Haven, CT, 1982.

6.188 **Hartford**, W. F., *Working People of Holyoke. Class and Ethnicity in a Massachusetts Mill Town, 1850–1960*, New Brunswick, NJ, 1990. Strongest on the making of Holyoke's working class in the textile industry in the nineteenth century, and examines the conflict between Yankees and French Canadian migrants.

6.189 **Knights**, P. R., *Yankee Destinies. The Lives of Ordinary Nineteenth Century Bostonians*, Chapel Hill, NC, 1991. Continues work that the author did in *The Plain People of Boston* in tracing the out-migration of Bostonians in the Civil War era.

6.190 **Levine**, L. W., *Highbrow, Lowbrow. The Emergence of Cultural Hierarchy in America*, Cambridge, MA, 1988. Traces the development of a distinct highbrow culture in the nineteenth century.

6.191 **Nelson**, B. C., *Beyond the Martyrs. A Social History of Chicago's Anarchists, 1870–1900*, New Brunswick, NJ, 1988.

6.192 **Reid**, J. P., *Law of the Elephant. Property and Social Behavior on the Overland Trail*, San Marino, CA, 1980.

6.193 **Rumbarger**, J. J., *Profits, Power, and Prohibition. Alcohol Reform and the Industrializing of America, 1800–1930*, Albany, NY, 1989. Finds that temperance and prohibition were weapons in a class war for the social control of America.

Gender relations

6.194 **Abelson**, Elaine S., *When Ladies Go a Thieving. Middle Class Shoplifters in the Victorian Department Store*, New York, 1989.

6.195 **Aron**, Cindy Sondik, *Ladies and Gentlemen of the Civil Service. Middle-Class Workers in Victorian America*, New York, 1987. Looks at the nineteenth century government office as the first workplace that integrated men and women employees, and suggests that this encounter helped break down the dominant middle class ideology of separate spheres.

6.196 **Bennion**, Sherilyn Cox, *Equal to the Occasion. Women Editors of the Nineteenth Century West*, Reno, NV, 1990.

6.197 **Birken**, L., *Consuming Desire. Sexual Science and the Emergence of a Culture of Abundance, 1871–1914*, Ithaca, NY, 1988.

6.198 **Boydston**, Jeanne, **Kelley**, Mary, and **Margolis**, Anne, (ed.), *The Limits of Sisterhood. The Beecher Sisters on Women's Rights and Women's Sphere*, Chapel Hill, NC, 1988. Explores the discussions and disagreements among the remarkable women of this prominent family.

6.199 **Braude**, Ann, *Radical Spirits. Spiritualism and Women's Rights in Nineteenth Century America*, Boston, 1989.

6.200 **Butler**, Anne, *Daughters of Joy, Sisters of Mercy. Prostitutes in the American West*, Urbana, IL, 1985. Reviews the history of prostitution from the perspectives of women's and western history.

6.201 **Bynum**, Victoria E., *Unruly Women. The Politics of Social and Sexual Control in the Old South*, Chapel Hill, NC, 1992.

6.202 **Carnes**, M. C., *Secret Ritual and Manhood in Victorian America*, New Haven, CT, 1989. A study of fraternal organizations and their sometimes bizarre initiation rites, and how membership in such groups was critical to male identity.

6.203 **Carnes**, M. C., and **Griffen**, C., (ed.), *Meanings for Manhood. Constructions of Masculinity in Victorian America*, Chicago, 1990.

6.204 **Clinton**, Catherine, and **Silber**, Nina, (ed.), *Divided Houses. Gender and the Civil War*, New York, 1992.

6.205 **Culpepper**, Marilyn Mayer, *Trials and Triumphs. Women of the American Civil War*, East Lansing, MI, 1991.

6.206 **Donnelly**, Mabel Collins, *The American Victorian Woman. The Myth and the Reality*, Westport, CT, 1986. A study that analyzes popular writing on womens' bodies and sets that analysis in cultural context.

6.207 **DuBois**, Ellen Carol, *Feminism and Suffrage. The Emergence of an Independent Women's Movement in America, 1848–1869*, Ithaca, NY, 1978.

6.208 **Dudden**, Faye E., *Serving Women. Household Service in Nineteenth-Century America*, Middletown, CT, 1983.

6.209 **Edwards**, G. T., *Sowing Good Seeds. The Northwest Suffrage Campaigns of Susan B. Anthony*, Portland, OR, 1990. Examines her travels to Oregon and Washington in three decades and the reaction of editors to her cause.

6.210 **Hewitt**, Nancy A., *Women's Activism and Social Change. Rochester, New York, 1822–1872*, Ithaca, NY, 1984. Investigates women's groups and finds diversity in background and aims in the upstate New York city that has become a favorite of scholars studying antebellum reform.

6.211 **Jameson**, Elizabeth, 'Toward a multicultural history of women in the western United States', *Signs*, XIII, 1988, 761–791.

6.212 **Jeffrey**, Julie Roy, *Frontier Women. The Trans-Mississippi West, 1840–1880*, New York, 1979.

6.213 **Lasser**, Carol, 'The domestic balance of power. Relations between mistress and maid in nineteenth century New England', *Labor History*, XXVIII, 1987, 5–22.

6.214 **Maher**, Mary Denis, *To Bind Up the Wounds. Catholic Sister Nurses in the U.S. Civil War*, Westport, CT, 1989. Links the history of women and religious orders, and shows how the war changed each.

6.215 **Marks**, Patricia, *Bicycles, Bangs, and Bloomers. The New Women in the Popular Press*, Lexington, KY, 1990. Concentrates on the 1880s and 1890s and looks at women in Great Britain and America, as seen in magazines.

6.216 **Marti**, D. B., *Women of the Grange. Mutuality and Sisterhood in Rural America, 1866–1920*, Westport, CT, 1991.

6.217 **Moldow**, Gloria, *Women Doctors in Gilded-Age Washington. Race, Gender, and Professionalization*, Urbana, IL, 1987.

6.218 **Montgomery**, Maureen E., '*Gilded Prostitution*'. *Status, Money, and Transatlantic Marriages, 1870–1914*, 1989. A history of wealthy American women who married British aristocrats.

6.219 **Motz**, Marilyn Ferris, *True Sisterhood. Michigan Women and their Kin, 1820–1920*, Albany, NY, 1983.

6.220 **Osterud**, Nancy Grey, *Bonds of Community. The Lives of Farm Women in Nineteenth Century New York*, Ithaca, NY, 1991.

6.221 **Pugh**, D. G., *Sons Of Liberty. The Masculine Mind in Nineteenth Century America*, Westport, CT, 1984.

6.222 **Riley**, Glenda, *The Female Frontier. A Comparative View of Women on the Prairie and the Plains*, Lawrence, KS, 1988. Maintains that the gender divide was so great that women's lives were not very different whether in settled communities or in sparsely populated frontier areas.

6.223 **Russert**, Cynthia Eagle, *Sexual Science. The Victorian Construction of Womanhood*, Cambridge, MA, 1989.

6.224 **Ryan**, Mary P., *Women in Public. Between Banners and Ballots, 1825–1880*, Baltimore, 1990.

6.225 **Samuels**, Shirley, (ed.), *The Culture of Sentiment. Race, Gender, and Sentimentality in 19th Century America*, New York, 1992.

6.226 **Smith-Rosenberg**, Caroll, *Disorderly Conduct. Visions of Gender in Victorian America*, New York, 1985. Eight essays on the diverging views of gender, sexuality, and deviance.

6.227 **Waller**, Altina L., *Reverend Beecher and Mrs. Tilton. Sex and Class in Victorian America*, Amherst, MA, 1982. An analysis of the well-publicized adultery case of Henry Ward Beecher.

6.228 **Wilson**, Margaret Gibbons, *The American Woman in Transition. The Urban Influence, 1870–1920*, Westport, CT, 1979.

Recreation, leisure, and sport

6.229 **Allen**, R. C., *Horrible Prettiness. Burlesque and American Culture*, Chapel Hill, NC, 1991. A cultural analysis of the nether world of the theater with its gender and class contradictions.

6.230 **Bogdan**, R., *Freak Show. Presenting Human Oddities for Amusement and Profit*, Chicago, 1988. An analysis of the mid-nineteenth century phenomenon of carnival displays that emphasizes the marketing savvy of the promoters.

6.231 **Duis**, P. R., *The Saloon. Public Drinking in Chicago and Boston, 1880–1920*, Urbana, IL, 1983. An analysis of working-class drinking habits and middle class efforts to stamp out the saloon by offering alternatives and through regulation.

6.232 **Fabian**, Ann, *Card Sharps, Dream Books, and Bucket Shops. Gambling in 19th Century America*, Ithaca, NY, 1990. Proposes that while gambling opponents were solidly bourgeois in their advocacy of work and accumulation, those who gambled in the North tended to be more marginal in society and the economy.

6.233 **Goldstein**, W., *Playing for Keeps. A History of Early Baseball*, Ithaca, NY, 1988. Traces the emergence of the professional game from the urban milieu of New York during the Civil War.

6.234 **Gorn**, E. J., *The Manly Art. Bare-Knuckle Prize Fighting in America*, Ithaca, NY, 1988. An examination of the emergence of boxing as one of the dominant popular sports in the nineteenth century.

6.235 **Green**, H., *Fit for America. Health, Fitness, Sport, and American Society*, Baltimore, 1986. Traces the unending quest by Americans for fitness from religious, even millenarian, sources, to racialist concerns later in the century.

6.236 **Greenhaigh**, P., *Ephemeral Vistas. The Expositions Universelles, Great Exhibitions, and World's Fairs, 1851–1939*, 1988.

6.237 **Isenberg**, M. T., *John L. Sullivan and His America*, Urbana, IL, 1988. A biography of the boxer who turned professional prize-fighting into a national mania.

6.238 **Levine**, P., *A. G. Spalding and the Rise of Baseball. The Promise of American Sport*, New York, 1985.

6.239 **McArthur**, B., *Actors and American Culture, 1880–1920*, Philadelphia, 1984. A study of the business of the theater from its disorganized and disreputable nineteenth century state through its emergence as a respectable business with actors becoming recognized stars in society.

6.240 **Rydell**, R. W., *All the World's a Fair. Visions of Empire at American International Expositions, 1876–1916*, Chicago, 1984. Explores the mix of business and tourism along with race and nationalism that was featured at world's fairs.

6.241 **Smith**, R. A., *Sports and Freedom. The Rise of Big-Time College Athletics*, New York, 1988. The definitive study of the origins of intercollegiate sports at the Ivy League schools and how player-centered games were altered to respond to the needs of coaches, alumni, and fans at large.

6.242 **Snyder**, R. W., *The Voice of the City. Vaudeville and Popular Culture in New York*, New York, 1989.

6.243 **Tawa**, N. E., *The Way to Tin Pan Alley. American Popular Song, 1866–1910*, New York, 1990.

Education

6.244 **Herbst**, J., *And Sadly Teach. Teacher Education and Professionalization in American Culture*, Madison, WI, 1989. A history of the origins of the normal school movement to train public school teachers, and how the institutions failed almost from the start to prepare teachers for the work in the classroom.

6.245 **Horowitz**, Helen Lefkowitz, *Alma Mater. Design and Experience in the Women's Colleges from their Nineteenth Century Beginnings to the 1930s*, New York, 1984. Looks at the interplay of architecture and gender relations among the so-called "Seven Sisters" colleges along with three other women's colleges.

6.246 **Jorgenson**, L. P., *The State and the Non-Public School, 1825–1925*, Columbia, MO, 1987. Examines the struggle over the control of the public school curriculum, particularly between Protestants and Catholics, and finds that the victory of Protestant doctrines in public education caused Catholics to withdraw into parochial schools.

6.247 **Kaufman**, Polly Welts, *Women Teachers on the Frontier*, New Haven, CT, 1984. Reviews the struggle for control of the spread of public education to the West, and the role that women played in propagating established notions of culture and order.

6.248 **Link**, W. A., *Hard Country and a Lonely Place. Schooling, Society, and Reform in Rural Virginia, 1870–1920*, Chapel Hill, NC, 1986.

6.249 **Marsden**, G. M., and **Lonfield**, B. J., (ed.), *The Secularization of the Academy*, New York, 1992.

6.250 **Mitchell**, T. R., *Political Education in the Southern Farmers' Alliance, 1887–1900*, Madison, WI, 1987.

6.251 **Oleson**, A., and **Voss**, J., (ed.), *The Organization of Knowledge in Modern America, 1860–1920*, Baltimore, 1979.

6.252 **Solomon**, Barbara Miller, *In the Company of Educated Women. A History of Women* and *Higher Education in America*, New Haven, CT, 1985. A survey of women in college that is strongest on the founding of nineteenth century women's colleges.

6.253 **Street**, D. R., 'The experiment system and land grant education. Antecedents to the Hatch Act', *Agricultural History*, LXII, 1988, 27–40.

6.254 **Vinovskis**, M. A., *The Origins of Public High Schools. A Reexamination of the Beverly High School Controversy*, Madison, WI, 1985. A quantitative reworking of Michael Katz's 1968 *Irony of Early School Reform*, Vinovskis finds other factors besides class struggle at the root of the choice made by nineteenth century Beverly, Massachusetts, to adopt mandatory high school attendance.

6.255 **Williams**, R. L., *The Origins of Federal Support for Higher Education. George W. Atherton and the Land-Grant College Movement*, University Park, PA, 1991. A study of how state colleges lobbied for federal support after the 1862 Morrill Act, and how a lasting relationship was built between the federal government and agricultural education.

Crime and punishment

6.256 **Ayers**, E. L., *Vengeance and Justice. Crime and Punishment in the 19th-Century American South*, New York, 1984. Looks at law and custom in Georgia before, during, and after the Civil War and finds that the war and the spread of market relations brought a much greater law enforcement presence in their wakes.

6.257 **Cresswell**, S., *Mormons & Cowboys, Moonshiners & Klansmen. Federal Law Enforcement in the South & West, 1870–1893*, Tuscaloosa, AL, 1991. Examines the records of the U.S. marshals in Mississippi and Utah to explain the federal role in law enforcement.

6.258 **Freedman**, Estelle B., *Their Sisters' Keepers. Women's Prison Reform in America, 1830–1930*, Ann Arbor, MI, 1981.

6.259 **Friedman**, L. M., and **Percival**, R. V., *The Roots of Justice. Crime and Punishment in Alameda County, California, 1870–1910*, Chapel Hill, NC, 1981.

6.260 **Harring**, S., *Policing a Class Society. The Experience of American Cities, 1865–1915*,

New Brunswick, NJ, 1983.

6.261 **Lane**, R., *Violent Death in the City. Suicide, Accident, and Murder in 19th Century Philadelphia*, Cambridge, MA, 1979. Links social change to differing rates of violent death; suicides rose and murder rates tended to fall.

RELIGION, BELIEFS, IDEAS, AND CULTURE

6.262 **Bremner**, R. H., *The Public Good. Philanthropy and Welfare in the Civil War Era*, New York, 1980.

6.263 **Bruce**, R. V., *The Launching of Modern American Science, 1846–1876*, Ithaca, NY, 1988.

6.264 **Cmiel**, K., *Democratic Eloquence. The Fight over Popular Speech in Nineteenth-Century America*, New York, 1990.

6.265 **Lubin**, D. M., *Acts of Portrayal. Eakins, Sargent, James*, New Haven, CT, 1985. An unusual blend of art and literary criticism that seeks to analyze the subjects and interpreters of portraits on canvas and in book form.

6.266 **Marling**, Karal Ann, *George Washington Slept Here. Colonial Revivals and American Culture, 1876–1986*, Cambridge, MA, 1988. Shows how Washington has been constantly reinvented by Americans, particularly starting in the late nineteenth century when a Washington fancy and a colonial revival in architecture and home furnishings helped distinguish Americans of older stock from immigrants.

6.267 **Mayo**, Louise A., *The Ambivalent Image. Nineteenth-Century America's Perception of the Jew*, Rutherford, NJ, 1988.

6.268 **Robertson**, D. M., *The Chicago Revival, 1876. Society and Revivalism in a Nineteenth Century City*, Metuchen, NJ, 1989.

6.269 **Thomas**, J. L., *Alternative America. Henry George, Edward Bellamy, Henry Demarest Lloyd and the Adversary Tradition*, Cambridge, MA, 1983.

6.270 **Turner**, J., *Without God, Without Creed. The Origins of Unbelief in America*, Baltimore, 1985. Examines the movement toward agnosticism and its sources in rationalism and other intellectual currents.

Denominations, North and South

6.271 **Angell**, S. W., *Bishop Henry McNeal Turner and African-American Religion in the South*, Knoxville, TN, 1992. Places its subject in the context of the development of the African Methodist Episcopal church in Georgia after the Civil War.

6.272 **Christiano**, K. J., *Religious Diversity and Social Change. American Cities, 1890–1906*, New York, 1987.

6.273 **Frankiel**, Sandra Sizer, *California's Spiritual Frontiers. Religious Alternatives in Anglo-Protestantism, 1850–1910*, Berkeley, CA, 1988.

6.274 **Hill**, S. S., *Varieties of Southern Religious Experience*, Baton Rouge, LA, 1988. Ten essays on the subject, most concerned with antebellum history.

6.275 **Moore**, J. T., *Through Fire and Flood. The Catholic Church in Frontier Texas*, College Station, TX, 1992.

6.276 **Moorhead**, J. H., *American Apocalypse. Yankee Protestants and the Civil War, 1860–1869*, New Haven, CT, 1978.

6.277 **Ownby**, T., *Subduing Satan. Religion, Recreation, and Manhood in the Rural South, 1865–1920*, Chapel Hill, NC, 1990.

6.278 **Spalding**, T. W., *The Premier See. A History of the Archdiocese of Baltimore, 1789–1989*, Baltimore, 1989. A history of the Catholic Church in Baltimore, strongest in the nineteenth century when for some time the archdiocese covered the entire United States.

6.279 **Spann**, E. K., *Brotherly Tomorrows. Movements for a Cooperative Society in America, 1820–1920*, New York, 1989.

6.280 **Stevenson**, Louise L., *Scholarly Means to Evangelical Ends. The New Haven Scholars and the Transformation of Higher Learning in America, 1830–1890*, Baltimore, 1986.

6.281 **Szasz**, F. M., *The Protestant Clergy in the Great Plains and Mountain West, 1865–1915*, Albuquerque, NM, 1988.

6.282 **Taves**, Ann, *The Household of Faith. Roman Catholic Devotions in Mid-Nineteenth Century America*, Notre Dame, IN, 1986. An examination of Catholic prayer books and the spirituality they reflect of Catholics.

6.283 **Tucker**, Cynthia Grant, *A Woman's Ministry. Mary Collison's Search for Reform as a Unitarian Minister, a Hull House Social Worker, and a Christian Science Practitioner*, Philadelphia, 1984.

Antislavery and proslavery thought

6.284 **Goodheart**, L. B., *Abolitionist, Actuary, Atheist. Elizur Wright and the Reform Impulse*, Kent, OH, 1990. Analyzes Wright's career in a host of nineteenth century reform movements, and charts his movement away from Christianity toward secular humanism.

6.285 **Martin**, S. D., *Black Baptists and African Missions. The Origins of a Movement, 1880–1915*, Macon, GA, 1989. Traces the missionary movement on the part of southern Baptists to spread the Gospel to Africa and to forge a new racial solidarity among blacks along religious lines.

6.286 **McKivigan**, J. R., *The War against Proslavery Religion. Abolitionism and the Northern Churches, 1830–1865*, Ithaca, NY, 1984. Traces the reception of abolitionist doctrines in various northern denominations and finds that evangelical churches tended to be more receptive to viewing slavery as a sin that required active church opposition.

6.287 **Nelson**, Jacquelyn S., *Indiana Quakers Confront the Civil War*, Indianapolis, IN, 1991. Shows that many Friends forsook pacifism for Union military service in the great conflict over slavery.

6.288 **Venet**, Wendy Hamand, *Neither Ballots nor Bullets. Women Abolitionists and the Civil War*, Charlottesville, VA, 1991.

6.289 **Walker**, C. E., *A Rock in a Weary Land. The African Methodist Episcopal Church During the Civil War and Reconstruction*, Baton Rouge, LA, 1982.

6.290 **Yee**, Shirley J., *Black Women Abolitionists. A Study in Activism, 1828–1860*, Knoxville, TN, 1992.

6.291 **Yellin**, Jean Fagan, *Women & Sisters. The Antislavery Feminists in American Culture*, New Haven, CT, 1989.

Social Darwinism and the Social Gospel

6.292 **Bannister**, R. C., *Social Darwinism. Science and Myth in Anglo-American Social*

Thought, Philadelphia, 1979.

6.293 **Bordin**, Ruth, *Woman and Temperance. The Quest for Power and Liberty, 1873–1900*, Philadelphia, 1981. An administrative history of the Woman's Christian Temperance Union and its charismatic leader, Frances Willard.

6.294 **Cashdollar**, C. D., *The Transformation of Theology, 1830–1890. Positivism and Protestant Thought in Britain and America*, Princeton, NJ, 1989.

6.295 **Curtis**, Susan, *A Consuming Faith. The Social Gospel and Modern American Culture*, Baltimore, 1991. Finds an irony in the thought of leading adherents of the Social Gospel. The study finds that they actually promoted the new culture of leisure and thereby undermined the Protestant Ethic as it had been known.

6.296 **Degler**, C. N., *In Search of Human Nature. The Decline and Revival of Darwinism in American Social Thought*, New York, 1991. A history of the nineteenth century spread of Social Darwinism and its surprising reappearance in the late twentieth century.

6.297 **Luker**, R. E., *The Social Gospel in Black and White. American Racial Reform, 1885–1912*, Chapel Hill, NC, 1991.

6.298 **Roberts**, J. H., *Darwinism and the Divine in America. Protestant Intellectuals and Organic Evolution, 1859–1900*, Madison, WI, 1988.

6.299 **White**, R. C., *Liberty and Justice for All. Racial Reform and the Social Gospel, 1877–1925*, San Francisco, 1990.

6.301 **David**, P., (ed.), *Reckoning With Slavery*, New York, 1976. A series of essays by new economic historians in response to Fogel and Engerman's *Time on the Cross*; the essay by Gavin Wright is particularly valuable.

6.302 **Fogel**, R. W., and **Engerman**, S. L., *Time on the Cross. The Economics of American Negro Slavery*, Boston, 1974, The manifesto of the self-proclaimed cliometricians, in two volumes; the first is narrative with charts, the second has the calculations, along with a quite complete bibliography of writings on slavery.

6.303 **Gallman**, R. E., and **Anderson**, R. V., 'Slaves as fixed capital. Slave labor and southern economic development', *Journal of American History*, LXIV, 1977, 24–46. Treats the idea of keeping slaves working at all times and the economic profitability of slavery.

6.304 **Hermann**, Janet Sharp, *The Pursuit of a Dream*, New York, 1981. An account of the Davis Bend plantation in Mississippi and how the older brother of Jefferson Davis tried to create a utopian, Owenite version of a slave plantation in the years before the Civil War.

6.305 **Lowe**, R. G., and **Campbell**, R. B., *Planters & Plain Folk. Agriculture in Antebellum Texas*, Dallas, TX, 1987.

6.306 **Owens**, H. P., *Steamboats and the Cotton Economy. River Trade in the Yazoo-Mississippi Delta*, Jackson, MS, 1990.

6.307 **Shore**, L., *Southern Capitalists. The Ideological Leadership of an Elite, 1832–1885*, Chapel Hill, NC, 1986.

6.308 **Tadman**, M., *Speculators and Slaves. Masters, Traders, and Slaves in the Old South*, Madison, WI, 1989.

WORK AND ENTERPRISE

Slavery as an economic system

6.300 **Coclanis**, P. A., *The Shadow of a Dream. Economic Life and Death in the South Carolina Low Country, 1670–1920*, New York, 1989. A history of rice culture, both under slavery and free labor, that emphasizes South Carolina's rise under favorable market conditions, and later fall in the face of intense world competition in rice production.

The emerging industrial giant

6.309 **Carlson**, W. B., *Innovation as a Social Process. Elihu Thomson and the Rise of General Electric, 1870–1900*, New York, 1991.

6.310 **Garnet**, R. W., *The Telephone Enterprise. The Evolution of the Bell System's Horizontal Structure, 1876–1909*, Baltimore, 1985. Finds that the technical demands of the telephone business required horizontal integration of the firm, but one tempered by the need to operate under state regulation.

6.311 **Heitmann**, J. A., *The Modernization of the Louisiana Sugar Industry, 1830–1910*, Baton Rouge, LA, 1987.

6.312 **Hounshell**, D. A., *From the American System to Mass Production, 1800–1932. The Development of Manufacturing Technology in the United States*, Baltimore, 1984.

6.313 **Ingham**, J. N., *Making Iron and Steel. Independent Mills in Pittsburgh, 1820–1920*, Columbus, OH, 1991.

6.314 **Judd**, R. W., *Aroostook. A Century of Logging in Northern Maine*, Orono, ME, 1989.

6.315 **Kilar**, J. W., *Michigan's Lumbertowns. Lumbermen and Laborers in Saginaw, Bay City, and Muskegon, 1870–1905*, Detroit, 1990.

6.316 **Marvin**, Carolyn, *When Old Technologies Were New. Thinking about Electric Communication in the Late Nineteenth Century*, New York, 1988.

6.317 **McGaw**, Judith A., *Most Wonderful Machine. Mechanization and Social Change in Berkshire Paper Making, 1801–1885*, Princeton, NJ, 1987. Examines the gradual technological change in the western Massachusetts paper industry, and the consequent changes in labor and community life.

6.318 **Millard**, A., *Edison and the Business of Innovation*, Baltimore, 1990.

6.319 **Thompson**, R., *The Path to Mechanized Shoe Production in the United States*, Chapel Hill, NC, 1989. Charts the role of secondary inventions, such as the sewing machine, in transforming the shoe industry from handicraft to mass production.

6.320 **Williams**, J. H., *A Great & Shining Road. The Epic Story of the Transcontinental Railroad*, New York, 1988.

6.321 **Yates**, JoAnne, *Control through Communication. The Rise of System in American Management*, Baltimore, 1989.

The agricultural giant

6.322 **Ferleger**, L., (ed.), *Agriculture and National Development. Views on the Nineteenth Century*, Ames, IA, 1990.

6.323 **Hahn**, S., *The Roots of Southern Populism. Yeoman Farmers and the Transformation of the Georgia Upcountry, 1850–1890*, New York, 1983. Examines how and why white southern farmers lost their lands and independence after the Civil War and followed freed blacks into sharecropping.

6.324 **Isern**, T. D., *Bull Threshers and Bindlestiffs. Harvesting and Threshing on the North American Plains*, Lawrence, KS, 1990.

6.325 **Klingaman**, D. C., *Essays on the Economy of the Old Northwest*, Athens, OH, 1987. Continues some of the econometric work done in the 1975 volume edited by the same two scholars.

6.326 **Klingaman**, D. C., and **Vedder**, R., *Essays in Nineteenth Century Economic History*, Athens, OH, 1975. Essays by leading practioners of the "new economic history" on the emergence of the Midwest as an agricultural power.

6.327 **Parker**, W. N., *America and the Wider World*, New York, 1991. Part of a larger series by one of the leaders of the "New Economic History", this volume focuses on the origins of American prosperity in its nineteenth century agricultural strength.

6.328 **Pinney**, T., *A History of Winemaking in America. From the Beginning to the Prohibition Era*, Berkeley, CA, 1989. Concentrates on the nineteenth century origins of the California viniculture.

6.329 **Ransom**, R. L., and **Sutch**, R., *One Kind of Freedom. The Economic Consequences of Emancipation*, New York, 1977. A "new economic history" treatment of sharecropping that finds it was an economic compromise between the wishes of the planters and the freedmen.

6.330 **Rikoon**, J. S., *Threshing in the Midwest, 1820–1940. A Study of Traditional Culture and Technological Change*, Bloomington, IN, 1988. Examines the tensions between communal forms of grain harvesting and the pressures toward individualism that followed in the wake of mechanization.

6.331 **Skaggs**, J. M., *Prime Cut. Livestock Raising and Meatpacking in the United States, 1607–1983*, College Station, TX, 1984. A survey of the ranching and meat industries with particular concentration on the nineteenth century cattle drives.

6.332 **Winters**, D. E., *Farmers Without Farms. Agricultural Tenancy in Nineteenth-Century Iowa*, Westport, CT, 1978.

The northern working class

6.333 **Angus**, D. L., and **Mirel**, J., 'From spellers to spindles: work-force entry by the

children of textile workers, 1888–1890',
Social Science History, IX, 1984, 123–144.

6.334 **Arnesen**, E., *Waterfront Workers of New Orleans. Race, Class, and Politics, 1863–1923*, New York, 1991.

6.335 **Blewett**, Mary H., *Men, Women, and Work. Class, Gender, and Protest in the New England Shoe Industry, 1780–1910*, Urbana, IL, 1988. Treats the history of Massachusetts women in the shoe industry, particularly after 1860 when production became concentrated in factories, and how the experience of women workers differed from male shoe workers.

6.336 **Cassity**, M., *Defending a Way of Life. An American Community in the Nineteenth Century*, Albany, NY, 1989.

6.337 **Cornford**, D. A., *Workers and Dissent in the Redwood Empire*, Philadelphia, 1988. Traces the evolution of a radical republican tradition among timber workers in nineteenth century California into resistance and then accommodation to corporate capitalism.

6.338 **Fink**, L., *Workingman's Democracy. The Knights of Labor and American Politics*, Urbana, IL, 1983. A study of five localities and the surge of labor voting power in the early 1880s, and the reasons for its demise after 1886.

6.339 **Fones-Wolf**, K., *Trade Union Gospel. Christianity and Labor in Industrial Philadelphia, 1865–1915*, Philadelphia, 1989.

6.340 **Gabler**, E., *The American Telegrapher. A Social History, 1860–1900*, New Brunswick, NJ, 1988.

6.341 **Hoover**, G. A., 'Supplemental family income sources: ethnic differences in nineteenth-century industrial America', *Social Science History*, IX, 1985, 293–306.

6.342 **Katzman**, D., *Seven Days a Week. Women and Domestic Service in Industrializing America*, New York, 1978.

6.343 **Keyssar**, A., *Out of Work. The First Century of Unemployment in Massachusetts*, New York, 1986. Makes use of the extensive state Bureau of Labor Statistics reports to reconstruct estimates of unemployment.

6.344 **Korver**, T., *The Factious Commodity. A Study of the U. S. Labor Market, 1880–1940*, New York, 1990. Examines how labor was recruited into the wage market and how struggle between

employers and workers began with the employment contract.

6.345 **Krause**, P., *The Battle for Homestead, 1880–1892. Politics, Culture, and Steel*, Pittsburgh, 1992.

6.346 **Lankton**, L. D., *Cradle to Grave. Life, Work and Death at the Lake Superior Copper Mines*, New York, 1991. A labor and community study of the copper miners of Michigan's Keweenaw Peninsula.

6.347 **Marks**, G., *Unions in Politics. Britain, Germany, and the United States in the Nineteenth and Early Twentieth Centuries*, Princeton, NJ, 1989.

6.348 **McLaurin**, M. A., *The Knights of Labor in the South*, Westport, CT, 1978.

6.349 **Oestreicher**, R. J., *Solidarity and Fragmentation. Working People and Class Consciousness in Detroit, 1875–1900*, Urbana, IL, 1986. Highlights the role of the Knights of Labor in building a class conscious Detroit labor movement, but one that could not survive the tumult of 1886 and soon declined into ethnic and craft divisions.

6.350 **Palladino**, Grace, *Another Civil War. Labor, Capital, and the State in the Anthracite Region of Pennsylvania, 1840–68*, Urbana, IL, 1990. Chronicles the use by mine owners of the U.S. Army to suppress labor organizing in Schuykill County, Pennsylvania.

6.351 **Ross**, S. J., *Workers on the Edge. Work, Leisure, and Politics in Industrializing Cincinnati, 1788–1890*, New York, 1985. An examination of how republican ideology among artisan producers early in nineteenth century Cincinnati was transformed by the process of industrialization.

6.352 **Schwantes**, C. A., *Coxey's Army. An American Odyssey*, Lincoln, NE, 1985. A reconstruction of the marchers led by Jacob Coxey in 1894 who travelled the United States with Washington, DC as their destination with the goal of demanding an end to unemployment.

6.353 **Stromquist**, S., *A Generation of Boomers. The Pattern of Railroad Labor Conflict in Nineteenth Century America*, Urbana, IL, 1987. An analysis of the pattern of railroad strikes between 1881 and 1894 and how the outcomes of these strikes reflected changing class relations.

6.354 **Walkowitz**, D. J., *Worker City, Company Town. Iron and Cotton-Worker Protest in*

Troy and Cohoes, New York, 1855–1884, Urbana, IL, 1978.

6.355 **Wallace**, A. F. C., *St. Clair. A Nineteenth Century Coal Town's Experience with a Disaster-Prone Industry*, New York, 1987. An anthropologist's account of a Pennsylvania anthracite town and the conflict between labor and capital in and outside the mines.

RACE AND IDENTITY

African-Americans

(a) FROM SLAVES TO FREEDMEN

6.356 **Abzug**, R. H., and **Maizlish**, S. E., (ed.), *New Perspectives on Race and Slavery in America. Essays in Honor of Kenneth M. Stampp*, Lexington, KY, 1986. A festschrift to honor the University of California historian who helped chart the field of slavery studies with his landmark 1956 book, *The Peculiar Institution*.

6.357 **Blackett**, R. J. M., *Beating Against the Barriers. Biographical Essays in Nineteenth Century Afro-American History*, Baton Rouge, LA, 1986.

6.358 **Blight**, D. W., *Frederick Douglass' Civil War. Keeping Faith in Jubilee*, Baton Rouge, LA, 1989. A biography of the black abolitionist that examines in particular his leadership during the Civil War.

6.359 **Campbell**, R. B., *An Empire for Slavery. The Peculiar Institution in Texas, 1821–1865*, Baton Rouge, LA, 1989. Treats the proliferation of slavery in Texas before the Civil War and the lives and culture of the slaves.

6.360 **Collins**, B., *White Society in the Antebellum South*, 1985. Examines the basis of white solidarity in the South and finds it in a mix of race and kinship ties.

6.361 **Fields**, Barbara Jeanne, *Slavery and Freedom on the Middle Ground. Maryland during the Nineteenth Century*, New Haven, CT, 1985. Traces the decline of slavery in Maryland and finds that the institution was incompatible with the free labor capitalist economy that was emerging in the state.

6.362 **Foster**, Frances Smith, *Witnessing Slavery. The Development of Ante-Bellum Slave Narratives*, Westport, CT, 1979. Reviews the genre of the slave narrative, the most important source for historians in understanding slavery from the viewpoint of the slave.

6.363 **Fuke**, R. P., 'Planters, apprenticeship, and forced labor: the black family under pressure in post-emancipation Maryland', *Agricultural History*, LXII, 1988, 57–74.

6.364 **Harris**, J. W., *Plain Folk and Gentry in a Slave Society. White Liberty and Black Slavery in Augusta's Hinterland*, Middletown, CT, 1985. A case study of rural Georgia and the ties that bound slaveholding and non-slaveholding whites into a racialist democracy.

6.365 **Howard**, V. B., *Black Liberation in Kentucky. Emancipation and Freedom, 1862–1884*, Lexington, KY, 1983.

6.366 **Jaynes**, G. D., *Branches without Roots. Genesis of the Black Working Class in the American South, 1862–1882*, New York, 1986. An analysis of a sample of Freedmen's Bureau labor contracts from across the postbellum South that shows the transition from slavery to contract labor to sharecropping.

6.367 **Johnson**, M. P., and **Roark**, J. L., *Black Masters. A Free Family of Color in the Old South*, New York, 1984. Considers the place of the Ellison family of South Carolina and its relations with whites and other free blacks.

6.368 **Jones**, H., *Mutiny on the Amistad. The Saga of a Slave Revolt and its Impact on American Abolition, Law and Diplomacy*, New York, 1978. Explores the role of natural and positive law in the unfolding of this 1841 case and argues that abolitionists did not fully appreciate the Constitution as an anti-slavery document.

6.369 **Luker**, R. E., ' "Under our own vine and fig tree". From African unionism to black denominationalism in Newport, Rhode Island, 1760–1876', *Slavery and Abolition*, XII, 1991, 23–48. A history of the church that emerged as the Free African Union of Newport.

6.370 **Owens**, L. H., *This Species of Property. Slave Life and Culture in the Old South*, New York, 1976.

6.371 **Schweninger**, L., *Black Property Owners in the South, 1790–1915*, Urbana, IL, 1990. Exhaustive work in the manuscript census returns shows that a surprising number of free blacks before the war owned property.

6.372 **Swift**, D. E., *Black Prophets of Justice. Activist Clergy before the Civil War*, Baton Rouge, LA, 1989. Examines the lives of six black clergymen and their views on the role of religion in the lives of free blacks and the enslaved.

6.373 **Van Deburg**, W. L., *Slavery and Race in American Popular Culture*, Madison, WI, 1984. Considers the representation of black people in popular iconography.

6.374 **Walker**, Juliet E. K., *Free Frank. A Black Pioneer on the Antebellum Frontier*, Lexington, KY, 1983.

6.375 **White**, Deborah Gray, *Ar'n't I a Woman? Female Slaves in the Plantation South*, New York, 1985. Shows the extensive difference in the experience of slave women from the more chronicled slave men.

(b) AFTER EMANCIPATION

6.376 **Anderson**, E., *Race and Politics in North Carolina, 1872–1901. The Black Second*, Baton Rouge, LA, 1981. A study of an eastern North Carolina congressional district's history after the Democratic party gained control of the state and how a bi-racial coalition operated up to the beginning of the new century.

6.377 **Anderson**, J. D., *The Education of Blacks in the South, 1865–1935*, Chapel Hill, NC, 1988. A book critical of the Tuskegee and Hampton experiments in determining the course of black education in the South for several generations after slavery's end.

6.378 **Bigham**, D. E., *We Ask Only a Fair Trial. A History of the Black Community of Evansville, Indiana*, Bloomington, IN, 1987.

6.379 **Billington**, M. L., *New Mexico's Buffalo Soldiers, 1860–1900*, Niwot, CO, 1991. The history of black troops, many of them Civil War veterans, dispatched to fight Native Americans in the Southwest.

6.380 **Litwack**, L. F., *Been in the Storm So Long. The Aftermath of Slavery*, New York, 1979. A social history of the freed people, with special emphasis on work and religion.

6.381 **McCaul**, R. L., *The Black Struggle for Public Schooling in Nineteenth-Century Illinois*, Carbondale, IL, 1987.

6.382 **Orser**, C. E., *The Material Basis of the Postbellum Tenant Plantation. Historical Archaeology in the South Carolina Piedmont*, Athens, GA, 1988.

6.383 **Painter**, Nell Irvin, *Exodusters. Black Migration to Kansas after Reconstruction*, New York, 1976.

6.384 **Rabinowitz**, H. N., *Race Relations in the Urban South, 1865–1890*, New York, 1978. Looks at five cities and finds that legalized segregation was actually a change for the better in the social conditions for black people.

6.385 **Rachleff**, P. J., *Black Labor in the South. Richmond, Virginia, 1865–1890*, Philadelphia, 1984.

6.386 **Savage**, W. S., *Blacks in the West*, Westport, CT, 1976. Considers the contributions of black people to the frontier tradition, especially in the Army and as cowboys.

6.387 **Toll**, W., *The Resurgency of Race. Black Social Theory from Reconstruction to the Pan-American Conferences*, Philadelphia, 1979.

6.388 **Williamson**, J., *The Crucible of Race. Black-White Relations in the American South Since Emancipation*, New York, 1984. Analyzes the social thought of white southerners in the 1880s as the basis for the lynching and segregation backlash of the 1890s.

Native Americans

6.389 **Anderson**, G. C., *Little Crow, Spokesman for the Sioux*, St. Paul, MN, 1986. Places in ethnohistorical context the Dakota (or Sioux) leader of the 1862 uprising on the northern Great Plains.

6.390 **Bailey**, J. W., *Pacifying the Plains. General Alfred Terry and the Decline of the Sioux, 1866–1890*, Westport, CT, 1979.

6.391 **Bender**, N. J., *'New Hope for the Indians'. The Grant Peace Policy and the Navajos in the 1870s*, Albuquerque, NM, 1989. A review of federal Indian policy as applied to the Southwest.

6.392 **Blaine**, Martha Royce, *Pawnee Passage, 1870–1875*, Norman, OK, 1990.

6.393 **Chalfant**, W. Y., *Without Quarter. The Wichita Expedition and the Fight on Crooked Creek*, Norman, OK, 1991. An account of the 1858 fighting between the U.S. and the Comanches from Texas north into Kansas.

6.394 **Gray**, J. S., *Custer's Last Campaign. Mitch Boyer and the Little Bighorn Reconstructed*,

Lincoln, NE, 1991. Part biography of Boyer, an Indian scout who served with Custer, and part an explanation of recent archaeological excavations at the battle site.

6.395 **Greene**, J. A., *Yellowstone Command. Colonel Nelson A. Miles and the Great Sioux War, 1876–1877*, Lincoln, NE, 1991.

6.396 **Hedren**, P. L., *Fort Laramie in 1876. Chronicle of a Frontier Post at War*, Lincoln, NE, 1988.

6.397 **Hurtado**, A. L., *Indian Survival on the California Frontier*, New Haven, CT, 1988.

6.398 **Hutton**, P. A., *Phil Sheridan and his Army*, Lincoln, NE, 1985. A thorough coverage of the soldiers and the Plains wars.

6.399 **Jensen**, R. E., (ed.), *Eyewitness at Wounded Knee*, Lincoln, NE, 1991. A photographic history of the 1890 massacre at Wounded Knee on the Pine Ridge Reservation.

6.400 **Madsen**, B. D., *The Shoshoni Frontier and the Bear River Massacre*, Salt Lake City, UT, 1985. An account of the 1863 massacre and of the series of continuing wars in the Great Basin at mid-century.

6.401 **Mcginnis**, A., *Counting Coup and Cutting Horses. Intertribal Warfare on the Northern Plains, 1738–1889*, Evergreen, CO, 1990.

6.402 **Murray**, K. A., *The Modocs and their War*, Norman, OK, 1984. The history of the California tribe and their 1873 war with the United States.

6.403 **Powell**, P. J., *People of the Sacred Mountain. A History of the Northern Cheyenne Chiefs and Warrior Societies, 1830–1879*, New York, 1979.

6.404 **Smith**, Sherry Lynn, *The View from Officer's Row. Army Perceptions of Western Indians*, Tucson, AZ, 1990.

6.405 **Sweeney**, E. S., *Cochise. Chiricahua Apache Chief*, Norman, OK, 1991. Traces the border war between the Apaches and Americans and Mexicans.

6.406 **Trafzer**, C. E., *The Kit Carson Campaign. The Last Great Navajo War*, Norman, OK, 1982.

6.407 **Weeks**, P., *Farewell, My Nation. The American Indian and the United States, 1820–1890*, Arlington Heights, IL, 1990. Surveys federal Indian policy toward American Indians, particularly the military encounters on the Great Plains.

6.408 **Wooster**, R., *The Military and United States Indian Policy, 1865–1903*, New Haven, CT, 1988.

(a) REFORMERS AND THE DAWES ACT

6.409 **Carlson**, L. A., *Indians, Bureaucrats and Land. The Dawes Act and the Decline of Indian Farming*, Westport, CT, 981.

6.410 **Churchill**, W., *Fantasies of the Master Race. Literature, Cinema and the Colonization of American Indians*, Monroe, ME, 1992.

6.411 **Coleman**, M. C., *Presbyterian Missionary Attitudes Toward American Indians, 1837–1893*, Jackson, MS, 1985. Focuses on the church's missions to the Choctaws of Mississippi and the Nez Perce of Idaho.

6.412 **Dippie**, B. W., *The Vanishing American. White Attitudes and U. S. Indian Policy*, Middletown, CT, 1982.

6.413 **Hagan**, W. T., *The Indian Rights Association. The Herbert Welsh Years, 1882–1904*, Tucson, AZ, 1985.

6.414 **Hoxie**, F. E., *A Final Promise. The Campaign to Assimilate the Indians, 1880–1920*, Lincoln, NE, 1984. Treats the determination of white reformers and government officials to combine education and land allotment into a policy of eradicating tribal culture and Indian identity.

6.415 **McBeth**, Sally J., *Ethnic Identity and the Boarding School Experience of West-Central Oklahoma Indians*, Washington, DC, 1983.

6.416 **Milner**, C. A., and **O'Neil**, F. A., (ed.), *Churchmen and the Western Indians, 1820–1920*, Norman, OK, 1985.

6.417 **Miner**, H. C., and **Unrau**, W. E., *The End of Indian Kansas. A Study of Cultural Revolution, 1854–1871*, Lawrence, KS, 1978.

6.418 **Prucha**, F. P., *The Churches and the Indian Schools, 1880–1912*, Lincoln, NE, 1979.

6.419 **Ruby**, R. H., and **Brown**, J. A., *Dreamer-Prophets of the Columbia Plateau, Smohall and Skolaskin*, Norman, OK, 1989. Biographical account of two prophets who were instrumental in revitalization movements in the nineteenth century Washington Territory.

6.420 **White**, R., *The Roots of Dependency. Subsistence, Environment, and Social Change among the Choctaws, Pawnees and Navajos*, Norman, OK, 1983.

European-Americans

6.421 **Alexander**, June Granatir, *The Immigrant Church and Community. Pittsburgh's Slovak Catholics and Lutherans, 1800–1915*, Pittsburgh, 1987. Concentrates mainly on the late nineteenth century Slovaks who maintained close ties to the homeland, mediated through the church.

6.422 **Ashkenazi**, E., *The Business of Jews in Louisiana, 1840–1875*, Tuscaloosa, AL, 1988.

6.423 **Berger**, D., (ed.), *The Legacy of Jewish Migration. 1881 and its Impact*, New York, 1983.

6.424 **Bodnar**, J., *The Transplanted. A History of Immigrants in Urban America*, Bloomington, IN, 1985. A new synthesis of immigration that stresses the culture that largely rural immigrants brought with them as they made their way to an urban capitalist life in the United States.

6.425 **Brownstone**, D. M., *Island of Hope, Island of Tears*, New York, 1979. A history of the immigration station at Ellis Island, New York.

6.426 **Cinel**, D., 'Sicilians in the deep South: the ironic outcome of isolation', *Studi Emigrazione*, XXVII, 1990, 55–86.

6.427 **Conzen**, Kathleen Neils, 'Immigrants, immigrant neighborhoods, and ethnic identity. Historical issues', *Journal of American History*, LXVI, 1979, 603–615.

6.428 **Debouzy**, Marianne, (ed.), *In the Shadow of the Statue of Liberty. Immigrants, Workers and Citizens in the American Republic, 1880–1920*, Paris, 1988. A French-language collection of essays inspired by the centennial of the Statue of Liberty.

6.429 **Diner**, Hasia R., *Erin's Daughters in America. Irish Immigrant Women in the Nineteenth Century*, Baltimore, 1983.

6.430 **Drinnon**, R., *Facing West. The Metaphysics of Indian-Hating and Empire Building*, Minneapolis, MN, 1980. A book in the American Studies tradition that links myth and symbol with racism and manifest destiny.

6.431 **Gjerde**, J., *From Peasants to Farmer. The Migration from Norway to the Upper Middle West*, New York, 1985. A detailed study of the people who left Balestrand, Norway, and the communities they built in Wisconsin and Minnesota.

6.432 **Greene**, V. R., *American Immigrant Leaders, 1800–1910. Marginality and Identity*, Baltimore, 1987. Examines the extent to which immigrants became American by writing about thirty-four leaders of the six largest immigrant groups.

6.433 **Higham**, J., *Strangers in the Land. Patterns of American Nativism, 1860–1925*, New Brunswick, NJ, 1988. The third edition of the 1963 classic, with an introduction that reviews new themes in the recent literature.

6.434 **Kamphoefner**, W. D., *The Westfalians. From Germany to Missouri*, Princeton, NJ, 1987.

6.435 **Keil**, H., *German Workers in Chicago. A Documentary History of Working-Class Culture from 1850 to World War I*, Urbana, IL, 1988. Part of the University of Munich's "Chicago Project" to write the history of the migration of Germans to America and the making of a German-American working class.

6.436 **Keil**, H., and **Jentz**, J. B., (ed.), *German Workers in Industrial Chicago, 1850–1910*, Urbana, IL, 1983. The first volume published by the collaboration between German and American scholars on the history of German immigrants in two worlds.

6.437 **Kipel**, V., 'Byelorussians in the United States', *Ethnic Forum*, IX, 1989, 75–90.

6.438 **Kraut**, A. M., *The Huddled Masses. The Immigrant in American Society, 1880–1921*, Arlington Heights, IL, 1982.

6.439 **Miller**, K. A., *Emigrants and Exiles. Ireland and the Irish Exodus to North America*, New York, 1985. A blend of quantitative and narrative evidence about the lives of the nineteenth century Irish immigrants.

6.440 **Miller**, K. A., and **Boling**, B. D., 'Golden streets, bitter tears. The Irish image of America during the era of mass migration', *Journal of American Ethnic History*, X, 1990–1991, 16–35.

6.441 **Moltmann**, G., 'Migrations from Germany to North America. New perspectives', *Reviews in American History*, XIV, 1986. A review of the recent German-authored literature.

6.442 **Mushkat**, J., *Fernando Wood. A Political Biography*, Kent, OH, 1990. Places the colorful antebellum New York City mayor in the social context of a burgeoning immigrant city.

6.443 **Nadel**, S., *Little Germany. Ethnicity, Religion, and Class in New York City,*

1845–1880, Urbana, IL, 1990. Considers mid-nineteenth century New York as the third leading German city, after Berlin and Vienna, and the tensions among Germans between competing class and ethnic loyalties.

6.444 **Pacyga**, D. A., and **Schelbert**, L., 'Polish emigration to the United States before World War One and capitalist development', *Polish American Studies*, XLVI, 1989, 10–18.

6.445 **Perlman**, R., *Bridging Three Worlds. Hungarian-Jewish Americans, 1848–1914*, Amherst, MA, 1991. A transnational study that analyzes the Hungarian scene from which Jews emigrated, and the American one to which the immigrants moved.

6.446 **Ramirez**, B., *On the Move. French-Canadian and Italian Migrants in the North Atlantic Economy, 1860–1914*, Toronto, ONT, 1991. Explores the rural to urban migrations of Quebecers and Italians to the United States, as well as the return migrations to the homeland.

6.447 **Sorin**, G., *The Prophetic Minority. American Jewish Immigrant Radicals, 1880–1920*, Bloomington, IN, 1985. A collective biography of more than one hundred Russian Jewish immigrant radicals that finds their socialism deeply grounded in traditional Jewish humanitarianism.

6.448 **Swierenga**, R. P., 'List upon list: the ship passenger records and immigration research', *Journal of American Ethnic History*, X, 1991, 42–53.

Asian-Americans

6.449 **Anderson**, D. L., *Imperialism and Idealism. American Diplomats in China, 1861–1898*, Bloomington, IN, 1986.

6.450 **Chan**, Sucheng, *This Bittersweet Soil. The Chinese in California Agriculture, 1860–1910*, Berkeley, CA, 1986. Shows that many immigrant Chinese became farm workers and truck gardeners and how the Chinese exclusion laws eventually forced them out of rural California.

6.451 **Peffer**, G. A., 'Forbidden families. Emigration experiences of Chinese women under the Page Law, 1875–1882', *Journal of American Ethnic History*, VI, 1986, 28–46.

6.452 **Russell**, J. M., *Atlanta, 1847–1890. City*

Building in the Old South and the New, Baton Rouge, LA, 1988.

6.453 **Tsai**, S. H., *The Chinese Experience in America*, Bloomington, IN, 1986.

SPACE, PLACE, AND MOVEMENT

The West

6.454 **Armitage**, Susan, and **Jameson**, Elizabeth, *The Women's West*, Norman, OK, 1987.

6.455 **Bakken**, G. M., *Practising Law in Frontier California*, Lincoln, NE, 1991.

6.456 **Barron**, H. S., *Those Who Stayed Behind. Rural Society in Nineteenth Century New England*, New York, 1984. Analyzes the people of a Vermont town who did not move west or migrate to the cities and finds a growing community cohesion alongside population stability.

6.457 **Billington**, R. A., *Land of Savagery, Land of Promise. The European Image of the American Frontier in the Nineteenth Century*, New York, 1981. The final publication of the great historian of the American West, the volume emphasizes the importance of the cultural ideas that Europeans brought with them about the type of America they expected to encounter.

6.458 **Boessenecker**, J., *Badge and Buckshot. Lawlessness in Old California*, Norman, OK, 1988.

6.459 **Cocks**, E. D., 'Land's end', *History of European Ideas*, VI, 1985, 129–151. A review of American thought about the social consequences of the end of the westward frontier.

6.460 **Fahey**, J., *Inland Empire. Unfolding Years, 1879–1923*, Seattle, 1986. Treats the region around Spokane, Washington in terms of the dominant business people who organized the agricultural and extractive industries of the northern Cascades region.

6.461 **Faragher**, J. M., *Women and Men on the Overland Trail*, New Haven, CT, 1979.

6.462 **Foote**, C. J., *Women of the New Mexico Frontier, 1846–1912*, Niwot, CO, 1990.

6.463 **Gates**, P. W., *Land and Law in California*.

Essays on Land Policies, Ames, IA, 1991. A collection of previously published essays by the foremost historian of the impact of the public lands on society; this volume shows the continuing effect of Mexican land policy on California once it became part of the U.S.

6.464 **Goetzman**, W. H., and **Goetzman**, W. N., *The West of the Imagination*, New York, 1986. A book, profusely illustrated with artworks by leading western artists, that concentrates on the frontier phase of western history. An extensive television series available on videocassette parallels this volume.

6.465 **Hamilton**, K. M., *Black Towns and Profit. Promotion and Development in the Trans-Appalachian West, 1877–1915*, Urbana, IL, 1991.

6.466 **Haywood**, C. R., *Victorian West. Class and Culture in Kansas Cattle Towns*, Lawrence, KS, 1991. Stresses the rapidity with which frontier cow towns were converted into orderly bourgeois outposts.

6.467 **Haywood**, C. R., *Cowtown Lawyers. Dodge City and Its Attorneys, 1876–1886*, Norman, OK, 1988.

6.468 **Hogan**, R., *Class and Community in Frontier Colorado*, Lawrence, KS, 1990.

6.469 **Hunt**, W. R., *Distant Justice. Policing the Alaskan Frontier*, Norman, OK, 1987.

6.470 **Hyde**, Anne Farrar, *An American Vision. Far Western Landscape and National Culture, 1820–1920*, New York, 1990. A work that argues that Americans had to develop their own aesthetic sense from the natural setting of the Rocky Mountain West, and once this identity was understood as different than the European landscape, then a separate American cultural identity could fully emerge.

6.471 **Ives**, E. D., *George Magoon and the Down East Game War. History, Folklore, and the Law*, Urbana, IL, 1988. Recounts the history of strife between game wardens and hunters in Maine as the state claimed ownership and sovereignty over wildlife.

6.472 **Lang**, W. L., (ed.), *Centennial West. Essays on the Northern Tier States*, Seattle, 1991.

6.473 **Limerick**, Patricia Nelson, *The Legacy of Conquest. The Unbroken Past of the American West*, New York, 1987. A work that contests older theories about the significance of the "frontier" by proposing a rival synthesis, namely, that the history of

the American West was one of combined economic conquest and ethnic dominance.

6.474 **Logue**, L. M., *A Sermon in the Desert. Belief and Behavior in Early St. George, Utah*, Urbana, IL, 1988. A community history of the southern Utah hamlet that was colonized by Mormons after 1860.

6.475 **McQuillan**, D. A., *Prevailing over Time. Ethnic Adjustment on the Kansas Prairies, 1875–1925*, Lincoln, NE, 1990. Shows how immigrant groups to the Great Plains created new ethnic identities based on merging their European heritage with the demands of their new environment.

6.476 **Miner**, H. C., *West of Wichita. Settling the High Plains of Kansas, 1865–1890*, Lawrence, KS, 1986.

6.477 **Nesbit**, R. C., *The History of Wisconsin. Urbanization and Industrialization, 1873–1893*, Madison, WI, 1985. Part of a six volume series on the history of the state.

6.478 **Paul**, R., *The Far West and the Great Plains in Transition, 1859–1900*, New York, 1988. Surveys the economic changes brought to the Great Plains and Mountain West by corporate mining interests and cattle raising, and the mix of ethnic people who moved into the region.

6.479 **Peterson**, F. W., *Homes in the Heartland. Balloon Frame Farmhouses of the Upper Midwest, 1850–1920*, Lawrence, KS, 1992.

6.480 **Pisani**, D. J., *From the Family Farm to Agribusiness. The Irrigation Crusade in California and the West, 1850–1931*, Berkeley, CA, 1984. Traces the history of state and federal irrigation policy as well as the ideological consequences of the changes in agriculture.

6.481 **Riley**, Glenda, 'The spectre of the savage. Rumors and alarmism on the Overland Trail', *Western Historical Quarterly*, 1984, XV, 427–444.

6.482 **Rohrbough**, M. J., *Aspen. The History of a Silver-Mining Town, 1879–1893*, New York, 1986.

6.483 **Slatta**, R. W., *Cowboys of the Americas*, New Haven, CT, 1990. Places the rise and fall of the cowboy of the American West within an international context; the comparison with Argentina is especially helpful.

6.484 **Slotkin**, R., *The Fatal Environment. The Myth of the Frontier in the Age of Industrialization, 1800–1980*, New York, 1985. A continuation of the author's *Regeneration Through Violence* that employs cultural anthropology to make sense of the central myth of American history, the frontier struggle as a source of continued renewal.

6.485 **Smith**, M. L., *Pacific Visions. California Scientists and the Environment, 1850–1915*, New Haven, CT, 1988.

6.486 **Thompson**, J., *Closing the Frontier. Radical Response in Oklahoma, 1889–1923*, Norman, OK, 1986. Interprets rural Oklahoma as a mix of midwestern wheat farmers and southern cotton growers, and locates the state's radical tradition in the problems associated with growing each crop.

6.487 **Underwood**, Kathleen, *Town Building on the Colorado Frontier*, Albuquerque, NM, 1987.

The American city

6.488 **Barth**, G., *City People. The Rise of Modern City Culture in Nineteenth Century America*, New York, 1980.

6.489 **Binford**, H. C., *The First Suburbs. Residential Communities on the Boston Periphery. 1815–1860*, Chicago, 1986. Studies the history of Somerville and Cambridge, Massachusetts before they became Boston suburbs and finds they had an independent commercial tie to the city before receiving a residential outflow.

6.490 **Blumin**, S. M., *The Emergence of the Middle Class. Social Experience in the American City. 1760–1900*, New York, 1989. Concentrates on the appearance of an urban bourgeoisie in Philadelphia and how its aspirations came to be central to American society.

6.491 **Conzen**, Kathleen Neils, *Immigrant Milwaukee, 1830–1840. Accommodation and Community in a Frontier City*, Cambridge, MA, 1976.

6.492 **Cronon**, W., *Nature's Metropolis. Chicago and the Great West*, New York, 1991. An environmental history of the nineteenth century rise of Chicago that argues the city's emergence was simultaneous to the development of the capitalist transformation of the Midwest's grain, livestock, and lumber resources.

6.493 **Davis**, H. E., *Henry Grady's New South. Atlanta, A Brave and Beautiful City*, Tuscaloosa, AL, 1990.

6.494 **Doyle**, D. H., *New Men, New Cities, New South. Atlanta, Nashville, Charleston, Mobile, 1860–1910*, Chapel Hill, NC, 1990.

6.495 **Gilbert**, J., *Perfect Cities. Chicago's Utopias of 1893*, Chicago, 1991. Links the Chicago World's Fair of 1893 to George Pullman's company town, and also to revivals.

6.496 **Hales**, P. B., *Silver Cities. The Photography of American Urbanization, 1839–1915*, Philadelphia, 1984. A study of photographers as a business group and how they reflected a new urban culture and at the same time helped shape that culture.

6.497 **Hershberg**, T., (ed.), *Philadelphia. Work, Space, Family, and Group Experience in the Nineteenth Century. Essays toward an Interdisciplinary History of the City*, New York, 1981. A collection of fourteen essays that make use of the database produced by the Philadelphia Social History Project in the study of the urban economy and the spatial development of the city.

6.498 **Lane**, R., *Roots of Violence in Black Philadelphia, 1860–1909*, Cambridge, MA, 1986. Argues that African-American criminal behavior in postbellum Philadelphia was rooted in the exclusion of blacks from the developing industrial economy.

6.499 **Lane**, R., *William Dorsey's Philadelphia and Ours. On the Past and Future of the Black City in America*, New York, 1991.

6.500 **Larsen**, L. H., *The Rise of the Urban South*, Lexington, KY, 1985. A survey of the nineteenth century origins of southern urbanization.

6.501 **Leighton**, Ann, *American Gardens of the Nineteenth Century. 'For Comfort and Affluence'*, Amherst, MA, 1987.

6.502 **McDonald**, T. J., *The Parameters of Urban Fiscal Policy. Socioeconomic Change and Political Culture in San Francisco, 1860–1906*, Berkeley, CA, 1986.

6.503 **McMurray**, Sally, *Families and Farmhouses in Nineteenth-Century America. Vernacular Design and Social Change*, New York, 1988. Looks at design plans in magazines oriented toward rural America and traces the changes in gender ideology as reflected in the house plans.

6.504 **Miller**, R., *American Apocalypse. The Great Fire and the Myth of Chicago*, Chicago, 1990. An architectural history of the city after the fire.

6.505 **Monkkonen**, E. H., *Police in Urban*

America, 1860–1920, New York, 1981.

6.506 **O'Gorman**, J. F., *H. H. Richardson. Architectural Forms for an American Society*, Chicago, 1987.

6.507 **Philpott**, T. L., *The Slum and the Ghetto. Neighborhood Deterioration and Middle-Class Reform, Chicago, 1880–1930*, New York, 1978.

6.508 **Rosenzweig**, R., *Eight Hours for What We Will. Workers & Leisure in an Industrial City, 1870–1920*, New York, 1983. The culture of the working class in Worcester, Massachusetts and its struggles over issues outside the workplace.

6.509 **Scherzer**, K. A., *The Unbounded Community. Neighborhood Life and Social Structure in New York City, 1830–1875*, Durham, NC, 1992.

6.510 **Schultz**, S. K., *Constructing Urban Culture. American Cities and City Planning, 1800–1920*, Philadelphia, 1989. Maintains that city planning in America long pre-dated the Columbian Exposition of 1893.

6.511 **Schuyler**, D., *The New Urban Landscape. The Redefinition of City Form in Nineteenth-Century Urban America*, Baltimore, 1986.

6.512 **Spann**, E. K., *The New Metropolis. New York City, 1840–1857*, New York, 1981.

6.513 **Teaford**, J. C., *The Unheralded Triumph. City Government in America, 1870–1900*, Baltimore, 1984. A defense of the efficiency in delivering services and balancing political demands shown by American cities, despite their vocal critics.

6.514 **Wade**, Louise Carroll, *Chicago's Pride. The Stockyards, Packingtown, and Environs in the Nineteenth Century*, Urbana, IL, 1987. A history of the origins of the meatpacking industry and surrounding neighborhoods on the South Side through the 1880s.

6.515 **Ward**, D., *Poverty, Ethnicity, and the American City, 1840–1925. Changing Conceptions of the Slum and the Ghetto*, New York, 1989. A study of successive investigations of ethnic urban neighborhoods and how outsiders saw the mix of poverty, immigration, and reform.

The South

6.516 **Bartley**, N. V., (ed.), *The Evolution of Southern Culture*, Athens, GA, 1988. Eight essays on the changes in the nineteenth century and early twentieth century South,

written by some of the leading historians of the region.

6.517 **Newby**, I. A., *Plain Folk in the New South. Social Change and Cultural Persistence, 1880–1915*, Baton Rouge, LA, 1989. A history of both the operatives and owners in the cotton textile industry, locating paternalism and worker passivity in the prior history of the white South.

6.518 **Siegel**, F. F., *The Roots of Southern Distinctiveness. Tobacco and Society in Danville, Virginia, 1780–1865*, Chapel Hill, NC, 1987. Insists that the nature of tobacco as a crop – rather than race or slavery – kept Danville and the Southside region of Virginia locked into an economy and society at odds with that of the North.

6.519 **Shifflett**, C. A., *Patronage and Poverty in the Tobacco South. Louisa County, Virginia, 1860–1900*, Knoxville, TN, 1982.

6.520 **Tullos**, A., *Habits of Industry. White Culture and the Transformation of the Carolina Piedmont*, Chapel Hill, NC, 1988. Studies the southern whites who controlled the New South textile mills in the Piedmont region, and locates their attitudes toward property and labor in the older history of Scotch-Irish Presbyterian settlers.

THE STATE AND THE PUBLIC REALM

The road to secession

6.521 **Ambrosius**, L. E., (ed.), *A Crisis of Republicanism. American Politics in the Civil War Era*, Lincoln, NE, 1990. A festschrift in University of Nebraska historian James Rawley's honor, this volume contains essays about the sectional crisis of the 1850s and after the war.

6.522 **Ash**, S. V., *Middle Tennessee Society Transformed, 1860–1870. War and Peace in the Upper South*, Baton Rouge, LA, 1988. A detailed look at the counties surrounding Nashville and why they chose the Confederacy in 1861 and the consequences they faced after defeat and occupation; the author finds local whites overwhelmingly preoccupied with race and racial control during the postwar period.

6.523 **Brandt**, N., *The Town That Started the Civil War*, Syracuse, NY, 1990. The story of Oberlin, Ohio and its role in the abolitionist movement.

6.524 **Bridges**, Amy, *A City in the Republic. Antebellum New York and the Origins of Machine Politics*, New York, 1984.

6.525 **Cooper**, W. J., *Liberty and Slavery. Southern Politics to 1860*, New York, 1983.

6.526 **Cooper**, W. J., (ed.), *A Master's Due. Essays in Honor of David Herbert Donald*, Baton Rouge, LA, 1985. A festschrift in honor of the Harvard historian and leader of the post-World War II movement away from Civil War revisionism.

6.527 **DeRosa**, M. L., *The Confederate Constitution. An Inquiry into American Constitutionalism*, Columbia, MO, 1991.

6.528 **Erlich**, W., *They Have No Rights. Dred Scott's Struggle for Freedom*, Westport, CT, 1979. Analyzes the legal thinking behind the Supreme Court's 1857 Dred Scott decision.

6.529 **Ferris**, N. B., *Desperate Diplomacy. William H. Seward's Foreign Policy*, Knoxville, TN, 1976. Covers the events of the tumultuous spring of 1861 when Seward devised various stratagems to preserve the old Union.

6.530 **Fogel**, R. W., *Without Consent or Contract. The Rise and Fall of American Slavery*, New York, 1989–1992. Continues the author's earlier calculations about slavery with a new discussion of the economics of antislavery and abolitionism. This work comes in three volumes. The first is a narrative, followed by two volumes of econometric and social science methods papers.

6.531 **Foner**, E., *Politics and Ideology in the Age of the Civil War*, New York, 1980.

6.532 **Ford**, L. K., *Origins of Southern Radicalism. The South Carolina Upcountry, 1800–1860*, New York, 1988.

6.533 **Gienapp**, W. E., *The Origins of the Republican Party, 1852–1856*, New York, 1987. An original interpretation of the formation of the Republican Party that weaves together the story of the 1850s political realignment, ethno-cultural developments and the coming of the Civil War.

6.534 **Holt**, M. F., *The Political Crisis of the 1850s*, New York, 1978. An interpretation by one of the leading exponents of the "ethnocultural" school of political historians.

6.535 **Holt**, M. F., *Political Parties and American Political Development. From the Age of Jackson to the Age of Lincoln*, Baton Rouge, LA, 1992.

6.536 **Huston**, J. L., *The Panic of 1857 and the Coming of the Civil War*, Baton Rouge, LA, 1987. Uses the financial panic in 1857 as a way of examining how the North and South reinforced rival visions of political economy and how their respective positions hardened.

6.537 **Inscoe**, J. C., *Mountain Masters, Slavery, and the Sectional Crisis in Western North Carolina*, Knoxville, TN, 1989. Details the economic and political connections between the largely non-slave portion of the state and the larger Slave South.

6.538 **Johannsen**, R. W., *The Frontier, the Union, and Stephen A. Douglas*, Urbana, IL, 1989. A collection of fifteen essays by the premier biographer of Douglas, including perceptive comments about Lincoln and frontier Illinois.

6.539 **Kenzer**, R. C., *Kinship and Neighborhood in a Southern Community. Orange County, North Carolina, 1849–1881*, Knoxville, TN, 1988. A study of the countryside surrounding present-day Durham, North Carolina, and how during the decades before the Civil War a local gentry dominated the county through family ties and trade relations and the war itself did little to change the arrangement of white society.

6.540 **Kruman**, M. W., *Parties and Politics in North Carolina, 1836–1865*, Baton Rouge, LA, 1983.

6.541 **Levine**, B., *Half Slave, Half Free. The Roots of Civil War*, New York, 1992.

6.542 **McCormick**, R. L., *The Party Period and Public Policy. American Politics from the Age of Jackson to the Progressive Era*, New York, 1986. An antidote to ethnocultural interpretations of political parties in the nineteenth century.

6.543 **McMurray**, Stephanie, 'The two faces of republicanism: gender and proslavery politics in antebellum South Carolina,' *Journal of American History*, LXXVIII, 1992, 1245–1264. Combines public and private spheres into the possibility of gendered history of politics.

6.544 **Norton**, Anne, *Alternative Americas. A Reading of Antebellum Political Culture*, Chicago, 1986. Contrasts the two political cultures of North and South through a wide reading of texts.

6.545 **Peterson**, M. D., *The Great Triumvirate. Webster, Clay and Calhoun*, New York, 1987. A biographical study of Daniel Webster, Henry Clay and John Calhoun, this work analyses the place of each statesman in the political history of the U.S. and concludes that ultimately none of them was fully suited to the republican, populist times in which they lived.

6.546 **Potter**, D. M., with **Fehrenbacher**, D. E., *The Impending Crisis, 1848–1861*, New York, 1976. A still useful volume on the politics of the road to Fort Sumter.

6.547 **Shields**, Johanna Nicol, *The Line of Duty. Maverick Congressmen and the Development of American Political Culture, 1836–1860*, Westport, CT, 1985. Uses quantitative scaling techniques to identify a group of "maverick" or fringe congressmen who emphasized personal honor and emerged as important committee leaders.

6.548 **Silbey**, J. H., *The American Political Nation, 1838–1893*, Stanford, CA, 1991. Argues that the old "second party system" lasted until the crisis of the 1890s and was the heyday of American parties.

6.549 **Stampp**, K. M., *America in 1857. A Nation on the Brink*, New York, 1990. Argues that 1857 was the critical point at which the old Union could have been saved without secession and war; the careful explication of the events in Kansas places central responsibility for the subsequent failure on President Buchanan.

6.550 **Summers**, M. W., *The Plundering Generation. Corruption and the Crisis of the Union, 1849–1861*, New York, 1987. Shows how a profusion of political and financial scandals caused voters in both North and South to lose faith in the old republic and seek mutually antagonistic solutions.

6.551 **Sutton**, R. P., *Revolution to Secession. Constitution Making in the Old Dominion*, Charlottesville, VA, 1989.

6.552 **Thornton**, J. M., *Politics and Power in a Slave Society. Alabama, 1800–1860*, Baton Rouge, LA, 1978.

6.553 **Woods**, J. M., *Rebellion and Realignment. Arkansas's Road to Secession*, Fayetteville, AR, 1987.

6.554 **Zarefsky**, D., *Lincoln, Douglas, and Slavery. In the Crucible of Public Debate*, Chicago, 1990.

The Civil War

6.555 **Cortada**, J. W., *Spain and the American Civil War. Relations at Mid-Century, 1855–1868*, Philadelphia, 1980.

6.556 **Griffith**, P., *Battle Tactics of the Civil War*, New Haven, CT, 1989. A rather scornful evaluation of the conflict that sets its place in history as the last Napoleonic war rather than the first modern war, in large part because the forces on both sides were merely armed rabble.

6.557 **Hess**, E. J., *Liberty, Virtue, and Progress. Northerners and Their War for the Union*, New York, 1988.

6.558 **Hughes**, N. C., *The Battle of Belmont. Grant Strikes Back*, Chapel Hill, NC, 1991. An account of the Missouri skirmish in 1861 that showed some of Grant's pluck as a battle leader.

6.559 **Jimerson**, R. C., *The Private Civil War. Popular Thought During the Sectional Conflict*, Baton Rouge, LA, 1988.

6.560 **Mitchell**, R., *Civil War Soldiers*, New York, 1988. One of the first books to apply the new social and cultural history of the nineteenth century to understanding the attitudes of the common soldiers in both armies.

6.561 **Paludan**, P. S., *Victims. A True Story of the Civil War*, Knoxville, TN, 1981.

6.562 **Robertson**, J. I., *Soldiers Blue and Gray*, Columbia, SC, 1988.

6.563 **Sewell**, R. H., *A House Divided. Sectionalism and the Civil War, 1848–1865*, Baltimore, 1988. A useful survey of the politics of the coming of the Civil War.

6.564 **Shattuck**, G. H., *A Shield and Hiding Place. The Religious Life of the Civil War Armies*, Macon, GA, 1987.

6.565 **Turner**, Maxine, *Navy Gray. A Story of the Confederate Navy on the Chattahoochee and Apalchicola Rivers*, Tuscaloosa, AL, 1988.

6.566 **Ward**, G. C., (ed.), *The Civil War. An Illustrated History*, New York, 1990. Book that accompanied a popular television series; many of the leading historians of the Civil War collaborated on the project.

6.567 **Warren**, G. H., *Fountain of Discontent. The Trent Affair and Freedom of the Seas*, Boston, 1981.

(a) STRATEGY: CAMPAIGNS ON THE VIRGINIA FRONT

6.568 **Bryant**, W. O., *Cahaba Prison and the 'Sultana' Disaster*, Tuscaloosa, AL, 1990. The story of a Confederate prisoner-of-war camp in Alabama and the unfortunate fate of the Union prisoners released after the war's end, only to be killed in a Mississippi River shipwreck.

6.569 **Furgurson**, E. B., *Chancellorsville, The Souls of the Brave*, New York, 1992. Battle narrative that examines the failings of Joe Hooker and the success of Robert E. Lee.

6.570 **Gallagher**, G. W., *Struggle for the Shenandoah. Essays on the 1864 Valley Campaign*, Kent, OH, 1991. Five essays on the importance of the Shenandoah campaign from June through November to the outcome of the war in the Virginia theater.

6.571 **Gallagher**, G. W., (ed.), *The First Day at Gettysburg. Essays on Confederate and Union Leadership*, Kent, OH, 1992.

6.572 **Hagerman**, E., *The American Civil War and the Origins of Modern Warfare. Ideas, Organization, and Field Command*, Bloomington, IN, 1988. Stresses the importance of long-range organization and coordination to make the mass citizen armies effective organizations in a modern sense.

6.573 **Hennessy**, J. J., *Return to Bull Run. The Campaign and Battle of Second Manassas*, New York, 1992. Battle narrative of the August 1862 campaign of John Pope that led to yet another Union defeat.

6.574 **Jones**, T. L., *Lee's Tigers. The Louisiana Infantry in the Army of Northern Virginia*, Baton Rouge, LA, 1987.

6.575 **Krick**, R. K., *Stonewall Jackson at Cedar Mountain*, Chapel Hill, NC, 1990. An account of the August 1862 clash between Jackson's corps and Union General John Pope's forces.

6.576 **Matter**, W. D., *If It Takes All Summer. The Battle of Spottsylvania*, Chapel Hill, NC, 1988. A thorough history of the May 1864 battle which the author argues was unrivalled for bloodiness until World War I.

6.577 **Priest**, J. M., *Antietam. The Soldier's Battle*, Shippensburg, PA, 1989.

6.578 **Robertson**, J. I., *Civil War Virginia. Battleground for a Nation*, Charlottesville, VA, 1991. A history of the state and its people from the secession crisis to the fall of Richmond.

6.579 **Robertson**, W. G., *Back Door to Richmond. The Bermuda Hundred Campaign, April-June 1864*, Newark, DE, 1987. Describes the failure of the campaign led by Benjamin Butler to approach the Confederate capital from the southeast and the subsequent lengthening of the war.

6.580 **Scott**, R. G., *Into the Wilderness with the Army of the Potomac*, Bloomington, IN, 1985. A battle history of the May 1864 Virginia campaign that gives full consideration to U. S. Grant's strategic initiative.

6.581 **Sears**, S. W., *Landscape Turned Red. The Battle of Antietam*, New York, 1983. Complete account of the 1862 Maryland battle in which Robert E. Lee's invading Confederates were turned back.

6.582 **Trudeau**, N. A., *Bloody Roads South. The Wilderness to Cold Harbor, May-June 1864*, Boston, 1989. A battle history of the fierce fighting in the Union offensive in the spring of 1864.

(b) STRATEGY: CAMPAIGNS ON THE WESTERN FRONT

6.583 **Castel**, A., *Decision in the West. The Atlanta Campaign of 1864*, New York, 1992. Battle narrative of Sherman's spring 1864 move on Atlanta that is critical of the Union leader; the author also emphasizes the critical nature of the campaign's outcome on the fall 1864 elections in the North that returned Lincoln to the White House and guaranteed the continuation of the war.

6.584 **Cimprich**, J., and **Mainfort**, R. C., Jr., 'The Fort Pillow Massacre. A statistical note', *Journal of American History*, LXXVI, 1989, 830–837. A look at the casualty figures for the infamous 1864 capture of Fort Pillow, Tennessee, and subsequent massacre of surrendered troops, by Confederate General Nathan Bedford Forrest, finds two-thirds of the black soldiers at the fort died while only one-third of the white Union troops were killed.

6.585 **Cozzens**, P., *No Better Place to Die. The Battle of Stones River*, Urbana, IL, 1990. Definitive account of the three-day engagement at Murfreesboro, Tennessee at the end of 1862 and how the Confederate defeat helped lead to greater Union success in 1863.

6.586 **Cozzens**, P., *This Terrible Sound. The Battle of Chickamauga*, Urbana, IL, 1992. Battle narrative of the Confederate victory outside Chattanooga in the fall of 1863.

6.587 **Fellman**, M., *Inside War. The Guerrilla Conflict in Missouri during the American Civil War*, New York, 1989. A social history of the bushwhacking and guerrilla attacks by southerners and the repression by federal forces in Missouri.

6.588 **Frank**, J. A., and **Reaves**, G. A., '*Seeing the Elephant*'. *Raw Recruits at the Battle of Shiloh*, Westport, CT, 1989. An account of how green troops fared under withering fire in the 1862 bloodletting at Shiloh.

6.589 **Gaines**, W. C., *The Confederate Cherokees. John Drew's Regiment of Mounted Rifles*, Baton Rouge, LA, 1989. Recounts the history of an Indian unit in the Civil War and ties the history of the war to internal tribal politics.

6.590 **Glatthaar**, J. T., *The March to the Sea and Beyond. Sherman's Troops in the Savannah and Carolinas Campaigns*, New York, 1985. A social history of the 60,000 men in the Union Army who devastated Georgia and South Carolina in the last six months of the war.

6.591 **Jones**, A., *Civil War Command and Strategy. The Process of Victory and Defeat*, New York, 1992.

6.592 **Josephy**, A. M., *The Civil War in the American West*, New York, 1991. A look at the battles and guerrilla war in the trans-Mississippi theater by a leading practitioner of the New Western History.

6.593 **Reed**, Rowena, *Combined Operations in the Civil War*, Annapolis, MD, 1978. A study of the joint Navy-Army offensives, both on the coast and on the inland rivers.

6.594 **Siepel**, K. H., *Rebel. The Life and Times of John Singleton Mosby*, New York, 1983.

6.595 **Thompson**, J., *Henry Hopkins Sibley. Confederate General of the West*, Natchitoches, LA, 1987. A biography of the Louisiana-born rebel who invaded New Mexico as a prelude to an envisioned occupation of the entire Far West.

6.596 **Woodworth**, S. E., *Jefferson Davis and His Generals. The Failure of Confederate Command in the West*, Lawrence, KS, 1990.

(c) WHY THE NORTH WON

6.597 **Adams**, M. C. C., *Our Masters the Rebels. A Speculation on Union Military Failure in the East, 1861–1865*, Cambridge, MA, 1978. Attributes repeated Union Army defeats in Virginia to psychological causes

6.598 **Bensel**, R. F., *Yankee Leviathan. The Origins of Central State Authority in America, 1859–1877*, New York, 1991. A volume on the Union government in the crisis of the war and Reconstruction that uses the insights of "state and society" sociology to make sense of the origins of th modern federal system.

6.599 **Bogue**, A. G., *The Congressman's Civil War*, New York, 1989. An analysis of the role of Capitol Hill in fighting the Civil War, complete with quantitative analysis of roll call votes and party discipline.

6.600 **Crawford**, M., *The Anglo-American Crisis of the Mid-Nineteenth Century. 'The Times' and America, 1850–1862*, Athens, GA, 1987. Looks at 'The Times' as a baromete of English opinion.

6.601 **Gallman**, J.M., *Mastering Wartime. A Social History of Philadelphia during the Civil War*, New York, 1990. As with McKay's study of New York, this volume finds a pattern of continuity and control i the urban North during the Civil War.

6.602 **Glatthaar**, J. T., *Forged in Battle. The Civil War Alliance of Black Soldiers and White Officers*, New York, 1990. Consider the social history of the regiments filled with black recruits and commanded by whites, both in and out of combat.

6.603 **Jones**, H., *Union in Peril. The Crisis over British Intervention in the Civil War*, Chape Hill, NC, 1992.

6.604 **Klement**, F. L., *Dark Lanterns. Secret Political Societies, Conspiracies, and Treason Trials in the Civil War*, Baton Rouge, LA, 1984. Downplays the extent and influence of pro-Southern groups in the North and considers the wartime moves against them as out of proportion.

6.605 **Linderman**, G. F., *Embattled Courage. Th Experience of Combat in the American Civil War*, New York, 1987. An examination of the "face of battle" as soldiers saw it during the Civil War that emphasizes the importance of a gendered sense of manliness and courage.

6.606 **McKay**, E. A., *The Civil War and New York City*, Syracuse, NY, 1990. Shows how the city's political and mercantile elites differed on the war, and despite the 1863 draft riot, the city power structure was little altered by the experience of the war and victory.

6.607 **McPherson**, J. M., *Abraham Lincoln and the Second American Revolution*, New York, 1990. Contains seven essays on the theme of tensions between "liberty" and "power" in the Civil War era.

6.608 **Neely**, M. E., 'Was the Civil War a total war?', *Civil War History*, XXXVII, 1991, 5–28. Answers the question in the negative by stressing the destructive nature of earlier European wars, and the disjuncture with twentieth century war without discrimination against civilian populations.

6.609 **Neely**, M. E., *The Fate of Liberty. Abraham Lincoln and Civil Liberties*, New York, 1991. Finds that after some initial confusion and recklessness, the Union government came to devise responsible methods to contain disloyal and pro-Confederate sentiment during the Civil War.

6.610 **Paludan**, P. S., 'A People's Contest'. *The Union at War, 1861–1865*, New York, 1988. Offers a view of the northern response to secession that is grounded in the social and cultural history of the region.

6.611 **Royster**, C., *The Destructive War. William Tecumseh Sherman, Stonewall Jackson, and the Americans*, New York, 1991. Argues, against recent interpretations that link Sherman with the twentieth century concept of "total war", that instead he, along with Jackson, was one of many who advocated and practised a hard war.

6.612 **Vinovskis**, M., (ed.), *Toward a Social History of the American Civil War. Exploratory Essays*, New York, 1990. A set of essays that applies the methods of the "New Social History" to the wartime North and the postbellum society.

6.613 **Wills**, G., *Lincoln at Gettysburg. The Words that Remade America*, New York, 1992. An analysis of the Gettysburg Address that claims Lincoln reinvigorated the equality premise of the Declaration of Independence as central to the Union's war aims.

(d) WHY THE SOUTH LOST

6.614 **Ball**, D. B., *Financial Failure and Confederate Defeat*, Urbana, IL, 1991. Contends that the South lost the war in its own Treasury Department and that a different set of policies would have produced a favorable outcome.

6.615 **Beringer**, R. E., *Why the South Lost the Civil War*, Athens, GA, 1986.

6.616 **Beringer**, R. E., *The Elements of Confederate Defeat. Nationalism, War Aims, and Religion*, Athens, GA, 1988.

6.617 **Boritt**, G. S., and **McPherson**, J. M., (ed.), *Why the Confederacy Lost*, New York, 1992. A collection of essays focusing on the political weaknesses of the southern republic.

6.618 **Crofts**, D. W., *Reluctant Confederates. Upper South Unionists in the Secession Crisis*, Chapel Hill, NC, 1989. A study of conditional unionists in the winter and spring of 1861.

6.619 **Current**, R. N., *Lincoln's Loyalists. Union Soldiers from the Confederacy*, Boston, 1992. Analyzes the makeup of Union Army units made up of white volunteers from seceding states, especially Tennessee and Virginia.

6.620 **DeCredico**, Mary A., *Patriotism for Profit. Georgia's Urban Entrepreneurs and the Confederate War Effort*, Chapel Hill, NC, 1990.

6.621 **Durrill**, W. K., *War of Another Kind. A Southern Community in the Great Rebellion*, New York, 1990. Shows how class conflict among whites, and between whites and blacks in Washington County, North Carolina undermined the Confederate bid for independence.

6.622 **Faust**, Drew Gilpin, *The Creation of Confederate Nationalism. Ideology and Identity in the Civil War South*, Baton Rouge, LA, 1988.

6.623 **Faust**, Drew Gilpin, 'Altars of sacrifice. Confederate women and the narratives of war', *Journal of American History*, LXXVI, 1990, 1200–1228. Argues that a key part of the answer to the question of why the South lost the Civil War is that southern women grew disenchanted with the Confederacy as the war dragged on.

6.624 **Hallock**, Judith Lee, *Braxton Bragg and Confederate Defeat, Vol. II*, Tuscaloosa, AL, 1991. Continues Grady McWhiney's 1968 pioneering inquiry into why the

Confederates fared so poorly in the West.

6.625 **Harter**, E. C., *The Lost Colony of the Confederacy*, Jackson, MS, 1985. The history of Confederate emigrés who set up a slave colony in Brazil.

6.626 **Lash**, J. N., *Destroyer of the Iron Horse. General Joseph E. Johnston and Confederate Rail Transport, 1861–1865*, Kent, OH, 1991.

6.627 **Lebergott**, S., 'Why the South lost. Commercial purpose in the Confederacy', *Journal of American History*, LXX, 1984, 58–74. Finds that the pursuit of private gain by individuals in the Confederacy helped doom the overall war effort.

6.628 **Losson**, C., *Tennessee's Forgotten Warriors. Frank Cheatham and his Confederate Division*, Knoxville, TN, 1989.

6.629 **McMurry**, R. M., *Two Great Rebel Armies. An Essay in Confederate Military History*, Chapel Hill, NC, 1989. A defense of Robert E. Lee's Army of Northern Virginia by way of contrast to the Confederates' unsuccesful Army of the Tennessee.

6.630 **McWhiney**, G., and **Jamieson**, P. D., *Attack and Die. Civil War Military Tactics and the Southern Heritage*, University, AL, 1982. A study of Civil War battles that links high casualties on the southern side to a combination of Napoleonic tactics and a lingering "Celtic" heritage of Scots-Irish descendants who felt most at home while making suicide charges.

6.631 **Neely**, M. E., **Holzer**, H., and **Boritt**, G. S., *The Confederate Image. Prints of the Lost Cause*, Chapel Hill, NC, 1987.

6.632 **Nolan**, A. T., *Lee Considered. General Robert E. Lee and Civil War History*, Chapel Hill, NC, 1991. Attacks the "marble man" image of Lee, and tries instead to portray him as a typical southern patriarch.

6.633 **Rable**, G. C., *Civil Wars. Women and the Crisis of Southern Nationalism*, Urbana, IL, 1989. A comprehensive study of southern women before and during the Civil War that finds continuity of gender roles.

6.634 **Smith**, E. H., 'Chambersburg. Anatomy of a Confederate reprisal', *American Historical Review*, XCVI, 1991, 432–455. Analyzes the 1864 raid of Confederates on a Pennsylvania town and finds that the wanton destruction was the result of a culture clash between civilian German immigrants and southern soldiers.

6.635 **Thomas**, E. M., *The Confederate Nation, 1861–1865*. New York, 1978. A one-volume survey of the rise and fall of the Confederates with particularly good analysis of the Confederate constitution and how the politics of the southern republic hampered its war effort.

6.636 **Thomas**, E. M., *et al.*, (ed.), *The Old South in the Crucible of War. Essays*, Jackson, MS, 1983.

6.637 **Wiley**, B. I., *Confederate Women*, Westport, CT, 1975. The leading historian of the social side of the war turns his attention to rebel women and their role in the war.

Reconstruction

6.638 **Ayers**, E.L., *The Promise of the New South Life after Reconstruction*, New York, 1992

6.639 **Beatty**, Bess, *A Revolution Gone Backward. The Black Response to National Politics, 1876–1896*, Westport, CT, 1987.

6.640 **Butchart**, R. E., *Northern Schools, Southern Blacks and Reconstruction. Freedman's Education*, Westport, CT, 1980.

6.641 **Carter**, D. T., *When the War Was Over. The Failure of Self-Reconstruction in the South, 1865–1867*, Baton Rouge, LA, 1985. Analyzes the near uniform antagonism of the ex-Confederates to reconciliation to the goals of presidential reconstruction.

6.642 **Cheek**, W., and **Cheek**, Aimee Lee, *John Mercer Langston and the Fight for Black Freedom, 1829–1865*, Urbana, IL, 1988. Examines the early life of the free black leader before his election to Congress during Reconstruction.

6.643 **Cohen**, W., *At Freedom's Edge. Black Mobility and the Southern White Quest for Racial Control, 1861–1915*, Baton Rouge, LA, 1991.

6.644 **Crouch**, B. A., *The Freedmen's Bureau and Black Texans*, Austin, TX, 1992.

6.645 **Current**, R. N., *Those Terrible Carpetbaggers. A Reinterpretation*, New York, 1988. A collective biography of ten prominent northern migrants to the postbellum South that emphasizes the economic interests that drew them southward, and how the personal business difficulties tended to draw them into Republican party politics.

6.646 **Curtis**, M. K., *No State Shall Abridge. The Fourteenth Amendment and the Bill of Rights*, Durham, NC, 1990. This work argues for the view that Congressional Republicans did intend for the Constitution to incorporate the Bill of Rights and apply it to the states.

6.647 **Drago**, E. L., *Black Politicians and Reconstruction in Georgia. A Splendid Failure*, Baton Rouge, LA, 1982.

6.648 **Field**, Phyllis F., *The Politics of Race in New York. The Struggle for Black Suffrage in the Civil War Era*, Ithaca, NY, 1982. Recounts the party positions on black voting up until the adoption of the Fifteenth Amendment.

6.649 **Fitzgerald**, M. W., *The Union League Movement in the Deep South. Politics and Agricultural Change During Reconstruction*, Baton Rouge, LA, 1989. Explains the League's role in the political mobilization of the freedmen in 1867, as well as its part in defending the freedmen in contractual relations with landowners.

6.650 **Foner**, E., *Reconstruction. America's Unfinished Revolution, 1863–1877*, New York, 1988. A magisterial survey of the end of slavery and the often heroic efforts made by the freedmen to make a new society and politics in the postwar South on the basis of the ideology of the triumphant northern Republicans.

6.651 **Foster**, G. M., *Ghosts of the Confederacy. Defeat, the Lost Cause, and the Emergence of the New South*, New York, 1987. This work explores the ways Southerners responded to the defeat of the Confederate Army from 1865 through 1913.

6.652 **Furtwangler**, A., *Assassin on Stage. Brutus, Hamlet, and the Death of Lincoln*, Urbana, IL, 1991. Places the assassination of Lincoln into the stage history of *Hamlet* and *Julius Caesar*, and links the tragedy of the war to the tragedy in Ford's Theater.

6.653 **Gillette**, W., *Retreat from Reconstruction, 1869–1879*, Baton Rouge, LA, 1979.

6.654 **Howard**, V. B., *Religion and the Radical Republican Movement, 1860–1870*, Lexington, KY, 1990.

6.655 **Jones**, Jacqueline, *Soldiers of Light and Love: Northern Teachers and Georgia Blacks, 1862–1875*, Chapel Hill, NC, 1980.

6.656 **Lanza**, M. L., *Agrarianism and Reconstruction Politics. The Southern Homestead Act*, Baton Rouge, LA, 1990. Analyzes why the Republican hopes for a transformation of the South through a restricted homestead measure did not come to pass.

6.657 **Lofgren**, C. A., *The Plessy Case. A Legal-Historical Interpretation*, New York, 1987. An analysis of the notorious 1896 "Plessy vs. Ferguson" case that established separate-but-equal as the law of the land, Lofgren's book explores the role of nineteenth century scientific racism in the process of judicial decision-making in this case.

6.658 **Maltz**, E. M., *Civil Rights, the Constitution, and Congress, 1863–1869*, Lawrence, KS, 1990. Studies the philosophy and politics behind the Fourteenth Amendment to the Constitution and finds that conservative Republicans in Congress wanted to limit the scope of the amendment's guarantee to equality of opportunity, not racial equality.

6.659 **McConnell**, S., *Glorious Contentment. The Grand Army of the Republic, 1865–1900*, Chapel Hill, NC, 1992.

6.660 **Moneyhon**, C. H., *Republicanism in Reconstruction Texas*, Austin, TX, 1980.

6.661 **Morris**, R. C., *Reading, 'Riting, and Reconstruction. The Education of Freedmen in the South, 1861–1870*, Chicago, 1982.

6.662 **Nelson**, W. E., *The Fourteenth Amendment. From Political Principle to Judicial Doctrine*, Cambridge, MA, 1988.

6.663 **Olsen**, O. H., (ed.), *Reconstruction and Redemption in the South*, Baton Rouge, LA, 1980.

6.664 **Perman**, M., *The Road to Redemption. Southern Politics, 1869–1879*, Chapel Hill, NC, 1984. A study of politics within the southern Democratic and Republican parties that shows the economic crisis of the mid-1870s led to an all-out effort by the Democrats to regain power on a racialist basis.

6.665 **Rable**, G. C., *But There Was No Peace. The Role of Violence in the Politics of Reconstruction*, Athens, GA, 1984. Catalogues the onslaught of white violence directed against blacks and the Republican party; the overwhelming extralegal force used serves to take historians to task for faulting northerners for half-way measures to reconstruct the South when all such actions would be resisted by armed vigilantes.

6.666 **Robinson**, A. L., 'Beyond the realm of social consensus: new meanings of Reconstruction for American history',

Journal of American History, LXVIII, 1981.

6.667 **Sawrey**, R. D., *Dubious Victory. The Reconstruction Debate in Ohio*, Lexington, KY, 1992.

6.668 **Seip**, T. L., *The South Returns to Congress. Men, Economic Measures, and International Relations, 1868–1879*, Baton Rouge, LA, 1983. Looks at the region's efforts to secure economic aid, particularly on the part of southern Republicans, through an analysis of voting patterns in Congress.

6.669 **Summers**, M. W., *Railroads, Reconstruction, and the Gospel of Prosperity. Aid Under the Radical Republicans, 1867–77*, Princeton, NJ, 1984. Underscores the efforts of southern Republicans to build a white base for the party on internal improvements, and how the failure of many railroad projects in the 1870s helped doom the party.

6.670 **Sutherland**, D. E., *The Confederate Carpetbaggers*, Baton Rouge, LA, 1988.

6.671 **Tunnell**, T., *Crucible of Reconstruction. War, Radicalism and Race in Louisiana, 1862–1877*, Baton Rouge, LA, 1984. Considers the politics of Louisiana reconstruction from Lincoln's wartime plan through the mobilization of black voters and eventual return to white domination.

6.672 **Wallenstein**, P., *From Slave South to New South. Public Policy in Nineteenth-Century Georgia*, Chapel Hill, NC, 1987. An analysis of public policy in nineteenth century Georgia centering on budgets and other financial matters.

6.673 **Wiggins**, Sarah Woolfolk, *The Scalawag in Alabama Politics, 1865–1881*, University, AL, 1977. A study of southern white Republicans.

6.674 **Wilson**, C. R., *Baptized in Blood. The Religion of the Lost Cause, 1865–1920*, Athens, GA, 1980.

The Big Barbecue

6.675 **Allswang**, J. M., *Bosses, Machines, and Urban Voters*, Baltimore, 1986.

6.676 **Avrich**, P., *The Haymarket Tragedy*, Princeton, NJ, 1984. The definitive study of the 1886 Chicago bombing and the repression against anarchists and radicals that followed.

6.677 **Campbell**, B. C., *Representative Democracy. Public Policy and Midwestern Legislatures in the Late Nineteenth Century*, Cambridge, MA, 1980.

6.678 **Carosso**, V. P., with **Carosso**, Rose C., *The Morgans. Private International Bankers, 1854–1913*, Cambridge, MA, 1987. A history of J. Pierpont Morgan and his father, Junius S. Morgan, based on internal Morgan records.

6.679 **Doenecke**, J. D., *The Presidencies of James A. Garfield & Chester A. Arthur*, Lawrence, KS, 1981.

6.680 **Feuer**, A. B., (ed.), *Combat Diary. Episodes from the History of the Twenty-Second Regiment, 1866–1905*, New York, 1991. Memoirs of a professional soldier who served in the U.S. Army in campaigns against the Indians in the Southwest, the Spanish in Cuba, and the Filipinos.

6.681 **Hoogenboom**, A. A., *The Presidency of Rutherford B. Hayes*, Lawrence, KS, 1988.

6.682 **Hyman**, H. M., *Equal Justice Under Law. Constitutional Development, 1835–1875*, New York, 1982. A survey of constitutional history in the Civil War era.

6.683 **Leonard**, T. C., *The Power of the Press. The Birth of American Political Reporting*, New York, 1986. Treats the emerging independence of journalists in the nineteenth century and the growing dependence of politicians on the press as a mediator.

6.684 **Miller**, W. R., *Revenuers and Moonshiners. Enforcing Federal Liquor Law in the Mountain South, 1865–1900*, Chapel Hill, NC, 1991. Locates the famed struggle over illegal alcohol in Appalachia in the outcome of Reconstruction.

6.685 **Pegram**, T. R., *Partisans and Progressives. Private Interest and Public Policy in Illinois, 1870–1922*, Urbana, IL, 1992.

6.686 **Schlesinger**, K. R., *The Power that Governs. The Evolution of Judicial Activism in a Midwestern State, 1840–1890*, New York, 1990. Looks at the regulation of railroads and other businesses in Illinois and links that history to the larger history of politics in the Civil War era.

6.687 **Shumsky**, N. L., *The Evolution of Political Protest and the Workingmen's Party of California*, Columbus, OH, 1991.

6.688 **Socolofsky**, H. E., and **Spetter**, A. B., *The Presidency of Benjamin Harrison*, Lawrence, KS, 1987.

6.689 **Varga**, N., 'America's patron saint.

Tammany', *Journal of American Culture*, X, 1987, 45–51.

6.690 **West**, R. S., *Satire on Stone. The Political Cartoons of Joseph Keppler*, Urbana, IL, 1988.

The Populist challenge

6.691 **Clanton**, G., *Populism. The Humane Preference in America, 1890–1900*, Boston, 1991. Takes the Populists at their word in finding that a commitment to human needs rather than to property rights was their guiding principle.

6.692 **Flynt**, W., *Poor but Proud. Alabama's Poor Whites*, Tuscaloosa, AL, 1989.

6.693 **Goodwyn**, L., *Democratic Promise. The Populist Moment in America*, New York, 1976.

6.694 **McMath**, R. C., *American Populism. A Social History, 1877–1898*, New York, 1993.

6.695 **McNall**, S. G., *The Road to Rebellion. Class Formation and Kansas Populism, 1865–1900*, Chicago, 1988.

6.696 **Miller**, W. R., *Oklahoma Populism. A History of the People's Party in the Oklahoma Territory*, Norman, OK, 1987.

6.697 **Palmer**, B., *'Man Over Money': The Southern Populist Critique of American Capitalism*, Chapel Hill, NC, 1980.

6.698 **Pollack**, N., *The Humane Economy. Populism, Capitalism, and Democracy*, New Brunswick, NJ, 1990. A distinguished historian of the movement argues that Populist leaders fashioned an ideology that envisioned a modified capitalism, but that the movement was not hostile to market relations.

6.699 **Pollack**, N., *The Just Polity. Populism, Law, and Human Welfare*, Urbana, IL, 1987. Continues the author's life of scholarship that defends the People's Party

from its critics, and finds that Populism still has much to offer twentieth century Americans.

6.700 **Smallwood**, F., *The Other Candidates. Third Parties in Presidential Elections*, Hanover, NH, 1983.

6.701 **Woods**, T. A., *Knights of the Plow. Oliver H. Kelley and the Origins of the Grange in Republican Ideology*, Ames, IA, 1991. Examines the origins of the Granger movement and places the thought of its leader in the larger tradition of republicanism.

Foreign relations

6.702 **Mattox**, H. E., *The Twilight of Amateur Diplomacy. The American Foreign Service and its Senior Officers in the 1890s*, Kent, OH, 1989. Utilizes a statistical survey to ascertain that U.S. diplomats who had no formal training were actually quite competent and not patronage hacks.

6.703 **Osborne**, T. J., *Empire Can Wait. American Opposition to Hawaiian Annexation, 1893–1898*, Kent, OH, 1981.

6.704 **Rosenstone**, R. A., *Mirror in the Shrine. American Encounters with Meiji Japan*, Cambridge, MA, 1988. A collective biography of Americans who lived in Japan and observed the emergence of the modern Japanese society.

6.705 **Schoonover**, T., (ed.), *Mexican Lobby. Matias Romero in Washington, 1861–1867*, Rutherford, NJ, 1986. Account of the Mexican ambassador to the U.S. amid the Civil War crisis.

6.706 **Wiley**, P. B., and **Ichiro**, K., *Yankees in the Land of the Gods. Commodore Perry and the Opening of Japan*, New York, 1990. A collaboration between an American and Japanese scholar on the two nations at the onset of their commercial and diplomatic contact.

7

THE ORGANIZATIONAL SOCIETY AND WORLD POWER, 1898–1945

GENERAL

7.1 **Carter**, P. A., *Another Part of the Twenties*, New York, 1977. An iconoclastic survey of the decade.

7.2 **Cashman**, S. D., *America in the Twenties and Thirties. The Olympian Age of Franklin Delano Roosevelt*, New York, 1989.

7.3 **Chafe**, W. H., *The Paradox of Change. American Women in the 20th Century*, New York, 1991. A revised and updated version of the author's influential 1972 book *The American Women*.

7.4 **Flink**, J. J., *The Automobile Age*, Cambridge, MA, 1988.

7.5 **Geller**, L. D., (ed.), *The American Field Service Archives of World War I, 1914–1917*, New York, 1989.

7.6 **Green**, D., *Shaping Political Consciousness. The Language of Politics in America from McKinley to Reagan*, Ithaca, NY, 1987. Strongest on the time before World War II when contradictions emerged between the use of older American forms of discourse and the ends to which political leaders put their words.

7.7 **Harr**, J. E., and **Johnson**, P. J., *The Rockefeller Century*, New York, 1988.

7.8 **Kennedy**, D. M., *Over Here: The First World War and American Society*, New York, 1980.

7.9 **Leonard**, T. C., *Above the Battle. War Making in America from Appomattox to Versailles*, New York, 1978.

7.10 **Ling**, P. J., *America and the Automobile. Technology, Reform, and Social Change*, 1990.

7.11 **Lippy**, C. H., (ed.), *Twentieth-Century Shapers of American Popular Religion*, Westport, CT, 1989.

7.12 **Marquis**, Alice Goldfarb, *Hope and Ashes. The Birth of Modern Times, 1929–1939*, New York, 1986.

7.13 **Mortimer**, E., *The World That FDR Built. Vision and Reality*, New York, 1989. Interviews with political leaders and journalists who came of age during World War II.

7.14 **Ogren**, K. J., *The Jazz Revolution. Twenties America and the Meaning of Jazz*, New York, 1989.

7.15 **Parrish**, M. E., *Anxious Decades. America in Prosperity and Depression, 1920–1941*, New York, 1992. Useful introduction to the period.

7.16 **Sklar**, M. J., *The United States as a Developing Country. Studies in U.S. History in the Progressive Era and the 1920s*, New York, 1992. A collection of essays on the theme of the emergence of a new state devoted to the service of corporate capitalism early in the twentieth century.

126

GUIDES TO SOURCES

Primary sources

7.17 **Bessie**, A., and **Prago**, A., (ed.), *Our Fight. Writings by Veterans of the Abraham Lincoln Brigade, Spain 1936–1939*, New York, 1987.

7.18 **Bland**, L. E., (ed.), *The Papers of George Catlett Marshall*, Baltimore, 1981– .

7.19 **Borus**, D. H., (ed.), *These United States. Portraits of America from the 1920s*, Ithaca, NY, 1992.

7.20 **Buhite**, R. D., and **Levy**, D. W., *FDR's Fireside Chats*, Norman, OK, 1992.

7.21 **Chan**, Sucheng, (ed.), *Quiet Odyssey. A Pioneer Korean Woman in America*, Seattle, 1991. The autobiography of Mary Paik Lee, who moved to California from Korea at the beginning of the century and lived as a farm worker.

7.22 **Chandler**, A. C., Jr., (ed.), *The Papers of Dwight David Eisenhower*, Baltimore, 1970– .

7.23 **Constantine**, J. R., (ed.), *Letters of Eugene V. Debs*, Urbana, IL, 1990. A three volume set of letters that spans the life of the socialist and labor leader.

7.24 **Cott**, Nancy F., (ed.), *A Woman Making History. Mary Ritter Beard through her Letters*, New Haven, CT, 1991. A collection of letters that shows Beard's attempt to build a women's history movement before its time.

7.25 **Courtwright**, D., **Joseph**, H., and **Jarlais**, D. D., *Addicts Who Survived. An Oral History of Narcotic Use in America, 1923–1965*, Knoxville, TN, 1989. Interviews with drug addicts and descriptions of the federal legal control of narcotics and the meager rehabilitation resources available to addicts.

7.26 **Earley**, Charity Adams, *One Woman's Army. A Black Officer Remembers the WAC*, College Station, TX, 1989.

7.27 **Fox**, S., *The Unknown Internment. An Oral History of the Relocation of Italian Americans during World War II*, Boston, 1990.

7.28 **Hilderbrand**, R. C., (ed.), *The Papers of Woodrow Wilson. The Complete Press Conferences, 1913–1919*, Princeton, NJ, 1985. Volume 50 of the *Papers* series.

7.29 **Hoffman**, Alice M., and **Hoffman**, H. S., *Archives of Memory. A Soldier Recalls World War II*, Lexington, KY, 1990.

7.30 **Hoopes**, R., *Americans Remember the Home Front. An Oral Narrative*, New York, 1977.

7.31 **Kimball**, W. F., (ed.), *Churchill and Roosevelt. The Complete Correspondence*, Princeton, NJ, 1984. A three volume set.

7.32 **Klejment**, Anne, and **Klejment**, Alice, *Dorothy Day and The Catholic Worker. A Bibliography and Index*, New York, 1986.

7.33 **Larner**, J. W., *The Papers of the Society of American Indians*, Wilmington, DE, 1986. A microform set of the papers of the records of the first lobbying group of Indian professionals; a guide and index is on the first reel of microfilm.

7.34 **Larner**, J. W., (ed.), *The Papers of Carlos Montezuma, M.D.*, Wilmington, DE, 1983. A microform series of the papers of one of the founders of the Society of American Indians.

7.35 **Le Guin**, C. A., (ed.), *A Home-Concealed Woman. The Diaries of Magnolia Wynn Le Guin, 1901–1913*, Athens, GA, 1990. A descendant's edition of his great-grandmother's diaries that shows a rural southern white woman's life was bounded by conception, birth, nursing, and household chores.

7.36 **Lester**, DeeGee, *Roosevelt Research. Collections for the Study of Theodore, Franklin and Eleanor*, Westport, CT, 1992. A reference work that guides the researcher to the various repositories holding collections on or about the presidents and Mrs. Roosevelt.

7.37 **Link**, A. S., (ed.), *The Papers of Woodrow Wilson*, Princeton, NJ, 1966–1993. Monumental sixty-eight volume set, with an additional index volume, that covers Wilson's life from boyhood through graduate school at Johns Hopkins, Princeton years, New Jersey statehouse, and, of course, his two terms in the White House.

7.38 **Litoff**, Judy Barrett, and **Smith**, D. C., *Since You Went Away. World War II Letters from American Women on the Home Front*, New York, 1991. A collection of letters from mothers, wives, sweethearts, etc. to their men overseas, showing the changes in the lives led at home.

7.39 **Markowitz**, G., and **Rosner**, D., (ed.), *'Slaves of the Depression'. Workers' Letters about Life on the Job*, Ithaca, NY, 1987. A collection of documents written by workers that emphasizes the emergence of a strong class consciousness and a strong sense that capitalists were to blame for mass unemployment and misery.

7.40 **McGuire**, P., *Taps for a Jim Crow Army. Letters from Black Soldiers in World War II*, Santa Barbara, CA, 1983.

7.41 **Owings**, L. C., *Environmental Values, 1860–1972. A Guide to Information Sources*, Detroit, 1976.

7.42 **Roley**, P., (ed.), *G Company's War. Two Personal Accounts of the Campaigns in Europe, 1944–1945*, Tuscaloosa, AL, 1992. Two diaries combined into one account of riflemen in the assault on Germany.

7.43 **Snyder**, L. L., *Historic Documents of World War I*, Westport, CT, 1977.

7.44 **Woirol**, G., (ed.), *In the Floating Army. F. C. Mills on Itinerant Life in California, 1914*, Urbana, IL, 1992. Reprints some of the writings of an economist who lived among farm workers on the new corporate farms of California.

7.45 **Zangrando**, R. L., (ed.), *Papers of the NAACP*, Frederick, MD, 1989. A microfilm collection that is in eighteen parts, complete with guides for each part.

Atlases, bibliographies, and dictionaries

7.46 **Baxter**, C. F., *The Normandy Campaign, 1944*, Westport, CT, 1992. Reviews more than five hundred entries on the topic, including some foreign language publications.

7.47 **Buenker**, J. D., (ed.), *Historical Dictionary of the Progressive Era, 1890–1920*, New York, 1988.

7.48 **Buenker**, J. D., and **Burckel**, N. C., *Progressive Reform. A Guide to Information Sources*, Detroit, 1980.

7.49 **Clements**, W. M., and **Malpezzi**, Frances M., *Native American Folklore, 1879–1979. An Annotated Bibliography*, Athens, OH, 1984.

7.50 **Coleman**, P. K., and **Lamb**, C. R., *The Non-Partisan League, 1915–1922: An Annotated Bibliography*, St. Paul, MN, 1985.

7.51 **Cooper**, J. M., and **Neu**, C. E., (ed.), *The Wilson Era. Essays in Honor of Arthur S. Link*, Arlington Heights, IL, 1991.

7.52 **Frederick**, R. G., *Warren G. Harding. A Bibliography*, Westport, CT, 1992. A guide to the literature about the president and about the history of the early 1920s.

7.53 **Graham**, O. L., and **Wander**, M. R., *Franklin D. Roosevelt. His Life and Times, An Encyclopedic View*, Boston, MA, 1985.

7.54 **Herwig**, H. H., *Biographical Dictionary of World War I*, Westport, CT, 1982.

7.55 **Killen**, Linda, and **Lael**, R. L., *Versailles and After. An Annotated Bibliography of American Foreign Relations, 1919–1933*, New York, 1983.

7.56 **Kirkendall**, R. S., (ed.), *The Harry S. Truman Encyclopedia*, Boston, 1989.

7.57 **Kyvig**, D. E., *New Day/ New Deal. A Bibliography of the Great American Depression, 1929–1941*, New York, 1988.

7.58 **Langman**, L., *Encyclopedia of American Film Comedy*, New York, 1987.

7.59 **Langman**, L., *Writers on the American Screen. A Guide to Film Adaptations of American and Foreign Literary Works*, New York, 1986.

7.60 **Meier**, A., and **Rudwick**, E., *Black History and the Historical Profession, 1915–1980*, Urbana, IL, 1986. A historiographical survey that traces the origins of black historical writing back to Carter Woodson, founder of the *Journal of Negro History*.

7.61 **Olson**, J. S., (ed.), *Historical Dictionary of the New Deal. From Inauguration to Preparation for War*, Westport, CT, 1985.

7.62 **Perry**, M., *The Harlem Renaissance. An Annotated Bibliography and Commentary*, New York, 1982.

7.63 **Schaffer**, R., *The United States in World War I. A Selected Bibliography*, Santa Barbara, CA, 1978.

7.64 **Schlacter**, Gail, and **Byrne**, Pamela R., (ed.), *World War II from an American Perspective. An Annotated Bibliography*, Santa Barbara, CA, 1983.

7.65 **Schlacter**, Gail, *The Great Depression. A Historical Bibliography*, Santa Barbara, CA, 1984.

7.66 **Smith**, M. J., *World War II. The European and Mediterranean Theaters. An Annotated Bibliography*, New York, 1984.

7.67 **Smith**, S. H., (ed.), *Investigations of the Attack on Pearl Harbor. Index to Government Hearings*, New York, 1990.

7.68 **Watson**, B. L., and **Watson**, Susan M., *United States Intelligence. An Encyclopedia*, New York, 1990.

7.69 **Woodward**, D. R., and **Maddox**, R. F., *America and World War I. A Selected Annotated Bibliography of English-*

Language Sources, New York, 1985.

Historiography

7.70 **Achenbaum**, W. A., 'W(h)ither social welfare history? A review essay', *Journal of Social History*, XXIV, 1990, 135–141. Reviews current methods of studying the history of social welfare.

7.71 **Baker**, Susan Stout, *Radical Beginnings. Richard Hofstadter and the 1930s*, Westport, CT, 1985. An intellectual biography of one of the leaders of the "consensus school" of history; the author finds continuity between Hofstadter's politics in the Great Depression and his postwar writings.

7.72 **Bowden**, H. W., *Church History in an Age of Uncertainty. Historiographical Patterns in the United States, 1906–1990*; Carbondale, IL, 1991. A thorough review of writings on American religious history this century.

7.73 **Dawidowicz**, Lucy S., *The Holocaust and the Historians*, Cambridge, MA, 1981.

7.74 **Escott**, P. D., *W. J. Cash and the Minds of the South*, Baton Rouge, LA, 1992. A fiftieth anniversary retrospective anthology about Cash's influence on southern thinking.

7.75 **Fasce**, F., 'American Labor History, 1973–1983. Italian Perspectives', *Reviews in American History*, XIV, 1986, 597–613. A review of writings by Italian scholars.

7.76 **Fink**, L., ' "Intellectuals" versus "Workers". Academic requirements and the creation of labor history', *American Historical Review*, XCVI, 1991, 395–421. A review of the "Wisconsin School" of labor historians in the early twentieth century and their legacy for today's writers.

7.77 **Fitzpatrick**, Ellen, 'Rethinking the intellectual origins of American labor history', *American Historical Review*, XCVI, 1991, 422–428.

7.78 **Ingham**, J. N., 'Business history: theory-driven and theory-starved', *Canadian Review of American Studies*, XXII, 1991, 101–109. Reviews the recent writings in business history and evaluates the impact of Alfred Chandler's work on the field.

7.79 **Lawson**, S. F., 'Freedom then, freedom now. The historiography of the civil rights movement', *American Historical Review*, XCVI, 1991, 456–471.

7.80 **Matsuda**, T., 'The coming of the Pacific war. Japanese perspectives', *Reviews in American History*, XIV, 1986, 629–652.

7.81 **Murphy**, Marjorie, 'What women have wrought', *American Historical Review*, XCIII, 1988, 653–663. Reviews recent books on women workers and the culture of work.

7.82 **Persons**, S., *Ethnic Studies at Chicago, 1905–1945*, Urbana, IL, 1987. Reviews the ideas and impact of the "Chicago School" of sociology and urban studies.

7.83 **Pfitzer**, G. M., *Samuel Eliot Morison's Historical World. In Quest of a New Parkman*, Boston, 1991. An intellectual biography of Morison that also chronicles much about the writing of history and the historical profession in this century.

7.84 **Puhle**, H.-J., 'Comparative approaches from Germany. The "New Nation" in advanced industrial capitalism, 1860–1940 – integration, stabilization and reform', *Reviews in American History*, XIV, 1986, 614–628. An article that compares state and society in Germany and the United States.

7.85 **Sadkovich**, J. J., *Reevaluating Major Naval Combatants of World War II*, New York, 1990.

7.86 **Scott**, Anne Firor. 'On seeing and not seeing: a case of historical invisibility', *Journal of American History*, LXXI, 1984, 7–21. Discusses the former invisibility of women's studies and calls for more women's history.

7.87 **Williams**, V. J., *From a Caste to a Minority. Changing Attitudes of American Sociologists Toward Afro-Americans, 1896–1945*, Westport, CT, 1989.

BIOGRAPHY

7.88 **Adams**, H. H., *Witness to Power. The Life of Fleet Admiral William D. Leahy*, Annapolis, MD, 1985.

7.89 **Aichele**, G. J., *Oliver Wendell Holmes, Jr. Soldier, Scholar, Judge*, Boston, 1989.

7.90 **Alexander**, C. C., *Ty Cobb*, New York, 1984. A biography of the early twentieth century baseball star that places his exploits in the context of the changing South of his youth and the city of Detroit where he starred.

7.91 **Alpern**, Sara, *Freda Kirchey. A Woman of The Nation*, Cambridge, MA, 1987. A biography of the woman who published *The Nation* magazine and made it into the foremost organ of American liberalism.

7.92 **Ambrose**, S. E., *Eisenhower. General of the Army, President-Elect, 1890–1952*, New York, 1983.

7.93 **Antler**, Joyce, *Lucy Sprague Mitchell. The Making of a Modern Woman*, New Haven, CT, 1987. Biography of the educator who worked with John Dewey on progressive education at the Bank Street College in New York.

7.94 **Ashby**, L., *William Jennings Bryan. Champion of Democracy*, Boston, 1987. A survey of Bryan's political life.

7.95 **Baker**, L., *Brandeis and Frankfurter. A Dual Biography*, New York, 1984. An account of the relationship between the two jurists that includes a full treatment of the actions of each on the Supreme Court.

7.96 **Baker**, Liva, *The Justice from Beacon Hill. The Life and Times of Oliver Wendell Holmes*, New York, 1991. Especially strong on Holmes's personal life, in addition to offering a full review of his legal thought.

7.97 **Baker**, W. J., *Jesse Owens. An American Life*, New York, 1986. A biography of the 1936 Olympic track star that follows him through the racial turmoil of his time and into the 1960s.

7.98 **Beasley**, M. H., *Eleanor Roosevelt and the Media. A Public Quest for Self-Fulfillment*, Urbana, IL, 1987.

7.99 **Bjork**, D. W., *William James. The Center of His Vision*, New York, 1988.

7.100 **Brittain**, J. E., *Alexanderson. Pioneer in American Electrial Engineering*, Baltimore, 1992. Biography of one of the pioneer inventor-entrepreneurs who made the General Electric Company a world power unto itself.

7.101 **Britton**, J. A., *Carleton Beals. A Radical Journalist in Latin America*, Albuquerque, NM, 1987. A biography of the leading American journalist who covered Latin American politics and society for an American audience that often chose to overlook his prophetic writings.

7.102 **Bruns**, R. A., *Preacher. Billy Sunday and Big-Time American Evangelism*, New York, 1992.

7.103 **Buckley**, K. W., *Mechanical Man. John Broadus Watson and the Beginnings of Behaviorism*, New York, 1989. Biography of the psychologist who insisted on the primacy of environmental forces in determining intelligence, and his subsequent career as an advertising executive.

7.104 **Bush**, G. W., *Lord of Attention. Gerald Stanley Lee and the Crowd Metaphor in Industrializing America*, Amherst, MA, 1991. A biography of an intellectual-turned-advertising man with reflections about the transformation of society from producers to consumers.

7.105 **Caro**, R. A., *The Years of Lyndon Johnson. Means of Ascent*, New York, 1990. An LBJ biography in Manichean terms, in which arch-segregationist Coke Stephenson becomes the hero to Johnson's villain in the 1948 election.

7.106 **Chesler**, Ellen, *Woman of Valor. Margaret Sanger and the Birth Control Movement in America*, New York, 1992.

7.107 **Clayton**, B., *W. J. Cash. A Life*, Baton Rouge, LA, 1991. Biography of the southern essayist who defined the South for the rest of the nation.

7.108 **Clayton**, B., *Forgotten Prophet. The Life of Randolph Bourne*, Baton Rouge, LA, 1984. A biography of one of the leading cultural critics of the pre-1914 era and one of the more prominent anti-war leaders.

7.109 **Cook**, Blanche Wiesen, *Eleanor Roosevelt*, New York, 1992.

7.110 **Cotkin**, G., *William James. Public Philosopher*, Baltimore, 1990.

7.111 **Cray**, E., *General of the Army. George C. Marshall, Soldier and Statesman*, New York, 1990. A one volume work that covers in detail Marshall's military career and gives thorough treatment to his accomplishments as Secretary of State in the critical opening years of the Cold War.

7.112 **Crosswell**, D. K. R., *The Chief of Staff. The Military Career of General Walter Bedell Smith*, Westport, CT, 1991.

7.113 **Dawson**, N. L., *Louis D. Brandeis, Felix Frankfurter, and the New Deal*, Hamden, CT, 1980.

7.114 **Donald**, D. H., *Look Homeward. A Life of Thomas Wolfe*, Boston, 1987.

7.115 **Dorsett**, L. W., *Billy Sunday and the Redemption of Urban America*, Grand Rapids, MI, 1991. A sympathetic biography of the revivalist that covers his rise and fall.

7.116 **Dorwart**, J. M., *Eberstadt and Forrestal. A*

National Security Partnership, 1909–1949, College Station, TX, 1991. A dual biography of Ferdinand Eberstadt and James Forrestal and how they managed through bureaucratic infighting to reshape the armed forces command structure after World War II.

7.117 **Duberman**, M. B., *Paul Robeson*, New York, 1988.

7.118 **Ernst**, R., *Weakness is a Crime. The Life of Bernard McFadden*, Syracuse, NY, 1991. A biography of the entrepreneur who promoted physical fitness, changes in diet, and in sexual practices.

7.119 **Falk**, Candace, *Love, Anarchy, and Emma Goldman*, New York, 1984.

7.120 **Ferrell**, R. H., *Woodrow Wilson and World War I, 1917–1921*, New York, 1985. A survey of the politics and diplomacy of Wilson's presidency.

7.121 **Fine**, S., *Frank Murphy. The Washington Years*, Ann Arbor, MI, 1984. The third volume of the author's biography finds Murphy as Attorney General and Supreme Court justice.

7.122 **Foster**, M. S., *Henry J. Kaiser. Builder in the Modern American West*, Austin, TX, 1989. A business biography of the shipbuilder, steelmaker, and health care provider whom the author sees as the most important businessman operating west of the Mississippi.

7.123 **Freidel**, F. B., *Franklin D. Roosevelt. A Rendezvous with Destiny*, Boston, 1990.

7.124 **Friedman**, L. J., *Menninger. The Family and the Clinic*, New York, 1990. Places the Topeka-based enterprise and its guiding family in the larger context of the history of American psychiatry.

7.125 **Goggin**, Jacqueline Anne, *Carter G. Woodson. A Life in Black History*, Baton Rouge, LA, 1993.

7.126 **Griffith**, Sally Foreman, *Home Town News. William Allen White and the Emporia Gazette*, New York, 1989. A biography of the Kansas editor and his influence on Republican Party politics.

7.127 **Hamilton**, N., *JFK. Reckless Youth*, New York, 1992. Yet another Kennedy biography, this first volume of a projected trilogy focuses on the subject's life through his election to Congress in 1946; the author finds that Kennedy overcame a childhood of neglect and abuse to emerge as public leader.

7.128 **Hardeman**, D. B., *Rayburn. A Biography*, Austin, TX, 1987. A biography of the Texas politician who rose to become the longtime Speaker of the House of Representatives.

7.129 **Harlan**, L. D., *Booker T. Washington. The Wizard of Tuskegee, 1901–1915*, New York, 1983. Completes the author's biography of the black leader.

7.130 **Healey**, Dorothy, with **Isserman**, M., *Dorothy Healey Remembers. A Life in the American Communist Party*, New York, 1990. An as-told-to autobiography of an influential Southern California communist.

7.131 **Hecht**, R. A., *Oliver La Farge and the American Indian. A Biography*, Metuchen, NJ, 1991. A biography of a twentieth century "friend" of American Indians, La Farge's life shows a transition in attitudes from the era of forced acculturation to that of cultural pluralism.

7.132 **Hecksher**, A., *Woodrow Wilson*, New York, 1991. Covers its subject's life from boyhood in the Reconstruction South through the presidency and the Versailles Conference; in his interpretation of Wilson the statesman, the author differs with other critics, finding that Wilson acted only from lofty motives, and not from overt consideration of American material interests.

7.133 **Hewlett**, R. G., *Jessie Ball Du Pont*, Gainesville, FL, 1992. Biography of the woman who became Mrs. Alfred Du Pont, and after her husband's death, a leading figure in American philanthrophy.

7.134 **Highsaw**, R. B., *Edward Douglass White. Defender of the Conservative Faith*, Baton Rouge, LA, 1981.

7.135 **Hirsch**, H. N., *The Enigma of Felix Frankfurter*, New York, 1981.

7.136 **Hodgson**, G., *The Colonel. The Life and Wars of Henry Stimson, 1867–1950*, New York, 1990.

7.137 **Howard**, F., *Wilbur and Orville. A Biography of the Wright Brothers*, New York, 1987.

7.138 **Hughes**, T. P., *Lewis Mumford. Public Intellectual*, New York, 1990. Concentrates on Mumford's views about the relationship of technology to civilization.

7.139 **Hyatt**, M., *Franz Boas, Social Activist. The Dynamics of Ethnicity*, Westport, CT, 1990. A biography of the anthropologist that focuses on his public battles against eugenics and racism.

7.140 **Iverson**, P., *Carlos Montezuma and the Changing World of American Indians*, Albuquerque, NM, 1982.

7.141 **Jeannsonne**, G., *Leander Perez. Boss of the Delta*, Baton Rouge, LA, 1977.

7.142 **Jeannsonne**, G., *Gerald L. K. Smith. Minister of Hate*, New Haven, CT, 1988. A full-length biography of the right-wing populist associated with Father Coughlin, and his turn toward outright anti-semitism before and after World War II.

7.143 **Keith**, Caroline H., *'For Hell and a Brown Mule'. The Biography of Senator Millard E. Tydings*, Lanham, MD, 1991. The life of a Maryland senator who was noteworthy for having been Joseph McCarthy's most prominent whipping boy in the 1950 campaign.

7.144 **Kessner**, T., *Fiorello H. LaGuardia and the Making of Modern New York*, New York, 1989. An astute measure of the famous mayor that on balance finds him to have been consistent in his fight for social justice.

7.145 **Kimball**, W. F., *The Juggler. Franklin Roosevelt as Wartime Statesman*, Princeton, NJ, 1991.

7.146 **Kirkby**, Diane, (ed.), *Alice Henry. The Power of Pen and Voice. The Life of an Australian-American Labor Reformer*, New York, 1991. Biography of the leader of the Women's Trade Union League that elucidates Henry's notion of an "industrial feminism".

7.147 **Kline**, R. R., *Steinmetz. Engineer and Socialist*, Baltimore, 1992.

7.148 **Lawren**, W., *The General and the Bomb. A Biography of General Leslie R. Groves, Director of the Manhattan Project*, New York, 1988.

7.149 **Lee**, D., *Sergeant York. An American Hero*, Lexington, KY, 1985. A sympathetic biography of a deeply religious southerner who emerged as the leading American hero of World War I and permanent enshrinement as a living symbol of American military prowess.

7.150 **Lee**, R. A., *Dwight D. Eisenhower. Soldier and Statesman*, Chicago, 1981.

7.151 **Levy**, D. W., *Herbert Croly of the New Republic. The Life and Thought of an American Progressive*, Princeton, NJ, 1984.

7.152 **Littlefield**, D. F., *Alex Posey. Creek Poet, Journalist, and Humorist*, Lincoln, NE, 1992.

7.153 **Loveland**, Anne C., *Lillian Smith, a Southerner Confronting the South. A Biography*, Baton Rouge, LA, 1986. A biography of the writer who daringly challenged white racism in the South during the 1930s and 1940s.

7.154 **MacKinnon**, Janice R., and **MacKinnon**, S. R., *Agnes Smedley. The Life and Times of an American Radical*, Berkeley, CA, 1988.

7.155 **Madison**, J. H., *Eli Lilly. A Life, 1885–1977*, Indianapolis, IN, 1989. A biography of the entrepreneur and philanthropist who made his fortune in the pharmaceutical business.

7.156 **Marks**, F. W., *Wind Over Sand. The Diplomacy of Franklin Roosevelt*, Athens, GA, 1988.

7.157 **McCormick**, J., *George Santayana. A Biography*, New York, 1987.

7.158 **McGuire**, P., *He, Too, Spoke for Democracy. Judge Hastie, World War II, and the Black Soldier*, Westport, CT, 1988. Looks at the legal treatment of black soldiers by the War Department through the career of William Hastie.

7.159 **McJimsey**, G., *Harry Hopkins. Ally of the Poor and Defender of Democracy*, Cambridge, MA, 1987. Concentrates on Hopkins' service as a diplomat during the war, as well as his New Deal days at several of the alphabet soup agencies.

7.160 **McMurry**, Linda O., *George Washington Carver. Scientist and Symbol*, New York, 1981.

7.161 **Meine**, C., *Aldo Leopold. His Life and Work*, Madison, WI, 1988. A full biography of the environmentalist who espoused a "land ethic" that stressed the importance of wilderness.

7.162 **Miller**, D. L., *Lewis Mumford. A Life*, New York, 1989. A biography that covers Mumford's entire life but concentrates on the cultural criticism and urban planning essays of the 1930s.

7.163 **Miller**, R. M., *Harry Emerson Fosdick. Preacher, Pastor, Prophet*, New York, 1985. A biography of the American Protestant leader.

7.164 **Morton**, Marian J., *Emma Goldman and the American Left. 'Nowhere at Home'*, New York, 1992. Concise biography of the anarchist leader.

7.165 **Myers**, G. E., *William James. His Life and Thought*, New Haven, CT, 1986.

7.166 **Namorato**, M. V., *Rexford G. Tugwell. A Biography*, New York, 1988. A biography of the New Dealer who was an important part of President Roosevelt's "Brains Trust".

7.167 **Nash**, G. H., *The Life of Herbert Hoover. The Humanitarian, 1914–1917*, New York, 1988. The second in a multi-volume biographical series on Hoover; the focus is on Hoover's work in helping occupied Belgium that in turn brought him to the national and world stage.

7.168 **Novick**, S. M., *Honorable Justice. The Life of Oliver Wendell Holmes*, Boston, 1989.

7.169 **Paper**, L. J., *Brandeis. An Intimate Biography of One of America's Truly Great Supreme Court Justices*, Englewood Cliffs, NJ, 1983. Another biography of the justice that gives full attention to his reform career and to his opinions from the bench.

7.170 **Payne**, Elizabeth Anne, *Reform, Labor, and Feminism. Margaret Dreier Robins and the Women's Trade Union League*, Urbana, IL, 1988.

7.171 **Perry**, Elisabeth Israels, *Belle Moskowitz. Feminine Politics and the Exercise of Power in the Age of Alfred E. Smith*, New York, 1987. A biography of Governor Smith's leading social welfare policy-maker in the 1920s, locating Moskowitz both in New York City's immigrant Jewish community and in the women's movement of the time.

7.172 **Petillo**, Carol Morris, *Douglas MacArthur, the Phillipine Years*, Bloomington, IN, 1981.

7.173 **Pfaff**, D. W., *Joseph Pulitzer II and the Post Dispatch. A Newspaperman's Life*. University Park, PA, 1991.

7.174 **Pfeffer**, Paula F., *A. Phillip Randolph. Pioneer of the Civil Rights Movement*, Baton Rouge, LA, 1990. Charts the evolution of the labor leader into a national civil rights leader among African-Americans.

7.175 **Phelan**, C., *William Green. Biography of a Labor Leader*, Albany, NY, 1989.

7.176 **Potter**, E. B., *Bull Halsey*, Annapolis, MD, 1985. A biography of the colorful naval officer in charge of American aircraft carriers early in the Pacific war, who later worked to support the island-hopping strategy.

7.177 **Rampersad**, A., *The Life of Langston Hughes*, New York, 1986–1988. A two volume biography of the black poet and leader of the Harlem Renaissance.

7.178 **Ritchie**, D. A., *James M. Landis. Dean of the Regulators*, Cambridge, MA, 1980.

7.179 **Rockefeller**, S. C., *John Dewey. Religious Faith and Democratic Humanism*, New York, 1991.

7.180 **Rosenbaum**, H. D., and **Bartelme**, Elizabeth, (ed.), *Franklin D. Roosevelt. The Man, the Myth, the Era, 1882–1945*, Westport, CT, 1987.

7.181 **Rouse**, Jacqueline Anne, *Lugenia Burns Hope. Black Southern Reformer*, Athens, GA, 1989.

7.182 **Salmond**, J. A., *Miss Lucy of the CIO. The Life and Times of Lucy Randolph Mason, 1882–1959*, Athens, GA, 1988. Chronicles the life of a woman reformer who was active in many causes, and in the 1930s signed on with the CIO in various attempts to organize southern workers.

7.183 **Salvatore**, N., *Eugene V. Debs. Citizen and Socialist*, Urbana, IL, 1982. Standard biography of the labor leader and presidential candidate of the Socialist Party.

7.184 **Samuels**, E., *Bernard Berenson. The Making of a Legend*, Cambridge, MA, 1987. Continues a 1979 biography of the art connoisseur, and in this book takes up Berenson's work in the interwar years.

7.185 **Saunders**, Frances Wright, *Eileen Axson Wilson. First Lady between Two Worlds*, Chapel Hill, NC, 1986. Biography of the wife of Woodrow Wilson.

7.186 **Schmidt**, H., *Maverick Marine. General Smedley D. Butler and the Contradictions of American Military History*, Lexington, KY, 1987. A biography of the general who led American forces frequently into interventions in Latin America and the Caribbean, and who then in the 1930s repudiated his earlier work.

7.187 **Schwarz**, J. A., *The Speculator. Bernard M. Baruch in Washington, 1917–1965*, Chapel Hill, NC, 1981.

7.188 **Schwarz**, J. A., *Liberal. Adolf A. Berle and the Vision of an American Era*, New York, 1987. A biography of the New Dealer that interprets him as a builder of a conservative state capitalism, rather than a corporate liberal.

7.189 **Shi**, D.E., *Matthew Josephson, Bourgeois Bohemian*, New Haven, CT, 1981. Biography of the influential author of the 1934 "Robber Barons" that locates the subject amidst Popular Front leftists of the Depression Era.

7.190 **Stein**, Judith, *The World of Marcus Garvey. Race and Class in Modern Society*, Baton Rouge, LA, 1986. Features the contradictions between the bourgeois drive of Garvey and his organization and yearning of the black masses for a racial movement.

7.191 **Stineman**, Esther Lanigan, *Mary Austin. Song of a Maverick*, New Haven, CT, 1989. Biography of the feminist, environmentalist, and Native American rights leader.

7.192 **Strumm**, Philippa, *Brandeis. Justice for the People*, Cambrige, MA, 1984. A biography that celebrates the progressivism of the justice and links him to the old republican tradition that became increasingly ignored as the justice aged.

7.193 **Theoharis**, A. G., and **Cox**, J. S., *The Boss. J. Edgar Hoover and the Great American Inquisition*, Philadelphia, 1988. The most thorough study of Hoover's career and how he served every presidential administration by a combination of blackmail and favors-trading.

7.194 **Trimble**, V. H., *The Astonishing Mr. Scripps. The Turbulent Life of America's Penny Press Lord*, Ames, IA, 1992.

7.195 **Urofsky**, M. I., *Felix Frankfurter. Judicial Restraint and Individual Liberties*, Boston, 1991.

7.196 **Urofsky**, M. I., *A Voice That Spoke for Justice*, Albany, NY, 1982. A biography of the leading rabbi and Zionist Stephen Wise.

7.197 **Wall**, J. F., *Alfred I. Du Pont. The Man and His Family*, New York, 1990. A biography that focuses on Du Pont's transformation of the family business into a giant chemicals corporation in the early twentieth century.

7.198 **Ward**, G.C., *Before the Trumpet. Young Franklin Roosevelt, 1882–1905*, New York, 1985. In the first of two volumes on Roosevelt's life before 1928, the author examines the family and social setting that molded FDR.

7.199 **Ward**, G. C., *A First Class Temperament. The Emergence of Franklin Roosevelt*, New York, 1989. Ward's second lengthy volume covers the major elements in Roosevelt's life before the White House, including marriage to Eleanor Roosevelt.

7.200 **Watkins**, T. H., *Righteous Pilgrim. The Life and Times of Harold L. Ickes, 1874–1952*, New York, 1990. A biography of the New Deal Secretary of the Interior, providing information on politics as well as on Ickes' life.

7.201 **Weinberg**, S., *Armand Hammer. The Untold Story*, Boston, 1989. A biography of the oilman and conduit to the Soviet Union from Lenin onward.

7.202 **Weinstein**, E. A., *Woodrow Wilson. A Medical and Psychological Biography*, Princeton, NJ, 1981.

7.203 **Westbrook**, R. B., *John Dewey and American Democracy*, Ithaca, NY, 1992. A biography of the education reformer that stresses his commitment to participatory democracy.

7.204 **Wexler**, Alice, *Emma Goldman in Exile. From the Russian Revolution to the Spanish Civil War*, Boston, 1989.

7.205 **White**, G., and **Maze**, J., *Harold Ickes of the New Deal. His Private Life and Public Career*, Cambridge, MA, 1985.

7.206 **Wynes**, C. E., *Charles Richard Drew. The Man and the Myth*, Urbana, IL, 1988.

7.207 **Youngs**, J. W. T., *Eleanor Roosevelt. A Personal and Public Life*, Boston, 1985.

7.208 **Zieger**, R. H., *John L. Lewis. Labor Leader*, Boston, 1988.

DEMOGRAPHY, FAMILY, AND HEALTH

7.209 **Apple**, Rima D., *Mothers and Medicine. A Social History of Infant Feeding, 1890–1950*, Madison, WI, 1987. Examines how a combination of physicians, nurses, and businessmen convinced American women to switch from breastfeeding to bottled formula.

7.210 **Berkowitz**, E. D., *Disabled Policy. America's Programs for the Handicapped*, New York, 1987.

7.211A **Brandt**, A. M., *No Magic Bullet. A Social History of Venereal Disease in the United States Since 1880*, New York, 1985.

7.211B **Caldwell**, M., *The Last Crusade. The War on Consumption, 1862–1954*, New York, 1988. A history of the medical and social struggle against tuberculosis with an emphasis on the sanitorium as the product of a soulless American medical establishment.

7.212 **Clark**, C. E., *The American Family Home, 1800–1960*, Chapel Hill, NC, 1986.

7.213 **Crosby**, A. W., *America's Forgotten Pandemic. The Influenza of 1918*, Westport, CT, 1976.

7.214 **Ettling**, J., *The Germ of Laziness. Rockefeller Philanthropy and Public Health in the New South*, Cambridge, MA, 1981.

7.215 **Fee**, Elizabeth, *Disease and Discovery. A History of the Johns Hopkins School of Hygiene and Public Health, 1916–1939*, Baltimore, 1987. Created as part of the Rockefeller Foundation's reform of American medical education, the work done at the public health school at Johns Hopkins, nonetheless, soon became considered of secondary importance to the agendas of physicians and other academics.

7.216 **Gallagher**, H. G., *FDR's Splendid Deception*, New York, 1985. Reviews the politics and public relations of how Franklin Roosevelt handled his polio, and considers the changes in the public perception of disabled people since FDR's death.

7.217 **Graebner**, W., *A History of Retirement. The Meaning and Function of an American Institution, 1885–1978*, New Haven, CT, 1980.

7.218 **Gratton**, B., *Urban Elders. Family, Work, and Welfare Among Boston's Aged, 1890–1950*, Philadelphia, 1986.

7.219 **Grob**, G. N., *Mental Illness and American Society, 1875–1940*, Princeton, NJ, 1983.

7.220 **Harden**, Victoria A., *Rocky Mountain Spotted Fever. History of a Twentieth Century Disease*, Baltimore, 1990.

7.221 **Hareven**, Tamara K., *Family Time and Industrial Time. The Relationship Between the Family and Work in a New England Industrial Community*, New York, 1982. A look at work, ethnicity, and family life among textile mill workers in Manchester, New Hampshire.

7.222 **Hollingsworth**, J. R., **Hage**, J., and **Hanneman**, R. A., *State Intervention in Medical Care. Consequences for Britain, France, Sweden and the United States, 1890–1970*, Ithaca, NY, 1990.

7.223 **Jones**, J. H., *Bad Blood. The Tuskegee Syphilis Experiment*, New York, 1981.

7.224 **Kevles**, D. J., *In the Name of Eugenics. Genetics and the Uses of Human Heredity*, New York, 1985. Traces the history of the eugenics movement in Britain and the United States and shows that the American version combined class prejudice with a racist underpinning.

7.225 **Levenstein**, H., *Revolution at the Table. The Transformation of the American Diet*, New York, 1988. A story of how Progressive Era home economists convinced Americans to eat less and eat differently from the corpulent diet of the Victorian Era.

7.226 **Ludmerer**, K. M., *Learning to Heal. The Development of American Medical Education*, New York, 1985. A comprehensive review of the origins of modern medical education in the American university and how this produced scientific medical practice as a result.

7.227 **Modell**, J., and **Steffey**, D., 'Waging war and marriage. Military service and family formation, 1940–1950', *Journal of Family History*, XIII, 1988, 195–218.

7.228 **Reilly**, P. G., *The Surgical Solution. A History of Involuntary Sterilization in the United States*, Baltimore, 1991. Ties forced sterilization laws into the larger history of eugenics and shows the persistence of such operations even after the eugenics movement receded.

7.229 **Rogers**, Naomi, *Dirt and Disease. Polio before FDR*, New Brunswick, NJ, 1992.

7.230 **Rothman**, D. J., *Conscience and Convenience: The Asylum and Its Alternatives in Progressive America*, Boston, 1980.

7.231 **Stearns**, P. N., and **Haggerty**, T., 'The role of fear. Transitions in American emotional standards for children, 1850–1950', *American Historical Review*, XCVI, 1991, 63–94. Examines fear as socially constructed, and how and why twentieth century parents have sought to protect their sons and daughters from fear, while nineteenth century parents expected their sons to confront and conquer fear.

7.232 **Stevens**, Rosemary, *In Sickness and in Wealth. American Hospitals in the Twentieth Century*, New York, 1989. A history of voluntary hospitals that finds an ongoing struggle within the hospital between community needs and the bureaucratic imperative to expand and generate income.

7.233 **Teller**, M. E., *The Tuberculosis Movement. A Public Health Campaign in the Progressive Era*, Westport, CT, 1988. Links the medical movement against TB to a Progressive Era ideology of expert-led change and the sometimes coercive use of state power.

7.234 **Zelizer**, Viviana A., *Pricing the Priceless Child. The Changing Social Value of Children*, New York, 1985. Analyzes court cases involving wrongful death or injury of children and how the legal system came to mirror social attitudes about children.

SOCIAL RELATIONS

Class and community

7.235 **Ames**, K. L., *Death in the Dining Room and Other Tales of Victorian Culture*, Philadelphia, 1992. Examines the material culture of late nineteenth century America.

7.236 **Dumenil**, Lynn, *Freemasonry and American Culture, 1880–1930*, Princeton, NJ, 1984. A look at Masonry as one expression of middle-class Protestant ideology, and how it changed from emphasizing bourgeois individualism in the nineteenth century to a twentieth century emphasis on collective and communal betterment.

7.237 **Fischer**, C. S., *America Calling. A Social History of the Telephone to 1940*, Berkeley, CA, 1992.

7.238 **Frankel**, Noralee, and **Dye**, Nancy S., (ed.), *Gender, Class, Race, and Reform in the Progressive Era*, Lexington, KY, 1991.

7.239 **Hammack**, D. C., *Power and Society. Greater New York at the Turn of the Century*, New York, 1982.

7.240 **Katz**, M. B., *In the Shadow of the Poorhouse. A Social History of Welfare in America*, New York, 1986. A survey of nineteenth- and twentieth-century approaches to welfare that stresses the intimate link between labor discipline and public assistance.

7.241 **Kelley**, R. D. G., 'Notes on deconstructing "The Folk" ', *American Historical Review*, XCVII, 1992, 1400–1408.

7.242 **Kirschner**, D. S., *The Paradox of Professionalism. Reform and Public Service in Urban America, 1900–1940*, Westport, CT, 1986. Evaluates the first generation of city social workers in light of the tension between their desire for change and doubts about their clientele.

7.243 **Lears**, T. J. J., 'Making fun of popular culture', *American Historical Review*, XCVII, 1992, 1417–1426. A comment on Lawrence Levine's AHR Forum piece.

7.244 **May**, L., *Screening Out the Past. The Birth of Mass Culture and the Motion Picture Industry*, New York, 1980.

7.245 **Nye**, D. E., *Electrifying America. Social Meanings of a New Technology, 1880–1940*, Cambridge, MA, 1990.

7.246 **Patterson**, J. T., *America's Struggle Against Poverty, 1900–1980*, Cambridge, MA, 1981.

7.247A **Reed**, Ueda, *Avenues to Adulthood. The Origins of the High School and Social Mobility in an American Suburb*, New York 1987.

7.247B **Susman**, W. I., *Culture as History. The Transformation of American Society in the Twentieth Century*, New York, 1984. A collection of essays published posthumously that represent the author's views on the culture clash between the culture of nineteenth century republicanism and the twentieth century consumer society.

7.248 **Trolander**, Judith Ann, *Professionalism and Social Change. From the Settlement House Movement to Neighborhood Centers, 1886 to the Present*, New York, 1987. Traces the history of urban social work focusing on the continuing tension between outside helpers and the self-help of local communities.

Gender relations

7.249 **Adams**, M. C. C., *The Great Adventure. Male Desire and the Coming of World War I* Bloomington, IN, 1990. Finds the roots of the Anglo-American involvement in the war among excessively differentiated gender roles resulting in the raising of over aggressive and warlike boys and men.

7.250 **Bailey**, Beth L., *From Front Porch to Back Seat. Courtship in Twentieth Century America*, Baltimore, 1988. An account of how male-female relations changed from mother-controlled and approved courtship to dating and automobile romance.

7.251 **Baker**, Paula, *The Moral Frameworks of Public Life. Gender, Politics, and the State in Rural New York, 1830–1970*, New York, 1991. Uses the methods of cultural history to understand American politics in terms of gender relations. The author expands the definition of politics to go beyond voting and elections to considerations of how decisions were made and in what cultural context.

7.252 **Becker**, Susan D., *The Origins of the Equal Rights Amendment. American Feminism Between the Wars*, Westport, CT, 1981.

7.253 **Benson**, Susan Porter, *Counter Cultures. Saleswomen, Managers, and Customers in American Department Stores, 1890–1940*, Urbana, IL, 1986.

7.254 **Berube**, A., *Coming Out Under Fire. The History of Gay Men and Women in World War II*, New York, 1990. Follows the different histories of homosexual men and women in the American armed forces during the war and finds both oppression and opportunity for gay soldiers.

7.255 **Boris**, Eileen, 'Regulating industrial homework. The triumph of "Sacred Motherhood" ', *Journal of American History*, LXXI, 1985, 745–763.

7.256 **Brown**, Dorothy M., *Setting a Course. American Women in the 1920s*, Boston, 1987. A useful survey of what it meant to be a "new woman" in the 1920s and how different that experience was depending on wider social differences among women.

7.257 **Brumberg**, Joan Jacobs, *Fasting Girls. The Emergence of Anorexia Nervosa as a Modern Disease*, Cambridge, MA, 1988. Finds that the origin of the eating disorder prevalent among well-to-do adolescent females was directly connected to cultural changes that denigrated young women.

7.258 **Buechler**, S. M., *The Transformation of the Woman Suffrage Movement. The Case of Illinois, 1850–1920*, New Brunswick, NJ, 1986. Shows how the feminist drive toward the vote became increasingly tame in Illinois from its more radical nineteenth century origins, as social class came to shape the perspective of suffragists.

7.259 **Cott**, Nancy F., *The Grounding of Modern Feminism*, New Haven, CT, 1987. Looks at the feminist movement of the 1910s and 1920s and finds that the ideas of the movement were largely fulfilled after suffrage was granted, and that the thought of the movement was an essential precursor to the feminism that emerged in the 1960s.

7.260 **Dye**, Nancy Schrom, *As Equals and As Sisters. Feminism, the Labor Movement, and the Women's Trade Union League of New York*, New York, 1980.

7.261 **Fitzpatrick**, Ellen, *Endless Crusade. Women Social Scientists and Progressive Reform*, New York, 1990.

7.262 **Ford**, Linda G., *Iron Jawed Angels. The Suffrage Militancy of the National Woman's Party, 1912–1920*, Lanham, MD, 1991. Analyzes the drive for women's suffrage and finds that the use of militant protest tactics by the National Woman's Party was highly effective.

7.263 **Glenn**, Susan A., *Daughters of the Shtetl. Life and Labor in the Immigrant Generation*, Ithaca, NY, 1990. A history of immigrant Jewish women that finds ethnic and class solidarity was of greater importance than gender in transforming their lives.

7.264 **Gluck**, Sherna Berger, *Rosie the Riveter Revisited. Women, the War, and Social Change*, Boston, 1987. Oral history based on interviews with women who gained employment in the Los Angeles area aircraft factories.

7.265 **Gordon**, Felice D., *After Winning. The Legacy of the New Jersey Suffragists, 1920–1947*, New Brunswick, NJ, 1986. Shows how women active in the suffrage movement continued in politics after 1920 pursuing two broadly separate goals, equal rights and moral reform.

7.266 **Gordon**, Lynn D., *Gender and Higher Education in the Progressive Era*, New Haven, CT, 1990.

7.267 **Gover**, C. Jane., *The Positive Image. Women Photographers in Turn of the Century America*, Albany, NY, 1988.

7.268 **Hunter**, Jane, *The Gospel of Gentility. American Women Missionaries in Turn-of-the-Century China*, New Haven, CT, 1984. Explores the contradictions between the ideology of separate spheres preached by American women in China and the actual lives they led.

7.269 **Kessler-Harris**, Alice, *A Woman's Wage. Historical Meanings and Social Consequences*, Lexington, KY, 1990. Analyzes how markets set the value of women's work earlier in the twentieth century in the context of current debates over comparable worth.

7.270 **Lunardini**, Christine A., *From Equal Suffrage to Equal Rights. Alice Paul and the National Women's Party, 1910–1928*, New York, 1986.

7.271 **Lutz**, T., *American Nervousness, 1903. An Anecdotal History*, Ithaca, NY, 1990. Looks at the outbreak of neurasthenia among writers and intellectuals in 1903 and the meaning for the old Victorian culture.

7.272 **Muncy**, Robyn, *Creating a Female Dominion in American Reform, 1890–1935*,

New York, 1991. A history of women's role in the social work movement and how it was transformed into a profession.

7.273 **Palmer**, Phyllis, *Domesticity and Dirt. Housewives and Domestic Servants in the United States, 1920–1945*, Philadelphia, 1990. Charts the work routine of domestic servants and finds, although their percentage within the female work force declined, servants remained an important part of the household economy.

7.274 **Pascoe**, P., *Relations of Rescue. The Search for Female Moral Authority in the American West, 1874–1939*, New York, 1990.

7.275 **Poling-Kempes**, Leslie, *The Harvey Girls. Women Who Opened the West*, New York, 1989.

7.276 **Rosen**, Ruth, *The Lost Sisterhood. Prostitution in America, 1900–1918*, Baltimore, 1982.

7.277 **Scharf**, Lois, *Eleanor Roosevelt. First Lady of American Liberalism*, Boston, 1987. A brief biography of Roosevelt that places her amidst other women reformers, both before and after the New Deal, and also appraises her actions in light of her family upbringing and marriage to Franklin Roosevelt.

7.278 **Tentler**, Leslie, *Wage-Earning Women. Industrial Work and Family Life in the United States, 1900–1930*, New York, 1979.

7.279 **Thomas**, Mary Martha, *The New Woman in Alabama. Social Reforms and Suffrage, 1890–1920*, Tuscaloosa, AL, 1992.

7.280 **Wagner**, Lilya, *Women War Correspondents of World War II*, New York, 1989.

7.281 **Wandersee**, Winifred D., *Women's Work and Family Values, 1920–1940*, Cambridge, MA, 1981.

7.282 **Ware**, Susan, *Beyond Suffrage. Women in the New Deal*, Cambridge, MA, 1981.

7.283 **Ware**, Susan, *Partner and I. Molly Dewson, Feminism, and New Deal Politics*, New Haven, CT, 1987. A biography of the Massachusetts-born reformer and her circle of women friends in New York, that made up an important part of the female leadership of the Democratic party.

7.284 **Wheeler**, Marjorie Spruill, *New Women of the New South. The Leaders of the Woman Suffrage Movement of the Southern States*, New York, 1993.

Education

7.285 **Barrow**, C. W., *Universities and the Capitalist State. Corporate Liberalism and the Reconstruction of American Higher Education, 1894–1928*, Madison, WI, 1990.

7.286 **Chapman**, P. D., *Schools as Sorters. Lewis M. Terman, Applied Psychology, and the Intelligence Testing Movement, 1890–1930*, New York, 1988.

7.287 **Cohen**, R. D., *Children of the Mill. Schooling and Society in Gary, Indiana, 1906–1960*, Bloomington, IN, 1990.

7.288 **Cohen**, S., 'Representations of history', *History of Education*, XX, 1991, 131–141. A review essay about the history of American high schools.

7.289 **Cuban**, L., *How Teachers Taught. Constancy and Change in American Classrooms, 1890–1980*, New York, 1984.

7.290 **Edel**, A., *The Struggle for Academic Democracy. Lessons from the 1938 'Revolution' in New York City's Colleges*, Philadelphia, 1990. A history of the development of faculty governance and academic freedom in the 1930s, as recalled by a participant, and how the new rights were subsequently overturned by a combination of budget cuts and anti-communist purges.

7.291 **Fass**, Paula, *The Damned and the Beautiful. American Youth in the 1920s*, New York, 1977.

7.292 **Fass**, Paula, *Outside In. Minorities and the Transformation of American Education*, New York, 1989. Analyzes the role that 'Americanization' drives have had on minority children throughout the twentieth century.

7.293 **Glen**, J. M., *Highlander. No Ordinary School, 1932–1962*, Lexington, KY, 1988.

7.294 **Hawkins**, H., *Banding Together. The Rise of National Associations in American Higher Education, 1887–1950*, Baltimore, 1992.

7.295 **Horn**, Margo, *Before It's Too Late. The Child Guidance Movement in the United States, 1922–1945*, Philadelphia, 1989.

7.296 **Kaestle**, C. F., *et al.*, *Literacy in the United States. Readers and Reading since 1880*, New Haven, CT, 1991. A collection of essays by Kaestle and his students on reading as a social act and the publishing business that has tried to gauge the reading public.

7.297 **Kliebard**, H. M., *The Struggle for the*

American Curriculum, 1893–1958, Boston, 1986. Covers the political and intellectual history of John Dewey's educational initiatives.

7.298 **Lagemann**, Ellen Condliffe, *The Politics of Knowledge. The Carnegie Corporation, Philanthropy, and Public Policy*, Middletown, CT, 1989.

7.299 **Margo**, R. A., *Race and Schooling in the South, 1880–1950. An Economic History*, Chicago, 1990. Elaborate quantitative study that argues the persistence of black poverty was caused by an unequal education system, and that the outmigration of blacks from the South led to some improvements even before the civil rights era.

7.300 **Murphy**, Marjorie, *Blackboard Unions. The AFT and the NEA, 1900–1980*, Ithaca, NY, 1991. A study of teachers and politics that focuses on the struggle for union recognition and periodic red scares, as well as the dealings between teachers and the parents of their students.

7.301 **Nash**, G. H., *Herbert Hoover and Stanford University*, Stanford, CA, 1988.

7.302 **Perlmann**, J., *Ethnic Differences. Schooling and Social Structure among the Irish, Italians, Jews and Blacks in an American City, 1880–1935*, New York, 1988. Based on a sample of more than 10,000 students who attended schools in Providence, Rhode Island, this study finds less difference in school achievement by ethnic group than the author expected.

7.303 **Peterson**, P. E., *The Politics of School Reform, 1870–1940*, Chicago, 1985. Concentrates on the groups that coalesced in support of the public high school.

7.304 **Raftery**, Judith Rosenberg, *Land of Fair Promise. Politics and Reform in Los Angeles Schools, 1885–1941*, Stanford, CA, 1992.

7.305 **Raymond**, Elizabeth, 'Country school legacy. Nevada's educational heritage', *Halcyon*, 1983, V, 107–118.

7.306 **Synnott**, Marcia Graham, *The Half-Opened Door. Discrimination and Admissions at Harvard, Yale, and Princeton, 1900–1970*, Westport, CT, 1979. Traces the development of anti-Semitic admissions policies at the premier Ivy League colleges and their eventual dismantlement.

7.307 **Taggart**, R. J., *Private Philanthropy and Public Education. Pierre S. du Pont and the Delaware Schools, 1890–1940*, Newark, DE, 1988.

7.308 **Wheatley**, S. C., *The Politics of Philanthropy. Abraham Flexner and Medical Philanthropy*, Madison, WI, 1988. Examines how the medical reformer connected physician training to universities and to the Rockefeller Foundation, as well as how Flexner's successors at the Foundation pursued other goals.

Crime and punishment

7.309 **Clark**, N., *Deliver Us From Evil. An Interpretation of American Prohibition*, New York, 1976. Unusual interpretation that stresses the success of Prohibition, both as a social movement, and as a political movement, through the efforts of Wayne Wheeler and the Anti-Saloon League.

7.310 **Fisher**, J., *The Lindbergh Case*, New Brunswick, NJ, 1987. A review of the famous kidnapping case that concludes that the convicted and executed Bruno Hauptmann was indeed guilty.

7.311 **Fox**, S., *Blood and Power. Organized Crime in Twentieth-Century America*, New York, 1989.

7.312 **Hobson**, Barbara, *Uneasy Virtue. The Politics of Prostitution and the American Reform Tradition*, New York, 1987.

7.313 **Lutholz**, M. W., *Grand Dragon. D. C. Stephenson and the Ku Klux Klan in Indiana*, West Lafayette, IN, 1991.

7.314 **Moore**, L. J., *Citizen Klansmen. The Ku Klux Klan in Indiana, 1921–1928*, Chapel Hill, NC, 1991.

7.315 **Nelli**, H. S., *The Business of Crime. Italians and Syndicate Crime in the United States*, New York, 1976.

7.316 **Seretan**, L. G., 'The new working class and social banditry in depression America', *Mid-America*, LXIII, 1981, 107–127. Links the eruption of spectacular crimes in the early years of the Depression to the economic downturn.

7.317 **Tucker**, R. K., *The Dragon and the Cross. The Rise and Fall of the Ku Klux Klan in Middle America*, Hamden, CT, 1991.

7.318 **Tyrrell**, I., *Woman's World/Woman's Empire. The Woman's Christian Temperance Union in International Perspective, 1880–1930*, Chapel Hill, NC, 1991. Places the organization's worldwide efforts into a larger discussion of imperialism.

Recreation, entertainment, and sport

7.319 **Chevigny**, P., *Gigs. Jazz and the Cabaret Laws in New York City*, New York, 1991.

7.320 **Crepeau**, R. C., *Baseball. America's Diamond Mind, 1919–1941*, Orlando, FL, 1980. Links changes in culture to the types of baseball heroes who emerged during the sport's "rabbit ball" era.

7.321 **Douglas**, Susan J., *Inventing American Broadcasting, 1899–1922*, Baltimore, 1987. Analyzes the changes in radio communication from the marine uses of the early wireless to the commercial medium that emerged in the 1920s.

7.322 **Guttman**, A., *The Olympics. A History of the Modern Games*, Urbana, IL, 1992.

7.323 **Kuklick**, B., *To Every Thing a Season. Shibe Park and Urban Philadelphia, 1909–1976*, Princeton, NJ, 1991. Analyzes the history of the baseball park where the Philadelphia Athletics and Phillies played, and how the surrounding neighborhood changed over the course of the century.

7.324 **Lieberman**, Robbie, *'My Song Is My Weapon'. People's Songs, American Communism, and the Politics of Culture, 1930–1950*, Urbana, IL, 1989.

7.325 **Lynes**, R., *The Lively Audience. A Social History of the Visual and Performing Arts in America, 1890–1950*, New York, 1985.

7.326 **Mrozek**, D. J., *Sport and American Mentality, 1880–1910*, Knoxville, TN, 1983. Utilizes the concept of regeneration to explain the fascination with sports in American society, and how sports were an essential part of the remaking of America.

7.327 **Peretti**, B. W., *The Creation of Jazz. Music, Race, and Culture in Urban America*, Urbana, IL, 1992.

7.328 **Riess**, S. A., *Touching Base. Professional Baseball and American Culture in the Progressive Era*, Westport, CT, 1980. Locates the game in its urban setting, and gives a careful study to the connection between city politics and stadium location.

7.329 **Roberts**, R., *Papa Jack. Jack Johnson and the Era of White Hopes*, New York, 1983.

7.330 **Roell**, C. H., *The Piano in America, 1890–1940*, Chapel Hill, NC, 1989. An institutional history that shows the influence of the instrument on American culture with ramifications for class and gender relations.

7.331 **Sanjek**, R., and **Sanjek**, D., *American Popular Music Business in the 20th Century*, New York, 1991. Covers the musicians as well as the business of music publishing.

7.332 **Scharff**, Virginia, *Taking the Wheel. Women and the Coming of the Motor Age*, New York, 1991.

7.333 **Schuller**, G., *The Swing Era. The Development of Jazz, 1930–1945*, New York, 1989. An encyclopedic appraisal of black and white swing music and its impact on America before and during the war.

The invention of Hollywood

7.334 **Gomery**, D., *Shared Pleasures. A History of Movie Presentation in the United States*, Madison, WI, 1992.

7.335 **Hansen**, Miriam, *Babel and Babylon. Spectatorship in American Silent Film*, Cambridge, MA, 1991.

7.336 **Harvey**, J., *Romantic Comedy in Hollywood, from Lubitsch to Sturges*, New York, 1987. An appreciation of the "screwball comedy" and its effect on mass society.

7.337 **Hilger**, M., *The American Indian in Film*, Metuchen, NJ, 1986. The origins and development of the other half of the "western" picture.

7.338 **Leff**, L. J., and **Simmons**, J. L., *The Dame in the Kimono. Hollywood, Censorship and the Production Code from the 1920s to the 1960s*, New York, 1990. A social history of censorship in the movies, particularly that imposed by the film producers' own Production Code Administration.

7.339 **Ray**, R. B., *A Certain Tendency of the Hollywood Cinema, 1930–1980*, Princeton, NJ, 1985. Uses structuralism and post-structuralism to understand films and American culture.

7.340 **Silk**, Catherine, and **Silk**, J., *Racism and Anti-Racism in American Popular Culture. Portrayals of African-Americans in Fiction and Film*, 1990. Concentrates on late nineteenth and early twentieth century fiction, and the films of the first half of the twentieth century.

7.341 **Sklar**, R., *City Boys. Cagney, Bogart, Garfield*, Princeton, NJ, 1992.

7.342 **Vaughn**, S., 'Morality and entertainment. The origins of the motion picture production code', *Journal of American*

History, LXXVII, 1990, 39–65. Examines the political debate about motion picture content, and shows how a conservative coalition successfully sought to implement a censor's code that had at its core the Ten Commandments.

The mass media

7.343 **Baughman**, J. L., *Henry R. Luce and the Rise of the American News Media*, Boston, 1987. A biography of the man the author calls America's "propaganda minister" and how his publications flourished in the 1930s and 1940s.

7.344 **Burnham**, J.C., *How Superstition Won and Science Lost. Popularizing Science and Health in the United States*, New Brunswick, NJ, 1987. Americans embraced mumbo-jumbo and superstition in place of science, largely through the misguided efforts of science popularizers, especially in medicine.

7.345 **Cohn**, Jan, *Creating America. George Horace Lorimer and the Saturday Evening Post*, Pittsburgh, PA, 1989.

7.346 **Heald**, M., *Transatlantic Vistas. American Journalists in Europe, 1900–1940*, Kent, OH, 1988.

7.347 **Marzolf**, Marion Tuttle, *Civilizing Voices. American Press Criticism, 1880–1950*, New York, 1991.

7.348 **Shore**, E., *Talkin' Socialism. J. A. Wayland and the Role of the Press in American Radicalism, 1890–1912*, Lawrence, KS, 1988. Looks at the career of the Great Plains editor of *Appeal to Reason* and his role in building and diffusing the socialism movement.

7.349 **Wallace**, J. M., *Liberal Journalism and American Education, 1914–1941*, New Brunswick, NJ, 1991.

RELIGION, BELIEFS, IDEAS, AND CULTURE

7.350 **Chinnici**, J. P., *Devotion to the Holy Spirit in American Catholicism*, New York, 1985. Finds that Americans created a distinctive

Roman Catholicism through their chosen emphasis on the Holy Spirit.

7.351 **Clymer**, K. J., *Protestant Missionaries in the Phillipines, 1896–1916. An Inquiry into the American Colonial Mentality*, Urbana, IL, 1986.

7.352 **Cooney**, T. A., *The Rise of the New York Intellectuals. Partisan Review and its Circle*, Madison, WI, 1986. Traces the origins of the famous New York magazine and its writers to disaffected Communists and followers of Trotsky, and to an emerging Jewish-American identity.

7.353 **Cravens**, H., *The Triumph of Evolution. American Scientists and the Heredity-Environment Controversy, 1900–1941*, Philadelphia, 1978.

7.354 **Gorrell**, D. K., *The Age of Social Responsibility. The Social Gospel in the Progressive Era, 1900–1920*, Macon, GA, 1988.

7.355 **Handy**, R. T., *Undermined Establishment. Church-State Relations in America, 1880–1920*, Princeton, NJ, 1991.

7.356 **Harris**, B., and **Broch**, A., 'Otto Fenichel and the Left Opposition in Psychoanalysis', *Journal of the History of the Behavioral Sciences*, XXVII, 1991, 157–165.

7.357 **Hutchison**, W. R., *Errand to the World. American Protestant Thought and Foreign Missions*, Chicago, 1987. Surveys the lengthy history of American missionaries abroad, and is strongest for the twentieth century with its peak of enthusiasm before World War I and the subsequent decline of the foreign evangelizing spirit thereafter.

7.358 **Hutchison**, W. R., *Between the Times. The Travail of the Protestant Establishment in America, 1900–1960*, New York, 1989.

7.359 **Karier**, C. J., *Scientists of the Mind. Intellectual Founders of Modern Psychology*, Urbana, IL, 1986. Treats the social origins of American psychology, particularly the influence of William James and the reception of Freud's views in America.

7.360 **Kuznick**, P. J., *Beyond the Laboratory. Scientists as Political Activists in 1930s America*, Chicago, 1987. Focuses on the years 1937 to 1939 and the activities of the American Association for the Advancement of Science (and other allied groups) that led some scientists to embrace calls for radical political change.

7.361 **Lunden**, R., *Business and Religion in the American 1920s*, Westport, CT, 1988.

7.362 **Marty**, M. E., *Modern American Religion. The Irony of It All, 1893–1919*, Chicago, 1986. The first of four volumes surveying the history of twentieth century American religion, this initial book covers nearly all faith at a time of great tumult in religious life.

7.363 **Marty**, M. E., *Modern American Religion. The Noise of Conflict, 1919–1941*, Chicago, 1991. The second volume of his series focuses on the connections between religion and public life, particularly the fundamentalist controversy of the 1920s.

7.364 **Orsi**, R. A., *The Madonna of 115th Street. Faith and Community in Italian Harlem, 1880–1950*, New Haven, CT, 1985. An Annales-influenced ethnohistory of the Italian immigrants and their devotion to the Madonna.

7.365 **Ottanelli**, F. M., *The Communist Party of the United States. From the Great Depression to World War II*, New Brunswick, NJ, 1991.

7.366 **Watts**, Sarah Lyons, *Order against Chaos. Business Culture and Labor Ideology in America, 1880–1915*, Westport, CT, 1991.

Fundamentalism and revivals

7.367 **Brereton**, Virginia Lieson, *Training God's Army. The American Bible School, 1880–1940*, Bloomington, IN, 1990. Studies the curriculum and instruction in the scores of fundamentalist bible schools that were started by evangelists like Dwight L. Moody.

7.368 **Goff**, J. R., *Fields White Unto Harvest. Charles F. Parham and the Missionary Origins of Pentecostalism*, Fayetteville, AR, 1988.

7.369 **Harris**, M. W., *The Rise of Gospel Blues. The Music of Thomas Andrew Dorsey in the Urban Church*, New York, 1991.

7.370 **Lewis**, J. W., *The Protestant Experience in Gary, Indiana, 1906–1975*, Knoxville, TN, 1992.

7.371 **Longfield**, B. J., *The Presbyterian Controversy. Fundamentalists, Modernists, and Moderates*, New York, 1991. Examines the doctrinal split within 1920s Presbyterianism and the leaders of the different camps within the church.

7.372 **MacRobert**, I., *The Black Roots and White Racism of Early Pentecostalism in the USA*, New York, 1988.

7.373 **Marsden**, G. M., *Fundamentalism and American Culture. The Shaping of Twentieth-Century Evangelicalism, 1870–1925*, New York, 1980.

7.374 **Trollinger**, W. V., *God's Empire. William Bell Riley and Midwestern Fundamentalism*, Madison, WI, 1990. A biography of a Minneapolis Baptist leader that shows how fundamentalism survived the 1920s and, by using new organizational techniques such as radio, built a new base in the 1930s and 1940s.

7.375 **Watt**, D. H., *A Transforming Faith. Explorations of Twentieth-Century American Evangelicalism*, New Brunswick, NJ, 1991.

7.376 **Watts**, Jill, *God, Harlem U.S.A., The Father Divine Story*, Berkeley, CA, 1992.

American Judaism

7.377 **Auerbach**, J. S., *Rabbis and Lawyers. The Journey from Torah to Constitution*, Bloomington, IN, 1990.

7.378 **Berman**, A., *Nazism, the Jews, and American Zionism, 1933–1948*, Detroit, 1990. A history of the Zionist movement in America that focuses on the tragic struggle between the ultimate goal of a homeland in Palestine and the more immediate imperative to rescue European Jewry.

7.379 **Brecher**, F. W., *Reluctant Ally. United States Foreign Policy toward the Jews from Wilson to Roosevelt*, Westport, CT, 1991.

7.380 **Cowan**, N. R., and **Cowan**, Ruth Schwartz, *Our Parents' Lives. The Americanization of Eastern European Jews*, New York, 1989.

7.381 **Klingenstein**, Susanne, *Jews in the American Academy, 1900–1940. The Dynamics of Intellectual Assimilation*, New Haven, CT, 1991.

7.382 **Levine**, P., *Ellis Island to Ebbets Field. Sport and the American Jewish Experience*, New York, 1992.

7.383 **Lindemann**, A. S., *The Jew Accused. Three Anti-Semitic Affairs*, Cambridge, 1991. Contrasts the lynching of Leo Frank in Georgia to the Dreyfuss Affair and the Beilis Affair in Czarist Russia, and finds America to have been less tolerant than France or Russia.

7.384 **Weinberg**, Sydney Stahl, *The World of Our Mothers. The Lives of Jewish Immigrant Women*, Chapel Hill, NC, 1988.

Progressivism

7.385 **Berman**, J. S., *Police Administration and Progressive Reform. Theodore Roosevelt as Police Commissioner of New York*, Westport, CT, 1987.

7.386 **Bulmer**, M., **Bales**, K., and **Sklar**, Kathryn Kish, (ed.), *The Social Survey in Historical Perspective, 1880–1940*, New York, 1991.

7.387 **Danbom**, D., *"The World of Hope". Progressives and the Struggle for an Ethical Public Life*, Philadelphia, 1987.

7.388 **Glassberg**, D., *American Historical Pageantry. The Uses of Tradition in the Early Twentieth Century*, Chapel Hill, NC, 1990. Uses an anthropological approach of "thick description" to analyze the cultural content of popular pageants in conjunction with the centralizing and nationalizing trends of the Progressive Era.

7.389 **Gordon**, Linda, 'Black and white visions of welfare: women's welfare activism, 1890–1945', *Journal of American History*, LXXVIII, 1991, 559–590. Looks at how white and black women viewed welfare differently and how they worked to establish a system of coverage.

7.390 **Grantham**, D. W., *Southern Progressivism. The Reconciliation of Progress and Tradition*, Knoxville, TN, 1983. Emphasizes the ties to the national reform impulse, particularly the strength of prohibitionism in the South.

7.391 **Handy**, R. T., *A History of Union Theological Seminary in New York*, New York, 1987. An institutional history of the nation's leading liberal seminary.

7.392 **Hyfler**, R., *Prophets of the Left. Socialist Thought in the Twentieth Century*, Westport, CT, 1984.

7.393 **Levinson**, H. S., *Santayana, Pragmatism, and the Spiritual Life*, Chapel Hill, NC, 1992.

7.394 **Link**, W. A., *The Paradox of Southern Progressivism, 1880–1930*, Chapel Hill, NC, 1992. The paradox involved the juxtaposition of reform energy from the state level and older traditions of local control and voluntary association.

7.395 **Madison**, J. H., 'Reformers and the rural church, 1900–1950', *Journal of American History*, LXXIII, 1986, 645–668. Analyzes the diagnosing and illuminating of rural churches and their reforms.

7.396 **Sealander**, Judith, *Grand Plans. Business Progressivism and Social Change in Ohio's Miami Valley, 1890–1929*, Lexington, KY, 1988.

7.397 **Tilman**, R., *Thorstein Veblen and His Critics, 1891–1963. Conservative, Liberal and Radical Perspectives*, Princeton, NJ, 1992.

7.398 **Wedell**, Marsha, *Elite Women and the Reform Impulse in Memphis, 1875–1915*, Knoxville, TN, 1991.

7.399 **West**, C., *The American Evasion of Philosophy. A Genealogy of Pragmatism*, Madison, WI, 1989. An essay on the meaning of John Dewey's philosophy in his time and ours.

7.400 **Wilson**, D. J., *Science, Community, and the Transformation of American Philosophy, 1860–1930*, Chicago, 1990. Traces the changes among American philosophers away from a theological orientation toward an incorporation of science and scientific methods in philosophical discourse.

7.401 **Wunderlin**, C. E., *Visions of a New Industrial Order. Social Science and Labor Theory in America's Progressive Era*, New York, 1992.

Realism and modernism

7.402 **Alexander**, C. C., *Here the Country Lies. Nationalism and the Arts in Twentieth Century America*, Bloomington, IN, 1980.

7.403 **Biehl**, S., *Independent Intellectuals in the United States, 1910–1945*, New York, 1992.

7.404 **Blake**, C. N., *Beloved Community. The Cultural Criticism of Randolph Bourne, Van Wyck Brooks, Waldo Frank, and Lewis Mumford*, Chapel Hill, NC, 1990. Locates the sources of ideas of influential twentieth century American intellectuals in the psychic history of their own upbringing.

7.405 **Brown**, C. C., *Niebuhr and His Age. Reinhold Niebuhr's Prophetic Rule in the Twentieth Century*, Philadelphia, 1992.

7.406 **Coben**, S., *Rebellion Against Victorianism. The Impetus for Cultural Change in 1920s America*, New York, 1991.

7.407 **Kalman**, Laura, *Legal Realism at Yale, 1927–1960*, Chapel Hill, NC, 1986. A study of the influential scholars at the Yale Law School who abandoned judicial formalism for a more critical approach to law and society.

7.408 **Marchand**, R., *Advertising the Dream.*

Making Way for Modernity, 1920–1940, Berkeley, CA, 1985. Uses tens of thousands of ads as a sort of text to examine the American psyche, particularly in the 1920s.

7.409 **Orvell**, M., *The Real Thing. Imitation and Authenticity in American Culture, 1880–1940*, Chapel Hill, NC, 1989. Considers the transition from Victorianism to modernism in architecture, photography, and literature.

7.410 **Peller**, D. P., *Hope Among Us Yet. Social Criticism and Social Solace in Depression America*, Athens, GA, 1987. A study of artists and writers in the 1930s and how the economic crisis produced cultural riches.

7.411 **Ross**, Dorothy, *The Origins of American Social Science*, New York, 1991. A look at the founding of the various social science disciplines and the late nineteenth and early twentieth century atmosphere of scientific method and American exceptionalism.

7.412 **Segal**, H. P., *Technological Utopianism in American Culture*, Chicago, 1985. Examines a number of writers and designers who sought to remake nature along Progressive Era lines.

7.413 **Stange**, Maren, *Symbols of Ideal Life. Social Documentary Photography in America, 1890–1950*, New York, 1989.

7.414 **Whiting**, Cecile, *Antifascism in American Art*, New Haven, CT, 1989.

WORK AND ENTERPRISE

The corporate economy

7.415 **Abel**, Marjorie, and **Folbre**, Nancy, 'A methodology for revising estimates. Female market participation in the U.S. before 1940', *Historical Methods*, XXIII, 1990, 167–176. Argues that a new concept called "market participation", rather than the older notion of labor-force participation, is needed to understand women's work before 1940.

7.416 **Horowitz**, D., *The Morality of Spending. Attitudes Toward the Consumer Society in America, 1875–1940*, Baltimore, 1985.

Traces the supplanting of the producer ethic in American life by a consumer ethos that had deep roots in American life.

7.417 **Kens**, P., *Judicial Power and Reform Politics. The Anatomy of Lochner v. New York*, Lawrence, KS, 1990.

7.418 **Rasmussen**, W. D., *Taking the University to the People. Seventy-Five Years of Cooperative Extension*, Ames, IA, 1989.

7.419 **Rosner**, D., and **Markowitz**, G., (ed.), *Dying for Work. Workers' Safety and Health in Twentieth-Century America*, Bloomington, IN, 1987. A collection of essays that charts the growing problem in the workplace of worker health from both traumatic job injury and long-term exposure to harmful substances.

7.420 **Wigmore**, B., *The Crash and Its Aftermath. A History of Securities Markets in the United States, 1929–1933*, Westport, CT, 1985.

Fordism: the assembly line in theory and practice

7.421 **Cherniack**, M., *The Hawk's Nest Incident. America's Worst Industrial Disaster*, New Haven, CT, 1986. A careful account of the silicosis and death that afflicted 700 miners who drilled the Hawk's Nest tunnel in West Virginia in the 1930s and the knowing disregard for worker safety on the part of the Union Carbide Corporation.

7.422 **Crouch**, T. D., *The Bishop's Boys. A Life of Wilbur and Orville Wright*, New York, 1989.

7.423 **Davis**, D. F., *Conspicuous Production. Automobiles and Elites in Detroit, 1899–1933*, Philadelphia, 1988. A business study of the growth of Detroit automobile firms that finds local merchants were active investors in the first wave of expansion.

7.424 **Gillespie**, R., *Manufacturing Knowledge. A History of the Hawthorne Experiments*, New York, 1991. A history of the industrial psychology department at a Western Electric plant, and the scientific foundations of modern personnel management.

7.425 **Harris**, H. J., *The Right to Manage. Industrial Relations Policies of American Business in the 1940s*, Madison, WI, 1982.

7.426 **Jakab**, P. L., *Visions of a Flying Machine. The Wright Brothers and the Process of Invention*, Washington, DC, 1990.

7.427 **Kraditor**, Aileen S., *'Jimmy Higgins'. The Mental World of the Rank and File Communist, 1930–1958*, Westport, CT, 1988. A portrait of a composite communist who stayed with the party through thick and thin.

7.428 **Lichtenstein**, N., and **Meyer**, S., (ed.), *On the Line. Essays in the History of Auto Work*, Urbana, IL, 1989.

7.429 **Meyer**, S., *The Five Dollar Day. Labor Management and Social Control in the Ford Motor Company, 1908–1921*, Albany, NY, 1981.

7.430 **Montgomery**, D., *Workers' Control in America. Studies in the History of Work, Technology, and Labor Struggles*, New York, 1979. A detailed look at several industries where the locus of class struggle was over knowledge essential to controlling the pace of production.

The polyglot American working class

7.431 **Altenbaugh**, R. J., *Education for Struggle. The American Labor Colleges of the 1920s and 1930s*, Philadelphia, 1990. A history of three independent colleges for workers, and the role of A. J. Muste in molding labor organizing.

7.432 **Barrett**, J. R., *Work and Community in the Jungle. Chicago's Packinghouse Workers, 1894–1922*, Urbana, IL, 1987.

7.433 **Beardsley**, E. H., *A History of Neglect. Health Care for Blacks and Mill Workers in the Twentieth-Century South*, Knoxville, TN, 1987. A bleak portrait of a multitude of health afflictions suffered by North and South Carolina textile workers that went largely unaddressed until the New Deal.

7.434 **Blewett**, Mary H., *The Last Generation. Work and Life in the Textile Mills of Lowell, Massachusetts, 1910–1960*, Amherst, MA, 1990. Continues the author's earlier volume on labor in Lowell with the primary sources for this book being oral histories of many of the workers and their children.

7.435 **Brody**, D., *Workers in Industrial America. Essays on the Twentieth Century Struggle*, New York, 1980.

7.436 **Cobble**, Dorothy Sue, *Dishing It Out. Waitresses and Their Unions in the Twentieth Century*, Urbana, IL, 1991.

7.437 **Cooper**, Patricia A., *Once a Cigar Maker.*

Men, Women, and Work Culture in American Cigar Factories, 1900–1919, Urbana, IL, 1987.

7.438 **Cumbler**, J. T., *Working-Class Community in Industrial America. Work, Leisure, and Struggle in Two Industrial Cities, 1880–1930*, Westport, CT, 1979. Analyzes the mixture of ethnicity and class in Fall River and Lynn, Massachusetts.

7.439 **DeVault**, Ileen A., *Sons and Daughters of Labor. Class and Clerical Work in Turn-of-the-Century Pittsburgh*, Ithaca, NY, 1990. A tour de force of quantitative history that studies almost two thousand women from their high school training through work and marriage.

7.440 **DeVries**, J. E., *Race and Kinship in a Midwestern Town. The Black Experience in Monroe, Michigan, 1900–1915*, Urbana, IL, 1984. Examines the history of race relations in a small town and finds strong similarities to southern segregation and attitudes.

7.441 **Eisenstein**, Sarah, *Give Us Bread, But Give Us Roses. Working Women's Consciousness in the United States, 1890 to the First World War*, 1983. A set of essays about the tensions between working class consciousness and domestic ideology that working women confronted.

7.442 **Emmons**, D., *The Butte Irish. Class and Ethnicity in an American Mining Town*, Urbana, IL, 1989. A study of the copper mining town of Butte, Montana and preeminent place held by Irish miners, still closely tied to Irish nationalism until the 1910s when new corporate owners transformed the industry and town by importing laborers from various parts of Europe, the American South, and Asia.

7.443 **Faue**, Elizabeth, *Community of Suffering & Struggle. Women, Men, and the Labor Movement in Minneapolis, 1915–1945*, Chapel Hill, NC, 1991. Stresses that the success of labor organizing in the 1930s was based on community issues that engaged women, and not just workplace solidarity.

7.444 **Fine**, Lisa M., *The Souls of the Skyscraper. Female Clerical Workers in Chicago, 1870–1930*, Philadelphia, 1990. Studies the redefinition of clerical work as women's work, and the women who did the work, in and out of the office.

7.445 **Hall**, Jacqueline Dowd, *et al.*, *Like a Family. The Making of a Southern Cotton Mill World*, Chapel Hill, NC, 1987. A social history of the emergence of a southern white working class in the Piedmont region textile mills, covering every topic from work on the mill floor to family and church, culminating in the great strike of 1934.

7.446 **Jensen**, Joan M., and **Davidson**, Sue, (ed.), *A Needle, a Bobbin, a Strike. Women Needle Workers in America*, Philadelphia, 1984. Examines the ethnic, class, and gender dimensions of women garment workers.

7.447 **Long**, Priscilla, *Where the Sun Never Shines. A History of America's Bloody Coal Industry*, New York, 1989.

7.448 **McHugh**, Cathy L., *Mill Family. The Labor System in the Southern Cotton Textile Industry, 1880–1915*, New York, 1988.

7.449 **Meyerowitz**, Joanne J., *Women Adrift. Independent Wage Earners in Chicago, 1880–1930*, Chicago, 1988.

7.450 **Nelson**, B., *Workers on the Waterfront. Seamen, Longshoremen, and Unionism in the 1930s*, Urbana, IL, 1988. An account of the culture of the workers who conducted the Pacific Coast strike of 1934.

7.451 **Rosner**, D., and **Markowitz**, G., *Deadly Dust. Silicosis and the Politics of Occupational Disease in Twentieth Century America*, Princeton, NJ, 1991.

Trade unions

7.452 **Babson**, S., *Building the Union. Skilled Workers and Anglo-Gaelic Immigrants in the Rise of the UAW*, New Brunswick, NJ, 1991.

7.453 **Derickson**, A., *Workers' Health, Workers' Democracy. The Western Miners' Struggle, 1891–1925*, Ithaca, NY, 1988. A history of the struggle to provide health care for members of the Western Federation of Miners.

7.454 **Dix**, K., *What's a Coal Miner to Do? The Mechanization of Coal Mining*, Pittsburgh, 1988.

7.455 **Fraser**, S., *Labor Will Rule. Sidney Hillman and the Rise of American Labor*, New York, 1991.

7.456 **Gitelman**, H. M., *Legacy of the Ludlow Massacre. A Chapter in American Industrial Relations*, Philadelphia, 1988. Describes the company unions that John D. Rockefeller, Jr., and the Canadian William Lyon Mackenzie King formed in Colorado

after the great massacre of the miners in 1914.

7.457 **Goldberg**, D. J., *A Tale of Three Cities: Labor Organization and Protest in Paterson, Passaic, and Lawrence, 1916–1921*, New Brunswick, NJ, 1989. Traces the complexities of local organizing by the American Textile Workers union during and after the war.

7.458 **Golin**, S., *The Fragile Bridge. Paterson Silk Strike, 1913*, Philadelphia, 1988.

7.459 **Kazin**, M., *Barons of Labor. The San Francisco Building Trades and Union Power in the Progressive Era*, Urbana, IL, 1987.

7.460 **Keeran**, R., *The Communist Party and the Auto Workers Unions*, Bloomington, IN, 1980.

7.461 **Korth**, P. A., and **Beegle**, Margaret R., *I Remember Like Today. The Auto-Lite Strike of 1934*, East Lansing, MI, 1988. Covers the Toledo, Ohio strike of auto parts workers that led to the formation of the United Auto Workers and the prominence of activist A. J. Muste.

7.462 **Lehrer**, Susan, *Origins of Protective Labor Legislation for Women, 1905–1925*, Albany, NY, 1987.

7.463 **Levenstein**, H. A., *Communism, Anticommunism, and the CIO*, Westport, CT, 1981.

7.464 **Lichtenstein**, N., *Labor's War at Home. The CIO in World War II*, New York, 1983.

7.465 **Meier**, A., and **Rudwick**, E., *Black Detroit and the Rise of the UAW*, New York, 1979.

7.466 **Meyer**, S., 'Stalin over Wisconsin'. The Making and Unmaking of Militant Unionism, 1900–1950*, Rutgers, NJ, 1992.

7.467 **Montgomery**, D., *The Fall of the House of Labor*, New York, 1987. Continues the author's *Workers' Control in America* and the argument that the drive toward scientific management fatally undermined the American labor movement and the possibility for greater social change.

7.468 **Nelson**, D., *American Rubber Workers and Organized Labor, 1900–1941*, Princeton, NJ, 1988. Analyzes the industrial workers in the rubber tire manufacturing sector, particularly in Akron, Ohio, and finds that loyalty to the CIO's United Rubber Workers formed only one aspect of a larger working-class outlook.

7.469 **Norwood**, S. H., *Labor's Flaming Youth. Telephone Operators and Worker Militancy, 1878–1923*, Urbana, IL, 1990.

7.470 **Rosenberg**, D., *New Orleans Dockworkers. Race, Labor, and Unionism, 1892–1923*, Albany, NY, 1988.

7.471 **Ruiz**, Vicki L., *Cannery Women, Cannery Lives. Mexican Women, Unionization, and the California Food Processing Industry, 1930–1950*, Albuquerque, NM, 1987.

7.472 **Schatz**, R. W., *The Electrical Workers. A History of Labor at General Electric and Westinghouse, 1923–1960*, Urbana, IL, 1983.

7.473 **Tomlins**, C. L., *The State and the Unions. Labor Relations, Law, and the Organized Labor Movement in America, 1880–1960*, New York, 1985. Contends that American organized labor made a fundamental mistake in seeking state support for an agreement with capitalism in the 1930s and 1940s.

7.474 **Tripp**, Anne Huber, *The I.W.W. and the Paterson Silk Strike of 1913*, Urbana, IL, 1987.

7.475 **Van Raaphorst**, Donna L., *Union Maids Not Wanted. Organizing Domestic Workers, 1870–1940*, Westport, CT, 1988.

7.476 **Winters**, D. E., *The Soul of the Wobblies. The I.W.W., Religion, and American Culture in the Progressive Era, 1905–1917*, Westport, CT, 1985.

7.477 **Zieger**, R. H., (ed.), *Organized Labor in the Twentieth Century South*, Knoxville, TN, 1991.

The new corporation

7.478 **Bowman**, J. R., *Capitalist Collective Action. Competition, Cooperation, and Conflict in the Coal Industry*, New York, 1989. The "conflict" in the alliterative title most interests the author in this study of how class solidarity among mine owners broke down over narrow self-interest.

7.479 **Burk**, R. F., *The Corporate State and the Broker State. The Du Ponts and American National Politics, 1925–1940*, Cambridge, MA, 1990.

7.480 **Chandler**, A. D., *Scale and Scope. The Dynamics of Industrial Capitalism*, Cambridge, MA, 1990. Continues *The Visible Hand* in a newer work that compares American corporate development with that in Germany and the U.K., and finds American and German firms prospered through integration of mass production and mass marketing.

7.481 **Cortada**, J. W., *Before the Computer. IBM, NCR, Burroughs, and Remington Rand and the Industry They Created, 1865–1956*, Princeton, NJ, 1993.

7.482 **Engelbourg**, S., *Power and Morality: American Business Ethics, 1840–1914*, Westport, CT, 1980.

7.483 **Galambos**, L., and **Pratt**, J., *The Rise of the Corporate Commonwealth. United States Business and Public Policy in the 20th Century*, New York, 1988. An examination of the changing relations between corporate power and federal power.

7.484 **Graham**, Margaret B. W., and **Pruitt**, Bettye H., *R&D for Industry. A Century of Technical Innovation at Alcoa*, New York, 1990.

7.485 **Henderson**, Alexa Benson, *Atlanta Life Insurance Company. Guardian of Black Economic Dignity*, Tuscaloosa, AL, 1990.

7.486 **Hounshell**, D. A., and **Smith**, J. K., *Science and Corporate Strategy. Du Pont R&D, 1902–1980*, New York, 1988.

7.487 **Hughes**, T. P., *Networks of Power. Electrification in Western Society, 1880–1930*, Chicago, 1983. The history of the development and spread of the American electric power grid, with contrasts to English and German history.

7.488 **Kane**, Nancy Frances, *Textiles in Transition. Technology, Wages, and Industry Relocation in the U.S. Textile Industry, 1880–1930*, Westport, CT, 1988. An econometric analysis of wage differences between New England and the Piedmont, as well as market segments, and why individual firms made general location decisions.

7.489 **Keller**, M., *Regulating a New Economy. Public Policy and Economic Change in America, 1900–1933*, Cambridge, MA, 1990. A description of the various forms of economic regulation employed from the Progressive Era to the New Deal. Arguing from a conservative standpoint, Keller explicitly rejects economic theory in favor of detailed description.

7.490 **Lamoreaux**, Naomi R., *The Great Merger Movement in American Business, 1895–1904*, New York, 1985. Traces corporate mergers at the turn of the century to a desire to limit competition and establish stability rather than from technical innovation leading to vertical integration.

7.491 **Lipartito**, K., *The Bell System and the Regional Business. The Telephone in the*

South, 1877–1920, Baltimore, 1989.

7.492 **McCraw**, T. K., *Prophets of Regulation. Charles Francis Adams, Louis D. Brandeis, James M. Landis, Alfred E. Kahn*, Cambridge, MA, 1984. Pulitzer-prize winning biographical study of these four major figures.

7.493 **Miranti**, P. J., *Accountancy Comes of Age. The Development of an American Profession, 1886–1940*, Chapel Hill, NC, 1990.

7.494 **Nash**, G. D., *A. P. Giannini and the Bank of America*, Norman, OK, 1992. History of the founding of the great California bank, as well as of its immigrant leader.

7.495 **Nelson**, D., *Frederick W. Taylor and the Rise of Scientific Management*, Madison, WI, 1980.

7.496 **Noble**, D. F., *America By Design. Science, Technology, and the Rise of Corporate Capitalism*, New York, 1977.

7.497 **Norris**, J. D., *Advertising and the Transformation of American Society, 1865–1920*, New York, 1990. Uses advertisements as a way of charting the fundamental change in American society from a nation of producers to one of consumers.

7.498 **Nye**, D. E., *Image Worlds. Corporate Identities at General Electric*, Cambridge, MA, 1985. Examines thousands of photographs taken by the GE company for both external advertising and internal company publications.

7.499 **Olien**, R. M., and **Olien**, Diana Davids, *Easy Money. Oil Promoters and Investors in the Jazz Age*, Chapel Hill, NC, 1990. Recounts the various schemes to attract investors in the 1920s to oil stocks.

7.500 **Reich**, L. S., *The Making of American Industrial Research. Science and Business at GE and Bell*, New York, 1985. Places the industrial laboratories of the two companies in the larger context of corporate goals and strategies.

7.501 **Scamehorn**, H. L., *Mill & Mine. The CF and I in the Twentieth Century*, Lincoln, NE, 1992. Business biography of the Colorado Fuel & Iron Company.

7.502 **Scranton**, P., *Figured Tapestry. Production, Markets, and Power in Philadelphia Textiles, 1885–1941*, New York, 1989. Continues the author's 1984 volume by looking at labor and production, and finds that the downfall of the Philadelphia textile business was due to changes in market structure.

7.503 **Sklar**, M. J., *The Corporate Reconstruction of American Capitalism, 1890–1916*, New York, 1988. Examines antitrust policy in the early twentieth century in the light of the momentous changes in the American economy due to the growth of oligopoly and monopoly.

7.504 **Smith**, G. D., *From Monopoly to Competition. The Transformation of Alcoa, 1888–1986*, New York, 1988.

7.505 **Smith**, G. D., *The Anatomy of a Business Strategy. Bell, Western Electric, and the Origins of the American Telephone Industry*, Baltimore, 1985. Considers the origins of vertical integration within the American Telephone and Telegraph Company.

7.506 **Swann**, J. P., *Academic Scientists and the Pharmaceutical Industry. Cooperative Research in Twentieth Century America*, Baltimore, 1988.

7.507 **Wasserman**, N. H., *From Invention to Innovation. Long-Distance Telephone Transmission at the Turn of the Century*, Baltimore, 1985. Examines the difficulty American Telephone and Telegraph faced in devising a technical solution to intercity telephony that did not disrupt other parts of the system.

7.508 **Whitten**, D. O., *The Emergence of Giant Enterprise, 1860–1914. American Commercial Enterprise and Extractive Industries*, Westport, CT, 1983.

7.509 **Yeager**, M., *Competition and Regulation. The Development of Oligopoly in the Meat Packing Industry*, Greenwich, CT, 1981.

7.510 **Zahavi**, G., *Workers, Managers, and Welfare Capitalism. The Shoe Workers and Tanners of Endicott Johnson, 1890–1950*, Urbana, IL, 1988. A history of how George Johnson brought techniques of mass production and mass distribution to the shoe industry, as well as personnel management techniques that kept the Endicott Johnson plants non-union.

7.511 **Zunz**, O., *Making America Corporate, 1870–1920*, Chicago, 1990. An inquiry into the origins of a distinct corporate culture in America.

The Great Depression and the New Deal

7.512 **Argersinger**, Ann E., *Toward a New Deal in Baltimore. People and Government in the Great Depression*, Chapel Hill, NC, 1988.

7.513 **Beito**, D. T., *Taxpayers in Revolt. Tax Resistance during the Great Depression*, Chapel Hill, NC, 1989.

7.514 **Bernstein**, M., *The Great Depression. Delayed Recovery and Economic Change in America, 1929–1939*, New York, 1987. A new explanation of the severity of the Depression that emphasizes that the timing of the long-term decline of older American industries coincided with the 1929 crash, and moreover, that the new industries were not sufficiently established to serve as engines of economic recovery.

7.515 **Best**, G. D., *Pride, Prejudice, and Politics. Roosevelt versus Recovery, 1933–1938*, New York, 1991. A conservative critique of the New Deal that argues recovery was retarded by government intervention in the market.

7.516 **Brock**, W. R., *Welfare, Democracy, and the New Deal*, New York, 1988.

7.517 **Daniel**, P., *Breaking the Land. The Transformation of Cotton, Tobacco, and Rice Cultures since 1880*, Urbana, IL, 1985. Compares the effect of New Deal federal agricultural policy in the South to the enclosure movement in its effect of ridding landlords of their black and white tenant farmers.

7.518 **Dawley**, A., *Struggles for Justice. Social Responsibility and the Liberal State*, Cambridge, MA, 1991. An account of the coming of the New Deal as the result of changes in control of the nation-state.

7.519 **Degen**, R. A., *The American Monetary System. A Concise Survey of its Evolution Since 1896*, Lexington, MA, 1987. A helpful guide through the complexities of monetary history.

7.520 **Fearon**, P., *War, Prosperity and Depression. The U.S. Economy, 1917–1945*, Lawrence, KS, 1987. A survey of the economic history of the U.S. through the Great Depression, including accounts by modern theorists about why the downturn was so long and so deep.

7.521 **Garraty**, J., *The Great Depression*, New York, 1986. Places the story of the American experience in the Depression against those of other European nations, particularly that of Germany, and finds that a narrow nationalism among all the industrialized world lengthened and worsened the slump.

7.522 **Gordon**, Linda, 'Social insurance and public assistance. The influence of gender in welfare thought in the United States, 1890–1935', *American Historical Review*, XCVII, 1992, 19–54. Examines the views of men and women social work reformers in implementing new systems designed to eliminate poverty without impairing the work ethic.

7.523 **Hodges**, J. A., *New Deal Labor Policy and the Southern Cotton Textile Industry, 1933–1941*, Knoxville, TN, 1986.

7.524 **Hunnicut**, B. K., *Work without End. Abandoning Shorter Hours for the Right to Work*, Philadelphia, 1988. Ties the end to agitation for a shorter work week to the change in cultural values from a producer society to a consumer society.

7.525 **Kornbluh**, Joyce L., *A New Deal for Workers' Education. The Workers' Service Program, 1933–1942*, Urbana, IL, 1987.

7.526 **Meikle**, J. L., *Twentieth Century Limited. Industrial Design in America, 1929–1939*, Philadelphia, 1979.

7.527 **Milkman**, Ruth, *Gender at Work. The Dynamics of Job Segregation by Sex during World War II*, Urbana, IL, 1987.

7.528 **Miller**, M. S., *The Irony of Victory. World War II and Lowell, Massachusetts*, Urbana, IL, 1988. Tells the story of World War II in the declining textile town as a missed opportunity for revitalization, based mainly on oral histories of those who lived in Lowell through the war.

7.529 **Mullins**, W. H., *The Depression and the Urban West Coast, 1929–1933. Los Angeles, San Francisco, Seattle, and Portland*, Bloomington, IN, 1991.

7.530 **Olney**, Martha L., *Buy Now, Pay Later. Advertising, Credit, and Consumer Durables in the 1920s*, Chapel Hill, NC, 1991. A detailed look at consumer credit and its role in facilitating the boom after 1920.

7.531 **Olson**, J. S., *Saving Capitalism. The Reconstruction Finance Corporation and the New Deal, 1933–1940*, Princeton, NJ, 1988. A close study of the obscure New Deal agency that the author contends was vital to the creation of a state-supported American capitalism that emerged in the 1930s.

7.532 **Schulz**, Constance, (ed.), *A South Carolina Album, 1936–1948. Documentary Photography in the Palmetto State from the Farm Security Administration, Office of War Information, and Standard Oil of New Jersey*, Columbia, SC, 1991. A volume of photographs of Depression and wartime

South Carolina with accompanying text that traces the changes in the aims and objects of the documentary photographers.

7.533 **Seely**, B. E., *Building the American Highway System. Engineers as Policy Makers*, Philadelphia, 1987.

7.534 **Smith**, D. L., *The New Deal in the Urban South*, Baton Rouge, LA, 1988.

7.535 **Spulber**, N., *Managing the American Economy from Roosevelt to Reagan*, Bloomington, IN, 1989.

7.536 **Wheelock**, D. C., *The Strategy and Consistency of Federal Reserve Monetary Policy, 1924–1933*, New York, 1991. Elaborate statistical test of the Fed's open market policies before and after the Crash; finds that the agency was not undone by a strategy change, but rather by its inability to comprehend the depth of the Depression.

The new agriculture

7.537 **Bader**, R. S., *Hayseeds, Moralizers, and Methodists. The Twentieth Century Image of Kansas*, Lawrence, KS, 1988.

7.538 **Creese**, W. L. T., *TVA's Public Planning. The Vision, the Reality*, Knoxville, TN, 1990. An architectural and environmental history of the Tennessee Valley Authority, the New Deal project to realize through public planning the revitalization of one of the most depressed regions in the United States.

7.539 **Danbom**, D. B., *The Resisted Revolution. Urban America and the Industrialization of Agriculture, 1900–1930*, Ames, IA, 1979.

7.540 **Danbom**, D. B., *'Our Purpose is to Serve'. The First Century of the North Dakota Agricultural Experiment Station*, Fargo, ND, 1990. A leading agricultural historian looks at an obscure agency and finds the intersection of farm policy, higher education, and science.

7.541 **Dunn**, D., *Cades Cove. The Life and Death of a Southern Appalachian Community, 1818–1937*, Knoxville, TN, 1988. A respectful account of social history of a mountain community that was destroyed as part of the making of Great Smoky Mountain National Park.

7.542 **Dyson**, L. K., *Red Harvest. The Communist Party and American Farmers*, Lincoln, NE, 1982. Examines how a self-styled proletarian party attempted to appeal to farmers and farm workers in the Great Depression.

7.543 **Fite**, G. C., *Cotton Fields No More. Southern Agriculture, 1865–1940*, Lexington, KY, 1984. Treats the transformation of the South away from cotton, in large part due to federal agricultural policy.

7.544 **Fitzgerald**, Deborah, *The Business of Breeding. Hybrid Corn in Illinois, 1890–1940*, Ithaca, NY, 1990.

7.545 **Friedberger**, M., *Farm Families and Change in Twentieth Century America*, Lexington, KY, 1988. Looks at family farming in California and Iowa and argues that it should be maintained as a valuable heritage.

7.546 **Kloppenburg**, J. R., *First the Seed. The Political Economy of Plant Biotechnology, 1492–2000*, New York, 1988. A critical look at how the hybrid seed industry arose, first in land grant universities, and then later in private industry.

7.547 **Petersen**, K. C., *Company Town. Potlatch, Idaho, and the Potlatch Lumber Company*, Pullman, WA, 1987.

7.548 **Sherow**, J. E., *Watering the Valley. Development along the High Plains, Arkansas River, 1870–1950*, Lawrence, KS, 1990.

7.549 **Stock**, Catherine McNicol, *Main Street in Crisis. The Great Depression and the Old Middle Class on the Northern Plains*, Chapel Hill, NC, 1992.

RACE AND ETHNIC IDENTITY

African-Americans

7.550 **Copeci**, D. J., Jr., *Race Relations in Wartime Detroit. The Sojourner Truth Housing Controversy of 1942*, Philadelphia, 1984. The story of a confrontation between would-be black migrants to a city housing project and the white demonstrators who stopped them, and how the tensions led to an outright race riot the next year.

7.551 **Copeci**, D. J., Jr., and **Wilkerson**, Martha, *Layered Violence. The Detroit*

Rioters of 1943, Jackson, MS, 1991. Analyzes the Detroit upheaval and finds it remarkable for the extent to which blacks fought back against white assailants both inside and outside black neighborhoods.

7.552 **Cortner**, R. C., *A Mob Intent on Death. The NAACP and the Arkansas Riot Cases*, Middletown, CT, 1988. Examines the 1919 Elaine, Arkansas labor conflict that led to a race riot with 200 dead and an aftermath of legal repression.

7.553 **Downey**, D. B., and **Hyser**, R. M., *No Crooked Death. Coatesville, Pennsylvania and the Lynching of Zachariah Walker*, Urbana, IL, 1991. An account of a 1911 northern lynching that ties race relations to local labor-management strife.

7.554 **Gatewood**, W. B., *Aristocrats of Color. The Black Elite, 1880–1920*, Bloomington, IN, 1990. Surveys upper-class blacks in northern and southern cities and finds them a relatively homogeneous group, bound by family and church ties, and fearful of the upheavals in the rural South.

7.555 **Grant**, N. L., *TVA and Black Americans. Planning for the Status Quo*, Philadelphia, 1990.

7.556 **Greenberg**, Cheryl Lynn, *'Or Does It Explode'. Black Harlem in the Great Depression*, New York, 1991. A history of how black New Yorkers responded to the economic and social crisis of the 1930s.

7.557 **Hine**, Darlene Clark, *Black Women in White. Racial Conflict and Cooperation in the Nursing Profession, 1890–1950*, Bloomington, IN, 1989.

7.558 **Holway**, J. B., *Black Diamonds. Life in the Negro Leagues from the Men Who Lived It*, Westport, CT, 1989.

7.559 **Homel**, M. W., *Down from Equality. Black Chicagoans and the Public Schools, 1920–1941*, Urbana, IL, 1984. Shows that a policy of school segregation coincided with a larger funding crisis in the city schools that worked to the disadvantage of the new black migrants and their children.

7.560 **Ingalls**, R. P., *Urban Vigilantes in the New South. Tampa, 1882–1936*, Knoxville, TN, 1988.

7.561 **Kelley**, R. D. G., *Hammer and Hoe. Alabama Communists during the Great Depression*, Chapel Hill, NC, 1990. Argues that the Communist Party in Alabama drew most of its strength from black workers, attracted to it more because of its anti-racist stance than because of its proletarianism.

7.562 **Lewis**, D. L., 'Parallels and divergences: assimilationist strategies of Afro-American and Jewish elites from 1910 to the early 1930s', *Journal of American History*, LXXI, 1984, 543–564. Deals with Afro-Americans and Jews who wanted to acculturate and assimilate to white society, to disappear.

7.563 **Lewis**, E., *In Their Own Interest. Race, Class, and Power in Twentieth-Century Norfolk, Virginia*, Berkeley, CA, 1991. Outlines an ongoing struggle for better lives on the part of black Norfolk, culminating in the civil rights movement.

7.564 **Lewis**, R. L., *Black Coal Miners in America. Race, Class and Community Conflict, 1780–1980*, Lexington, KY, 1987. A history of black miners in Appalachia, strongest for the early twentieth century when the West Virginia fields were opened and when opportunity existed for blacks, despite segregation.

7.565 **Litwack**, L. F., 'Trouble in mind. The Bicentennial and the Afro-American experience', *Journal of American History*, LXXVII, 1987, 315–337. Discusses the experience of Afro-Americans in their struggle for equality.

7.566 **McMillen**, N. R., *Dark Journey. Black Mississippians in the Age of Jim Crow*, Urbana, IL, 1989. Treats race relations from the 1890s up to the Civil Rights movement in the most resolutely white supremacist state, and finds that black people maintained various forms of resistance.

7.567 **Natanson**, N., *The Black Image in the New Deal. The Politics of FSA Photography*, Knoxville, TN, 1992. Finds that the much-praised realism of Farm Security Administration photography did not extend to race relations.

7.568 **Neverdon-Morton**, Cynthia, *Afro-American Women of the South and the Advancement of the Race, 1895–1925*, Knoxville, TN, 1989.

7.569 **Schwieder**, Dorothy, **Hraba**, J., and **Schwieder**, E., *Buxton. Work and Racial Equality in a Coal Mining Community*, Ames, IA, 1987. The history of an Iowa mining town, one-half of whose population was black, and by the authors' account was a model of interracial harmony, in large part because the company that owned the town wanted it so.

7.570 **Singh**, A., **Shriver**, W., and **Brodwin**, S., (ed.), *The Harlem Renaissance. Revaluations*, New York, 1989.

7.571 **Sitkoff**, H., *A New Deal for Blacks. The Emergence of Civil Rights as a National Issue*, New York, 1978.

7.572 **Trotter**, J. W., Jr., *Black Milwaukee. The Making of an Industrial Proletariat, 1914–1945*, Urbana, IL, 1985. Uses class analysis to show how black migrants to Milwaukee entered the industrial work force in the 1920s and devised their own working-class culture.

7.573 **Trotter**, J. W., Jr., *Coal, Class, and Color. Blacks in Southern West Virginia, 1915–1932*, Urbana, IL, 1990. The story of black coal miners in the heart of Appalachia, this books focuses on the development of race consciousness within the mining communities.

7.574 **Waldrep**, C., *Night Riders. Defending Community in the Black Patch, 1890–1915*, Durham, NC, 1993.

7.575 **Williamson**, J., *New People. Miscegenation and Mulattoes in the United States*, New York, 1980. A survey of race relations that finds the distinction between blacks and mulattoes ended early in the twentieth century.

7.576 **Zangrando**, R. L., *The NAACP Crusade Against Lynching, 1909–1950*, Philadelphia, 1980.

Native Americans

7.577 **Bernstein**, A. R., *American Indians and World War II. Toward a New Era in Indian Affairs*, Norman, OK, 1991. Shows how the war transformed the lives of veterans and war workers and was an important transition from the Indian New Deal to the postwar federal effort to end its trust relationship to the tribes.

7.578 **Biolsi**, T., *Organizing the Lakota. The Political Economy of the New Deal on the Pine Ridge and Rosebud Reservations*, Tucson, AZ, 1992. An account of how the Indian Reorganization Act of 1934 continued to foster dependence on federal authority on two big South Dakota reservations, despite the legislative intent of promoting self-reliance.

7.579 **Farr**, W. E., *The Reservation Blackfeet, 1883–1945. A Photographic History of Cultural Survival*, Seattle, 1984. A remarkable set of photographs of the Montana people.

7.580 **Fienup-Riordan**, Ann, *The Real People and the Children of Thunder. The Yup'ik Eskimo Encounter with Moravian Missionaries John and Edith Kilbruck*, Norman, OK, 1991. The story of an Indian mission to the Alaska Yup'ik and how missions served as intercultural waystations.

7.581 **Foster**, M. W., *Being Comanche. A Social History of an American Indian Community*, Tucson, AZ, 1991. Shows how the Comanches retained an Indian identity through the new use of peyote worship and the powwow despite the many changes around them in Oklahoma.

7.582 **Iverson**, P., (ed.), *The Plains Indians of the Twentieth Century*, Norman, OK, 1985.

7.583 **Kersey**, H. A., *The Florida Seminoles and the New Deal, 1933–1942*, Boca Raton, FL, 1989.

7.584 **Krupat**, A., *For Those Who Came After. A Study of Native American Autobiography*, Berkeley, CA, 1985.

7.585 **McDonnell**, Janet A., *The Dispossession of the American Indian, 1887–1934*, Bloomington, IN, 1991. Treats the continuing assault on tribalism that followed in the wake of the 1887 General Allotment Act.

7.586 **Meyer**, Melissa A., ' "We can not get a living as we used to". Dispossession and the White Earth Anishinaabeg, 1889–1920', *American Historical Review*, XCVI, 1991, 368–394. Tells the story of intratribal conflict on the White Earth, Minnesota, Chippewa Indian Reservation and how the reservation's land base was lost to non-Indians.

7.587 **Parman**, D. L., *The Navajos and the New Deal*, New Haven, CT, 1976.

7.588 **Stewart**, O. C., *Peyote Religion. A History*, Norman, OK, 1987. Considers the origin of the sacrament, and its spread as hybrid pan-Indian religion in the twentieth century.

7.589 **Unrau**, W. E., *Mixed Bloods and Tribal Dissolution. Charles Curtis and the Quest for Indian Identity*, Lawrence, KS, 1989.

7.590 **Unrau**, W. E., and **Miner**, C. H., *Tribal Dispossession and the Ottawa Indian University Fraud*, Norman, OK, 1985. A case study of a land rip-off involving the Ottawas of Kansas.

European-Americans

7.591 **Barkan**, E., *The Retreat of Scientific Racism. Changing Concepts of Race in Britain and the United States between the World Wars*, New York, 1992.

7.592 **Blee**, Katherine M., *Women of the Klan. Racism and Gender in the 1920s*, Berkeley, CA, 1991. Studies the women's auxiliary within the Ku Klux Klan in Indiana and finds that the women who joined were similar in motivation to male Klansmen.

7.593 **Bukowczyk**, J. J., *And My Children Did Not Know Me. A History of the Polish-Americans*, Bloomington, IN, 1987.

7.594 **Coser**, L. A., *Refugee Scholars in America. Their Impact and Their Experiences*, New Haven, CT, 1984.

7.595 **Ewen**, Elizabeth, *Immigrant Women in the Land of Dollars. Life and Culture on the Lower East Side, 1890–1925*, New York, 1985.

7.596 **Gabbacia**, Donna, *Militants and Migrants. Rural Sicilians Become American Workers*, New Brunswick, NJ, 1988.

7.597 **Gerlach**, L. R., *Blazing Crosses in Zion. The Ku Klux Klan in Utah*, Logan, UT, 1982.

7.598 **Heilbut**, A., *Exiled in Paradise. German Refugee Artists and Intellectuals in America, from the 1930s to the Present*, New York, 1983.

7.599 **Heinze**, A. R., *Adapting to Abundance. Jewish Immigrants, Mass Consumption, and the Search for an American Identity*, New York, 1990.

7.600 **Jenkins**, W. D., *Steel Valley Klan. The Ku Klux Klan in Ohio's Mahoning Valley*, Kent, OH, 1990.

7.601 **Kuropas**, M. B., *The Ukrainian Americans. Roots and Aspirations, 1884–1954*, Toronto, ONT, 1991.

7.602 **Lay**, S., (ed.), *The Invisible Empire in the West. Toward a New Historical Appraisal of the Ku Klux Klan of the 1920s*, Urbana, IL, 1992.

7.603 **Lehmann**, H., and **Sheehan**, J. J., *An Interrupted Past. German-Speaking Refugee Historians in the United States after 1933*, New York, 1991. A set of essays that examines the generation of immigrant historians, their work on German history, and their impact on the American academy.

7.604 **Moore**, Deborah Dash, *At Home in America. Second Generation New York Jews*, New York, 1981.

7.605 **Morawaska**, Ewa, *For Bread with Butter. The Life-World of East Central Europeans in Johnstown, Pennsylvania, 1890–1940*, New York, 1985.

7.606 **Orsi**, R. A., 'The fault of memory: southern Italy in the imagination of immigrants and the lives of their children in Italian Harlem, 1920–1945', *Journal of Family History*, XV, 1990, 133–147.

7.607 **Schultz**, April, ' "The pride of the race had been touched." The 1925 Norse-American immigration centennial and ethnic identity', *Journal of American History*, LXXVII, 1991, 1265–1295. Analyzes conflicting views about how Norwegian-Americans saw themselves in 1925, and how internal debates reflected the tensions about assimilation and ethnicity.

7.608 **Smith**, Judith E., *Family Connections. A History of Italian and Jewish Immigrant Lives in Providence, Rhode Island, 1900–1940*, Albany, NY, 1985.

7.609 **Soike**, L. J., *Norwegian Americans and the Politics of Dissent, 1880–1924*, Northfield, MN, 1991. Looks at Norwegian politicians and leaders who left the Republican Party for various reform movements in the Midwest.

7.610 **Yans-McLaughlin**, Virginia, *Family and Community. Italian Immigrants to Buffalo, 1880–1930*, Ithaca, NY, 1977.

Asian-Americans

7.611 **Daniels**, R., *Asian Americans. Chinese and Japanese in the United States since 1850*, Seattle, 1988. Chronicles the creation of separate racial communities, mainly in the American West, with an epilogue about Japanese and Chinese Americans in the present.

7.612 **Ichioka**, Y., *The Issei. The World of the First Generation Japanese Immigrants, 1885–1924*, New York, 1988. Uses Japanese language sources, both from the U.S. and Japan, to tell the history of the emigrants who left their homeland for Hawaii and California and the life they encountered.

7.613 **Jensen**, Joan M., *Passage from India. Asian Indian Immigrants in North America*, New Haven, CT, 1988.

7.614 **LaCroix**, S. J., and **Roumasset**, J., 'The evolution of private property in nineteenth century Hawaii', *Journal of Economic History*, L, 1990, 829–852.

7.615 **Limerick**, Patricia Nelson, 'The multicultural islands', *American Historical Review*, XCVII, 1992, 121–135. A review of the recent literature on the various ethnic groups that came to make up modern Hawaii.

7.616 **McKee**, D. L., *Chinese Exclusion Versus the Open Door Policy, 1900–1977. Clashes Over China Policy in the Roosevelt Era*, Detroit, 1977.

7.617 **Moriyama**, A. T., *Imingaisha. Japanese Emigration Companies and Hawaii, 1894–1908*, Honolulu, 1985. Tells the story of the 125,000 contract laborers and other immigrants who made their way from Japan to work on the sugar plantations of American-controlled Hawaii.

7.618 **Okihiro**, G. Y., *Cane Fires. The Anti-Japanese Movement in Hawaii, 1865–1945*, Philadelphia, 1991. Explores the racial conflict between Japanese and other groups that led to the imposition of martial law in Hawaii at the outset of World War II.

7.619 **Parker**, Linda S., *Native American Estate. The Struggle over Indian and Hawaiian Lands*, Honolulu, 1989.

7.620 **Patterson**, W., *The Korean Frontier in America. Immigration to Hawaii, 1896–1910*, Honolulu, 1988. A study of the complex diplomacy and labor relations surrounding Korean migrant workers to the Hawaiian sugar plantations and the subsequent conflicts.

7.621 **Teodor**, L. V., *Out of this Struggle. The Filipinos in Hawaii*, Honolulu, 1983.

7.622 **Yu**, R., *To Save China, to Save Ourselves. The Chinese Hand Laundry Alliance of New York*, Philadelphia, 1992. A history of the organization that was part labor union, part mutual assistance society, and how it was ultimately undermined by a combination of FBI intimidation and Chinese-American merchants.

Hispanic-Americans

7.623 **Blackwelder**, Julia Kirk, *Women of the Depression. Caste and Culture in San Antonio, 1929–1939*, College Station, TX, 1984.

7.624 **Chavez**, J. R., *The Lost Land. The Chicano Image of the Southwest*, Albuquerque, NM, 1984.

7.625 **Daniel**, C., *Chicano Workers and the Politics of Fairness. The FEPC in the Southwest, 1941–1945*, Austin, TX, 1991.

7.626 **DeLeon**, A., *Ethnicity in the Sunbelt. A History of Mexican-Americans in Houston*, Houston, 1989. Finds that the crucial period in the formation of a Mexican-American identity was the 1930s when acculturation into the larger Houston began.

7.627 **Deutsch**, Sara, *No Separate Refuge. Culture, Class, and Gender on an Anglo-Hispanic Frontier in the American Southwest, 1880–1940*, New York, 1987. A study of the meeting of two cultures in Texas, New Mexico, and Colorado, particularly as mediated by family and gender.

7.628 **Forrest**, Suzanne, *The Preservation of the Village. New Mexico's Hispanics and the New Deal*, Albuquerque, NM, 1989.

7.629 **Garcia**, R. A., *Rise of the Mexican American Middle Class. San Antonio, 1929–1941*, College Station, TX, 1991.

7.630 **Korrol**, Virginia E. Sanchez, *From Colonia to Community. The History of Puerto Ricans in New York City, 1917–1948*, Westport, CT, 1983.

7.631 **Romo**, R., *East Los Angeles. History of a Barrio*, Austin, TX, 1983.

7.632 **San Miguel**, G., *'Let All of Them Take Heed'. Mexican Americans and the Campaign for Educational Equality in Texas, 1910–1981*, Austin, TX, 1987.

SPACE, MOVEMENT, AND PLACE

The great migrations

7.633 **Athearn**, R. G., *The Mythic West in Twentieth Century America*, Lawrence, KS, 1986. A personal view by a leading western historian about the changes in the region since the early part of the century.

7.634 **Cinel**, D., *From Italy to San Francisco. The Immigrant Experience*, Stanford, CA, 1982.

7.635 **Cinel**, D., *The National Integration of Italian Return Migration, 1870–1929*, New York, 1991.

7.636 **Gregory**, J. N., *American Exodus. The*

Dust Bowl Migration and Okie Culture in California, New York, 1989. A treatment of the actual people behind Steinbeck's *Grapes of Wrath*, with the focus as much on the plurality of migrants who moved to Los Angeles.

7.637 **Grossman**, J. R., *Land of Hope. Chicago, Black Southerners, and the Great Migration*, Chicago, 1989. Illuminates the structure of the great movement of rural southern blacks to Chicago, as well as the city life they encountered.

7.638 **Grossman**, J. R., and **Gabbacia**, Donna, *Teaching the History of Immigration and Ethnicity*, Chicago, 1993.

7.639 **Kelley**, R. L., *Battling the Inland Sea. American Political Culture, Public Policy, and the Sacramento Valley, 1850–1986*, Berkeley, CA, 1989. This work celebrates the political culture that produced internal improvements such as railroads and irrigation projects in support of individual enterprise.

7.640 **Lee**, L. B., *Reclaiming the American West. An Historiography and Guide*, Santa Barbara, CA, 1980. Covers the history and writings about irrigation and hydro projects funded by the U.S. Bureau of Reclamation.

7.641 **Lemann**, N., *The Promised Land. The Great Black Migration and How It Changed America*, New York, 1991. A study that focuses on the migration of African-Americans from Mississippi to Chicago, and how the culture of the rural South influenced the new city.

7.642 **Lowitt**, R., *The New Deal and the West*, Bloomington, IN, 1984. Looks at the effects of Interior and Agriculture Department policies on the western states and their culture of individualism.

7.643 **Marks**, Carole, *Farewell – We're Good and Gone. The Great Black Migration*, Bloomington, IN, 1989.

7.644 **Nash**, G. D., *The American West Transformed. The Impact of the Second World War*, Bloomington, IN, 1985. First of two volume set that argues World War II and direct federal spending created the modern American West, especially the urban West.

7.645 **Nash**, G. D., *World War II and the West. Reshaping the Economy*, Lincoln, NE, 1990. Second volume of the author's work on the role of the federal transformation of the American West.

7.646 **Starr**, K., *Inventing the Dream. California Through the Progressive Era*, New York, 1985. Continues the author's series that explores how California emerged as the definer of twentieth century American culture, particularly as exemplified in the new Hollywood film industry.

7.647 **Stevens**, J. E., *Hoover Dam. An American Adventure*, Norman, OK, 1988. Combines the construction history of the dam with its transforming effect on nearby Las Vegas and on southern California.

7.648 **Stratton**, D. H., (ed.), *Spokane and the Inland Empire. An Interior Pacific Northwest Anthology*, Pullman, WA, 1991.

7.649 **Thomas**, R. W., *Life for Us Is What We Make It. Building Black Community in Detroit, 1915–1945*, Bloomington, IN, 1992.

7.650 **Trotter**, J. W., (ed.), *The Great Migration in Historical Perspective. New Dimensions of Race, Class, and Gender*, Bloomington, IN, 1991. A set of essays by leading scholars of the black migration from the South to northern cities.

Urban America

7.651 **Bauman**, J. F., *Public Housing, Race and Renewal. Urban Planning in Philadelphia, 1920–1974*, Philadelphia, 1987.

7.652 **Berner**, R. C., *Seattle, 1900–1920. From Boomtown, Urban Turbulence, to Restoration*, Seattle, 1991. The first of two planned volumes on the history of the Emerald City up to World War II.

7.653 **Bogart**, Michele H., *Public Sculpture and the Civil Ideal in New York City, 1890–1930*, Chicago, 1989.

7.654 **Bottles**, S. L., *Los Angeles and the Automobile. The Making of the Modern City*, Berkeley, CA, 1987.

7.655 **Buder**, S., *Visionaries and Planners. The Garden City Movement and the Modern Community*, New York, 1990. Analyzes the impact of Ebenezer Howard's ideas on urban planning in Europe and North America.

7.656 **Crooks**, J. B., *Jacksonville after the Fire, 1901–1919. A New South City*, Jacksonville, FL, 1991.

7.657 **Cumbler**, J. T., *A Social History of Economic Decline. Business, Politics, and Work in Trenton*, New Brunswick, NJ, 1989. Traces the origins of the New Jersey city's industrial decline to the disappearance of local capitalists after World War I.

7.658 **Fairbanks**, R. B., *Making Better Citizens. Housing Reform and the Community Development Strategy in Cincinnati, 1890–1960*, Urbana, IL, 1989. Traces the changing mix of planning and housing construction in Cincinnati.

7.659 **Feagin**, J. R., *Free Enterprise City. Houston in Political and Economic Perspective*, New Brunswick, NJ, 1988. A critical view of the effects of unrestrained capitalism and dependence on the oil business as reflected in the rise of Houston in the interwar years.

7.660 **Garner**, J. S., (ed.), *The Midwest in American Architecture*, Urbana, IL, 1991.

7.661 **Ghirardo**, Diane, *Building New Communities. New Deal America and Fascist Italy*, Princeton, NJ, 1989.

7.662 **Grese**, R. E., *Jens Jensen. Maker of Natural Parks and Gardens*, Baltimore, 1992. Account of a Danish immigrant landscape architect who was most influential in designing public parks in turn of the century Chicago.

7.663 **Issel**, W., and **Cherny**, R. W., *San Francisco, 1865–1932. Politics, Power, and Urban Development*, Berkeley, CA, 1986. Analyzes the shifting conflict for power between working class organizations and business elites.

7.664 **Kuhn**, C. M., **Joye**, H. E., and **West**, E. B., *Living Atlanta. An Oral History of the City, 1914–1948*, Athens, GA, 1990. A summary of hundreds of hours of interviews with Atlantans who remember the city in the era of segregation.

7.665 **Melvin**, Patricia Mooney, *The Organic City. Urban Definition and Neighborhood Organization, 1880–1920*, Lexington, KY, 1987.

7.666 **Mormino**, G. R., *Immigrants on the Hill. Italian-Americans in St. Louis, 1882–1982*, Urbana, IL, 1986.

7.667 **Mormino**, G. R., and **Pozzetta**, G. E., *The Immigrant World of Ybor City. Italians and their Latin Neighbors in Tampa, 1885–1985*, Urbana, IL, 1987.

7.668 **Platt**, H. E., *The Electric City. Energy and the Growth of the Chicago Area, 1880–1930*, Chicago, 1991.

7.669 **Riess**, S. A., *City Games. The Evolution of American Urban Society and the Rise of Sports*, Urbana, IL, 1989. Argues that modern professional American sports were

intertwined with urban growth through a combination of boss politics, transit economics, and even organized crime.

7.670 **Slayton**, R. A., *Back of the Yards. The Making of a Local Democracy*, Chicago, 1986. An ethnographic study of the Eastern European immigrants and their children who worked in Chicago's meatpacking plants and built a culture of unionism and community solidarity between the wars.

7.671 **Stilgoe**, J. R., *Metropolitan Corridor. Railroads and the American Scene*, New Haven, CT, 1983. A book that lovingly recreates how the railroads shaped the environment of cities and the rural areas through which they passed.

7.672 **Tobey**, R., **Wetherell**, C., and **Brigham**, J., 'Moving out and settling in. Residential mobility, home owning, and the public enframing of citizenship, 1921–1950', *American Historical Review*, 1990, VC, 1395–1422. Analyzes geographical mobility from a study of electrical utility bills, and finds that the dramatic growth of home ownership due to eased federal mortgage lending practices led to a sharp decline in movement.

7.673 **Van Tassel**, D. D., and **Grabowski**, J. J., (ed.), *Cleveland. A Tradition of Reform*, Kent, OH, 1986. Eight essays on different reform movements in the Ohio city.

7.674 **Ward**, D., and **Zunz**, O., (ed.), *The Landscape of Modernity. Essays on New York City, 1900–1940*, New York, 1992.

7.675 **Wilson**, W. H., *The City Beautiful Movement*, Baltimore, 1989. Traces the movement for urban grace and style back to Frederick Law Olmstead and includes a cogent analysis of the influence of the 1893 World's Fair on the thought of urban planners.

7.676 **Wolfe**, Margaret Ripley, *Kingsport, Tennessee. A Planned American City*, Lexington, KY, 1987. The story of one of the first planned cities, how it attracted investment capital after World War I, and how it was later buffeted by the problems of Cold War America.

7.677 **Worley**, W. S., *J. C. Nichols and the Shaping of Kansas City. Innovation in Planned Residential Communities*, Columbia, MO, 1990. Shows how the developer used deed restrictions and homeowner associations to build and maintain the Country Club district of Kansas City.

The emergence of suburbia

7.678 **Ebner**, M. H., *Creating Chicago's North Shore. A Suburban History*, Chicago, 1988. Traces the development of the set of Chicago suburbs that emerged in the early twentieth century, how they related to the city, and to one another.

7.679 **Jackson**, K. T., *The Crabgrass Frontier. The Suburbanization of the United States*, New York, 1985. Contrasts American urban history with Europe's and finds that a mix of market and government forces, particularly in the 1920s and 1930s, helped bring about a radical decentralization of U.S. cities.

7.680 **Keating**, Ann Durkin, *Building Chicago. Suburban Developers and the Creation of a Divided Metropolis*, Columbus, OH, 1989. Considers the origins of separate suburban political development within the context of class and race.

7.681 **Marsh**, Margaret, *Suburban Lives*, New Brunswick, NJ, 1990. Traces the emergence of American suburbs through the 1920s and links suburban growth to conservative gender and family trends.

7.682 **Stilgoe**, J. R., *Borderland. Origins of the American Suburb, 1820–1939*, New Haven, CT, 1988. A history of suburbia written by a landscape historian that emphasizes the importance of the physical landscape as a deliberate construct between city and country life.

The South

7.683 **Cobb**, J. C., *Industrialization and Southern Society, 1877–1984*, Lexington, KY, 1984. Argues that industrialization had a shallow effect on southern society due to long-term regional features that persist up to today.

7.684 **Conkin**, P. K., *The Southern Agrarians*, Knoxville, TN, 1988. An intellectual biography of the Nashville twelve and their defense of a southern rural way of life in the Great Depression.

7.685 **Kirby**, J. T., *Rural Worlds Lost. The American South, 1920–1960*, Baton Rouge, LA, 1987. Shows how federal policies during the Great Depression fundamentally changed the Black Belt South and how World War II changed the Appalachian and Ozark white South.

7.686 **McWilliams**, T. S., *The New South Faces the World. Foreign Affairs and the Southern Sense of Self, 1877–1950*, Baton Rouge, LA, 1988. Explores southern opposition to American imperial ambitions as a legacy of the Civil War, and how that legacy disappeared by World War II.

7.687 **Ragsdale**, K. B., *The Year America Discovered Texas. Centennial '36*, College Station, TX, 1987.

7.688 **Shifflett**, C. A., *Coal Towns. Life, Work, and Culture in Company Towns of Southern Appalachia, 1880–1960*, Knoxville, TN, 1991.

7.689 **Wright**, G., *Old South, New South. Revolutions in the Southern Economy since the Civil War*, New York, 1986. Argues that the South's rigid racial segregation cordoned the region off from the national labor market and hampered development until the shocks of the Great Depression and World War II.

THE STATE AND THE PUBLIC REALM

Politics and elections

7.690 **Avrich**, P., *Sacco and Vanzetti. The Anarchist Background*, Princeton, NJ, 1991. Makes use of Italian-language materials to place the two martyrs in the larger history of transatlantic anarchism.

7.691 **Bensel**, R. F., *Sectionalism and American Political Development, 1880–1980*, Madison, WI, 1984.

7.692 **Brinkley**, A., *Voices of Protest. Huey Long, Father Coughlin, and the Great Depression*, New York, 1982.

7.693 **Broderick**, F. L., *Progressivism at Risk. Electing a President in 1912*, Westport, CT, 1989.

7.694 **Broesamle**, J. J., *Reform and Reaction in Twentieth Century American Politics*, Westport, CT, 1990.

7.695 **Craig**, D. B., *After Wilson. The Struggle for the Democratic Party, 1920–1934*, Chapel Hill, NC, 1992.

7.696 **Critchlow**, D. T., *Socialism in the Heartland. The Midwestern Experience*,

1900–1925, Notre Dame, IN, 1986.

7.697 **Eagles**, C. W., *Democracy Delayed. Congressional Reapportionment and Urban-Rural Conflict in the 1920s*, Athens, GA, 1990. Analyzes the politics in Congress over the Census of 1920 and the subsequent failure to reapportion the House of Representatives.

7.698 **Feinman**, R. L., *Twilight of Progressivism. The Western Republican Senators and the New Deal*, Baltimore, 1981. Analyzes the actions of twelve senior Republican senators in response to the domestic and foreign initiatives of the New Deal.

7.699 **Gamm**, G. H., *The Making of New Deal Democrats. Voting Behavior and Realignment in Boston, 1920–1940*, Chicago, 1989.

7.700 **Gould**, L. I., *The Presidency of Theodore Roosevelt*, Lawrence, KS, 1991.

7.701 **Gould**, L. I., *The Presidency of William McKinley*, Lawrence, KS, 1980.

7.702 **Grantham**, D. W., *The Life and Death of the Solid South. A Political History*, Lexington, KY, 1988. Traces the emergence of the postbellum South dominated by the whites-only Democratic party and its planter elite, and how the New Deal and the eventual national Democratic commitment to civil rights ended the one-party South.

7.703 **Green**, J. R., *Grass-roots Socialism. Radical Movements in the Southwest, 1895–1943*, Baton Rouge, LA, 1978.

7.704 **Jensen**, R. J., *Grass Roots Politics. Parties, Issues, and Voters, 1854–1983*, Westport, CT, 1983.

7.705 **Kleppner**, P., *Continuity and Change in Electoral Politics, 1893–1928*, Westport, CT, 1987. A defense of the argument that the presidential election of 1896 was one of "realignment" despite recent criticisms of that model.

7.706 **Kraditor**, Aileen S., *The Radical Persuasion, 1890–1917. Aspects of the Intellectual History and the Historiography of Three American Radical Organizations*, Baton Rouge, LA, 1981.

7.707 **Mitchell**, G., *The Campaign of the Century. Upton Sinclair's Race for Governor of California and the Birth of Media Politics*, New York, 1992. Argues that a conglomeration of business and show-business ganged up to defeat the leftist candidate Upton Sinclair in a 1934 California election.

7.708 **Leff**, M. H., *The Limits of Symbolic Reform. The New Deal and Taxation, 1933–1939*, New York, 1984. Maintains that Roosevelt's administration shunned actual tax policies that would significantly redistribute wealth and income in favor of talk and symbols about economic royalism.

7.709 **McCormick**, R. L., *From Realignment to Reform. Political Change in New York State, 1893–1910*, Ithaca, NY, 1981.

7.710 **Mintz**, F. R., *The Liberty Lobby and the American Right. Race, Conspiracy, and Culture*, Westport, CT, 1985.

7.711 **Oestreicher**, R. J., 'Urban working-class political behavior and theories of American electoral politics, 1870–1940', *Journal of American History*, LXXIV, 1988, 1257–1286. Discusses working-class voters and their party affiliation.

7.712 **Pinderhughes**, Dianne M., *Race and Ethnicity in Chicago Politics. A Reexamination of Pluralist Theory*, Urbana, IL, 1987. A political scientist looks at Chicago's twentieth century history and finds that the race question superseded all other group loyalties.

7.713 **Reynolds**, J. F., *Testing Democracy. Electoral Behavior and Progressive Reform in New Jersey, 1880–1920*, Chapel Hill, NC, 1988.

7.714 **Ribuffo**, L. P., *The Old Christian Right. The Protestant Far Right from the Great Depression to the Cold War*, Philadelphia, 1983.

7.715 **Ribuffo**, L. P., *Right Center Left. Essays in American History*, New Brunswick, NJ, 1992. Collected essays on fringe movements and their leaders in the twentieth century.

7.716 **Sarasohn**, D., *The Party of Reform. Democrats in the Progressive Era*, Jackson, MS, 1989.

7.717 **Savage**, S. J., *Roosevelt. The Party Leader, 1932–1945*, Lexington, KY, 1991. Examines how FDR worked with urban party bosses to solidify the Democrats as the major national party.

7.718 **Scott**, Anne Firor, and **Scott**, A. M., *One Half the People. The Fight for Woman Suffrage*, Urbana, IL, 1982.

7.719 **Thorsen**, N. A., *The Political Thought of Woodrow Wilson, 1875–1910*, Princeton, NJ, 1988.

7.720 **Tobin**, E. M., *Organize or Perish. Independent Progressives, 1913–1933*, New York, 1986.

.721 **VanderMeer**, P. R., *The Hoosier Politician. Officeholding and Political Culture in Indiana, 1896–1920*, Urbana, IL, 1985.

Government

7.722 **Braeman**, J., *Before the Civil Rights Revolution. The Old Court and Individual Rights*, New York, 1988.

7.723 **Buenker**, J. D., *The Income Tax and the Progressive Era*, New York, 1985.

7.724 **Burton**, D. H., *The Learned Presidency. Theodore Roosevelt, William Howard Taft, Woodrow Wilson*, Rutherford, NJ, 1988.

7.725 **Donner**, F. J., *Protectors of Privilege. Red Squads and Police Repression in Urban America*, Berkeley, CA, 1990. Looks at local spying on left-wing and labor organizations by metropolitan police departments.

7.726 **Judd**, R. W., *Socialist Cities. Municipal Politics and the Grass Roots of American Socialism*, Albany, NY, 1989.

7.727 **Silverman**, R. A., *Law and Urban Growth. Civil Litigation in the Boston Trial Courts, 1880–1900*, Princeton, NJ, 1981.

7.728 **Talbert**, R., *Negative Intelligence. The Army and the American Left, 1917–1941*, Jackson, MS, 1991.

7.729 **Welch**, R. E., *The Presidencies of Grover Cleveland*, Lawrence, KS, 1988.

The modern state

7.730 **Achenbaum**, W. A., *Social Security. Visions and Revisions*, New York, 1986.

7.731A **Adams**, J. A., *Damming the Colorado. The Rise of the Lower Colorado River Authority, 1933–1939*, College Station, TX, 1990.

7.731B **Brand**, D. R., *Corporatism and the Rule of Law. A Study of the National Recovery Administration*, Ithaca, NY, 1988.

7.732 **Clements**, K. A., *The Presidency of Woodrow Wilson*, Lawrence, KS, 1991.

7.733 **Cobb**, J. C., and **Namorato**, M. V., (ed.), *The New Deal and the South*, Jackson, MS, 1984. A collection of essays on the effects of policy and politics on the South.

7.734 **Coleman**, P. J., *Progressivism and the World of Reform. New Zealand and the Origins of the American Welfare State*, Lawrence, KS, 1987.

7.735 **Critchlow**, D. T., and **Hawley**, E. W., (ed.), *Federal Social Policy. The Historical Dimension*, University Park, PA, 1988.

7.736 **Curtis**, J., *Mind's Eye, Mind's Truth. FSA Photography Reconsidered*, Philadelphia, 1989. A study of the work of four famous photographers, Walker Evans, Dorothea Lange, Arthur Rothstein, and Russell Lee, and the Farm Security Administration that employed them in the late 1930s.

7.737 **Cutler**, Phoebe, *The Public Landscape of the New Deal*, New Haven, CT, 1985.

7.738 **Friendly**, F. W., *Minnesota Rag. The Dramatic Story of the Landmark Supreme Court Case That Gave New Meaning to Freedom of the Press*, New York, 1981. A journalist's account of a 1931 Supreme Court decision that held prior restraint of the press unconstitutional by state governments as well as the federal one.

7.739 **Hamilton**, D. E., *From New Day to New Deal. American Farm Policy from Hoover to Roosevelt, 1928–1933*, Chapel Hill, NC, 1991.

7.740 **Harden**, Victoria A., *Inventing the NIH. Federal Biomedical Research Policy, 1887–1937*, Baltimore, 1986. An institutional history of the various federal laboratories that came to make up the National Institute of Health.

7.741 **Higgs**, R., *Crisis and Leviathan. Critical Episodes in the Growth of American Government*, New York, 1987. A conservative attack on the origins of the modern state that emphasizes the lost freedoms and reduced power of the market.

7.742 **Karl**, B., *The Uneasy State. The United States from 1915 to 1945*, Chicago, 1983. An account of the various ways in which the federal government sought to keep up with and shape the changes in twentieth century American life.

7.743 **Marling**, Karal Ann, *Wall-to-Wall America. A Cultural History of Post-Office Murals in the Great Depression*, Minneapolis, MN, 1982. Examines the politics and aesthetics of a decade's worth of federally funded art in federal buildings, most notably post offices.

7.744 **Mavigliano**, G. J., and **Lawson**, R. A., *The Federal Art Project in Illinois, 1935–1943*, Carbondale, IL, 1990.

7.745 **May**, C. N., *In the Name of War. Judicial Review and the War Powers Since 1918*, Cambridge, MA, 1989.

7.746 **Meyer**, H. C., *Airshipmen, Businessmen, and Politics, 1890–1940*, Washington, DC, 1991.

7.747 **Nash**, G. D., (ed.), *Social Security. The First Half-Century*, Albuquerque, NM, 1988.

7.748 **Park**, Marlene, and **Markowitz**, G. E., *Democratic Vistas. Post Offices and Public Art in the New Deal*, Philadelphia, 1985. A favorable appraisal of the intent and value of the federally funded art project of the 1930s.

7.749 **Perry**, Barbara A., *A 'Representative' Supreme Court? The Impact of Race, Religion, and Gender on Appointments*, Westport, CT, 1991. Looks at such issues as the emergence and disappearance of a "Jewish" seat on the Supreme Court, and other political considerations about appointments.

7.750 **Powers**, R. G., *Secrecy and Power. The Life of J. Edgar Hoover*, New York, 1987. A cultural history of Hoover and the FBI that, while not denying the agency's abuses of constitutional rights, ties the Bureau's growth to the positive ethos of federal action in the Great Depression.

7.751 **Quadagno**, Jill, *The Transformation of Old Age Security. Class and Politics in the American Welfare State*, Chicago, 1988. An account of the development of old age pensions under the 1935 Social Security Act that emphasizes the failure of private corporate pensions in the 1920s and an upsurge of labor militancy in the Depression decade.

7.752 **Reid**, R. L., *Picturing Minnesota, 1936–1943. Photographs from the Farm Security Adminstration*, St. Paul, MN, 1989. Features 171 photographs of rural life in Depression-Era Minnesota.

7.753 **Sautter**, U., *Three Cheers for the Unemployed. Government and Unemployment Before the New Deal*, New York, 1992. Maintains that unemployment programs and income maintenance schemes had been accepted by reformist policy-makers before 1929 and that their implementation in the Depression was relatively smooth.

7.754 **Schwartz**, Bonnie Fox, *The Civil Works Administration, 1933–1934*, Princeton, NJ, 1984. A history of the federal agency created to alleviate mass unemployment during the winter of 1933–1934.

7.755 **Semonche**, J. E., *Charting the Future. The Supreme Court Responds to a Changing Society, 1890–1920*, Westport, CT, 1978.

7.756 **Temin**, P., *Taking Your Medicine. Drug Regulation in the United States*, Cambridge, MA, 1980. An economist's skeptical view of twentieth century federal regulation of prescription and non-prescription medicine that finds fault with governmental attempts to replace caveat emptor with central fiat.

7.757 **Tulis**, J. K., *The Rhetorical Presidency*, Princeton, NJ, 1987. Finds that Theodore Roosevelt and Woodrow Wilson modernized the presidency as a locus of persuasion.

7.758 **Wilson**, Margaret Gibbon, *Floridians and Work. Yesterday and Today*, Macon, GA, 1989. Blends photographs of Depression-Era Florida taken by the Farm Security Administration with text from Works Progress Administration oral histories of Florida residents.

7.759 **Winfield**, Betty Houchin, *FDR and the News Media*, Urbana, IL, 1990. Utilizes the transcripts of the President's weekly press conferences to analyze how FDR made effective use of the press.

7.760 **Young**, J. H., *Pure Food. Securing the Federal Food and Drug Acts of 1906*, Princeton, NJ, 1989. Traces the political coalition of manufacturers and reformers that came together long before Upton Sinclair's *The Jungle* to press for federal protection and inspection of the nation's food supply.

Warfare

7.761 **Bradford**, J. C., (ed.), *Admirals of the New Steel Navy. Makers of the American Naval Tradition, 1880–1930*, Annapolis, MD, 1990.

7.762 **May**, E. R., (ed.), *Knowing One's Enemies. Intelligence Assessment Before the Two World Wars*, Princeton, NJ, 1985. A set of essays that shows the problem with military intelligence was not so much in the failure to provide warning of the adversary's intent, but rather in the assessment of the meaning of intelligence.

7.763 **Powaski**, R. E., *Toward an Entangling Alliance. American Isolationism, Internationalism, and Europe, 1901–1950*, Westport, CT, 1991. A useful synthesis of how and why American diplomacy reversed Washington's famous "no entangling alliances" formula.

7.764 **Reardon**, Carol, *Soldiers and Scholars. The U.S. Army and the Uses of Military History, 1865–1920*, Lawrence, KS, 1990. Analyzes the curriculum at the Army's officer training schools and the relationship to university instruction.

(a) SPANISH-AMERICAN WAR

7.765 **Devine**, M. J., *John W. Foster and Diplomacy in the Imperial Era, 1873–1917*, Athens, OH, 1981.

7.766 **Linn**, B. M., *The U.S. Army and Counterinsurgency in the Philippine War, 1899–1902*, Chapel Hill, NC, 1989.

7.767 **Offner**, J. L., *An Unwanted War. The Diplomacy of the United States and Spain over Cuba, 1895–1898*, Chapel Hill, NC, 1992.

7.768 **O'Toole**, G. J. A., *The Spanish War. An American Epic – 1898*, New York, 1984.

7.769 **Trask**, D. F., *The War with Spain in 1898*, New York, 1981.

7.770 **Welch**, R. E., *Response to Imperialism. The United States and the Philippine-American War, 1899–1902*, Chapel Hill, NC, 1979.

(b) WORLD WAR I

7.771 **Ambrosius**, L. E., *Wilsonian Statecraft. Theory and Practice of Liberal Internationalism during World War I*, Wilmington, DE, 1991.

7.772 **Calhoun**, F. S., *Power and Principle. Armed Intervention in Wilsonian Foreign Policy*, Kent, OH, 1986.

7.773 **Chambers**, J. W., *To Raise an Army. The Draft Comes to Modern America*, New York, 1987. Examines how wartime expediency caused the Wilson administration to embrace a national draft run on a local level, and thus fell short of the measures called for by some progressives for citizenship linked to universal military service.

7.774 **Chrislock**, C. H., *Watchdog of Loyalty. The Minnesota Commission of Public Safety during World War I*, St. Paul, MN, 1991. How an agency chartered by state government used its police powers to suppress dissent and promote support for the war.

7.775 **Coogan**, J. W., *The End of Neutrality. The United States, Britain, and Maritime Rights,*

1899–1915, Ithaca, NY, 1981.

7.776 **Gardner**, L. C., *Safe for Democracy. The Anglo-American Response to Revolution, 1913–1923*, New York, 1984. An account of the emerging concorde between the U.S. and Great Britain to eliminate revolutionary challenges to liberal capitalism, first in Mexico and above all in Russia.

7.777 **Gibbs**, C. C., *The Great Silent Majority. Missouri's Resistance to World War I*, Columbia, MO, 1988.

7.778 **Greenwald**, Maurine Weiner, *Women, War, and Work. The Impact of World War I on Women Workers in the United States*, Westport, CT, 1980.

7.779 **Kennett**, L. B., *The First Air War, 1914–1918*, New York, 1991.

7.780 **Knock**, T. J., *To End All Wars. Woodrow Wilson and the Quest for a New World Order*, New York, 1992.

7.781 **Murphy**, P. L., *World War I and the Origin of Civil Liberties in the United States*, New York, 1979.

7.782 **Polenberg**, R., *Fighting Faiths. The Abrams Case, the Supreme Court, and Free Speech*, New York, 1987. An account of the World War I radicals who were sentenced to prison under the Sedition Act for opposing U.S. intervention against the Bolshevik Revolution, and particularly how the Supreme Court refused to overturn the convictions.

7.783 **Speed**, R. B., *Prisoners, Diplomats, and The Great War. A Study in the Diplomacy of Captivity*, Westport, CT, 1990. Looks at how all the belligerents treated POWs, including the U.S.

7.784 **Unterberger**, Betty Miller, *The United States, Revolutionary Russia, and the Rise of Czechoslovakia*, Chapel Hill, NC, 1989. Ties the Czech and Slovak national movements to emigré politics in the United States, and after 1917, to the Czech Legion in Russia and ultimate intervention on behalf of an independent Czechoslovakia by President Wilson.

7.785 **Walworth**, A., *Wilson and His Peacemakers. American Diplomacy at the Paris Peace Conference, 1919*, New York, 1988.

7.786 **Wiegand**, W. A., *'An Active Instrument for Propaganda'. The American Public Library During World War I*, Westport, CT, 1989.

(c) AFTER VERSAILLES

7.787 **Alonso**, Harriet Hyman, *The Women's Peace Union and the Outlawry of War, 1921–1942*, Knoxville, TN, 1989.

7.788 **Bennett**, E. M., *Franklin D. Roosevelt and the Search for Security. American-Soviet Relations, 1933–1939*, Wilmington, DE, 1985. Examines how the World War I debt issue, State Department anti-communism, and a general isolationism helped derail the early years of a U.S.-Soviet rapprochement.

7.789 **Cole**, W. S., *Norway and the United States, 1905–1955. Two Democracies in Peace and War*, Ames, IA, 1989.

7.790 **Costigliola**, F., *Awkward Dominion. American Political, Economic, and Cultural Relations with Europe, 1919–1933*, Ithaca, NY, 1985. Examines the burst of American influence on postwar Europe.

7.791 **Dunne**, M., *The United States and the World Court, 1920–1935*, New York, 1988.

7.792 **Hall**, C., *Britain, America and Arms Control, 1921–1937*, New York, 1987.

7.793 **Jablon**, H., *Crossroads of Decision. The State Department and Foreign Policy, 1933–1937*, Lexington, KY, 1983. A critical view of the State Department's career diplomats and their shortcomings in the turbulent world of the 1930s.

7.794 **Kaufman**, R. G., *Arms Control during the Pre-Nuclear Era. The United States and Naval Limitation between the Two World Wars*, New York, 1990.

7.795 **Killen**, Linda, *The Russian Bureau. A Case Study in Wilsonian Diplomacy*, Lexington, KY, 1983. Uses a small federal agency directed to coordinate public and private business with the Soviet republic; its records show the Wilson Administration's thinking about future dealings with the U.S.S.R.

7.796 **Lentin**, A., *Lloyd George, Woodrow Wilson and the Guilt of Germany. An Essay in the Pre-History of Appeasement*, Baton Rouge, LA, 1985. Faults Lloyd George for insisting on a harsh treaty without the means of enforcing permanent German compliance and finds the world a loser for not having had Wilson's vision triumph at Versailles.

7.797 **Little**, D., *Malevolent Neutrality. The United States, Great Britain, and the Origins of the Spanish Civil War*, Ithaca, NY, 1985. Traces American hostility to the Spanish Republic during the Civil War to an earlier fear of the Spanish Left in the early 1930s.

7.798 **Margulies**, H. F., *The Mild Reservationists and the League of Nations Controversy in the Senate*, Columbia, MO, 1989.

7.799 **McKercher**, B. J. C., (ed.), *Anglo-American Relations in the 1920s. The Struggle for Supremacy*, Edmonton, ALB, 1990.

7.800 **Pease**, N., *Poland, the United States, and the Stabilization of Europe, 1919–1933*, New York, 1986. Covers the history of how Poland failed to win substantial American financing after the war.

7.801 **Schwabe**, K., translated by Rita and R. Kimber, *Woodrow Wilson, Revolutionary Germany, and Peacemaking, 1918–1919. Missionary Diplomacy and the Realities of Power*, Chapel Hill, NC, 1985. A thorough analysis of Wilson's policy toward the German republic and how that policy was received by Germans.

7.802 **Truscott**, L. K., *The Twilight of the U.S. Cavalry. Life in the Old Army, 1917–1942*, Lawrence, KS, 1989.

7.803 **Widenor**, W. C., *Henry Cabot Lodge and the Search for an American Foreign Policy*, Berkelely, CA, 1980.

(d) WORLD WAR II

7.804 **Bennett**, E. M., *Franklin D. Roosevelt and the Search for Victory. American-Soviet Relations, 1939–1945*, Wilmington, DE, 1990.

7.805 **Cole**, W. S., *Roosevelt and the Isolationists, 1932–1945*, Lincoln, NE, 1983.

7.806 **Dwyer**, T. R., *Strained Relations. Ireland at Peace and the USA at War, 1941–1945*, Totowa, NJ, 1988.

7.807 **Fussell**, P., *Wartime. Understanding and Behavior in the Second World War*, New York, 1989.

7.808 **Gregory**, R., *America 1941. A Nation at the Crossroads*, New York, 1988.

7.809 **Heinrichs**, W., *Threshold of War. Franklin D. Roosevelt and American Entry into World War II*, New York, 1988. A narrative that combines the story of Anglo-American cooperation in the Atlantic with the deterioration of U.S.-Japanese relations in the Pacific, leading to December, 1941.

7.810 **Hess**, G. R., *The United States at War, 1941–1945*, Arlington Heights, IL, 1986.

7.811 **Hilderbrand**, R.C., *Dumbarton Oaks. The Origins of the United Nations and the Search* *for Postwar Security*, Chapel Hill, NC, 1990. A consideration of the conference that preceded establishment of the U.N., the author finds some ground for believing in a postwar Anglo-American-Soviet entente, but that good intentions ran afoul over the fate of Poland.

7.812 **Jones**, V. C., *Manhattan. The Army and the Atomic Bomb*, Washington, DC, 1985.

7.813 **Kennett**, L. B., *A History of Strategic Bombing*, New York, 1982.

7.814 **Larrabee**, E., *Commander in Chief. Franklin Delano Roosevelt, His Lieutenants, and Their War*, New York, 1987. A volume full of praise for FDR's wartime leadership of the armed forces, and of the men who helped formulate American strategy.

7.815 **Peters**, G., *There's a War to be Won. The United States Army in World War II*, New York, 1991.

7.816 **Rock**, W. R., *Chamberlain and Roosevelt. British Foreign Policy and the United States, 1937–1940*, Columbus, OH, 1988. Reviews Anglo-American relations up to the spring of 1940 and finds fault chiefly with Chamberlain for his decision to ignore a possible American alliance.

7.817 **Schneider**, J. C., *Should America Go to War? The Debate over Foreign Policy in Chicago, 1939–1941*, Chapel Hill, NC, 1989.

7.818 **Sherry**, M. S., *The Rise of American Air Power. The Creation of Armageddon*, New Haven, CT, 1987.

7.819 **Shulman**, Holly Cowan, *The Voice of America. Propaganda and Democracy, 1941–1945*, Madison, WI, 1990.

7.820 **Soley**, L. C., *Radio Warfare. OSS and CIA Subversive Propaganda*, New York, 1989.

7.821 **Vander Meulen**, J. A., *The Politics of Aircraft. Building an American Military Industry*, Lawrence, KS, 1991.

7.822 **Willmott**, H.P., *The Great Crusade. A New Complete History of the Second World War*, New York, 1990. A comprehensive survey of both the European and Pacific wars with an emphasis on economic power as the decisive advantage for the Allied side.

7.823 **Wyman**, D. S., *The Abandonment of the Jews. America and the Holocaust, 1941–1945*, New York, 1984.

(i) WAR IN THE PACIFIC

7.824 **Barnhart**, M. A., *Japan Prepares for Total War. The Search for Economic Security, 1919–1941*, Ithaca, NY, 1987.

7.825 **Bartsch**, W. H., *Doomed at the Start. American Pursuit Pilots in the Philippines, 1941–1942*, College Station, TX, 1992. Tells the story of how the Army Air Force was quickly destroyed in the first month of the Philippines campaign.

7.826 **Conroy**, Hilary, and **Conroy**, W., (ed.), *Pearl Harbor Examined: Prologue to the Pacific War*, Honolulu, 1990. A collection of essays by leading diplomatic historians from the U.S. and Japan about the buildup to warfare. The anthology is noteworthy for the continuing disagreement between the two nations about the proper course of Japanese and American diplomacy in the late 1930s and early 1940s.

7.827 **Corbett**, P. S., *Quiet Passages. The Exchange of Civilians between the United States and Japan during the Second World War*, Kent, OH, 1987. A study of the "Special Division" of the State Department during the war that dealt with third countries representing American interests to Japan, including civilians interned and American prisoners of war.

7.828 **Dower**, J. W., *War Without Mercy. Race and Power in the Pacific War*, New York, 1986. Examines the savage nature of the fighting in the Pacific theater and finds that a high level of racism and xenophobia on both sides explains the nature of the conflict and the resulting atrocities.

7.829 **Ford**, D., *Flying Tigers. Claire Chennault and the American Volunteer Group*, Washington, DC, 1991.

7.830 **Frank**, R. B., *Guadacanal*, New York, 1990.

7.831 **Gailey**, H. A., *Bougainville, 1943–1945. The Forgotten Campaign*, Lexington, KY, 1991.

7.832 **Hays**, O., *Home from Siberia. The Secret Odysseys of Interned American Airmen in World War II*, College Station, TX, 1990. An account of American aviators who landed in the Soviet Union and were detained in camps until August 1945 out of respect for Soviet neutrality toward Japan.

7.833 **Iriye**, A., *Power and Culture. The Japanese-American War, 1941–1945*, Cambridge, MA, 1981. An attempt to use the tools of cultural anthropology to understand the wartime struggle between the U.S. and Japan, and finds a surprising agreement between the combatants on the goals of international relations.

7.834 **Iriye**, A., and **Cohen**, W., (ed.), *American, Chinese, and Japanese Perspectives on Wartime Asia, 1931–1949*, Wilmington, DE, 1990. A collection of essays by ten historians who met periodically in the 1980s to talk about the three nations and their parts in World War II, the Chinese Revolution, and the Cold War.

7.835 **Lauren**, P. G., (ed.), *The China Hands' Legacy. Ethics and Diplomacy*, Boulder, CO, 1987. A collection of essays by scholars and former diplomats about the dilemma of the State Department professionals who candidly reported the truth about the Kuomintang at the ultimate cost of their jobs.

7.836 **Leary**, W. M., (ed.), *We Shall Return. MacArthur's Commanders and the Defeat of Japan, 1942–1945*, Lexington, KY, 1988.

7.837 **Miller**, E. S., *War Plan Orange. The U.S. Strategy to Defeat Japan, 1897–1945*, Annapolis, MD, 1991. Shows how American military and naval planners foresaw the course of a Pacific war against Japan as early as 1912 and how the actual war closely followed that plan.

7.838 **Pearlman**, M., *To Make Democracy Safe for America. Patricians and Preparedness in the Progressive Era*, Urbana, IL, 1984. Traces the origins of the drive for universal male military training and shows how it was linked to a Progressive impulse to redefine national purpose.

7.839 **Rogers**, P. P., *The Good Years. MacArthur and Sutherland*, New York, 1990. The first of two volumes examining the wartime relationship up to 1943 of Douglas MacArthur and his chief of staff, as recalled by an enlisted man on the general's staff.

7.840 **Rogers**, P. P., *The Bitter Years. MacArthur and Sutherland*, New York, 1990.

7.841 **Sigal**, L. V., *Fighting to a Finish. The Politics of War Termination in the United States and Japan, 1945*, Ithaca, NY, 1988.

7.842 **Slackman**, M., *Target – Pearl Harbor*, Honolulu, 1990. The most up-to-date account of Japanese planning for the attack on Hawaii, and the carelessness on the part of American commanders in Washington and Honolulu in preparing for war.

7.843 **Spector**, R. H., *Eagle Against the Sun. The American War with Japan*, New York, 1985. A survey of the combined operations in the Pacific.

7.844 **Thorne**, C., *The Issue of War. States, Societies, and the Far Eastern Conflict of 1941–1945*, New York, 1985. A cultural and social history of the war in the Pacific told from the vantage point of all the combatants.

7.845 **Utley**, J. G., *Going to War with Japan, 1937–1941*, Knoxville, TN, 1985. A study critical of American diplomacy in its dealings with Japan.

(ii) THE EUROPEAN THEATER

7.846 **Gelb**, N., *Desperate Venture. The Story of Operation Torch, the Allied Invasion of North Africa*, New York, 1992.

7.847 **Gilbert**, M., *Auschwitz and the Allies*, New York, 1981.

7.848 **Hearden**, P. J., *Roosevelt Confronts Hitler. America's Entry into World War II*, Dekalb, IL, 1987.

7.849 **Hurtsfield**, J. G., *America and the French Nation, 1939–1945*, Chapel Hill, NC, 1986. Shows how Franklin Roosevelt himself directed a policy of working with the Vichy government and shunning the Gaullists until after D-Day.

7.850 **Levine**, A. J., *The Strategic Bombing of Germany, 1940–1945*, Westport, CT, 1992.

7.851 **McFarland**, S. L., and **Newton**, W. P., *To Command the Sky. The Battle for Air Superiority over Germany, 1942–1944*, Washington, DC, 1991.

(iii) THE HOME FRONT

7.852 **Anderson**, Karen, *Wartime Women. Sex Roles, Family Relations, and the Status of Women During World War II*, Westport, CT, 1981.

7.853 **Campbell**, D'Ann, *Women at War with America. Private Lives in a Patriotic Era*, Cambridge, MA, 1984.

7.854 **Hacker**, B. C., *The Dragon's Tail. Radiation Safety in the Manhattan Project, 1942–1946*, Berkeley, CA, 1987. Studies the precautions and occasional lack of precautions to safeguard exposure to radiation, including after the war in the early South Pacific tests.

7.855 **Jakeman**, R. J., *The Divided Skies. Establishing Segregated Flight Training at Tuskegee, Alabama, 1934–1942*, Tuscaloosa, AL, 1992.

7.856 **James**, T., *Exile Within. The Schooling of Japanese Americans, 1942–1945*,

Cambridge, MA, 1987. Tells the story of the federal effort to provide education to the 30,000 Japanese-American children interned during the war, both from the viewpoint of the War Relocation Authority, and from that of the camp inmates.

7.857 **Kesselman**, Amy, *Fleeting Opportunities. Women Shipyard Workers in Portland and Vancouver During World War II and Reconversion*, Albany, NY, 1990.

7.858 **Koppes**, C. R., and **Black**, G. D., *Hollywood Goes to War. How Politics, Profits and Propaganda Shaped World War II Movies*, New York, 1987. Story of the movie industry's cooperation with the Office of War Information over their mutual interests during wartime.

7.859 **Leff**, M. H., 'The politics of sacrifice on the American home front during World War II', *Journal of American History*, LXXVI, 1991, 1296–1318, Analyzes the political debate over who would have to curb customary behavior at home, i.e., "sacrifice".

7.860 **Lipstadt**, Deborah E., *Beyond Belief. The American Press and the Coming of the Holocaust, 1933–1945*, New York, 1986.

7.861 **Lowenstein**, Sharon R., *Token Refuge. The Story of the Jewish Refugee Shelter at Oswego, 1944–1946*, Bloomington, IN, 1986.

7.862 **Neusner**, J., *Stranger at Home. 'The Holocaust', Zionism, and American Judaism*, Chicago, 1981.

7.863 **Schneider**, J. G., *The Navy V-12 Program. Leadership for a Lifetime*, Boston, 1987. Details how the Navy recruited officer candidates into leading American colleges in wartime and then into active service.

7.864 **Stack**, J. F., *International Conflict in an American City. Boston's Irish, Italians, and Jews, 1935–1944*, Westport, CT, 1979. Considers the effects of international affairs on local politics in Boston.

The American empire

7.865 **Anderson**, I. H., *Aramco, the United States, and Saudia Arabia. A Study of the Dynamics of Foreign Oil Policy, 1933–1950*, Princeton, NJ, 1981.

7.866 **Blumenthal**, H., *Illusion and Reality in Franco-American Diplomacy, 1914–1945*, Baton Rouge, LA, 1986. Treats the major episodes of U.S.-French affairs in both wars and the period between the wars.

7.867 **Buckley**, T. H., and **Strong**, E. B., *American Foreign and National Security Policies, 1914–1945*, Knoxville, TN, 1987.

7.868 **Collin**, R. H., *Theodore Roosevelt, Culture, Diplomacy and Expansion. A New View of American Imperialism*, Baton Rouge, LA, 1985.

7.869 **Dobson**, J., *Reticent Expansionism. The Foreign Policy of William McKinley*, Pittsburgh, 1988.

7.870 **Graebner**, N. A., *America as a World Power. A Realist Appraisal from Wilson to Reagan*, Wilmington, DE, 1984. A critique of idealist foreign policy by a leading realist scholar.

7.871 **Lake**, D. A., *Power, Protection, and Free Trade. International Sources of U.S. Commercial Strategy, 1887–1939*, Ithaca, NY, 1988.

7.872 **Stoff**, M. B., *Oil, War and American Security. The Search for a National Policy on Foreign Oil, 1941–1947*, New Haven, CT, 1980.

7.873 **Turk**, R. W., *The Ambiguous Relationship. Theodore Roosevelt and Alfred Thayer Mahan*, Westport, CT, 1987. Highlights the differences in views between the naval theorist and the policy-maker, and finds that Roosevelt was far more belligerent in his use and understanding of naval power than Mahan.

7.874 **Weintraub**, S., *A Marriage of Convenience. Relationships Between Mexico and the United States*, New York, 1990.

7.875 **Woods**, R. B., *A Changing of the Guard. Anglo-American Relations, 1941–1946*, Chapel Hill, NC, 1990. An analysis of U.S.-British economic relations that faults the Americans for driving such a hard bargain against Great Britain in such areas as currency, trade, and Lend-Lease, and for not recognizing that the principal postwar menace was Stalinism rather than colonialism.

(a) THE U.S. AND THE PACIFIC

7.876 **Brands**, H. W., *Bound to Empire. The United States and the Philippines*, New York, 1992.

7.877 **Darby**, P., *Three Faces of Imperialism. British and American Approaches to Asia and Africa, 1870–1970*, New Haven, CT, 1987. Considers the American empire as a successor to the British one, and evaluates it in terms of its own geopolitical motivation, moral imperative, and economic interest, with the finding that economic motivation was least important.

7.878 **Karnow**, S., *In Our Image. America's Empire in the Philippines*, New York, 1989.

7.879 **Noble**, D. L., *The Eagle and the Dragon. The United States Military in China, 1901–1937*, Westport, CT, 1990. A social history of garrison life for American soldiers and sailors in China.

7.880 **Robert**, Priscilla, (ed.), *Sino-American Relations since 1900*, Hong Kong, 1991.

7.881 **Taylor**, Sandra C., *Advocate of Understanding. Sidney Gulick and the Search for Peace with Japan*, Kent, OH, 1984. Contrasts the career of missionary Gulick and other Americans who lobbied for Japan against the more numerous Americans who worked in China.

7.882 **Walker**, W. O., *Opium and Foreign Policy. The Anglo-American Search for Order in Asia, 1912–1954*, Chapel Hill, NC, 1991.

(b) THE CARIBBEAN

7.883 **Baptiste**, F. A., *War, Cooperation, and Conflict. The European Possessions in the Caribbean, 1939–1945*, Westport, CT, 1988.

7.884 **Benjamin**, J. R., *The United States and the Origins of the Cuban Revolution. An Empire of Liberty in an Age of National Liberation*, Princeton, NJ, 1990.

7.885 **Collin**, R. H., *Theodore Roosevelt's Caribbean. The Panama Canal, the Monroe Doctrine, and the Latin American Context*, Baton Rouge, LA, 1990. A spirited defense of American imperial expansion in the Roosevelt Administration, concluding with the creation of a Panama under American control.

7.886 **Perez**, L. A., *Cuba and the United States. Ties of Singular Intimacy*, Athens, GA, 1990.

7.887 **Plummer**, Brenda Gayle, *Haiti and the Great Powers, 1902–1915*, Baton Rouge, LA, 1988.

7.888 **Yerxa**, D. A., *Admirals and Empire. The United States Navy and the Caribbean, 1898–1945*, Columbia, SC, 1991.

(c) LATIN AMERICA

7.889 **Hall**, Linda B., *Revolution on the Border. The United States and Mexico, 1910–1920*, Albuquerque, NM, 1988.

7.890 **Krenn**, M. L., *U.S. Policy toward Economic Nationalism in Latin America, 1917–1929*, Wilmington, DE, 1990. Finds the U.S. was consistently hostile to national attempts to regulate American capital from World War I onward.

7.891 **Lael**, R. L., *Arrogant Diplomacy. U.S. Policy toward Colombia, 1903–1922*, Wilmington, DE, 1987. The arrogance stemmed from the American role in fostering the breakaway of Panama, and the subsequent construction of the canal.

7.892 **Leonard**, T. M., *Central America and the United States. The Search for Stability*, Athens, GA, 1991.

7.893 **Musicant**, I., *The Banana Wars. A History of United States Military Intervention in Latin America from the Spanish-American War to the Invasion of Panama*, New York, 1990. Concentrates on the assorted U.S. military interventions up to 1934 with postscripts on Grenada and Panama.

8

THE COLD WAR AND ITS CONTRADICTIONS, 1945–1992

GENERAL

8.1 **Blum**, J. M., *Years of Discord. American Politics and Society, 1961–1974*, New York, 1991.

8.2 **Boyer**, P., *By The Bomb's Early Light. American Thought and Culture at the Dawn of the Atomic Age*, New York, 1985. A survey of the impact of the atomic bomb on American life.

8.3 **Brookeman**, C., *American Culture and Society Since the 1930s*, New York, 1984.

8.4 **Brown**, T., *JFK, History of an Image*, Bloomington, IN, 1988.

8.5 **Carter**, P. A., *Another Part of the Fifties*, New York, 1983. The author tackles the fifties, as he has other decades, with an iconoclastic view; he finds more creativity and ferment than other historians.

8.6 **Carter**, P. A., *Politics, Religion, and Rockets. Essays in Twentieth Century American History*, Tucson, AZ, 1991.

8.7 **Chafe**, W. H., *America Since 1945*, Washington, DC, 1990.

8.8 **Chalmers**, D., *And the Crooked Places Made Straight. The Struggle for Social Change in the 1960s*, Baltimore, 1991.

8.9 **Daniel**, P., *Standing at the Crossroads. Southern Life in the Twentieth Century*, New York, 1986.

8.10 **Diggins**, J. P., *The Proud Decades. America in War and Peace, 1941–1960*, New York, 1988. A survey of the war years and the Cold War struggles at home over the New Deal legacy.

8.11 **Graebner**, W., *The Age of Doubt. American Thought and Culture in the 1940s*, Boston, 1991.

8.12 **Hollander**, P., *Anti-Americanism. Critiques at Home and Abroad, 1965–1990*, New York, 1992.

8.13 **Inglis**, F., *The Cruel Peace. Everyday Life in the Cold War*, New York, 1991.

8.14 **Kapstein**, E. B., *The Insecure Alliance. Energy Crises and Western Politics since 1944*, New York, 1990. A synthesis of world politics since World War II that places the onus for rise and fall of American dominance on the direct control of petroleum.

8.15 **Mayo**, J. M., *War Memorials as Political Landscape. The American Experience and Beyond*, New York, 1988. A consideration of the intersection of politics and art, particularly in the case of the Vietnam Memorial.

8.16 **McQuaid**, K., *The Anxious Years. America in the Vietnam-Watergate Era*, New York, 1989. A survey of the 1960s and early 1970s that is explicitly critical of political leaders for a general crisis of the nation.

8.17 **Merelman**, R. M., *Partial Visions. Culture and Politics in Britain, Canada, and the United States*, Madison, WI, 1991.

8.18 **O'Neill**, W. L., *American High. The Years of Confidence, 1945–1960*, New York, 1987. Finds much worthy of praise in the 1950s as a necessary prelude to the opening of American society in the following decade.

8.19 **Schaller**, M., *Reckoning with Reagan. America and Its President in the 1980s*,

New York, 1992.

8.20 Schulzinger, R. D., *American Diplomacy in the Twentieth Century*, New York, 1990. The second edition of an influential survey.

8.21 Shaw, M., (ed.), *The Modern Presidency. From Roosevelt to Reagan*, New York, 1987. A look at American political leadership by a collection of British scholars.

8.22 Ungar, S., *The Rise and Fall of Nuclearism. Fear and Faith as Determinants of the Arms Race*, University Park, PA, 1992.

8.23 Whitfield, S. J., *The Culture of the Cold War*, Baltimore, 1991. A synthesis of the era with a special focus on Hollywood, both the blacklist, and the film output.

8.24 Yergin, D., *The Prize. The Epic Quest for Oil, Money and Power*, New York, 1990. A history of the oil business in the twentieth century, especially strong on the central place of oil and diplomacy since World War II.

GUIDES TO SOURCES

Primary sources

8.25 Boyle, P. G., (ed.), *The Churchill-Eisenhower Correspondence, 1953–1955*, Chapel Hill, NC, 1990.

8.26 Carson, C., (ed.), *Malcolm X. The FBI File*, New York, 1991. Reproduces the original documents from the released FBI files; particular coverage is on Malcolm's last year of life when he broke with the Nation of Islam.

8.27 Carson, C., (ed.), *The Papers of Martin Luther King, Jr.*, Berkeley, CA, 1992. Volume one of this series appeared in 1992. See also the collection of documents compiled by David Garrow.

8.28 Galambos, L., *et al.*, (ed.), *The Papers of Dwight David Eisenhower*, Baltimore, 1970– .

8.29 Garrow, D. J., *Martin Luther King, Jr. and the Civil Rights Movement*, Brooklyn, NY, 1989. An eighteen volume set; seven volumes consist of republished secondary source writings on King and the movement, while the remaining volumes reproduce contemporary documents.

8.30 Glennon, J. P., *et al.*, (ed.), *Foreign Relations of the United States*, Washington, DC, 1989. Massive publishing program carried out by the State Department, but years behind on declassifying Cold War materials of the 1950s.

8.31 Lehrack, O. J., (ed.), *No Shining Armor. The Marines at War in Vietnam. An Oral History*, Lawrence, KS, 1992.

8.32 Oudes, B., (ed.), *From: The President. Richard Nixon's Secret Files*, New York, 1989. Presidential papers sealed after Nixon's resignation now made public over his repeated objections, these papers confirm what is already known about Nixon's obsession with real and imagined enemies.

8.33 Smith, J. E., (ed.), *The Papers of General Lucius D. Clay*, Bloomington, IN, 1974. A two volume set that covers Clay's years as military governor of the U.S. zone in occupied Germany.

Atlases, bibliographies, and encyclopedias

8.34 Addis, Patricia K., *Through a Woman's I. An Annotated Bibliography of American Women's Autobiographical Writings, 1946–1976*, Metuchen, NJ, 1983.

8.35 Black, J. L., *Origins, Evolution, and Nature of the Cold War. An Annotated Bibliographic Guide*, Santa Barbara, CA, 1986.

8.36 Blackstock, P. W., *Intelligence, Espionage, Counterespionage, and Covert Operations. A Guide to Information Sources*, Detroit, 1978.

8.37 Bohananon, R. D., *Dwight D. Eisenhower. A Selected Bibliography of Periodical and Dissertation Literature*, Abilene, KS, 1981.

8.38 Briscoe, Mary Louise, *American Autobiography, 1945–1980. A Bibliography*, Madison, WI, 1982.

8.39 Burns, R. D., (ed.), *The Wars in Vietnam, Cambodia, and Laos, 1945–1982. A Bibliographic Guide*, Santa Barbara, CA, 1983.

8.40 Burns, R. D., *Harry S. Truman. A Bibliography of His Times and Presidency*, Wilmington, DE, 1984.

8.41 Burns, R. D., *Arms Control and Disarmament. A Bibliography*, Santa Barbara, CA, 1977.

8.42 Burt, R., *Congressional Hearings on American Defense Policy, 1947–1971. An*

Annotated Bibliography, Lawrence, KS, 1974.

8.43 **Casper**, D. E., *Richard Nixon. A Bibliographic Exploration*, New York, 1988.

8.44 **Cordasco**, F., *The New American Immigration. Evolving Patterns of Legal and Illegal Emigration. A Bibliography of Selected References*, New York, 1987.

8.45 **Danky**, J. P., (ed.), *Index to Wisconsin Native American Periodicals, 1897–1981*, Westport, CT, 1983. Strongest on newspapers that were published during the "Red Power" era of the 1960s and 1970s.

8.46 **Davis**, L. G., *Malcolm X. A Selected Bibliography*, Westport, CT, 1984.

8.47 **Feinberg**, R., *The Equal Rights Amendment. An Annotated Bibliography of the Isssues, 1976–1985*, New York, 1986.

8.48 **Guth**, D. J., and **Wrone**, D. R., *The Assassination of John F. Kennedy. A Comprehensive Historical and Legal Bibliography*, Westport, CT, 1980.

8.49 **Jackson**, Rebecca, *The 1960s. An Annotated Bibliography of Social and Political Movements*, Westport, CT, 1992. Lists more than a thousand entries, both contemporary and retrospective.

8.50 **Lankevich**, G. J., (ed.), *Gerald R. Ford, 1913– . Chronology, Documents, Bibliographical Aids*, Dobbs Ferry, NY, 1977.

8.51 **Lobb**, M. L., *Native American Youth and Alcohol. An Annotated Bibliography*, New York, 1989.

8.52 **MacCorkle**, Lyn, *Cubans in the United States. A Bibliography for Research in the Social and Behavioral Sciences, 1960–1983*, Westport, CT, 1984.

8.53 **McFarland**, K. D., *The Korean War. An Annotated Bibliography*, New York, 1986.

8.54 **Menendez**, A. J., *School Prayer and Other Religious Issues in American Public Education. A Bibliography*, New York, 1985.

8.55 **Olson**, J. S., (ed.), *Dictionary of the Vietnam War*, New York, 1988.

8.56 **Parish**, D. W., *Changes in American Society, 1960–1978. An Annotated Bibliography of Offical Government Publications*, Metuchen, NJ, 1980.

8.57 **Peake**, L. A., *The United States in the Vietnam War, 1954–1975. A Selected, Annotated Bibliography*, New York, 1986.

8.58 **Pyatt**, S. E., *Martin Luther King, Jr. An Annotated Bibliography*, New York, 1986.

8.59 **Sicherman**, Barbara, and **Green**, C. H., (ed.), *Notable American Women. The Modern Period. A Bibliographical Directory*, Cambridge, MA, 1980.

8.60 **Smith**, M. J., (ed.), *Watergate. An Annotated Bibliography of Sources in English, 1972–1982*, Metuchen, NJ, 1983.

8.61 **Stapleton**, M. L., *The Truman and Eisenhower Years, 1945–1960. A Selective Bibliography*, Metuchen, NJ, 1973.

8.62 **Sublette**, J. R., *J. D. Salinger. An Annotated Bibliography*, New York, 1984.

Historiography

8.63 **Bender**, T., 'Wholes and parts: the need for synthesis in American history', *Journal of American History*, LXXIII, 1986, 120–136. Discusses synthesis in American history.

8.64 **Berger**, M. T., 'The limits of power and the lessons of history: North American neo-liberalism, and the U.S. crisis of empire in Central America', *Australasian Journal of American Studies*, IX, 1990, 57–69.

8.65 **Berthoff**, R., 'Peasants and artisans, puritans and republicans: personal liberty and communal equality in American history', *Journal of American History*, LXIX, 1982, 579–598. Discusses the ebb and flow of republican feeling throughout U.S. history.

8.66 **Chambers**, C. A., 'Toward a redefinition of welfare history', *Journal of American History*, LXXIII, 1986, 407–433. Looks at welfare history and writes about its importance and why it should be studied.

8.67 **Cohen**, S., 'American education. The metropolitan experience', *Historical Studies in Education*, I, 1989, 307–326. Reviews the opus of education historian Lawrence Cremin.

8.68 **Degler**, C. N., 'Remaking American history', *Journal of American History*, XLVII, 1980, 7–25. Discussion of the changes that have occurred in the field of American history since World War II.

8.69 **Ebner**, M. H., 'Urban history: retrospect and prospect', *Journal of American History*, LXVIII, 1981, 69–84. Discusses urban history, its rise and its importance.

8.70 **Fry**, M., (ed.), *History, the White House and the Kremlin. Statesmen as Historians*, 1991. A set of essays that collectively shows that history is more likely to be pressed into the service of existing policies and ideologies than it is to be studied with a fresh eye.

8.71 **Gleason**, P., 'Identifying identity: a semantic history', *Journal of American History*, LXIX, 1982, 910–931. Analyzes the history of the word "identity".

8.72 **Harding**, H., and **Ming**, Y., (ed.), *Sino-American Relations, 1945–1955. A Joint Reassessment of a Critical Decade*, Wilmington, DE, 1989. Published anthology of a conference of U.S. and Chinese scholars on the history of U.S. involvement in the Chinese Revolution and the onset of the Cold War.

8.73 **Hollinger**, D. A., The problem of pragmatism in American history', *Journal of American History*, LXVII, 1980, 88–107. Analyzes pragmatism and its pros and cons in American history.

8.74 **Hounshell**, D. A., 'Commentary. On the discipline of the history of American technology', *Journal of American History*, LXVII, 1981, 854–865. Discusses the rise and importance of the history of American technology.

8.75 **Isserman**, M., 'The not-so-dark and bloody ground. New works on the 1960s', *American Historical Review*, XCIV, 1989, 990–1010. Reviews books on and about the New Left and its enduring impact.

8.76 **Jervis**, R., 'The military history of the cold war', *Diplomatic History*, XV, 1991, 91–113. Reviews the recent literature on the arms race.

8.77 **Kiernan**, B., 'The Vietnam War. Alternative endings', *American Historical Review*, XCVII, 1992, 1118–1137. A review article of some of the recent secondary literature on American involvement in the war.

8.78 **Lerner**, Gerda, 'The necessity of history and the professional historian', *Journal of American History*, LXIX, 1982, 7–20. Calls for the pursuance of history and the expanding role of the professional historian.

8.79 **Leuchtenburg**, W. E., 'The pertinence of political history: reflections on the significance of the state in America', *Journal of American History*, LXXIII, 1986, 585–600. A call for the study of political history since it has been neglected as of late.

8.80 **Matthews**, F., 'Hobbesian populism. Interpretive paradigms and moral vision in American historiography', *Journal of American History*, LXXII, 1985, 92–115. Takes a look at the state of recent American history and historiography.

8.81 **May**, L., (ed.), *Recasting America. Culture and Politics in the Age of Cold War*, Chicago, 1989. A collection of essays on a variety of topics about the 1950s.

8.82 **Mohl**, R. A., 'Towards a history of Cuban exiles in the United States', *Journal of American Ethnic History*, X, 1991, 62–65.

8.83 **Neustadt**, R. E., and **May**, E. R., *Thinking in Time. The Uses of History for Decision-Makers*, New York, 1986. Ruminations from two academics who have periodically advised presidents for more than three decades.

8.84 **Noble**, D. W., *The End of American History. Democracy, Capitalism, and the Metaphor of Two Worlds in Anglo-American Historical Writing, 1880–1980*, Minneapolis, MN, 1985.

8.85 **Okroi**, L. J., *Galbraith, Harrington, Heilbroner. Economics and Dissent in an Age of Optimism*, Princeton, NJ, 1988.

8.86 **Pious**, R. M., 'Prerogative power and the Reagan presidency: a review essay', *Political Science Quarterly*, CVI, 1991, 499–510. Reviews the writings on the Reagan years by journalists and scholars and focuses on the delegation of power by Reagan to various associates.

8.87 **Platt**, A. M., *E. Franklin Frazier Reconsidered*, New Brunswick, NJ, 1991. Sympathetic biography of the black social scientist that defends his views on the history and twentieth century dilemma of the black family.

8.88 **Rosenstone**, R. A., 'History in images/history in words. Reflections on the possibility of really putting history onto film', *American Historical Review*, XCIII, 1988, 1173–1185. Introduces an AHR Forum about the relationship of the historian to film.

8.89 **West**, P., 'Interpreting the Korean War', *American Historical Review*, XCIV, 1989, 878–896. Reviews the recent literature on the origins and outcome of the Korean War and describes an emerging postrevisionist synthesis.

8.90 **White**, H., 'Historiography and historiophoty', *American Historical Review*, XCIII, 1988, 1193–1199. Part of an AHR Forum on the relationship of film and history.

8.91 **Wiener**, J. M., 'Radical historians and the crisis in American history, 1959–1980', *Journal of American History*, LXXVI, 1989, 399–434. Wiener looks at radical history, its origins, rise, and place in today's historical profession.

8.92 **Williams**, J. A., 'Public history and local history', *Public Historian*, XI, 1989, 103–111.

BIOGRAPHY

8.93 **Abrahamson**, R., *Spanning the Century. The Life of W. Averell Harriman*, New York, 1992. Biography of the railroad heir, diplomat, and Democratic Party politician.

8.94 **Ambrose**, S. E., *Eisenhower. The President*, New York, 1984. The second volume of a biography that is part of a general scholarly reappraisal and upgrading of Ike and his legacy.

8.95 **Ambrose**, S. E., *Nixon. The Education of a Politician, 1913–1962*, New York, 1987. The first of a three-volume work that characterizes Nixon as the product of the new Southern California, a man committed to the free enterprise system, a foe of the New Deal, and a skillful politician who rode the anti-communist crusade to the vice presidency.

8.96 **Ambrose**, S. E., *Nixon. The Triumph of a Politician, 1962–1972*, New York, 1989. This second volume of the author's trilogy on Nixon stresses his comeback from political oblivion after 1962 and his accomplishments in his first presidential term.

8.97 **Ashmore**, H. S., *Unseasonable Truths. The Life of Robert Maynard Hutchins*, Boston, 1989. A biography of the educator-reformer that covers his presidency at the University of Chicago and his leadership of various private philanthropies.

8.98 **Brinkley**, D., *Dean Acheson. The Cold War Years, 1953–1971*, New Haven, CT, 1992. A biography of the diplomat's public career after he left the State Department, particularly strong on Acheson's influence on Kennedy Administration thinking.

8.99 **Callahan**, D., *Dangerous Capabilities. Paul Nitze and the Cold War*, New York, 1990. A biography of the Wall Street banker and his role in formulating American policy toward the Soviet Union.

8.100 **Currey**, C. B., *Edward Lansdale. The Unquiet American*, Boston, 1988. Biography of the special warfare officer who was active in Vietnam before the escalation into the American-dominated war.

8.101 **Dallek**, R., *Lone Star Rising. Lyndon Johnson and his Times, 1908–1960*, New York, 1991. The first of two planned volumes on the life of Johnson, this volume carries the story through LBJ's career in the Senate and his nomination to run for the vice presidency in 1960. The author is notably more sympathetic to his subject than Caro.

8.102 **Dierenfield**, B. J., *Keeper of the Rules. Congressman Howard B. Smith of Virginia*, Charlottesville, VA, 1987.

8.103 **Dzuback**, Mary Ann, *Robert M. Hutchins. Portrait of an Educator*, Chicago, 1991. Biography of the University of Chicago president who shook up academe with a host of unusual ideas.

8.104 **Fite**, G. C., *Richard B. Russell, Jr., Senator from Georgia*, Chapel Hill, NC, 1991. Biography of the powerful Georgia Democrat and longtime chairman of the Senate Agriculture Committee.

8.105 **Flynn**, G. Q., *Lewis B. Hershey. Mr. Selective Service*, Chapel Hill, NC, 1985. A biography of the general who administered the draft from World War II through the Vietnam War, and who helped fashion a system that accommodated political interests until the inequities apparent in the 1960s led to its abolition.

8.106 **Fox**, R. W., *Reinhold Niebuhr. A Biography*, New York, 1985.

8.107 **Frazer**, W., *Power and Ideas. Milton Friedman and the Big U-Turn*, Gainesville, FL, 1988. A two volume biography of the libertarian economist and his influence on conservative thought and politics.

8.108 **Freyer**, T. A., *Hugo L. Black and the Dilemma of American Liberalism*, Glenview, IL, 1990. A biography of the Alabamian on the Supreme Court that links his policy views with the social history of the New South.

8.109 **Garrow**, D. J., *Bearing the Cross. Martin Luther King, Jr. and the Southern Christian Leadership Conference*, New York, 1986. A lengthy biography of King that grounds his leadership in the southern black church.

8.110 **Goldman**, R., *Thurgood Marshall. Justice for All*, New York, 1992. Biography of the first black justice on the Supreme Court.

8.111 **Gosnell**, H. F., *Truman's Crises. A Political Biography of Harry S. Truman*, Westport, CT, 1980.

8.112 **Hamilton**, C. V., *Adam Clayton Powell, Jr. The Political Biography of an American Dilemma*, New York, 1991. Biography of the Harlem congressman that shows him to have been a complex mix of public bluster and private expediency.

8.113 **Henggeler**, P. A., *In His Steps. Lyndon Johnson and the Kennedy Mystique*, Chicago, 1991.

8.114 **Hiss**, A., *Recollections of a Life*, New York, 1988. Autobiography involving the most celebrated case of the postwar spy scare, with Hiss still insisting that he was framed.

8.115 **Hixson**, W. L., *George Kennan. Cold War Iconoclast*, New York, 1989. A survey of the public career of the State Department official credited with originating the Cold War policy of "containment".

8.116 **Hoopes**, T., and **Brinkley**, D., *Driven Patriot. The Life and Times of James Forrestal*, New York, 1992.

8.117 **James**, D. C., *The Years of MacArthur. Triumph and Disaster, 1945–1964*, Boston, 1985. The third and final volume of the author's biography.

8.118 **Jenkins**, R., *Truman*, New York, 1986. The Labour statesman appraises the Truman presidency and lauds him for his foreign policy, particularly the Marshall Plan to rebuild Europe.

8.119 **Jezer**, M., *Abbie Hoffman. American Rebel*, New Brunswick, NJ, 1992. Biography of the Yippie leader that follows his life through the Movement and the drug culture.

8.120 **Kalman**, Laura, *Abe Fortas. A Biography*, New Haven, CT, 1990. Biography of the lawyer-jurist and confidant of Lyndon Johnson.

8.121 **Kurtz**, M. L., and **Peoples**, M. D., *Earl K. Long. The Saga of Uncle Earl and Louisiana Politics*, Baton Rouge, LA, 1990.

8.122 **McCullough**, D., *Truman*, New York, 1992. Massive biography of the Man from Missouri that finds him correct on nearly every decision of his presidency.

8.123 **McKeever**, P., *Adlai Stevenson. His Life and Legacy*, New York, 1989.

8.124 **Meilinger**, P. S., *Hoyt S. Vandenberg. The Life of a General*, Bloomington, IN, 1989.

A biography of the first chief of staff of the newly independent Air Force, and how he helped shape the service into a leading element of Cold War strategy.

8.125 **Morris**, R., *Richard Milhous Nixon. The Rise of an American Politician*, New York, 1990. A biography of Nixon up to his election as vice president in 1952, written by a former staff assistant who stresses his subject's ceaseless striving for fame and honor.

8.126 **Newman**, R. P., *The Cold War Romance of Lillian Hellman and John Melby*, Chapel Hill, NC, 1989. Traces the love affair of the writer and diplomat from wartime Moscow up through Hellman's subpoena to testify before the House Un-American Activities Committee in 1952.

8.127 **Nunnelly**, W. A., *Bull Connor*, Tuscaloosa, AL, 1991. A biography of the Birmingham, Alabama police chief and his rise to power as a dedicated segregationist.

8.128 **Pach**, C. J., *The Presidency of Dwight D. Eisenhower*, Lawrence, KS, 1991. Agrees with other recent biographers that Ike was a shrewd occupant of the Oval Office, but differs in finding few accomplishments at home or abroad during his eight years in office.

8.129 **Parmet**, H., *Richard Nixon and his America*, Boston, 1990. A biography of Nixon that places him at the center of a decades-long effort to overturn the New Deal, at home and abroad.

8.130 **Pemberton**, W. E., *Harry S. Truman. Fair Dealer and Cold Warrior*, Boston, 1989. Helpful survey of Truman's years in the White House.

8.131 **Philipson**, Ilene, *Ethel Rosenberg. Beyond the Myths*, New York, 1988. An account of the accused 'atom spy' that sets her within the sometimes overlapping worlds of New York Jewish life and New York Communist Party politics.

8.132 **Pogue**, F. C., *George C. Marshall. Statesman, 1945–1959*, New York, 1987. The final part of the author's biographical series, concentrating on Marshall's role in formulating the containment policy and the working out of an American commitment to Europe through the Marshall Plan.

8.133 **Pohl**, Frances K., *Ben Shahn. New Deal Artist in a Cold War Climate, 1947–1954*, Austin, TX, 1989.

8.134 **Reeves**, T. C., *A Question of Character. A*

Life of John F. Kennedy, New York, 1991.
Evaluates Kennedy in the light of his
personal character and finds the late
president very much wanting and very
much under the control of his domineering
father, Joseph P. Kennedy.

8.135 **Rivlin**, B., (ed.), *Ralph Bunche. The Man
and His Times*, New York, 1990. A
biography of the African-American
diplomat that gives due attention to his
career as a scholar.

8.136 **Rogin**, M. P., *Ronald Reagan, the Movie,
and Other Episodes in Political Demonology*,
Berkeley, CA, 1987. Reviews Reagan's
film and political career and finds the link
between the two in the character that
Reagan portrayed in *King's Row*.

8.137 **Rummel**, R. W., *Howard Hughes and
TWA*, Washington, DC, 1991. Covers the
years from 1939 to 1960 when the
billionaire controlled the airline, written by
a former TWA employee with inside
knowledge of the corporation and the man.

8.138 **Salmond**, J. A., *The Conscience of a
Lawyer. Clifford J. Durr and American Civil
Liberties, 1899–1975*, Tuscaloosa, AL,
1990. An Australian historian looks at the
Alabama lawyer who defended many
communists and radicals in the
McCarthyite Era purges.

8.139 **Schapsmeier**, E. L., and **Schapsmeier**, F.
H., *Gerald R. Ford's Date with Destiny. A
Political Biography*, New York, 1989.

8.140 **Scobie**, Ingrid Winther, *Center Stage.
Helen Gahagan Douglas, A Life*, New
York, 1992. A biography of the actress and
politician who was defeated in a nasty 1950
Senate race in California by Richard
Nixon.

8.141 **Simon**, J. F., *Independent Journey. The
Life of William O. Douglas*, New York,
1980. Biography of the New Dealer and
Supreme Court Justice.

8.142 **Steel**, R., *Walter Lippman and the American
Century*, Boston, 1980.

8.143 **Stoler**, M. A., *George C. Marshall. Soldier-
Statesman of the American Century*, Boston,
1989.

8.144 **Talbott**, S., *The Master of the Game. Paul
Nitze and the Nuclear Peace*, New York,
1988.

8.145 **Wicker**, T., *One of Us. Richard Nixon and
the American Dream*, New York, 1991.
Links Nixon's political career to his
difficult and unhappy childhood and finds
that his emotional drive led to many

effective accomplishments before his
downfall in the Watergate affair.

DEMOGRAPHY, FAMILY, AND HEALTH

8.146 **Byerly**, G., *The Baby Boom. A Selective
Annotated Bibliography*, Lexington, MA,
1985.

8.147 **Coontz**, Stephanie, *The Way We Never
Were. American Families and the Nostalgia
Trap*, New York, 1992. A spirited attack
on the conservative yearning for a return to
an imagined golden age of the family.

8.148 **Cutright**, P., and **Smith**, H. L., 'Declining
family size and the number of children in
poor families in the United States:
1964–1983', *Social Science Research*, XV,
1986, 256–288.

8.149 **Duberman**, M. B., *About Time. Exploring
the Gay Past*, New York, 1986.

8.150 **Fishman**, Sylvia Barack, 'The changing
American Jewish family in the 80s',
Contemporary Jewry, IX, 1988, 1–33.

8.151 **Fox**, D. M., *Health Policies, Health
Politics. The British and American
Experience, 1911–1965*, Princeton, NJ,
1986. Finds surprising similarities between
the health care systems of the two
countries, despite the obvious gap
separating private health care in the U.S.
and National Health Service in Great
Britain; the chief similarity was the
crowning of the scientific hospital as the
center of health care distribution.

8.152 **Graebner**, W., *Coming of Age in Buffalo.
Youth and Authority in the Postwar Era*,
Philadelphia, 1990.

8.153 **Grob**, G. N., *From Asylum to Community.
Mental Health Policy in Modern America*,
Princeton, NJ, 1991. Continues the
author's history of mental health treatment
with a look at the postwar period,
particularly deinstitutionalization after
1963.

8.154 **Hollingsworth**, J. R., *A Political Economy
of Medicine. Great Britain and the United
States*, Baltimore, 1986. A sociological
perspective on the development of
twentieth century health care systems in

the two countries that stresses class as the reason Britain has universal access and the United States has limited, private access to health care.

8.155 **Liachowitz**, Claire H., *Disability as a Social Construct. Legislative Roots*, Philadelphia, 1988.

8.156 **May**, Elaine Tyler, *Homeward Bound. American Families in the Cold War Era*, New York, 1988. Finds that the distinctive features of postwar family life, such as the baby boom and domesticity for women, were in part responses to the conformity demanded of all Americans in the battle against communism.

8.157 **Modell**, J., *Into One's Own. From Youth to Adulthood in the United States, 1920–1975*, Berkeley, CA, 1989.

8.158 **Patterson**, J. T., *The Dread Disease. Cancer and Modern American Culture*, Cambridge, MA, 1987. A history of the origins and conduct of the "war on cancer" that shows the tensions between a large medical bureaucracy and a counter-culture looking elsewhere for miracle cures.

8.159 **Riley**, Glenda, *Divorce. An American Tradition*, New York, 1991. A survey of divorce law and custom with a focus on the twentieth century.

8.160 **Rosewater**, Ann, 'Child and family trends: beyond the numbers', *Proceedings of the Academy of Political Science*, XXXVII, 1989, 4–19.

8.161 **Serow**, W. J., *Population Aging in the United States*, New York, 1990.

8.162 **Skolnick**, Arlene S., *Embattled Paradise. The American Family in an Age of Uncertainty*, New York, 1991. Looks at the changes in the postwar family.

8.163 **Smith**, Jane S., *Patenting the Sun. Polio and the Salk Vaccine*, New York, 1990. A history of the scientific quest for a polio cure, grounded in a cultural history of America in the Cold War years.

8.164 **Thompson**, Maxine Seaborn, and **Ensminger**, Margaret E., 'Psychological well-being among mothers with school age children. Evolving family structures', *Social Forces*, LXVII, 1989, 715–730. A study of black single parent mothers in Chicago and the stresses of child-raising in the 1960s and 1970s.

8.165 **Tyor**, P. L., and **Bell**, L. V., *Caring for the Retarded in America. A History*, Westport, CT, 1984. Concentrates on the twentieth century and the movement away from mass institutionalization of the mentally retarded toward decentralized care and treatment.

8.166 **Van Horn**, Susan Householder, *Women, Work, and Fertility, 1900–1986*, New York, 1988.

SOCIAL RELATIONS

Class and community

8.167 **Baritz**, L., *The Good Life. The Meaning of Success for the American Middle Class*, New York, 1989. A jeremiad against modern American middle-class culture, particularly its feminization within the family.

8.168 **Berkowitz**, E. D., *America's Welfare State. From Roosevelt to Reagan*, Baltimore, 1992.

8.169 **Haveman**, R. H., *Poverty Policy and Poverty Research. The Great Society and the Social Sciences*, Madison, WI, 1987. Examines the impact of the War on Poverty on social scientists undertaking new research on the poor.

8.170 **Katznelson**, I., *City Trenches. Urban Politics and the Patterning of Class in America*, New York, 1981.

8.171 **Levine**, D., *Poverty and Policy. The Growth of the American Welfare State in International Comparison*, New Brunswick, NJ, 1989. Contrasts the development of social programs in the U.S. to those in the U.K., Germany, and Denmark, and finds the tardiness in American development due to the persistence of states' rights.

8.172 **Silver**, H., and **Silver**, Pamela, *An Educational War on Poverty. American and British Policy-Making, 1960–1980*, New York, 1991. Contrasts the U.S. movement to fight poverty through the Head Start program with subsequent British efforts along similar lines.

8.173 **Wenocur**, S., and **Reisch**, M., (ed.), *From Charity to Enterprise. The Development of American Social Work in a Market Economy*, Urbana, IL, 1989. Traces the emergence of social work as a profession from the urban settlement houses to casework-based bureaucracies.

Gender relations

8.174 **Berry**, Mary Frances, *Why ERA Failed. Politics, Women's Rights, and the Amending Process of the Constitution*, Bloomington, IN, 1986. Contrasts the political success of earlier amendments with the failure to achieve political consensus behind the Equal Rights Amendment.

8.175 **Breines**, Wini, *Young, White, Miserable. Growing up Female in the Fifties*, Boston, 1992.

8.176 **Fox-Genovese**, Elizabeth, *Feminism without Illusions. A Critique of Individualism*, Chapel Hill, NC, 1991. The illusions to be dispensed with include the liberal heritage of individualism of the past three centuries and how it influences society today.

8.177 **Goldin**, Claudia Dale, *Understanding the Gender Gap. An Economic History of American Women*, New York, 1990. A thorough study of twentieth century labor force participation by women and of the persisting gap in wages between men and women; the author explains much of the discrimination in wage rates by reference to employers' "bars" against retaining married women, and also to the changing experience of different birth cohorts of women.

8.178 **Harrison**, Cynthia, *On Account of Sex. The Politics of Women's Issues, 1945–1968*, Berkeley, CA, 1988. Treats the origins of the political movement for the Equal Rights Amendment.

8.179 **Jeffords**, Susan, *The Remasculinization of America. Gender and the Vietnam War*, Bloomington, IN, 1989. A study of Vietnam War literature (fiction, memoirs, and films) that finds an underlying renewed assertion of masculinity at the heart of what is seen as a gendered conflict.

8.180 **Kaledin**, Eugenia, *Mothers and More. American Women in the 1950s*, Boston, 1984.

8.181 **Kessler-Harris**, Alice, 'Equal Employment Opportunity Commission v. Sears, Roebuck and Co. A personal account', *Radical History Review*, XXXV, 1986, 57–79. Recounts the author's experience as an expert witness in the celebrated lawsuit by the federal agency against the retailer charging a lengthy pattern of gender discrimination against female employees at Sears.

8.182 **Lamphere**, Louise, *From Working Daughters to Working Mothers. Immigrant Women in a New England Industrial Community*, Ithaca, NY, 1987. Contrasts the different experiences of immigrant women to a Rhode Island textile town, starting with early nineteenth century women wage laborers up to today's Portugese immigrant women.

8.183 **Mansbridge**, Jane J., *Why We Lost the ERA*, Chicago, 1986. Uses group theory to examine why the Equal Rights Amendment was defeated, with particular focus on the issue of women's likely eligibility for a military draft.

8.184 **Mathews**, D. G., and **De Hart**, Jane Sherron, *Sex, Gender, and the Politics of ERA*, New York, 1990. Tells the history of the failed "Equal Rights Amendment" to the Constitution, and links the failure to a general conservative backlash, as well as to mistaken tactics and strategy by the amendment's proponents.

8.185 **Morden**, Bettie J., *The Women's Army Corps, 1945–1978*, Washington, DC, 1990.

8.186 **Perrone**, Bobette, **Stockel**, H. Henrietta, and **Krueger**, Victoria, *Medicine Women, Curanderas, and Women Doctors*, Norman, OK, 1989. An unusual cross-cultural study across the races to look at women and healing.

8.187 **Rakow**, Lana F., *Gender on the Line. Women, the Telephone, and Community Life*, Urbana, IL, 1992. Social history of the differences in how men and women used the telephone.

8.188 **Wandersee**, Winifred D., *On the Move. American Women in the 1970s*, Boston, 1988.

8.189 **Warren**, Carol A. B., *Madwives. Schizophrenic Women in the 1950s*, New Brunswick, NJ, 1987. Finds that psychiatry was used as an instrument of control in a case study of women inmates at the Napa State Hospital in California.

Education

8.190 **Best**, J. H., 'The revolution of markets and management: toward a history of American higher education since 1945', *History of Education Quarterly*, XXVIII, 1988, 177–189.

8.191 **Bloom**, A. D., *The Closing of the American Mind*, New York, 1987. A best-selling blast at the downfall of western civilization, due in part to the failure of American colleges to require its study.

8.192 **Brint**, S., and **Karabel**, J., *The Diverted Dream. Community Colleges and the Promise of Educational Opportunity in America, 1900–1985*, New York, 1989. Traces the emergence of junior colleges and their struggle to find a role in the higher education system.

8.193 **Fitzgerald**, Frances, *America Revised. History Schoolbooks in the Twentieth Century*, Boston, 1979. A study of American culture through the lens of history textbooks for children; the author finds the recent trend has been away from genuine narrative and too much toward pabulum.

8.194 **Freeland**, R. M., *Academia's Golden Age. Universities in Massachusetts, 1945–1970*, New York, 1992.

8.195 **Gilbert**, J., *A Cycle of Outrage. America's Reaction to the Juvenile Delinquent in the 1950s*, New York, 1986. Connects the backlash of the anti-communism crusade to an increased scrutiny of American youth in the postwar period.

8.196 **Gurock**, J. S., *The Men and Women of Yeshiva. Higher Education, Orthodoxy, and American Judaism*, New York, 1988. An institutional account of Yeshiva University and its role as intellectual center of Orthodox Jewry.

8.197 **Illick**, J. E., *At Liberty. The Story of a Community and a Generation. The Bethlehem, Pennsylvania, High School Class of 1952*, Knoxville, TN, 1989.

8.198 **Jacoby**, R., *The Last Intellectuals. American Culture in the Age of Academe*, New York, 1987. Decries the disappearance of leftist intellectuals in the United States after World War II and ascribes the irrelevance of the Left in part to its isolation in universities.

8.199 **Katz**, M. B., *Reconstructing American Education*, Cambridge, MA, 1987. Reflections on the modern public school system by one of the leading historians of the new social history of education.

8.200 **Lloyd**, Susan McIntosh, *The Putney School. A Progressive Experiment*, New Haven, CT, 1987. Contrasts the ideals of the Vermont private school that flourished in the 1940s and 1950s with the high-handed administration of its founder, Carmelita Hinton.

8.201 **McGee**, L., *Education of the Black Adult in the United States*, Westport, CT, 1985.

8.202 **Ravitch**, Diane, *The Troubled Crusade. American Education, 1945–1980*, New York, 1983. A history of the national controversies surrounding public education, particularly racial integration of the schools, written by a scholar-politician.

8.203 **Wiener**, J., *Professors, Politics, and Pop*, New York, 1991. Reflections on the changes in campus life and the role of the professoriat.

Recreation, entertainment, and sport

8.204 **Balio**, T., *United Artists. The Company that Changed the Film Industry*, Madison, WI, 1987. Continues the author's series on the history of United Artists, and in this volume focuses on how the studio survived the difficult 1950s by negotiating agreements with independent producers and becoming primarily a film distributor.

8.205 **Baughman**, J. L., *The Republic of Mass Culture. Journalism, Filmmaking, and Broadcasting in America since 1941*, Baltimore, 1992.

8.206 **Klein**, A. M., *Sugarball. The American Game, the Dominican Dream*, New Haven, CT, 1991. Traces the Dominican connection from sandlot fields on the island to major league baseball on the mainland.

8.207 **Rader**, B., *In Its Own Image. How Television Has Transformed Sports*, New York, 1984. A history of how television altered nearly every American sport and in almost every case for the worse.

8.208 **Raskin**, M., *et al.*, 'JFK and the culture of violence', *American Historical Review*, XCVIII, 1992, 487–511. Collected reviews of Oliver Stone's film with attention to the problem of historians working with filmmakers.

8.209 **Rees**, D., and **Crampton**, L., (ed.), *Rock Movers and Shakers*, Santa Barbara, CA, 1991. A biographical directory of rock and roll stars.

8.210 **Roberts**, R., and **Olson**, J. F., *Winning is the Only Thing. Sports in America since 1945*, Baltimore, 1989. Examines how pervasive sports has become in modern American culture and how it has been shaped by capitalism and the Cold War.

8.211 **Rosenthal**, D., *Hard Bop. Jazz and Black Music, 1955–1965*, New York, 1992. A history of the musicians and the influence of their music.

Television culture

8.212 **Balio**, T., (ed.), *Hollywood in the Age of Television*, Boston, 1990. Sixteen essays that maintain the motion picture industry sought a close involvement with television.

8.213 **Boddy**, W., *Fifties Television. The Industry and its Critics*, Urbana, IL, 1990. Revises the notion that the 1950s were a "Golden Age" of American television, arguing instead that the medium was dominated by commercial sponsors who tightly controlled programming.

8.214 **Sanderson**, G., and **MacDonald**, F., (ed.), *Marshall McLuhan. The Man and his Message*, Golden, CO, 1989. A mix of McLuhan's writings and writings about his work that seeks to portray him as a major cultural critic of the twentieth century.

8.215 **Tichi**, Cecelia, *Electronic Hearth. Creating an American Television Culture*, New York, 1991. Focuses on the social and psychological changes in the American family, especially its children, due to the pervasiveness of television.

8.216 **Watson**, Mary Ann, *The Expanding Vista. American Television in the Kennedy Years*, New York, 1990. Reviews the important uses of television by President Kennedy and how the networks adjusted to criticism by the Federal Communications Commission.

8.217 **Zelizer**, Barbie, *Covering the Body. The Kennedy Assassination, the Media, and the Shaping of Collective Memory*, Chicago, 1992.

Crime and punishment

8.218 **Allen**, F. A., *The Decline of the Rehabilitative Ideal. Penal Policy and Social Purpose*, New Haven, CT, 1981. Links the general crisis in postwar American society to a pessimism about the possibility of changing the behavior of prisoners.

8.219 **Bedau**, H. A., *Death is Different. Studies in the Morality, Law and Politics of Capital Punishment*, Boston, 1987. A collection of essays by the leading scholarly critic of the recent death penalty revival in the U.S.

8.220 **Bowers**, W. J., *et al.*, *Legal Homicide. Death and Punishment in America, 1864–1982*, Boston, 1984. Particularly strong on the postwar connection between race and capital punishment.

8.221 **Brannigan**, A., 'Moral panics and juvenile delinquents in Britain and America', *Criminal Justice History*, VIII, 1987, 18.1–191. Reviews the recent literature on the postwar fear of juvenile delinquency.

8.222 **Inglis**, B., *The Forbidden Game. A Social History of Drugs*, New York, 1975.

8.223 **Irons**, P., *The Courage of Their Convictions*, New York, 1988. A study of major Supreme Court cases involving free speech questions or the rights of unpopular minorities.

8.224 **Wright**, J. D., *et al.*, *Under the Gun. Weapons, Crime, and Violence in America*, New York, 1983.

RELIGION, BELIEFS, IDEAS, AND CULTURE

8.225 **Boyer**, P., *When Time Shall Be No More. Prophecy Belief in Modern American Culture*, Cambridge, MA, 1992.

8.226 **Irvin**, Dona L., *The Unsung Heart of Black America. A Middle-Class Church at Midcentury*, Columbia, MO, 1992. A history of a black church in Oakland, California in the midst of the civil rights era.

8.227 **Nielsen**, N. C., 'The advancement of religion versus teaching about religion in the public schools', *Journal of Church and State*, XXVI, 1984, 105–116.

8.228 **Pells**, R. H., *The Liberal Mind in a Conservative Age. American Intellectuals in the 1940s and 1950s*, New York, 1985. Analyzes the writings of postwar intellectuals who retained a critical view of American culture, but also made their peace with capitalism.

8.229 **Torrey**, E. F., *Freudian Fraud. The Malignant Effect of Freud's Theory on American Thought and Culture*, New York, 1992.

8.230 **Warner**, R. S., *New Wine in Old Wineskins. Evangelicals and Liberals in a Small-Town Church*, Berkeley, CA, 1988.

8.231 **Wilcox**, C., *God's Warriors. The Christian Right in Twentieth Century America*, Baltimore, 1992.

8.232 **Wuthnow**, R., *The Restructuring of American Religion. Society and Faith Since World War II*, Princeton, NJ, 1988. Shows how denominational differences among Americans, particularly between Catholics and Protestants, have faded since World War II in favor of two competing views of religion in society, a liberal one emphasizing peace and justice versus a conservative one stressing a prescriptive moral code.

Catholicism

8.233 **Fisher**, J. T., *The Catholic Counterculture in America, 1933–1962*, Chapel Hill, NC, 1989.

8.234 **Gleason**, P., *Keeping the Faith. American Catholicism Past and Present*, Notre Dame, IN, 1987. An intellectual history of Catholic education and theology in the twentieth century and how the 1960s shook the faith.

8.235 **Hunt**, R. P., and **Grasso**, K. L., *John Courtney Murray and the American Civil Conversation*, Grand Rapids, MI, 1992. Narrative of how the Catholic theologian Murray helped bridge the chasm between Protestants and Catholics after World War II.

8.236 **Leahy**, W. P., *Adapting to America. Catholics, Jesuits, and Higher Education in the Twentieth Century*, Washington, DC, 1991.

8.237 **McNeal**, Patricia, *Harder than War. Catholic Peacemaking in Twentieth-Century America*, New Brunswick, NJ, 1992.

American Judaism after the Holocaust

8.238 **Burstin**, Barbara Stern, *After the Holocaust. The Migration of Polish Jews and Christians to Pittsburgh*, Pittsburgh, 1989.

8.239 **Gal**, A., *David Ben-Gurion and the American Alignment for a Jewish State*, Bloomington, IN, 1991.

8.240 **Kaufman**, M., *An Ambiguous Partnership. Non-Zionists and Zionists in America, 1939–1948*, Jerusalem, 1991.

8.241 **Whitfield**, S. J., *Into the Dark. Hannah Arendt and Totalitarianism*, Philadelphia, 1980.

8.242 **Whitfield**, S. J., *American Space, Jewish Time*, Hamden, CT, 1988.

Modernism and post-modernism

8.243 **Bloom**, A., *Prodigal Sons. The New York Intellectuals and their New World*, New York, 1986. An account of the writers for the *Partisan Review* that stresses their commitment to anti-Stalinism and the narrowing space they found after World War II.

8.244 **Cantor**, N. F., *Twentieth Century Culture. Modernism to Deconstruction*, New York, 1988.

8.245 **Crane**, Diana, *The Transformation of the Avant-Garde. The New York Art World, 1940–1985*, Chicago, 1987.

8.246 **Hoeveler**, J. D., *Watch on the Right. Conservative Intellectuals in Post-Modern America*, Madison, WI, 1991.

8.247 **Jumonville**, N., *Critical Crossings. The New York Intellectuals in Postwar America*, Berkeley, CA, 1991.

8.248 **Lasch**, C., *The Minimal Self. Psychic Survival in Troubled Times*, New York, 1984.

8.249 **Lasch**, C., *The True and Only Heaven. Progress and its Critics*, New York, 1991. An extended essay about the gap between the beliefs of intellectuals in the death of progress and the persistence of that idea among those the author calls petit-bourgeois.

8.250 **Marling**, Karal Ann, and **Wetenhall**, J., *Iwo Jima. Monuments, Memories, and the American Hero*. Cambridge, MA, 1991. An account of the politics behind the building in Washington of the Iwo Jima monument, and how memories of the battle were constructed and reconstructed after the war.

8.251 **Matthews**, F., 'The attack on "historicism". Allan Bloom's indictment of contemporary American historical scholarship', *American Historical Review*, XCV, 1990, 429–447. A critical review of Bloom's attack on modern scholarship and a defense of the relativism that is at the heart of modern history.

8.252 **Ross**, A., *No Respect. Intellectuals and Popular Culture*, New York, 1989.

8.253 **Schwartz**, L. H., *Creating Faulkner's Reputation. The Politics of Modern Literary Criticism*, Knoxville, TN, 1988.

8.254 **Senie**, Harriet F., *Contemporary Public Sculpture. Tradition, Transformation, and Controversy*, New York, 1992.

The counter-culture

8.255 **Buhle**, P., *History and the New Left. Madison, Wisconsin, 1950–1970*, Philadelphia, 1990. An intellectual history of some of the University of Wisconsin historians and how they made their campus the center of leftist thought.

8.256 **Caute**, D., *The Year of the Barricades. A Journey through 1968*, New York, 1988.

8.257 **Farber**, D., *Chicago, '68*, Chicago, 1988.

8.258 **Gitlin**, T., *The Sixties. Years of Hope, Days of Rage*, New York, 1987.

8.259 **Isserman**, M., *If I Had a Hammer . . . The Death of the Old Left and the Birth of the New Left*, New York, 1987. Follows the twists and turns of the Left from the Trotskyites to the Schactmanites and on to SDS.

8.260 **Matusow**, A. J., *The Unraveling of America. A History of Liberalism in the 1960s*, New York, 1984. A wide-ranging survey that covers politics and culture.

8.261 **Maynard**, J. A., *Venice West. The Beat Generation in Southern California*, New Brunswick, NJ, 1991.

8.262 **Miller**, T., *The Hippies and American Values*, Knoxville, TN, 1991.

8.263 **Morgan**, E. P., *The 60's Experience. Hard Lessons about Modern America*, Philadelphia, 1991.

8.264 **Tischler**, Barbara I., (ed.), *Sights on the Sixties*, New Brunswick, NJ, 1992.

WORK AND ENTERPRISE

Rise and fall of the labor movement

8.265 **Fink**, L., and **Greenberg**, B., *Upheaval in the Quiet Zone. A History of Hospital Workers' Union, Local 1199*, Urbana, IL, 1989.

8.266 **Freeman**, J. B., *In Transit. The Transport Workers Union in New York City, 1933–1966*, New York, 1989.

8.267 **Gabin**, Nancy F., *Feminism in the Labor Movement. Women and the United Auto Workers, 1935–1975*, Ithaca, NY, 1990.

8.268 **Gall**, G. J., *The Politics of Right to Work. The Labor Federations as Special Interests, 1943–1979*, Westport, CT, 1988. Analyzes the successful business counter-offensive to break the closed shop, and the failure of organized labor to roll back right-to-work legislation.

8.269 **Gerstle**, G., *Working-Class Americanism. The Politics of Labor in a Textile City, 1914–1960*, New York, 1989. Analyzes the workers of Woonsockett, Rhode Island and finds a continuing struggle between radical and Catholic ideas that vied for the loyalty of French Canadian immigrant workers.

8.270 **Goldfield**, M., *The Decline of Organized Labor in the United States*, Chicago, 1987. Focuses on the business counter-offensive after World War II as the main cause of the decline of the labor movement.

8.271 **Green**, J. R., *The World of the Worker. Labor in Twentieth Century America*, New York, 1980. A history of organized and unorganized labor that focuses on militancy on and off the shop floor.

8.272 **Griffith**, Barbara S., *The Crisis of American Labor. Operation Dixie and the Defeat of the CIO*, Philadelphia, 1988. The story of the CIO attempt to organize southern industry, particularly the Cannon textile mills after World War II and how that failure permanently set back the labor movement.

8.273 **Halpern**, M., *UAW Politics in the Cold War Era*, Albany, NY, 1988.

8.274 **Kimeldorf**, H., *Reds or Rackets? The Making of Radical and Conservative Unions on the Waterfront*, Berkeley, CA, 1988. Contrasts the political orientation of the West and East coast longshoremen unions.

8.275 **McColloch**, M., *White Collar Workers in Transition. The Boom Years, 1940–1970*, Westport, CT, 1983.

8.276 **Palladino**, Grace, *Dreams of Dignity, Workers of Vision. A History of the International Brotherhood of Electrical Workers*, Washington, DC, 1991.

8.277 **Renshaw**, P., *American Labor and Consensus Capitalism, 1935–1990*, Jackson, MS, 1991. Details the rise and fall of a social compact between business, the state, and organized labor after the New Deal.

8.278 **Rhinehart**, Marilyn D., *A Way of Work and a Way of Life. Coal-Mining in Thurber, Texas, 1888–1926*, College Station, TX, 1992.

8.279 **Rosswurm**, S., (ed.), *The CIO's Left-Led Unions*, New Brunswick, NJ, 1992. Essays on various unions in the CIO and how communist leadership came under attack before and after World War II.

8.280 **Zieger**, R. H., *American Workers, American Unions, 1920–1985*, Baltimore, 1986. Concentrates on the post-World War II period when mass unions became bureaucratized and particularistic.

The American economy in a world system

8.281 **Bromley**, S., *American Hegemony and World Oil. The Industry, the State System and the World Economy*, New York, 1991.

8.282 **Butsch**, R., (ed.), *For Fun and Profit. The Transformation of Leisure into Consumption*, Philadelphia, 1990. A collection of nine essays explores the relationship between culture, consumers, and mass marketers, finding that although corporations dominate and exploit popular culture, the relationship is not one of complete hegemony.

8.283 **Fuechtmann**, T.C., *Steeples and Stacks. Religion and Steel, Crisis in Youngstown*, New York, 1989. Chronicles the struggle of a religious coalition of clergy and laity in the 1970s to promote worker ownership of the failed steel mills of Youngstown, Ohio.

8.284 **Hall**, P. D., *Inventing the Nonprofit Sector and Other Essays on Philanthropy, Voluntarism, and Nonprofit Organizations*, Baltimore, 1992.

8.285 **Hirsh**, R. F., *Technology and Transformation in the American Electric Utility Industry*, New York, 1989.

8.286 **Morris**, P. J. T., *The American Synthetic Rubber Research Program*, Philadelphia, 1989.

8.287 **Noble**, D. F., *Forces of Production. A Social History of Industrial Automation*, New York, 1984. Argues that politics and class struggle was at the heart of the postwar effort to develop an automatic machine tool that could be programmed by management.

8.288 **Robert**, J. C., *Ethyl. A History of the Corporation and the People Who Made It*, Charlottesville, VA, 1983. The Virginia-based chemicals corporation and the twists and turns in its fortunes.

8.289 **Rodman**, K. A., *Sanctity versus Sovereignty. The United States and the Nationalization of Natural Resource Investments*, New York, 1988.

8.290 **Sloan**, J. W., *Eisenhower and the Management of Prosperity*, Lawrence, KS, 1991. An account that finds Ike presided over sound economic policy, and moreover was quite interested in the topic.

8.291 **Strasser**, Susan, *Satisfaction Guaranteed. The Making of the American Mass Market*, New York, 1989. Argues that between 1880 and 1920, corporations devised ways of bypassing wholesalers and jobbers to market their products directly to local retailers and consumers, thereby creating a new consumer-led economy.

8.292 **Tedlow**, R. S., *New and Improved. The Story of Mass Marketing in America*, New York, 1990. Builds on Alfred Chandler's concept of a growing revolution in the mass distribution of products, and using several corporate case studies, argues that marketing was the key to the successful creation of consumer demand.

8.293 **Tugwell**, F., *The Energy Crisis and the American Political Economy. Politics and Markets in the Management of Natural Resources*, Stanford, CA, 1988.

8.294 **Vietor**, R. H. K., *Energy Policy in America since 1945. A Study of Business-Government Relations*, New York, 1984. Traces the role of the federal government in supplementing market decisions about the overall mix of solid and liquid fuels, as well as the mix of domestic and foreign production.

8.295 **Wall**, B. H., *Growth in a Changing Environment. A History of Standard Oil Company Exxon Corporation, 1950–1975*, New York, 1988.

8.296 **Waring**, S. P., *Taylorism Transformed. Scientific Management Theory since 1945*, Chapel Hill, NC, 1991.

RACE AND
ETHNIC IDENTITY

African-Americans and
the civil rights movement

8.297 **Branch**, T., *Parting the Waters. America in the King Years, 1954–1963*, New York, 1988.

8.298 **Button**, J. W., *Blacks and Social Change. Impact of the Civil Rights Movement in Southern Communities*, Princeton, NJ, 1989. A political science study of how power changed in the South after the 1960s.

8.299 **Carson**, C., 'Martin Luther King, Jr.: charismatic leadership in a mass struggle', *Journal of American History*, LXXIV, 1987, 448–454. Discusses King's role in the civil rights movement and myths that abound about him.

8.300 **Chestnut**, J. L., Jr., and **Cass**, Julia, *Black in Selma. The Uncommon Life of J. L. Chestnut, Jr.*, New York, 1990.

8.301 **Colburn**, D. R., *Racial Change and Community Crisis. St. Augustine, Florida, 1877–1980*, New York, 1985. A history that focuses on the failed 1964 campaign of the Southern Christian Leadership Conference to integrate the city and the subsequent legal battles to end segregation.

8.302 **Cone**, J. H., *Martin and Malcolm and America. A Dream or a Nightmare*, Maryknoll, NY, 1991.

8.303 **Cone**, J. H., 'Martin Luther King, Jr., and the Third World', *Journal of American History*, LXXIV, 1987, 455–467. Discusses King's significance to the Third World and their significance for him.

8.304 **Fairclough**, A., *To Redeem the Soul of America. The Southern Leadership Conference and Martin Luther King, Jr.*, Athens, GA, 1987. A work that focuses more on the institutional framework of the civil rights movement and King's place as its leader.

8.305 **Fine**, S., *Violence in the Model City. The Cavanagh Administration, Race Relations, and the Detroit Riot of 1967*, Ann Arbor, MI, 1989. Recounts the history of the worst urban uprising of the 1960s in a city with an administration pledged to racial harmony, yet one that was plagued by a heavy-handed police force.

8.306 **Freyer**, T. A., *The Little Rock Crisis. A Constitutional Interpretation*, Westport, CT, 1984. A study of the conflict between states' rights and federal power in the 1957 desegregation of Central High School in Little Rock, Arkansas.

8.307 **Garrow**, D. J., 'Martin Luther King, Jr., and the spirit of leadership', *Journal of American History*, LXXIV, 1987, 438–447. Charts King's rise to leadership in Montgomery, Alabama.

8.308 **Garrow**, D., *The Montgomery Bus Boycott and the Women who started it. The Memoir of Jo Ann Gibson Robinson*, Knoxville, TN, 1987.

8.309 **Graham**, H. D., *The Civil Rights Era. Origins and Development of National Policy*, New York, 1990. Looks at federal policy-makers, especially in the Equal Employment Opportunity Commission, and how they developed affirmative action programs.

8.310 **Grimshaw**, W. J., *Bitter Fruit. Black Politics and the Chicago Machine, 1931–1991*, Chicago, 1992.

8.311 **Harding**, V. G., 'Beyond amnesia: Martin Luther King, Jr., and the future of America', *Journal of American History*, LXXIV, 1987, 468–476. Remembers King and what he accomplished and strove for.

8.312 **Harding**, V. G., *Hope and History. Why We Must Share the Story of the Movement*, Maryknoll, NY, 1990. Part memoir and part history, this volume is directed mainly to teachers thinking about how to teach the civil rights era to students born after its end.

8.313 **Hirsch**, A. R., *Making the Second Ghetto. Race and Housing in Chicago, 1940–1960*, New York, 1983.

8.314 **Huggins**, N. I., 'Martin Luther King, Jr.: charisma and leadership', *Journal of American History*, LXXIV, 1987, 477–481. Discusses King and the leadership role he played.

8.315 **King**, R. H., *Civil Rights and the Idea of Freedom*, New York, 1992.

8.316 **Kleppner**, P., *Chicago Divided. The Making of a Black Mayor*, DeKalb, IL, 1985. Traces the 1983 electoral triumph of Harold Washington in Chicago to the emergence of a unified black voting electorate.

8.317 **Lipsitz**, G., *A Life in the Struggle. Ivory Perry and the Culture of Opposition*, Philadelphia, 1988.

8.318 **McAdam**, D., *Freedom Summer*, New

York, 1988.

8.319 **Metcalf**, G. R., *From Little Rock to Boston. The History of School Desegregation*, Westport, CT, 1983.

8.320 **O'Reilly**, K., *Racial Matters. The FBI's Secret File on Black America, 1960–1972*, New York, 1989. Documents FBI Director J. Edgar Hoover's massive spying on civil rights leaders and his disdain for their movement for racial justice.

8.321 **Pratt**, R. A., *The Color of Their Skin. Education and Race in Richmond, Virginia, 1954–1989*. Charlottesville, VA, 1992.

8.322 **Sikora**, F., *Until Justice Rolls Down. The Birmingham Church Bombing Case*, Tuscaloosa, AL, 1991. A reporter's account of the 1963 dynamiting that killed four black children, and how the perpetrators were ultimately prosecuted in the 1970s.

8.323 **Sitkoff**, H., *The Struggle for Black Equality, 1954–1980*, New York, 1981.

8.324 **Southern**, D. W., *Gunnar Myrdal and Black-White Relations. The Use and Abuse of An American Dilemma, 1944–1969*, Baton Rouge, LA, 1987.

8.325 **Thelen**, D., 'Becoming Martin Luther King, Jr.: plagiarism and originality. A round table', *Journal of American History*, LXXVIII, 1991, 11–123. Contains essays on Martin Luther King, Jr., on different aspects of his life, with a special focus on interpreting his actions in plagiarizing his doctoral dissertation from another student's work.

8.326 **Thompson**, D. C., *A Black Elite. A Profile of Graduates of UNCF Colleges*, New York, 1986.

8.327 **Tygiel**, J., *Baseball's Great Experiment. Jackie Robinson and His Legacy*, New York, 1983. Recounts the story of the first black athlete to play major league baseball in the twentieth century, and the social ramifications that followed the integration of the sport.

8.328 **Walton**, H., *When the Marching Stopped. The Politics of Civil Rights Regulatory Agencies*, Albany, NY, 1988.

8.329 **Weisbrot**, R., *Freedom Bound. A History of America's Civil Rights Movement*, New York, 1990. A brief synthesis of the civil rights movement that continues the story past Selma and the 1965 Voting Rights Act through the Reagan years.

8.330 **Weiss**, Nancy J., *Whitney M. Young, Jr., and the Struggle for Civil Rights*, Princeton, NJ, 1989.

8.331 **Whitfield**, S. J., *A Death in the Delta. The Story of Emmett Till*, New York, 1988. A dramatic account of a 1955 lynching in Mississippi of a black Chicago teenager, and the resulting uproar that was part of the emerging civil rights movement in the South.

8.332 **Wolters**, R., *The Burden of Brown. Thirty Years of School Desegregation*, Knoxville, TN, 1984.

8.333 **Zweigenhaft**, R. L., and **Domhoff**, G. W., *Blacks in the White Establishment? A Study of Race and Class in America*, New Haven, CT, 1991. Reviews the history of recruiting efforts by prep schools and elite colleges to attract black students in the early 1960s, and the impressive measure of success achieved by the alumni.

Native Americans

8.334 **Ambler**, Marjane, *Breaking the Iron Bonds. Indian Control of Energy Development*, Lawrence, KS, 1990.

8.335 **Burton**, L., *American Indian Water Rights and the Limits of Law*, Lawrence, KS, 1991.

8.336 **Campisi**, J., *The Mashpee Indians. Tribe on Trial*, Syracuse, NY, 1991. The story of the 1977 trial between the tribe and Massachusetts localities over land control, as told by a witness for the tribe.

8.337 **Cornell**, S. E., *The Return of the Native. American Indian Political Resurgence*, New York, 1988.

8.338 **Danziger**, E. J., *Survival and Regeneration. Detroit's American Indian Community*, Detroit, 1991.

8.339 **Doherty**, R., *Disputed Waters. Native Americans and the Great Lakes Fishery*, Lexington, KY, 1990. A review of the litigation between the Michigan bands of Chippewa Indians and the State of Michigan over control of Lake Michigan deep-water fishing.

8.340 **Fixico**, D. L., *Termination and Relocation. Federal Indian Policy, 1945–1960*, Albuquerque, NM, 1986. Covers the postwar policy of the federal government to end formal tribal identity and to move rural Native Americans from reservations to designated cities.

8.341 **Hauptman**, L. M., *Formulating American Indian Policy in New York State*,

1970–1986, Albany, NY, 1988.

8.342 **Hornung**, R., *One Nation under the Gun*, New York, 1992. An account of reservation violence among Mohawks in New York State and Canada.

8.343 **Howard**, J. H., *Oklahoma Seminoles. Medicines, Magic, and Religion*, Norman, OK, 1984.

8.344 **Kelley**, Jane Holden, *Yacqui Women. Contemporary Life Histories*, Lincoln, NE, 1978. Women's lives and enduring tribal customs of the Arizona Yacqui.

8.345 **Lawson**, M. L., *Dammed Indians. The Pick-Sloan Plan and the Missouri River Sioux, 1944–1980*, Norman, OK, 1982. Evocative title that refers to the series of irrigation and power dams that flooded several Sioux (Lakota) reservations, and the tribal response.

8.346 **Porter**, F. W., III, (ed.), *Nonrecognized American Indian Tribes. An Historical and Legal Perspective*, Chicago, 1983. A set of papers about tribal groups who maintain an Indian identity but are not recognized by the Bureau of Indian Affairs.

8.347 **Rosenthal**, H. D., *Their Day in Court. A History of the Indian Claims Commission*, New York, 1990. Written by the Commission's own staff historian, this work is critical of the termination philosophy that underlay the work of the ICC.

8.348 **Shattuck**, G. C., *The Oneida Land Claims. A Legal History*, Syracuse, NY, 1991. The story of more than two decades of litigation over the remaining rights to millions of acres in central New York state, as told by the tribal attorney.

8.349 **Sutton**, I., (ed.), *Irredeemable America. The Indians' Estate and Land Claims*, Albuquerque, NM, 1985.

8.350 **Vecsey**, C., and **Starna**, W. A., (ed.), *Iroquois Land Claims*, Syracuse, NY, 1988.

8.351 **Voget**, F. W., *The Shoshoni-Crow Sun Dance*, Norman, OK, 1984. The history and practice of one of the most important ceremonies of the Plains tribes, banned for much of the twentieth century by U.S. authority.

8.352 **Weibel-Orlando**, Joan, *Indian Country, L. A. Maintaining Ethnic Community in Complex Society*, Urbana, IL, 1991. A study of Native Americans who relocated to Los Angeles.

European-Americans

8.353 **Formisano**, R. P., *Boston Against Busing. Race, Class, and Ethnicity in the 1960s and 1970s*, Chapel Hill, NC, 1991.

8.354 **Jasso**, G., and **Rosenzweig**, M. R., *The New Chosen People. Immigrants in the United States*, New York, 1990.

8.355 **Simpson**, C., *Blowback. America's Recruitment of Nazis and its Effects on the Cold War*, New York, 1988.

8.356 **Sollors**, W., (ed.), *The Invention of Ethnicity*, New York, 1989. A collection of essays on the theme of ethnic identity as a social construct.

8.357 **Yans-McLaughlin**, Virginia, *Immigration Reconsidered. History, Sociology, and Politics*, New York, 1990. Reflections about immigration on the occasion of the centennial of the Statue of Liberty.

Hispanic-Americans

8.358 **Camarillo**, A., *Chicanos in California. A History of Mexican Americans in California*, San Francisco, 1984.

8.359 **Garcia**, M. T., *Mexican Americans. Leadership, Ideology, and Identity, 1930–1960*, New Haven, CT, 1989. Shows how labor leaders and intellectuals prefigured the Chicano movement of the 1960s and 1970s.

8.360 **Gurak**, D. T., 'Family formation and marital selectivity among Colombian and Dominican immigrants in New York City', *International Migration Review*, XXI, 1987, 275–298.

8.361 **Levine**, B. B., (ed.), *The Caribbean Exodus*, New York, 1987.

8.362 **Marin**, Marguerite V., *Social Protest in an Urban Barrio. A Study of the Chicano Movement, 1966–1974*, Lanham, MD, 1991.

8.363 **Masud-Piloto**, F. R., *With Open Arms. Cuban Migration to the United States*, Totowa, NJ, 1988.

8.364 **Rockett**, I. R. H., 'American immigration policy and ethnic selection: an overview', *Journal of Ethnic Studies*, X, 1983, 1–26.

8.365 **Scruggs**, O. M., *Braceros, 'Wetbacks', and the Farm Labor Problem. Mexican Agricultural Labor in the United States, 1942–1954*, New York, 1988.

SPACE, MOVEMENT, AND PLACE

The space race

8.366 **Bulkeley**, R., *The Sputniks Crisis and Early United States Space Policy. A Critique of the Historiography of Space*, Bloomington, IN, 1991. Both a history of the space program in the 1950s and a defense of the Eisenhower Administration for trying as best as possible to follow scientific suggestions rather than giving in to Cold War pressures.

8.367 **Burrows**, W. E., *Exploring Space. Voyages in the Solar System and Beyond*, New York, 1990.

8.368 **Koppes**, C. R., *JPL and the American Space Program. A History of the Jet Propulsion Laboratory*, New Haven, CT, 1982.

8.369 **Mack**, Pamela E., *Viewing the Earth. The Social Construction of the Landsat Satellite System*, Cambridge, MA, 1990.

8.370 **McDougall**, W. A., . . . *the Heavens and the Earth. A Political History of the Space Age*, New York, 1985. Shows that the space race was at all times before and after Sputnik another front in the Cold War.

The American city in crisis

8.371 **Bennett**, L., *Fragments of Cities. The New American Downtown and Neighborhoods*, Columbus, OH, 1990. Contrasts the considerable postwar investment in American urban central business districts with a parallel disinvestment in outlying city neighborhoods.

8.372 **Bernard**, R. M., (ed.), *Snowbelt Cities. Metropolitan Politics in the Northeast and Midwest Since World War II*, Bloomington, IN, 1990. Sixteen essays on the scramble for political power in declining cities.

8.373 **Crepeau**, R. C., *Melbourne Village. The First Twenty-Five Years, 1946–1971*, Orlando, FL, 1988. Community study of a planned village with communitarian ideals and how it was torn apart by internal strife and surrounding growth.

8.374 **Davis**, M., *City of Quartz. Excavating the Future in Los Angeles*, New York, 1990. Interprets Los Angeles as a postmodern text to be deconstructed through the analytical use of race, class, and gender.

8.375 **Doyle**, D. H., *Nashville Since the 1920s*, Knoxville, TN, 1985. Completes the author's history of the city that emerged as the country music capital.

8.376 **Elazar**, D. J., *et al.*, (ed.), *Cities of the Prairies Revisited. The Closing of the Metropolitan Frontier*, Lincoln, NE, 1986.

8.377 **Kelly**, Barbara M., *Suburbia Re-Examined*, Westport, CT, 1989.

8.378 **Klein**, N. M., and **Schiesl**, M. J., (ed.), *20th Century Los Angeles. Power, Promotion, and Social Conflict*, Claremont, CA, 1990. Seven essays on the history of the city, and while predating the 1992 uprising, make clear the racial and social divides in L.A.

8.379 **Kling**, R., **Oliver**, S., and **Poster**, M., (ed.), *Posturban CA. The Transformation of Orange County Since World War II*, Berkeley, CA, 1991. Ten essays that chart the growth of the county south of Los Angeles into a "posturban" metropolis of two million people with a distinctive politics and culture.

8.380 **Maharidge**, D., and **Williamson**, M., *And Their Children After Them*, New York, 1989. A social history of several Alabama families in the style of James Agee's work.

8.381 **Markusen**, Ann, *The Rise of the Gunbelt. The Military Remapping of Industrial America*, New York, 1991. Looks at the historical geography of the military industrial complex, especially how the aerospace industry left the Midwest for southern California.

8.382 **Miller**, Z. L., *Suburb. Neighborhood and Community in Forest Park, Ohio, 1935–1976*, Knoxville, TN, 1981.

8.383 **Pratt**, J. A., *The Growth of a Refining Region*, Greenwich, CT, 1980. Explores the emergence of a vertically integrated oil business in the Gulf States.

8.384 **Schulman**, B. J., *From Cotton Belt to Sunbelt. Federal Policy, Economic Development, and the Transformation of the South, 1938–1980*, New York, 1991. Argues that only federal power upset the rule of the planters in the South, particularly the power of defense spending.

8.385 **Teaford**, J. C., *The Rough Road to Renaissance. Urban Revitalization in America, 1940–1985*, Baltimore, 1990. A critical history of urban renewal efforts in a dozen northeastern cities that finds poor local leadership throughout much of the postwar era and a persistently intrusive and counter-productive federal presence.

The fouling of the American landscape

8.386 **Cronon**, W., 'Modes of prophecy and production: placing nature in history', *Journal of American History*, LXXVI, 1990, 1122–1131. Critique of Donald Worster and his approaches to environmental history.

8.387 **Crosby**, A. W., 'An enthusiastic second', *Journal of American History*, LXXVI, 1990, 1107–1110. Recommends that agroecological history be given more study because it is an important topic.

8.388 **Dunlap**, T. R., *DDT. Scientists, Citizens, and Public Policy*, Princeton, NJ, 1981.

8.389 **Elbers**, Joan S., *Changing Wilderness Values, 1930–1990: An Annotated Bibliography*, New York, 1991.

8.390 **Graf**, W. L., *Wilderness Preservation and the Sagebrush Rebellions*, Savage, NJ, 1990. An account of the 1970s and 1980s conflict over control of public land in the West between environmentalists and ranchers.

8.391 **Hays**, S. P., and **Hays**, Barbara D., *Beauty, Health, and Permanence. Environmental Politics in the United States, 1955–1985*, New York, 1987. Traces the emergence of modern environmentalism as a consumer movement separate from the older conservationism.

8.392 **Lacey**, M. J., (ed.), *Government and Environmental Politics. Essays on Historical Developments since World War Two*, Washington, DC, 1992.

8.393 **McGucken**, W., *Biodegradable. Detergents and the Environment*, College Station, TX, 1991.

8.394 **Merchant**, Carolyn, 'Gender and environmental history', *Journal of American History*, LXXVI, 1990, 1117–1121. Makes a case for adding a gender perspective to environmental history.

8.395 **Nash**, R. F., *The Rights of Nature. A History of Environmental Ethics*, Madison, WI, 1989. Connects the twentieth century environmental movement to the older American tradition of liberalism through the idea of rights.

8.396 **Pyne**, S. J., 'Firestick history', *Journal of American History*, LXXVI, 1990, 1132–1141. Essay treating the history of fire and its role in the environment.

8.397 **White**, R., 'Environmental history, ecology, and meaning', *Journal of American History*, LXXVI, 1990, 1111–1116. Critiques Donald Worster's view of how environmental history should be studied.

8.398 **Worster**, D., *Rivers of Empire. Water, Aridity, and the Growth of the American West*, New York, 1985. A history of western reclamation projects, grounded in a theoretical framework of "hydrological societies".

8.399 **Worster**, D., 'Transformations of the earth. Toward an agroecological perspective in history', *Journal of American History*, LXXVI, 1990, 1087–1106. Takes an new approach to history by looking at environmental history and its rise.

8.400 **Worster**, D., 'Seeing beyond culture', *Journal of American History*, LXXVI, 1990, 1142–1147. Response to criticism of his views of the direction environmental history scholarship should be taking.

THE STATE AND THE PUBLIC REALM

Warfare – Korea

8.401 **Appleman**, R. E., *Disaster in Korea. The Chinese Confront MacArthur*, College Station, TX, 1989. Treats the period immediately after the Chinese intervened in late 1950, and finds a breakdown of much of the American Army.

8.402 **Appleman**, R. E., *Escaping the Trap. The US Army X Corps in Northeast Korea, 1950*, College Station, TX, 1990.

8.403 **Appleman**, R. E., *Ridgway Duels for Korea*, College Station, TX, 1990. A self-avowed 'combat history' of the fighting in the first half of 1951.

8.404 **Blair**, C., *The Forgotten War. America in Korea, 1950–53*, New York, 1987.

8.405 **Foot**, Rosemary, *The Wrong War. American Policy and the Dimensions of the Korean Conflict, 1950–1953*, Ithaca, NY,

1985. Argues for a more belligerent and expansive American policy toward Korea than that seen in the public statements about the police action.

8.406 **Foot**, Rosemary, *A Substitute for Victory. The Politics of Peacemaking at the Korean Armistice Talks*, Ithaca, NY, 1990.

8.407 **Kaufman**, B. I., *The Korean War. Challenges in Crisis, Credibility, and Command*, Philadelphia, 1986. Treats the conflict as a genuine civil war within Korean society that soon became a part of the larger international struggle.

8.408 **MacDonald**, C. A., *Korea. The War Before Vietnam*, New York, 1986. Comprehensive history of the Korean Conflict that focuses on both the combat and negotiations to end the war.

8.409 **Matray**, J. I., *The Reluctant Crusade. American Foreign Policy in Korea, 1941–1950*, Honolulu, 1985.

8.410 **Stueck**, W. W., Jr., *The Road to Confrontation. American Policy toward China and Korea, 1947–1950*, Chapel Hill, NC, 1981. A work that examines the making of American foreign policy about the Korean peninsula and, once war broke out in 1950, about American policy toward Chinese involvement.

8.411 **Whelan**, R., *Drawing the Line. The Korean War, 1950–1953*, Boston, 1990.

Warfare – Vietnam

8.412 **Adams**, Judith Porter, *Peacework. Oral Histories of Women Peace Activists*, Boston, 1991.

8.413 **Anderson**, D. L., *Trapped by Success. The Eisenhower Administration and Vietnam, 1953–1961*, New York, 1991.

8.414A **Arnold**, J. R., *The First Domino. Eisenhower, the Military, and America's Intervention in Vietnam*, New York, 1991.

8.414B **Berman**, L., *Lyndon Johnson's War*, New York, 1989. A policy history of presidential decisions on Vietnam between 1965 and 1968 that emphasizes the divisions within the Administration over the conduct and outcome of the war, especially leading up to the Tet Offensive.

8.415 **Berman**, W. C., *William Fulbright and the Vietnam War. The Dissent of a Political Realist*, Kent, OH, 1988. Traces the evolution of the Arkansas senator's opposition to the Vietnam War, and argues that Fulbright came to his stance from a belief that American participation did not fulfill genuine security needs in Asia.

8.416 **Billings-Yun**, Melanie, *Decision Against War. Eisenhower and Dien Bien Phu, 1954* New York, 1988.

8.417 **Buckingham**, W. A., Jr., *Operation Ranch Hand. The Air Force and Herbicides in Southeast Asia, 1961–1971*, Washington, DC, 1982. Part of the Air Force's official history of the war, this volume concentrates on the aerial defoliation campaign in South Vietnam and the military and environmental consequences

8.418 **Cable**, L., *Unholy Grail. The US and the Wars in Vietnam, 1965–8*, New York, 1991

8.419 **Cincinnatus**, *Self-Destruction. The Disintegration and Decay of the United State Army during the Vietnam Era*, New York, 1981. A pseudonymous contribution by an army officer about how the Army's own personnel policies helped disrupt small unit cohesion in the field, and how internal corruption led to an active trade with the enemy.

8.420 **Clarke**, J. J., *United States Army in Vietnam*, Washington, DC, 1988. An official history of the war by the Army that examines the strategic folly of the American part in the conflict.

8.421 **DeBenedetti**, C., with **Chatfield**, C., (ed.), *An American Ordeal. The Antiwar Movement of the Vietnam Era*, Syracuse, NY, 1990. An encyclopedic account of the antiwar movement, written by one of its leaders.

8.422 **Dietz**, T., *Republicans and Vietnam, 1961–1968*, New York, 1986.

8.423 **DiLeo**, D. L., *George Ball, Vietnam, and the Rethinking of Containment*, Chapel Hill, NC, 1991.

8.424 **Franklin**, H. B., *MIA or Mythmaking in America*, New York, 1992. Reviews the politics and culture behind the persistent belief that American servicemen remain held against their will in Southeast Asia.

8.425 **Gardner**, L. C., *Approaching Vietnam. From World War II through Dienbienphuy*, New York, 1988. A history of the making of American foreign policy in Southeast Asia during and after World War II, and why the decisions made in the name of anti-communism led to later military intervention.

8.426 **Hallin**, D. C., *The 'Uncensored War'. The Media and Vietnam*, New York, 1986.

A review of television news footage about the war that shows a slow evolution from an uncritical Cold War perspective in 1965 toward a barrage of images that reflected the uncertainty of the war by 1968.

8.427 **Herring**, G. C., *America's Longest War. The United States and Vietnam, 1950–1975*, Philadelphia, 1986. A highly critical examination of U.S. policy.

8.428 **Hess**, G. R., *The United States' Emergence as a Southeast Asian Power, 1940–1950*, New York, 1987.

8.429 **Hess**, G. R., *Vietnam and the United States. Origins and Legacy of War*, Boston, 1990.

8.430 **Isaacs**, A. R., *Without Honor. Defeat in Vietnam and Cambodia*, Baltimore, 1983.

8.431 **Kaplan**, L. S., (ed.), *Dien Bien Phu and the Crisis of Franco-American Relations, 1954–1955*, Wilmington, DE, 1990.

8.432 **Karnow**, S., *Vietnam. A History*, New York, 1983.

8.433 **Kinnard**, D., *The Certain Trumpet. Maxwell Taylor & the American Experience in Vietnam*, Washington, DC, 1991.

8.434 **Kolko**, G., *Anatomy of a War. Vietnam, the United States, and the Modern Historical Experience*, New York, 1985. A history of the war in all its aspects from a committed socialist scholar who finds that the social organization of the Vietnamese Revolution was able to overcome the technological firepower of the United States.

8.435 **Olson**, J. S., and **Roberts**, R., *Where the Domino Fell. America and Vietnam, 1945 to 1990*, New York, 1991.

8.436 **Palmer**, B., Jr., *The 25-Year War. America's Military Role in Vietnam*, Lexington, KY, 1984. A critical account of the American political leadership written by one of General Westmoreland's aides.

8.437 **Rorabaugh**, W. J., *Berkeley at War, the 1960s*, New York, 1989. A local history that contrasts the anti-war movement springing from the campus of the University of California with the great movement of soldiers and material from the East Bay docks.

8.438 **Rotter**, A. J., *The Path to Vietnam. Origins of the American Commitment to Southeast Asia*, Ithaca, NY, 1987. Argues that Vietnam became central to American foreign policy in Asia after 1949 because the United States decided upon a containment policy toward China, and at the same time, a policy of combating nationalist movements in the rest of Asia.

8.439 **Shafer**, D. M., (ed.), *The Legacy. The Vietnam War in the American Imagination*, Boston, 1990. A volume of essays about the war and its aftermath, including a review of refugees from Southeast Asia to the U.S.

8.440 **Small**, M., *Johnson, Nixon, and the Doves*, New Brunswick, NJ, 1988.

8.441 **Small**, M., and **Hoover**, W. D., (ed.), *Give Peace a Chance. Exploring the Vietnam Antiwar Movement*, Syracuse, NY, 1992.

8.442 **Spector**, R. H., *United States Army in Vietnam. Advice and Support. The Early Years, 1941–1960*, Washington, DC, 1984. Volume one of the Army's own history of the war.

8.443 **Tonnesson**, S., *The Vietnamese Revolution of 1945. Roosevelt, Ho Chi Minh and de Gaulle in a World at War*, Oslo, 1991. A work noteworthy for the author's having consulted archival sources on three continents, the book focuses on the building of a popular movement in the interim between the fall of the Vichy regime and the surrender of the Japanese.

8.444 **Turner**, Kathleen J., *Lyndon Johnson's Dual War. Vietnam and the Press*, Chicago, 1985. Examines the adversarial relationship between LBJ and the media over Vietnam that was popularly known as the credibility gap.

8.445 **VanDeMark**, B., *Into the Quagmire. Lyndon Johnson and the Escalation of the Vietnam War*, New York, 1991. A survey of the actions taken by the Johnson Administration in 1964 and 1965.

8.446 **Young**, Marilyn B., *The Vietnam Wars. 1945–1990*, New York, 1991. Covers in a short volume the conflict in Indochina from the end of World War II onward, but concentrates on American involvement and the aftereffects on Vietnam and the United States.

The Cold War

(a) GENERAL HISTORIES

8.447 **Coker**, C., *Reflections on American Foreign Policy Since 1945*, New York, 1989.

8.448 **Funigiello**, P. J., *American-Soviet Trade in the Cold War*, Chapel Hill, NC, 1988.

8.449 **Gaddis**, J. L., *The Long Peace. Inquiries into the History of the Cold War*, New York, 1987.

8.450 **Hogan**, M. J., (ed.), *The End of the Cold*

War. Its Meaning and Implications, New York, 1992.

8.451 **Neilson**, K. and **Haycock**, R. G., *The Cold War and Defense*, New York, 1990.

8.452 **Paterson**, T. G., *Meeting the Communist Threat. Truman to Reagan*, New York, 1988. A collection of essays on the centrality of the Cold War to American foreign policy and domestic leadership since 1945.

8.453 **Schulzinger**, R. D., *The Wise Men of Foreign Affairs. The History of the Council on Foreign Relations*, New York, 1984.

8.454 **Schulzinger**, R. D., *Henry Kissinger. Doctor of Diplomacy*, New York, 1989. Weighs Kissinger's accomplishments in foreign policy against his ruthless and immoral use of power at home and abroad.

8.455 **Smith**, G., *Morality, Reason, and Power. American Diplomacy in the Carter Years*, New York, 1986.

8.456 **Snyder**, J., *Myths of Empire. Domestic Politics and International Ambition*, Ithaca, NY, 1991. Connects the defense of empires, including the American one, to a brand of ideology and economy that is expressed in politics at home.

8.457 **Stoessinger**, J. C., *Crusaders and Pragmatists. Movers of Modern American Foreign Policy*, New York, 1979.

(b) ORIGINS AND EARLY YEARS

8.458 **Bills**, S. L., *Empire and Cold War. The Roots of US-Third World Antagonism, 1945–1947*, New York, 1990.

8.459 **Brands**, H. W., *Inside the Cold War. Loy Henderson and the Rise of the American Empire, 1918–1961*, New York, 1991.

8.460 **Brands**, H. W., *Cold Warriors. Eisenhower's Generation and American Foreign Policy*, New York, 1988.

8.461 **Brands**, H. W., 'The age of vulnerability. Eisenhower and the national insecurity state', *American Historical Review*, XCIV, 1989, 963–989. An article that finds confusion and misunderstanding at the heart of Eisenhower's foreign and military policy, not the masterful behind-the-scenes Ike of other work.

8.462 **Chern**, K. S., *Dilemma in China. America's Policy Debate, 1945*, Hamden, CT, 1980.

8.463 **Cohen**, M. J., *Truman and Israel*, Berkeley, CA, 1990. An account of Truman's uneasy relationship with American Zionists, and how he balanced domestic political considerations with foreign policy objectives.

8.464 **Cohen**, T., *Remaking Japan. The American Occupation as New Deal*, New York, 1987. The story of the U.S. occupation of the Japanese from the point of view of the occupation's labor policy chief.

8.465 **Cook**, Blanche Wiesen, *The Declassified Eisenhower. A Divided Legacy*, Garden City, NY, 1981.

8.466 **DeSantis**, H., *The Diplomacy of Silence. The American Foreign Service, the Soviet Union, and the Cold War, 1933–1947*, Chicago, 1980. A focus on the State Department career officials who helped shape U.S. foreign policy toward the U.S.S.R. during the Roosevelt and Truman Adminstrations.

8.467 **Divine**, R. A., *The Sputnik Challenge. Eisenhower's Response to the Soviet Satellite*, New York, 1993.

8.468 **Divine**, R. A., *Eisenhower and the Cold War*, New York, 1981. One of a series of studies that found Eisenhower much more engaged in the making and execution of policy than was popularly thought in the 1950s.

8.469 **Edmonds**, R., *Setting the Mould. The United States and Britain, 1945–1950*, New York, 1986. A consideration of the "special relationship" from the viewpoint of the British with special attention paid to the Greek crisis and the question of atomic weapons.

8.470 **Gaddis**, J. L., *Strategies of Containment. A Critical Appraisal of Postwar American National Security Policy*, New York, 1982.

8.471 **Gallicchio**, M. S., *The Cold War Begins in Asia. American East Asian Policy and the Fall of the Japanese Empire*, New York, 1988.

8.472 **Gormly**, J. L., *From Potsdam to the Cold War. Big Three Diplomacy, 1945–1947*, Wilmington, DE, 1990.

8.473 **Gormly**, J. L., *The Collapse of the Grand Alliance, 1945–1948*, Baton Rouge, LA, 1987. Examines the change in circumstances after the war when Britain became a junior partner to the Americans, and how the Labour Government maneuvered to maintain British interests.

8.474 **Graebner**, N. A., (ed.), *The National Security. Its Theory and Practice, 1945–1960*, New York, 1986.

8.475 **Harries**, M., and **Harries**, Susie, *Sheathing the Sword. The Demilitarization of*

Postwar Japan, New York, 1987. Emphasizes the permanence of the postwar demilitarization for Japanese life and aims to negate 1980s fears of an armed Japanese resurgence.

8.476 **Hogan**, M. J., *The Marshall Plan. America, Britain, and the Reconstruction of Western Europe, 1947–1952*, New York, 1987. Takes the story of the American foreign aid initiative away from an exclusively anti-Soviet cast, and instead interprets it in the context of American domestic politics and British imperial politics.

8.477 **Immerman**, R. H., (ed.), *John Foster Dulles and the Diplomacy of the Cold War*, Princeton, NJ, 1990.

8.478 **Isaacson**, W., and **Thomas**, E., *The Wise Men. Six Friends and the World They Made*, New York, 1986.

8.479 **Kepley**, D. R., *The Collapse of the Middle Way. Senate Republicans and the Bipartisan Foreign Policy, 1948–1952*, Westport, CT, 1988.

8.480 **Kunz**, Diane B., *The Economic Diplomacy of the Suez Crisis*, Chapel Hill, NC, 1991.

8.481 **Lauren**, P. G., (ed.), *The China Hands' Legacy. Ethics and Diplomacy*, Boulder, CO, 1987. A collection of essays by scholars and former diplomats about the dilemma of the State Department professionals who candidly reported the truth about the Kuomintang at the ultimate cost of their jobs.

8.482 **Leffler**, M. P., *A Preponderance of Power. National Security, the Truman Administration, and the Cold War*, Stanford, CA, 1992. Judicious and closely argued survey of the origins of the Cold War, written self-consciously at its close; one of the definitive writings of the post-revisionist school.

8.483 **Maddox**, R. J., *From War to Cold War. The Education of Harry S. Truman*, Boulder, CO, 1988.

8.484 **Mayers**, D. A., *George Kennan and the Dilemmas of US Foreign Policy*, New York, 1988.

8.485 **McAliffe**, Mary S., 'Commentary/Eisenhower, the president', *Journal of American History*, LXVIII, 1981, 625–632. Discusses Eisenhower and the different interpretations of him and his presidency.

8.486 **McCoy**, D. R., *The Presidency of Harry S. Truman*, Lawrence, KS, 1984. Stresses the success of his containment policy abroad

and the relative failure of his Fair Deal at home.

8.487 **Miscamble**, W. D., *George F. Kennan and the Making of American Foreign Policy, 1947–1950*, Princeton, NJ, 1992.

8.488 **Nadeau**, R., *Stalin, Churchill, and Roosevelt Divide Europe*, New York, 1990.

8.489 **Ninkovich**, F. A., *The Diplomacy of Ideas. U.S. Foreign Policy and Cultural Relations, 1938–1950*, New York, 1981. Searches for the origins of official American cultural exchanges and finds that World War II marked the beginning of the export of American students and teachers as a deliberate instrument of American foreign policy.

8.490 **Pach**, C. J., *Arming the Free World. The Origins of the United States Military Assistance Program, 1945–1950*, Chapel Hill, NC, 1991. Shows the discontinuity between Lend-Lease and the Cold War containment program of military assistance.

8.491 **Pisani**, Sallie, *The CIA and the Marshall Plan*, Lawrence, KS, 1991.

8.492 **Pollard**, R. A., *Economic Security and the Origins of the Cold War, 1945–1950*, New York, 1985. A postrevisionist account that chiefly blames the Soviets for the onset of the Cold War.

8.493 **Reardon-Anderson**, J., *Yenan and the Great Powers. The Origins of Chinese Communist Foreign Policy, 1944–1946*, New York, 198

8.494 **Russell**, G., *Hans J. Morgenthau and the Ethics of American Statecraft*, Baton Rouge, LA, 1990.

8.495 **Ryan**, H. B., *The Vision of Anglo-America. The US-UK Alliance and the Emerging Cold War, 1943–1946*, New York, 1987. Looks at how British foreign policy under Churchill and the Labour Government feared a postwar American retreat into isolationism, and how British policy-makers sought to develop an entente against Soviet power.

8.496 **Stephanson**, A., *Kennan and the Art of Foreign Policy*, Cambridge, MA, 1989. A survey of the thought of one of the architects of American Cold War policy; Kennan was more the idealist trying to save the legacy of western civilization than the realist he saw himself as.

8.497 **Tusa**, Ann, and **Tusa**, J., *The Berlin Airlift*, New York, 1988.

8.498 **Woods**, R. B., and **Jones**, H., *Dawning*

of the Cold War. The United States' Quest for Order, Athens, GA, 1991.

8.499 **Yergin**, D., *Shattered Peace. The Origins of the Cold War and the National Security State*, Boston, 1977. One of the first attempts at a postrevisionist synthesis of the origins of the Cold War debate.

(c) LATER PHASES

8.500 **Beschloss**, M., *The Crisis Years. Kennedy and Khruschev, 1960–1963*, New York, 1991. A consideration of US-Soviet relations that stresses Kennedy's caution in dealing with Khruschev and makes the late president out as less of a hardline Cold Warrior.

8.501 **Bornet**, V. D., *The Presidency of Lyndon B. Johnson*, Lawrence, KS, 1983. A generally positive assessment of LBJ as president that lauds his domestic accomplishments and goes lightly on his handling of the Vietnam War.

8.502 **Burner**, D., *John F. Kennedy and a New Generation*, Boston, 1988. A part of Little, Brown's "Library of American Biography" series, this volume credits Kennedy for his style but faults his foreign policy.

8.503 **Cohen**, W. I., *Dean Rusk*, Totowa, NJ, 1980. A biography of the career of the Secretary of State in the Kennedy and Johnson Administrations that shows how Rusk repeatedly put aside his own skeptical views of foreign policy in Asia and thereby aided in the Vietnam debacle.

8.504 **Divine**, R. A., *The Cuban Missile Crisis*, New York, 1988. Second edition of a 1971 volume, updated in this book with reviews of recent scholarship.

8.505 **Firestone**, B. J., *The Quest for Nuclear Stability. John F. Kennedy and the Soviet Union*, Westport, CT, 1982.

8.506 **Firestone**, B. J., and **Vogt**, R. C., (ed.), *Lyndon Baines Johnson and the Uses of Power*, Westport, CT, 1988.

8.507 **Giglio**, J. N., *The Presidency of John F. Kennedy*, Lawrence, KS, 1991. Part of the publisher's "American Presidents" series, the author separates Kennedy's cautious public actions as president from his private character.

8.508 **Paterson**, T. G., (ed.), *Kennedy's Quest for Victory. American Foreign Policy, 1961–1963*, New York, 1989. Eleven essays on different aspects of Kennedy's foreign policy with the stress on the

president's aggressive expansion of the Cold War.

(d) OVERSEAS ANTI-COMMUNIST ALLIANCES

(i) EUROPE

8.509 **Coleman**, P., *The Liberal Conspiracy. The Congress for Cultural Freedom and the Struggle for the Mind of Postwar Europe*, New York, 1989. A history of the CIA-sponsored organization by an Australian who worked for a CCF-funded journal.

8.510 **Dastrup**, B. L., *Crusade in Nuremberg. Military Occupation, 1945–1949*, Westport, CT, 1985. Analyzes the denazification program implemented by the American occupying forces in the area around Nuremberg, and how Germans alternately cooperated and resisted the campaign.

8.511 **Frazier**, R., *Anglo-American Relations with Greece. The Coming of the Cold War, 1942–1947*, New York, 1991.

8.512 **Ireland**, T. P., *Creating the Entangling Alliance. The Origins of the North Atlantic Treaty Organization*, Westport, CT, 1981.

8.513 **Jones**, H., *'A New Kind of War'. America's Global Strategy and the Truman Doctrine in Greece*, New York, 1989.

8.514 **Kaplan**, L. S., *NATO and the United States. The Enduring Alliance*, Boston, 1988.

8.515 **Ninkovich**, F. A., *Germany and the United States. The Transformation of the German Question since 1945*, Boston, 1988.

8.516 **Schwartz**, T. A., *America's Germany. John J. McCloy and the Federal Republic of Germany*, Cambridge, MA, 1991.

8.517 **Wall**, I. M., *The United States and the Making of Postwar France, 1945–1954*, New York, 1991.

8.518 **Whitnah**, D. R., and **Erickson**, E. L., *The American Occupation of Austria. Planning and Early Years*, Westport, CT, 1985. Examines how the Allies discussed and then implemented the occupation of Austria by zones, as well as the politics behind the decision to define Austria as a nation conquered by the Nazis.

8.519 **Winks**, R. W., *Cloak & Gown. Scholars in the Secret War, 1939–1961*, New York, 1987. Recounts the history of spies recruited from Yale into the OSS and CIA.

(ii) ASIA

8.520 **Bain**, D. H., *Sitting in Darkness. Americans in the Philippines*, Boston, 1984.

8.521 **Borg**, Dorothy, and **Heinrichs**, W., (ed.), *Uncertain Years. Chinese-American Relations, 1947–1950*, New York, 1980.

8.522 **Brown**, B. T. ' "The very thing we feared most". American images of China in a decade of war and revolution, 1945–1955', *Maryland Historian*, VIII, 1987, 1–21.

8.523 **Cohen**, W. I., and **Iriye**, A., (eds.), *The Great Powers in East Asia, 1953–1960*, New York, 1990. A collection of essays by U.S., Russian, Japanese, and Chinese scholars on the Cold War in Asia.

8.524 **Finn**, R. B., *Winners in Peace. MacArthur, Yoshida, and Postwar Japan*, Berkeley, CA, 1992. A participant's account of the remaking of the Japanese polity after 1945.

8.525 **Iriye**, A., and **Cohen**, W. I., *The United States and Japan in the Postwar World*, Lexington, KY, 1989.

8.526 **Martin**, E. W., *Divided Counsel. The Anglo-American Response to Communist Victory in China*, Lexington, KY, 1986. Finds that both Britain and the United States were frozen out of potential relations with communist China because of the dogmatism of the new rulers in Beijing.

8.527 **Mayers**, D. A., *Cracking the Monolith. U.S. Policy Against the Sino-Soviet Alliance, 1949–1955*, Baton Rouge, LA, 1986. In contrast to Martin above, this book argues for a skillful application of American diplomacy in the 1950s as part of the basis for the eventual Sino-Soviet split.

8.528 **Merrill**, D., *Bread and the Ballot. The United States and India's Economic Development, 1947–1963*, Chapel Hill, NC, 1990.

8.529 **Neils**, Patricia, *China Images in the Life and Times of Henry Luce*, Savage, NJ, 1990. Downplays the importance of the *Time* magazine publisher as a shaper of American policy toward China.

8.530 **Schaller**, M., *The American Occupation of Japan. The Origins of the Cold War in Asia*, New York, 1985. Shows how the American Army worked with the existing Japanese state in the postwar period in trying to eradicate militarism.

8.531 **Schaller**, M., *Douglas MacArthur. The Far Eastern General*, New York, 1989. Shows that MacArthur's knowledge of Asia and Asians was shallow and often shaped by domestic American political considerations.

8.532 **Schonberger**, H. B., *Aftermath of War. Americans and the Remaking of Japan, 1945–1952*, Kent, OH, 1989. A look at how the Occupation Force leaders worked within Japanese society to refashion the polity.

8.533 **Tucker**, Nancy Bernkopf, *Patterns in the Dust. Chinese-American Relations and the Recognition Controversy, 1949–1950*, New York, 1983.

(iii) THE MIDDLE EAST

8.534 **Bain**, K. R., *The March to Zion. United States Policy and the Founding of Israel*, College Station, TX, 1979.

8.535 **Bill**, J. A., *The Eagle and the Lion. The Tragedy of American-Iranian Relations*, New Haven, CT, 1988. The book's title refers to an ongoing attempt by Americans to manipulate Iranians within an unequal relationship that ultimately led to the Islamic Revolution.

8.536 **Brands**, H. W., *The Specter of Neutralism. The United States and the Emergence of the Third World, 1947–1960*, New York, 1989. Looks at Egypt as an example of how the U.S. responded to neutralism.

8.537 **Ganin**, Z., *Truman, American Jewry, and Israel, 1945–1948*, New York, 1979.

8.538 **Gasiorowski**, M. J., *U.S. Foreign Policy and the Shah. Building a Client State in Iran*, Ithaca, NY, 1991. An account that covers the turmoil in Iran in the 1950s and the U.S. role in undermining the popular regime and returning the Shah to power.

8.539 **Goode**, J. F., *The United States and Iran, 1946–1951. The Diplomacy of Neglect*, New York, 1989. Maintains that the U.S. had minimal interest in helping the Shah's regime in the period before the nationalist uprising.

8.540 **Hahn**, P. L., *The United States, Great Britain, and Egypt, 1945–1956. Strategy and Diplomacy in the Early Cold War*, Chapel Hill, NC, 1991.

8.541 **Kuniholm**, B. R., *The Origins of the Cold War in the Near East: Great Power Conflict and Diplomacy in Iran, Turkey, and Greece*, Princeton, NJ, 1980.

8.542 **Miller**, A. D., *Search for Security. Saudi Arabian Oil and American Foreign Policy, 1939–1949*, Chapel Hill, NC, 1980.

8.543 **Painter**, D. S., *Oil and the American*

Century. *The Political Economy of U.S. Foreign Oil Policy, 1941–1954*, Baltimore, 1986. Traces the development of foreign policy in light of the overseas reach of American oil companies.

8.544 **Rubin**, B., *Paved with Good Intentions. The American Experience in Iran*, New York, 1981. An examination of how American foreign policy makers from World War II onward used the Shah of Iran for larger Cold War purposes and how the military buildup contributed to the internal weakness of the Pahlavi regime.

8.545 **Wilson**, E. M., *Decision on Palestine. How the U.S. Came to Recognize Israel*, Stanford, CA, 1979.

(iv) LATIN AMERICA
AND THE CARIBBEAN

8.546 **Carothers**, T., *In the Name of Democracy. U. S. Policy toward Latin America in the Reagan Years*, Berkeley, CA, 1991. A State Department employee under President Reagan gives an insider account of the making of policy toward Nicaragua and El Salvador.

8.547 **Cobbs**, Elizabeth Anne, *The Rich Neighbor Policy. Rockefeller and Kaiser in Brazil*, New Haven, CT, 1992.

8.548 **Haines**, G. K., *The Americanization of Brazil. A Study of U.S. Cold War Diplomacy in the Third World, 1945–1954*, Wilmington, DE, 1989.

8.549 **Martz**, J. D., *United States Policy in Latin America. A Quarter Century of Crisis and Challenge, 1961–1986*, Lincoln, NE, 1988.

8.550 **Morley**, M. H., *Imperial State and Revolution. The United States and Cuba, 1952–1986*, New York, 1987. Uses a Marxist analysis to trace the unrelenting attempts of the United States to control Cuba, both before and after the Cuban Revolution.

8.551 **Rabe**, S. G., *Eisenhower and Latin America. The Foreign Policy of Anticommunism*, Chapel Hill, NC, 1988.

8.552 **Tulchin**, J. S., *Argentina and the United States. A Conflicted Relationship*, Boston, 1990.

8.553 **Welch**, R. E., Jr., *Response to Revolution. The United States and the Cuban Revolution, 1959–1961*, Chapel Hill, NC, 1985. Stresses internal Cuban factors for why the new Castro regime became more radical after 1959.

The nuclear arms race

8.554 **Balogh**, B., *Chain Reaction. Expert Debate and Public Participation in American Commercial Nuclear Power, 1945–1975*, New York, 1991.

8.555 **Baucom**, D. R., *The Origins of SDI, 1944–1983*, Lawrence, KS, 1992. Links anti-missile technology with the ideology of deterrence and fear.

8.556 **Bernstein**, B. J. 'From the A-bomb to Star Wars: Edward Teller's history', *Technology and Culture*, XXXI, 1990, 846–861, A critical review of the life's work of Teller, the so-called 'father of the H-Bomb', and a physicist actively engaged in politics.

8.557 **Botti**, T. J., *The Long Wait. The Forging of the Anglo-American Nuclear Alliance, 1945–1958*, Westport, CT, 1987.

8.558 **Brown**, M. E., *Flying Blind. The Politics of the U.S. Strategic Bomber Program*, Ithaca, NY, 1992.

8.559 **Bundy**, M., *Danger and Survival. Choices about the Bomb in the First Fifty Years*, New York, 1988. A history of policy choices on nuclear weapons made by American leaders, and written by a former National Security advisor, starting with a defense of the Truman Administration's decisions in the summer of 1945.

8.560 **Gerber**, M. S., *On the Home Front. The Cold War Legacy of the Hanford Nuclear Site*, Lincoln, NE, 1992.

8.561 **Herken**, G., *The Winning Weapon. The Atomic Bomb in the Cold War, 1945–1950*, New York, 1980.

8.562 **Herken**, G., *Counsels of War*, New York, 1985. A review of the early strategists of nuclear war fighting and prevention.

8.563 **Leslie**, S. W., *The Cold War and American Science. The Military-Industrial-Academic Complex at MIT and Stanford*, New York, 1993.

8.564 **Moss**, N., *Klaus Fuchs. The Man Who Stole the Atom Bomb*, New York, 1987. A biography of the German-born scientist who worked on nuclear research for Great Britain, and who passed on American and British atomic secrets to Soviet agents; this work uses unclassified American documents to answer the question of why Fuchs betrayed his adopted Britain.

8.565 **Rosenthal**, J. H., *Righteous Realists. Political Realism, Responsible Power, and American Culture in the Nuclear Age*, Baton Rouge, LA, 1991. An admiring account of

George Kennan and other Cold War strategists that finds their thought and actions to be consistent with American ideals of democracy and morality.

8.566 **Sherwin**, M. J., *A World Destroyed. The Atomic Bomb and the Grand Alliance*, New York, 1975.

8.567 **Walker**, J. S., *Containing the Atom. Nuclear Regulation in a Changing Environment, 1963–1971*, Berkeley, CA, 1992.

8.568 **Williams**, R. C., *Klaus Fuchs, Atom Spy*, Cambridge, MA, 1987. A work highly critical of British intelligence for allowing Fuchs to be in a position to receive and transmit secret nuclear research data to the Soviets.

The maturing welfare state

8.569 **Barrow**, Deborah J., and **Walker**, T. G., *A Court Divided. The Fifth Circuit of Appeals and the Politics of Judicial Reform*, New Haven, CT, 1988.

8.570 **Belknap**, M. R., *Federal Law and Southern Order. Racial Violence and Constitutional Conflict in the Post-Brown South*, Athens, GA, 1987. Focuses on the constitutional and political debate that led to the 1968 Civil Rights Act which gave the federal government the power to act against local instances of white terrorism in the South.

8.571 **Belz**, H., *Equality Transformed. A Quarter Century of Affirmative Action*, New Brunswick, NJ, 1991.

8.572 **Bernstein**, I., *Promises Kept. John F. Kennedy's New Frontier*, New York, 1991.

8.573 **Epstein**, L., *Political Parties in the American Mold*, Madison, WI, 1985. A survey of twentieth century American political parties.

8.574 **Gillon**, S. M., *Politics and Vision. The ADA and American Liberalism, 1947–1985*, New York, 1987.

8.575 **Hamby**, A. L., *Liberalism and its Challengers. From FDR to Bush*, New York, 1992. The second edition of a survey of twentieth century American politics.

8.576 **Howard**, J. W., *Courts of Appeal in the Federal Judicial System. A Study of the Second, Fifth, and District of Columbia Circuits*, Princeton, NJ, 1981.

8.577 **Jones**, C. O., *The Trusteeship Presidency. Jimmy Carter and the United States Congress*, Baton Rouge, LA, 1988.

8.578 **Kallina**, E. F., *Courthouse over White House. Chicago and the Presidential Election of 1960*, Orlando, FL, 1988. Argues that any vote fraud committed in Chicago in 1960 was directed against a local Republican opponent of Democratic Mayor Daley, and that Nixon was an incidental loser, too.

8.579 **Lewis**, A., *Make No Law. The Sullivan Case and the First Amendment*, New York, 1991. A look at the libel case decided by the Supreme Court in such a way as to give wide latitude to the press in covering public figures.

8.580 **Mayhew**, D. R., *Divided We Govern. Party Control, Lawmaking, and Investigations, 1946–1990*, New Haven, CT, 1991.

8.581 **Murphy**, B. A., *Fortas. The Rise and Ruin of a Supreme Court Justice*, New York, 1988. Concentrates on the political maneuvering by President Johnson in 1968 to elevate his close political advisor, Associate Justice Abraham Fortas, to the Chief Justice's position, and how the prevarications of Johnson and Fortas himself led to a confirmation defeat in the Senate.

8.582 **Spitzer**, R. J., *President and Congress. Executive Hegemony at the Crossroads of American Government*, Philadelphia, 1993. Outlines the recent tendency toward presidential dominance of the federal government, in large part due to the increased importance of foreign relations.

8.583 **Weir**, Margaret, **Orloff**, Anna Shola, and **Skocpol**, Theda, (ed.), *The Politics of Social Policy in the United States*, Princeton, NJ, 1988. A collection of essays mainly by sociologists that contrasts American social welfare policy with other nations, essentially finding American practices rooted in conservative control of politics and the economy.

8.584 **Yarbrough**, T. E., *Mr. Justice Black and His Critics*, Durham, NC, 1988. Connects Justice Hugo Black's legal posivitist approach to his defense of civil liberties and especially his views on the First Amendment guarantee of freedom of speech.

Politics and elections

8.585 **Carlson**, J., *George C. Wallace and the Politics of Powerlessness. The Wallace Campaigns for the Presidency, 1964–1976*,

New Brunswick, NJ, 1981.

8.586 **Fraser**, S., and **Gaestle**, G., (ed.), *The Rise and Fall of the New Deal Order, 1930–1980*, Princeton, NJ, 1989. A collection of essays about the failure of social democracy to take root in America since the 1930s.

8.587 **Graebner**, W., *The Engineering of Consent. Democracy and Authority in Twentieth-Century America*, Madison, WI, 1987. Looks at the work of figures such as the public relations pioneer Edward Bernays as a way of determining how politics and political discourse have been replaced by manipulation.

8.588 **Lamis**, A. P., *The Two-Party South*, New York, 1984. Surveys the politics of the South as the Republicans emerged as the stronger national party while the Democrats built bi-racial coalitions for local and statewide victories.

8.589 **Newman**, S. L., *Liberalism at Wit's End. The Libertarian Revolt Against the Modern State*, Ithaca, NY, 1984. A critique of the philosophical origins of the current libertarian movement.

8.590 **Page**, B. I., and **Shapiro**, R. Y., *The Rational Public. Fifty Years of Trends in Americans' Policy Preferences*, Chicago, 1992. Analyzes polling data with the conclusion that the public is both well-informed and well-disposed toward sensible policy choices.

8.591 **Pleasants**, J. M., and **Burns**, A. M., *Frank Porter Graham and the 1950 Senate Race in North Carolina*, Chapel Hill, NC, 1990.

8.592 **Rae**, Nicol C., *The Decline and Fall of the Liberal Republicans. From 1952 to the Present*, New York, 1989.

8.593 **Shafer**, B. E., *Bifurcated Politics. Evolution and Reform in the National Party Convention*, Cambridge, MA, 1988.

8.594 **Staggenborg**, Suzanne, *The Pro-Choice Movement. Organization and Activism in the Abortion Conflict*, New York, 1991.

8.595 **Tananbaum**, D., *The Bricker Amendment Controversy. A Test of Eisenhower's Political Leadership*, Ithaca, NY, 1988.

8.596 **Walker**, S., *In Defense of American Liberties. A History of the ACLU*, New York, 1990. An organizational history of the American Civil Liberties Union that stresses the group's absolute defense of the First Amendment right to free speech, despite the frequent unpopularity of such a position.

McCarthyism and the national security state at home

8.597 **Bayly**, E. R., *Joe McCarthy and the Press*, Madison, WI, 1981.

8.598 **Boll**, M. M., *National Security Planning. Roosevelt through Reagan*, Lexington, KY, 1988.

8.599 **Broadwater**, J., *Eisenhower & the Anti-Communist Crusade*, Chapel Hill, NC, 1992.

8.600 **Davis**, J. K., *Spying on America. The FBI's Domestic Counterintelligence Program*, New York, 1992.

8.601 **Diamond**, S., *Compromised Campuses. The Collaboration of Universities with the Intelligence Community, 1945–1955*, New York, 1992. An indictment of the weakness of the American academy before the domestic spy agencies, written by one who was a victim of the witch hunt.

8.602 **Donner**, F. J., *The Age of Surveillance*, New York, 1981.

8.603 **Fried**, R. M., *Nightmare in Red. The McCarthy Era in Perspective*, New York, 1990.

8.604 **Gottfried**, P., and **Fleming**, T., *The Conservative Movement*, Boston, 1988.

8.605 **Holmes**, D. R., *Stalking the Academic Communist. Intellectual Freedom and the Firing of Alex Novikoff*, Hanover, NH, 1989.

8.606 **Isserman**, M., *Which Side Were You On? The American Communist Party During the Second World War*, Urbana, IL, 1983.

8.607 **Kazin**, M., 'The grass-roots right. New histories of U.S. conservatism in the twentieth century', *American Historical Review*, XCVII, 1992, 136–155. Reviews the recent secondary literature that looks at the ideology and makeup of the modern conservative movement.

8.608 **Keller**, W. W., *The Liberals and J. Edgar Hoover. Rise and Fall of a Domestic Intelligence State*, Princeton, NJ, 1989. Argues that the FBI's domestic spying was part of a larger national security state that was the inevitable result of the liberal accommodation to anti-communism.

8.609 **O'Brien**, M., *McCarthy and McCarthyism in Wisconsin*, Columbia, MO, 1980.

8.610 **Reinhard**, D. W., *The Republican Right since 1945*, Lexington, KY, 1983.

8.611 **Schrecker**, Ellen W., *No Ivory Tower. McCarthyism and the Universities*, New York, 1986. Covers the crackdown on communists and suspected subversives in universities and schools; the author finds that in almost every instance academic freedom lost out to the red-hunters.

8.612 **Schultz**, B., and **Schultz**, Ruth, *It Did Happen Here. Recollections of Political Repression in America*, Berkeley, CA, 1989. An account of postwar domestic spying and harassment, from the Hollywood Ten through the Chicago Seven.

8.613 **Sharlitt**, J. H., *Fatal Error. The Miscarriage of Justice that Sealed the Rosenbergs' Fate*, New York, 1989.

8.614 **Theoharis**, A., (ed.), *The Truman Presidency. The Origins of the Imperial Presidency and the National Security State*, Stanfordville, NY, 1979. A collection of essays that looks at how spying and domestic political intelligence in the early days of the Cold War became entrenched in American political life.

The Watergate crisis

8.615 **Ball**, H., *'We Have a Duty'. The Supreme Court and the Watergate Tapes Litigation*, Westport, CT, 1990.

8.616 **Firestone**, B. J., and **Ugrinsky**, A., (ed.), *Gerald R. Ford and the Politics of Post-Watergate America*, Westport, CT, 1993. A two volume set that resulted from a conference on the history of the Ford presidency.

8.617 **Kutler**, S. I., *The Wars of Watergate. The Last Crisis of Richard Nixon*, New York, 1990.

8.618 **Schudson**, M., *Watergate in American Memory. How We Remember, Forget, and Reconstruct the Past*, New York, 1992.

INDEX OF AUTHORS, EDITORS AND COMPILERS

Numbers refer to items in the bibliography.

Gottlieb, S. E., 1.830
Gougeon, L., 5.171
Gough, R. J., 3.276, 5.99
Gould, L. I., 7.700, 7.701
Gover, C. Jane, 7.267
Grabbe, H.-J., 5.302
Graber, M. A., 1.832
Grabowski, J. J., 7.673
Graebner, N. A., 7.870, 8.474
Graebner, W., 7.217, 8.11, 8.152, 8.587
Graf, W. L., 8.390
Graff, H. J., 1.413
Gragg, L., 3.46, 3.187
Graham, H. D., 8.309
Graham, Margaret B. W., 7.484
Graham, O. L., 7.53
Grant, N. L., 7.555
Grantham, D. W., 1.357, 7.390, 7.702
Grasmick, Mary K., 2.52
Grasso, K. L., 8.235
Gratton, B., 7.218
Gray, J., 1.128
Gray, J. S., 6.394
Greber, Naomi 2.113
Green, C. H., 8.59
Green, D., 7.6
Green, H., 6.235
Green, J. R., 7.703, 8.271
Green, M. D., 2.29, 5.292
Green, Rayna, 1.129
Greenbaum, F., 4.146
Greenberg, A. M., 2.111
Greenberg, B., 8.265
Greenberg, Cheryl Lynn, 7.556
Greenberg, D., 3.120
Greenberg, K. S., 5.207
Greenblatt, S., 3.8
Greene, J. A., 6.395
Greene, J. P., 1.206, 3.9, 3.11, 4.235, 4.45, 4.59
Greene, V. R., 6.432
Greenhaigh, P., 6.236
Greenstein, F. I., 1.207
Greenwald, Maurine Weiner, 7.778
Gregory, J. N., 7.636
Gregory, R., 7.808
Grenz, S., 1.557
Grese, R. E., 7.662
Greven, P. J., 3.66, 3.67
Gridley, Marion Eleanor, 2.74
Griffen, C., 6.185, 6.203
Griffen, Sally, 6.185
Griffin, Patricia, 4.199
Griffith, B. W., 5.277
Griffith, Barbara S., 8.272
Griffith, P., 6.556
Griffith, Sally Foreman, 7.126
Grim, R. E., 1.173, 1.208
Grimshaw, Patricia, 5.110
Grimshaw, W. J., 8.310

Grinde, D. A., 4.320
Griswold de Castillo, R., 1.414, 6.147, 6.148
Grob, G. N., 7.219, 8.153
Groneman, Carol, 1.482
Grossberg, M., 6.149
Grossman, J. R., 7.637, 7.638
Grover, Kathryn, 1.483, 1.484
Grubb, F., 4.173, 4.174, 4.96
Grumet, R. S., 2.30, 2.59
Guarneri, C. J., 5.172
Guelzo, A. C., 3.173
Guggisberg, H. R., 1.263
Guice, J. W., 5.312
Gundersen, Joan R., 4.112
Gunn, L. R., 5.350
Gura, P. F., 3.157, 4.130
Gurak, D. T., 8.360
Gurock, J. S., 1.130, 8.196
Guth, D. J., 8.48
Guthrie, J. W., 1.466
Gutierrez, R. A., 3.103
Guttman, A., 1.302, 1.485, 1.486, 7.322
Gyory, A., 1.102

Haakenson, Bergine, 1.56
Haas, Marilyn L., 2.31
Haber, Carole, 1.415
Haber, S., 1.61
Hacker, B. C., 7.854
Hackett, D. G., 1.558
Haefele, W. R., 4.262
Haegert, Dorothy, 2.60
Hagan, K. J., 1.833, 1.834
Hagan, W. T., 6.413
Hage, J., 7.222
Hagerman, E., 6.572
Haggerty, T., 7.231
Hahn, P. L., 8.540
Hahn, S., 5.100, 6.186, 6.323
Haines, G. K., 1.374, 8.548
Haines, M. R., 6.166
Halbrook, S., 4.321
Hale, D. K., 1.760
Hales, P. B., 6.496
Hall, C., 7.792
Hall, D. D., 3.12, 3.158
Hall, Gwendolyn Midlo, 3.224
Hall, Jacqueline Dowd, 7.445.
Hall, K. L., 1.358, 1.375, 5.351
Hall, Linda B., 7.889
Hall, M. G., 3.47
Hall, P. D., 8.284
Hall, R., 1.835
Hall, R. L., 3.225
Hall, T. D., 1.761
Haller, J. S., 6.150
Halley, P. L., 5.307
Hallin, D. C., 8.426
Hallock, Judith Lee, 6.624
Halpern, M., 8.273

Halttunen, Karen, 6.187
Haltzel, M. H., 1.852
Hamby, A. L., 8.575
Hamer, D., 5.324
Hamerow, T. S., 1.264, 1.265
Hamilton, C. H., 6.181
Hamilton, C. V., 8.112
Hamilton, D. E., 7.739
Hamilton, K. M., 6.465
Hamilton, N., 7.127
Hamm, T. D., 1.559
Hammack, D. C., 7.239
Hammel, G. R., 3.255
Hampel, R. L., 5.173
Handlin, Lilian, 1.379, 4.161
Handlin, O., 1.162, 1.379, 4.161
Handy, R. T., 7.355, 7.391
Hanke, L., 1.8
Hankins, Jean F., 4.276
Hann, J. H., 2.61, 2.117
Hanneman, R. A., 7.222
Hansen, J. M., 1.836
Hansen, K. J., 5.196
Hansen, Miriam, 7.335
Hanson, G. T., 1.174
Hansot, Elisabeth, 5.132
Hardeman, D. B., 7.128
Hardeman, N. P., 5.224
Harden, Victoria A., 7.220, 7.740
Harding, H., 8.72
Harding, R. H., 3.306
Harding, V. G., 8.311, 8.312
Hardman, K., 5.154
Hardt, H., 1.60
Hardy, B. C., 5.197
Hareven, Tamara K., 1.293, 1.416, 6.151, 6.152, 7.221
Hargrove, R. J., 4.76
Harlan, D., 1.315, 3.39
Harlan, L. D., 6.87, 7.129
Harr, J. E., 7.7
Harries, M., 8.475
Harries, Susie, 8.475
Harring, S., 6.260
Harris, B., 7.356
Harris, H. J., 7.425
Harris, J. W., 6.364
Harris, M. W., 7.369
Harris, R. L., Jr., 1.343
Harris, Trudier, 6.23
Harrison, Cynthia, 8.178
Harter, E. C., 6.625
Hartford, W. F., 6.188
Hartog, H., 5.325
Harvey, A. McG., 1.417
Harvey, J., 7.336
Haskell, J. D., 1.175
Haskell, T. L., 1.344
Haskins, L., 1.266
Haslach, R. D., 3.310
Hassler, W. W., 1.837
Hatch, N. O., 1.617, 3.174, 5.155

INDEX OF SUBJECTS

A note to the researcher: This subject index supplements the arrangement of the bibliography. The bibliography is arranged in categories familiar to historians. The subject index, on the other hand, covers those categories by which Americans classify themselves – ethnicity, religion, job, place, name, and institution. Numbers refer to items in the bibliography.

Abraham Lincoln Brigade, 7.717
Accomac County, VA, 3.96, 3.205
Accountants, 7.493
Acheson, Dean, 8.98
Actors, *see* Entertainers
Adams, Abigail, 5.118
Adams, Charles Francis, 7.492
Adams, Henry, 6.116
Adams, John, 4.71, 4.264, 5.19, 5.56
Adams, John Quincy, 5.71, 5.405
Adams, Louisa, 5.118
Adams, Samuel, 4.216
African-Americans
  American Revolution, 4.295
  artifacts, 1.669, 3.91
  culture, 1.120, 1.128, 1.151, 5.260,
    7.62, 7.554, 7.556, 7.570
  education, 5.263, 6.377, 6.655,
    6.661, 7.60, 8.201
  emancipation, 4.187, 4.189, 6.641,
    6.644
  families, 1.26, 1.27, 1.34, 1.35,
    6.158, 8.164
  Federal Bureau of Investigation,
    8.320
  free people during slavery 3.22,
    4.188, 5.269
  in film, 1.115, 7.340
  migration, 7.550, 7.569, 7.637,
    7.649, 7.650
  music, 1.157
  naming practices, 3.220
  organizations, 7.45
  politics and elections, 1.134, 1.839,
    6.376
  psychology, 5.274
  relations with Native Americans,
    1.687, 1.693, 3.3, 3.36, 3.203,

3.245, 5.280
  religion, 1.320, 1.465, 1.535,
    1.550, 1.576, 1.586, 5.263,
    6.271, 6.289, 7.376, 8.226
  riots, 7.550–7.553, 7.560, 7.574,
    7.576
  sailors, 1.668, 5.262
  slave revolts, 1.679, 3.219, 3.222,
    3.225, 3.232, 5.271
  soldiers, 6.11, 6.584, 6.602, 7.40,
    7.158
  women, 1.154, 1.685
  workers, 1.705, 7.465, 7.557,
    7.564, 7.569, 7.572, 7.573
Aged, *see* Senior citizens
Akron, OH, 7.468
Alabama, 2.19, 5.269, 5.317, 6.673,
    7.279, 8.380
Alaska, 1.104, 1.711, 6.469
Albany, NY, 1.558, 3.268
Aluminum Company of America,
    7.484, 7.504
Alvarez, Manuel, 5.52
American Association for the
    Advancement of Science, 7.360
American Civil Liberties Union,
    8.596
American Federation of Teachers,
    7.300
American Sunday School Union,
    5.163
American Telephone & Telegraph
    Co., 6.310, 7.491, 7.500, 7.505,
    7.507
Americans for Democratic Action,
    8.574
Anarchists, 6.181, 6.191, 6.676,
    7.690

Anglicans, *see* Episcopal Church
Annapolis, MD, 3.282
Anthony, Susan B., 6.125
Antietam, Battle of, 6.577, 6.581
Anti-Saloon League, 7.309
Apaches, 1.716, 2.40, 6.78, 6.405
Appalachia, 1.751, 1.780
Arab-Americans, 1.143
Arikara, 2.12
Arizona, 1.189, 1.414, 2.120, 8.344
Arkansas, 1.174, 6.553, 7.552
Arnold, Benedict, 4.85, 4.291
Arrington, Leonard J., 1.325
Arthur, Chester A., 6.679
Artists, 7.402, 7.414, 8.245
Aspen, CO, 6.482
Athletes, 1.453, 1.483–1.486, 1.516,
    6.23–6.38, 6.97, 6.233, 6.234,
    7.320, 7.322, 7.323, 7.328,
    7.383, 7.558, 8.206, 8.327
Atlanta, GA, 6.493, 6.494, 6.500,
    6.583, 7.534, 7.664
Atlanta Life Insurance Co., 7.485
Audubon Society, 1.109
Augusta, GA, 6.364
Austin, Mary, 7.191

Bache, Benjamin Franklin, 4.89,
    4.156
Bailyn, Bernard, 3.14, 4.57
Baldwin, Alice, 6.43
Baldwin, Frank, 6.43
Ball, George, 8.423
Baltimore, MD, 3.225, 4.227, 5.133,
    5.149, 6.278, 7.512
Bank of America, 7.494
Baptist Church, 3.143, 7.374
Barton, Clara, 6.113

225